PROGRAMS
FOR PROFIT

To
Albert and Margaret Carbonneau

PROGRAMS
FOR PROFIT
HOW TO
REALLY MAKE
MONEY WITH A
PERSONAL
COMPUTER

RICHARD ZBORAY AND DAVID SACHS

McGraw-Hill Book Company

New York   St. Louis   San Francisco   Auckland   Bogotá
Guatemala   Hamburg   Johannesburg   Lisbon   London
Madrid   Mexico   Montreal   New Delhi   Panama   Paris
San Juan   São Paulo   Singapore   Sydney   Tokyo   Toronto

The authors of the programs provided with this book have carefully reviewed them to ensure their performance in accordance with the specifications described in the book. Neither the authors nor McGraw-Hill, however, makes any warranties whatever concerning the programs. They assume no responsibility or liability of any kind for errors in the programs or for the consequences of any such errors.

PROGRAMS FOR PROFIT: How to Really Make Money with a Personal Computer

A BYTE Book.

1 2 3 4 5 6 7 8 9 0 D O C D O C 8 9 3 2 1 0 9 8 7 6 5 4

ISBN 0-07-072785-6

LIBRARY OF CONGRESS CATALOGING IN PUBLICATION DATA

Zboray, Richard.
  Programs for profit.

  (McGraw-Hill/VTX series) (A BYTE book)
  Includes index.
  1. Business—Data processing. 2. Microcomputers—
Programming. I. Sachs, David, date/   . II. Title.
III. Series. IV. Series: BYTE books.
HF5548.2.Z33   1984   001.64   83-17542
ISBN 0-07-072785-6

The editor for this book was Jeffrey McCartney;
and the editing supervisor was Charles P. Ray.
Text designed by Sharkey Design.

TABLE OF
CONTENTS

CHAPTER SIX
PROFITS FROM EXPENSES:
AN ACCOUNTS PAYABLE PROGRAM   86

CHAPTER SEVEN
HOW MUCH DO I CHARGE?   149

CHAPTER EIGHT
PROFITS ON THE BOOKS:
AN ACCOUNTS RECEIVABLE PROGRAM   166

CHAPTER NINE
SELLING SOFTWARE   251

CHAPTER TEN
SELLING INFORMATION:
A FOOTBALL INFORMATION PROGRAM   262

CHAPTER THIRTEEN
SELLING HARDWARE   331

CHAPTER FOURTEEN
PUTTING IT ALL TOGETHER   337

APPENDIXES   **347**

PREFACE

Programs For Profit is for those interested in profiting from personal computers. You don't have to be a programmer to make money with a personal computer. You don't even have to own a personal computer; you just need to want to make money with one. *Programs For Profit* shows you how to make money and provides the software to get you started.

If you already have a business, *Programs For Profit* presents programs that will increase your profits and save you the expense of paying somebody else for many services. If you don't have a business now and have no intention of ever starting one, however, *Programs For Profit* is also for you because it can help advance your career.

If you're not a programmer, you'll be happy to know the software for making money is already written. If you are a programmer, you'll be happy when you find software that you can make even more profitable by adding your own special features.

Programs For Profit is for everybody!

EQUIPMENT YOU'LL NEED

Programs For Profit includes programs designed to enable you to make money with a personal computer, disk drive, and printer.

All software is written in Microsoft BASIC Version 5.21 and can be run without modification on any IBM or IBM compatible personal computer, or any CP/M-based personal computer.

Minimum memory for efficient use of these programs is 64K. Two disk drives are recommended for actual business use. Any printer that can run on your system will work with these programs.

CHAPTER ONE
PREPARING TO MAKE MONEY

People buy personal computers (PCs) for many reasons. They want to play games, learn programming, acquaint their children with them, or use them in a business. To some people, PCs are so novel that they buy them without the faintest idea of what they'll do. After awhile, though, the computer loses its novelty. Games are no longer compelling. Children prefer television. Business applications don't "fit" a business, though much money has been spent looking for software that might. Programming, it turns out, is easy to master, but what do you do with the skill, anyhow? Dust starts to collect on the computer. Finally, the owner decides to turn the PC into cash. A tag sale is held and the machine sold.

Stop! Don't sell your personal computer. Brush off the dust. If you don't have a PC, get one. Start using it for profits.

WHO CAN MAKE MONEY?

For years software has been written so that people who know nothing about programming languages can slip a disk (or tape) into a computer to access its power. On its screen, the computer projects questions, which usually are brief and in English, and you type responses. Until recently, however, computers cost so much that only good-sized businesses could afford them. Personal computers have changed all that, however, because they are within most people's reach. Today, *anybody* can use a computer. By literally giving power to the people, personal computers promise countless new and revolutionary applications.

What you do with this power is shaped by how you think of a PC. If you think of it as a toy, you will be on the lookout for games. If you think of it as a learning device, you'll buy educational books and software, but games won't be of much interest. If you think of it as a money-making tool, you'll be alert for ways to make it profitable, and that's when questions begin to arise.

Just how do you go about translating your desire to make a PC profitable into money? Where do you start? What do you need? How do you know if you even can afford to try to make money?

You certainly need to know what a personal computer can do as a money-making tool—and be able to make it do it. The more capabilities you know about, the more you have to work with, and the more valuable the computer becomes. Costs, unfortunately, are still so high for application software that it's impossible to explore what's available.

Money-making software systems usually *start* in the hundreds of dollars. Not many people are willing to risk that kind of money on the chance that an application might be interesting and the software complete. Without hands-on experience in an application, you can't know if it's right for you, and you can't get the experience without first buying the software. You can't even know the capabilities you really need to buy until after you've had experience using software for the application. What if you spend too much on the wrong software?

As if this doesn't present enough of a problem, the fact is that the best software in the world is not enough to make money. You also must be able to figure out how to use the software to make a personal computer profitable.

Suppose you have software for an efficient bookkeeping system. What do you do with it? What do you do after you get the flash of inspiration that tells you how to creatively use the software?

Michael, a brilliant computer scientist I know, often calls me up and says, "This time I've really got a way to make money with a PC." He sounds eager, and is more familiar with the ins and outs of computer technology than anyone else I know, so I always listen attentively. His ideas are invariably real money makers, but he just as invariably never makes any money from them.

Once, I pointed out to Michael that he never bothers to flesh out the details of a profitable plan. "I've done all the creative work," he said. "Why don't you take care of the mechanics and we'll split the profits?" I told him we hadn't reached the "mechanics" stage yet. The creative effort was just beginning. "What do you mean?" he asked. "Who would buy what we were offering?" I asked. "How would we let people know about our offering? What would we charge?" "Isn't that stuff pretty straightforward?" he asked. No! The truth is, that it takes every bit as much creativity as the original idea. Michael wasn't interested in going on. These same types of problems stop most people from starting *any* kind of business.

Confronting the unknown is always intimidating. Do you just sit and wait for a profitable angle to hit you? How long should you wait? What kinds of ideas do you need, anyhow? Just how much do you charge?

Just becoming aware of opportunities for making money with a PC is a problem that's not easy to overcome because there are so many possibilities. To add to the confusion, software products, hardware products, services, and support may be combined. How do you decide on a business that's both suited to you and profitable?

For the beginner, making money with a PC is an undertaking filled with perplexity. *Programs For Profit* is designed to help you through this puzzling initiation.

WHAT YOU CAN EXPECT

By now, you've probably flipped through *Programs For Profit* and found it actually does contain what's needed to really make money with a personal computer. If you haven't, you're in store for a very pleasant surprise. You will find a survey of money-making opportunities, practical techniques for effectively and professionally conducting your business, software, and operating instructions.

The survey of opportunities is broad.

The business techniques have proven to be profitable and are appropriate to any business.

The software is designed to be productive and easy to use. It offers flexibility and expandability.

Unlike other software books you may have encountered, *Programs For Profit* provides operating instructions for *the user*. You do not need to understand code to operate the systems. Consequently, you may use the programs even if you're not a programmer.

If you do know BASIC, program documentation is clearly provided in REMARK statements in the code, so you can easily customize the software to your specific needs.

By allowing you to use a variety of business software without paying a lot of money, and by showing you how to use that software and your own skills profitably, *Programs For Profit* will help you overcome the traditional barriers to making money in the markets opened by PCs.

WHERE WE'RE GOING

Techniques for starting a business, meeting with prospective customers, figuring out how much to charge, and how to collect will be presented. The profitable opportunities that personal computers have opened will be explored. You will learn how to use the business software that is included for making money.

The presentation moves from single opportunities to packaging comprehensive offerings. You will become aware of problems that may be encountered and solutions you can use to resolve them. You also will gain a realistic perspective on profitable expectations.

A variety of pursuits will be explored, but the primary focus of *Programs For Profit* is on opportunities requiring minimal start-up costs and time to get you profitably in business—without risking a lot.

I strongly suggest you read the chapters as presented and avoid skipping around. The programs, on the other hand, may be operated in any order you like. You can use as many or as few programs as you want. I urge you to try some programs as you read. Choose the program that looks most interesting to you and start typing the program on a disk *after* you read Chap. 2, which presents general operations relevant to *all* programs. Then, start using the program with your own data so that when you finish reading, you'll be ready to put your business knowledge to use.

HOW MUCH MONEY ARE WE TALKING ABOUT?

Before I began work on *Programs For Profit*, I read all I could on the opportunities that PCs opened up. With the information I realistically could use, I would be hard-pressed to earn pin money. So I think it only fair if you ask how much money you can expect to make with this book.

My answer is that I don't know. For some readers, *Programs For Profit* will be the beginning of a full-time business. Others will use it to add capabilities to existing businesses, supplement their incomes, or advance their careers. You might be satisfied just knowing about the money-making opportunities these computers have introduced.

I do know markets exist for the businesses under consideration. According to the Small Business Administration, businesses have changed their work habits. To increase profits, big businesses reduce overhead costs by farming out work to small businesses specializing in such areas as mailing services and word processing. In difficult economic times, medium-sized and small businesses do the same. Paradoxically, the worst of times, when people are frightened about unemployment, is the best time to start a small business—and you'll have the knowledge and software to start yours.

WHAT YOU'LL NEED TO DO

Making money requires that you act. *Programs For Profit* opens possibilities for you, but you will have to turn them into profits. To do this, you must define your objectives, analyze your abilities, and decide how much effort you're willing to exert. Only you can decide how much money, if any, you want to make.

If your goal is solely to expand your mind and become acquainted with the profitable opportunities PCs have introduced, I hope you enjoy the experience of reading *Programs For Profit*. On the other hand, if making money is your real objective, you can use *Programs For Profit* as your guide. You'll have to take the steps necessary to reach that objective. Each step you take is, in a very real sense, liberating, and if you take them all, the experience may be very profitable.

CHAPTER

TWO

GENERAL

OPERATIONS

The programs in *Programs For Profit* share many characteristics. Instead of reading through repetitious descriptions for each new program, you'll find what they have in common fully spelled out in this chapter.

YOUR MONEY-MAKING TOOL

Your money-making tool is really three separate pieces of computer equipment: a personal computer, at least one disk drive, and a printer.

The software in *Programs For Profit* is designed to run on:

1. Any IBM PC or IBM-compatible personal computer running IBM BASIC 1.1 or any of the upperward compatible versions of IBM BASIC 1.1.

2. Or, any personal computer with a CP/M operating system and Microsoft BASIC Version 5.21. These computers include KAYPROS, DECs, Eagles, and Xerox 820s. The programs run on many old as well as new machines, so you can start a business very inexpensively. You can pick up an inexpensive original Osborne (which still is supported by Xerox), use it to start your business, and, later, when you begin making money, upgrade to one of the latest machines.

Many personal computers meet these criteria. Figures 2-1 through 2-4 show representative ones. This multiplicity, however, makes it impossible to

Fig. 2-1   IBM personal computer and printer.

Fig. 2-2   KAYPRO Model 4 featuring a detachable keyboard and 9-inch screen.

Fig. 2-3 Digital Equipment Corporation's Rainbow 100 personal computer and printer.

present basic procedures (such as starting up) for every make and model. You're assumed to know how to operate and care for your equipment.

NOTE:

The *Programs For Profit* programs will run with data stored on floppy or hard disks. All specifications are for *floppy* disks. A hard disk will significantly increase these specifications. A 5Mb hard disk, for example, will provide 15 times as much storage as specified.

The disk used for these specifications is a *single*, commonly used, double-density, double-sided disk. If you operate with another type of disk, your specifications will be different.

ABOUT THE PROGRAMS

The programs display English language prompts that step you through each procedure. Your response to a prompt is typed and sent by pressing the

Fig. 2-4 The original Osborne portable personal computer.

carriage return (or ENTER key on a numeric pad). Any line can be corrected before you send it. (See your personal computer user manual.)

The programs were written in Microsoft BASIC. Standard features allow the programs to be used exactly as presented. If your machine meets the criteria above, you will not need to make any program modifications.

The programs are fully documented with REMARK statements so the programmer readily will grasp the structure and "flow" of the code.

ABOUT THE EXAMPLES

Examples are used extensively to illustrate operations. In the examples, a prompt and a typical user response are shown on a single line. The user response is shown in **BOLDFACE** to distinguish it from the prompt:

ENTER NAME: **ROY GREEN**

The prompt is ENTER NAME: and the response is **ROY GREEN**. You do not need to respond exactly as shown. You can enter *any* name.

While each response must be ended by a carriage return (⟨CR⟩), the key is indicated in examples only when it is the only response made to a prompt:

ENTER NAME: ⟨**CR**⟩

In the above example, no information is typed; the user responds by pressing the carriage return.

ENTERING A PROGRAM

Before a program can become operable, you need to store it on a disk.

Code is provided at the end of each chapter in which a program is described. REMARK statements have been included as a guide through the code. You do not have to type these REMARK statements (a REMARK statement is indicated by REM at the beginning of a line). All other code *(including line numbers)* must be typed exactly as shown. Any mistake jeopardizes operation. Each line, consequently, should be verified before you press the carriage return. Though this care takes time, you'll save a lot of time avoiding error searches ("debugging"). If a mistake is entered, use your system editor to correct it. (Consult your BASIC manual for editing features.)

The printouts of the *Programs For Profit* programs have been adjusted to fit within margins. If you encounter a program line that does *not* start with a line number, it is simply a continuation of the line before it. When typing it in, simply type the first line (the one with the line number) and then continue typing the second *without* pressing a return between the lines. Though the following line, for example, is shown as three lines in *Programs For Profit*, you'll type it as one:

380 FIELD #1, 1 AS TTYPEF$, 2 AS SEASONF$, 2 AS WEEKF$, 30 AS
       TEAMAF$, 30 AS TEAMBF$, 1 AS WEATHERF$, 4 AS PTSAF$, 4
       AS PTSBF$, 1 AS FAVOREDF$, 4 AS SPREADF$

That is, for the entire line, you'll press the carriage return only *after* you type SPREADF$.

The resulting disk (source code) can be run only on personal computer models disk-compatible with the one on which it was originally entered. If you change machines, you'll need to reenter the entire program. If you type your code with an IBM Personal Computer, for example, you cannot use that disk on a DEC personal computer, which is not compatible. The disk could be used with a com PAQ, a machine that is compatible.

Although not required, a text editing or word processing system will be exceptionally helpful when you enter a program. If you use such a system, be sure it allows programs to be entered. Some word processing systems translate lines to an internal code for storage that changes the program.

Many applications may be expanded by interfacing a program and a word processing system. An interface program, which enables *Programs For Profit* records to be used in a word processing program, is provided in Appendix A.

If you'll be using more than one disk drive, you can store more than one application on a single disk. If you'll be using only a single disk drive, store only one application on a disk—you'll need the remaining space for your data.

To enter a program, load BASIC, then type and store the code. You may use the following general procedure:

1. Load the BASIC system disk into the disk drive.
2. Turn on the computer.
3. If necessary, boot up according to standard procedure.
4. In response to the system prompt, type **BASIC**.
5. In response to OK (or READY), type **AUTO**. Line numbers will be generated automatically by 10, so you don't type them.
6. Type the first line of code. Do not type the line number. Review and correct the line, if necessary. Press the carriage return. A new line number will be generated. Type the next line, and continue in this way until all lines are typed.
7. The computer will generate one more line number.
8. In response to the last line number, press the CTRL and C keys.
9. Type **SAVE "A:MAILLIST"**. MAILLIST is the name of the Mail List Program presented in Chap. 4. Each program has a different name which you'll use as a replacement for MAILLIST.

This procedure, illustrated in Fig. 2-5, stores the program on your BASIC disk. The program, however, may be stored on *any* disk. (See your operating system manual under "Copying.")

The WordStar word processing system is widely used today. The general procedure for entering a program with it is:

1. Access the WordStar system.

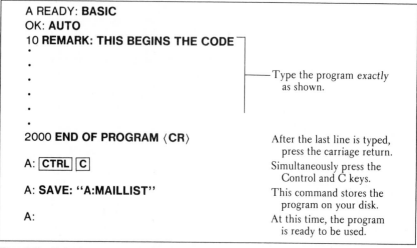

Fig. 2-5 Entering a program (IBM procedure).

2. Enter the NONDOCUMENT MODE. (Go into N.)
3. In response to NAME OF FILE TO EDIT, type:

MAILLIST.BAS

MAILLIST is the name of the Mail List Program. Replace MAILLIST with the name of other programs as necessary.

4. Type the program. Line numbers must be entered. WordStar operates as usual in this mode, except that there is no right-hand justification, wordwrap, or pagination. Instead of page, line, and column number, the status line now shows column and cursor location.
5. When the last line is typed, review your work for mistakes. Correct any mistakes with the WordStar editing features.
6. When you're ready to permanently save the program on your disk, simultaneously press the CTRL, K, and D keys.
7. In response to the NO-FILE menu, type **X**.

The program now may be operated.

OPERATING A PROGRAM

You must know how to access, detach, and communicate with a program.

ACCESSING A PROGRAM

Program operation will be simplified if you rename your BASIC command RUN. To access a program, respond to your system prompt:

RUN MAILLIST

You'll replace MAILLIST with the particular program you want to access. *All examples assume BASIC.COM is renamed RUN.COM.* The program you requested will be loaded and you will be prompted for the disk drive where your data file is:

ENTER THE DRIVE THAT THE DATAFILE WILL BE ON:

Each drive is identified by a letter, A through P. To respond, type the letter of the drive with the disk you'll be using for data. *You must type the single letter as a capital.*

Data may be stored on the same disk as your program or on a different one. For most applications, you should store data on a different disk to make realistic storage space available. All *Programs For Profit* storage specifications assume data will be stored on a separate data disk.

Whenever you first use a program, you will be prompted for the dimensions of your screen. Since programs may be used with many different personal computers, this setting adjusts displays to your particular screen size. The screen's width and height are defined by two responses:

1. HOW MANY CHARACTERS WIDE IS YOUR SCREEN?   Type a number. The smallest number that can be entered is 0, which will show nothing. The largest width normally manufactured today shows 132 characters across the screen. If you wish a helpful reminder, respond by typing ? and a description of what the program expects will be shown.
2. HOW MANY CHARACTERS TALL IS YOUR SCREEN?   Type a number. For reference, the standard screen shows 24 characters from top to bottom, and a legal-length word processor shows 66.

If you make a mistake and need to change the parameters once they are stored, reach your BASIC prompt and type:

KILL "PARAMTER.FIL"

NOTE:

Parameter is spelled P-A-R-A-M-T-E-R.

The response clears your parameter settings and allows you to start over. Any program code or data you may have on the disk remains intact.

DETACHING A PROGRAM

Each program provides an EXIT command that you'll use to end operation. You then remove your disk and turn off your equipment.

COMMUNICATING WITH A PROGRAM

You'll direct the operation of each program. Each program operates at two distinct levels: the Menu Level and the Command Level. Operation always starts and ends at the Menu Level.

The Menu Level

At the Menu Level, a menu of commands that can be used with the program is displayed. A prompt for a selection is also displayed at the bottom of the screen:

```
* * * * * * * * * * * * * * * * * * * * * * * * * * * * * * * * * * * * * * * * * *
                              MAIL LIST

                        AVAILABLE COMMANDS ARE:

                        1 – ADD      2 – CHANGE
                        3 – DELETE   4 – SELECT
                        5 – COUNT    6 – SEARCH
                        7 – LABELS   8 – EXIT
* * * * * * * * * * * * * * * * * * * * * * * * * * * * * * * * * * * * * * * * * *
                COMMAND SELECTION [ 1–8 OR ?1–?8 ]
```

The prompting line asks you to choose a command. The commands are numbered to save you typing. As an aid, responses that can be typed are shown in parentheses. For the Mail List menu, for example, the program expects you to type either number 1 through 8 or ?1 through ?8. A ? before a number indicates that a helpful description of the command can be displayed.

To use the Mail List Program ADD command, for instance, you will respond by typing 1. On the other hand, if you type ?1, only a brief description of the ADD command will be displayed, but the ADD operation will not be started:

COMMAND SELECTION [1–8 OR ?1–?8]:**?1**
THE ADD COMMAND
ALLOWS YOU TO ADD NEW INFORMATION TO THE
MAIL LIST AND PROMPTS AS IT GOES.
PRESS RETURN TO CONTINUE . . .

To clear the description from the screen and return to the Menu Level, press the carriage return.

The Command Level

Each command starts a computer operation. You will be fully prompted through the procedure for this operation and returned to the Menu Level. Formats for required data are shown in parentheses at the end of the prompts.

NOTE:

Various programs provide ADD and CHANGE commands. You must complete the procedures for each command. If a procedure is prematurely terminated in any way (e.g., a power failure), any data you may have attempted to store may be *permanently* inaccessible.

In responding during a command procedure, you may use upper- and lowercase letters for data. It is strongly recommended, however, that you use only uppercase letters. The capabilities of several programs allow you to specify data that then is matched to the information you have stored. These matches are exact. If you use upper and lowercase for data (e.g., Single Male), any variation in capitalization (e.g., single Male) is not considered an *exact* match, with the result that some of your data will be ignored.

Commas may be used in your data only when your response to a prompt begins with a quote, e.g.,

ENTER NAME: **"WILES, JOHN**

The closing quote is unnecessary.

Entering Special Data

When entering dates, telephone numbers, names of states, and zip codes for a procedure, you must observe the following rules.

ENTERING DATES.   Dates always are entered in the order:

MONTH DAY YEAR

Neither slashes nor spaces separate the entries. All entries must be specified by two digits. December 1, 1986, for example, is specified:

120186

As you can see, a zero is used with the day entry (01) to satisfy the two-digit rule.

ENTERING TELEPHONE NUMBERS.   The telephone number (203) 555-6666 is entered:

2035556666

The area code is always entered, but never enclosed in parentheses. If you are entering only local calls, you must leave three blank spaces (press the space bar three times) at the beginning of the number. The 1 long-distance designation is not entered. A space does not separate the code from the number. A dash does not separate the numbers.

ENTERING STATES.   States are entered as two-letter postal abbreviations. Periods are not used. The postal abbreviation for each state is listed in Appendix B.

ENTERING ZIP CODES. Zip Codes may be entered as either 5 or 9 digits.

You may wish to use the Zip plus 4 expanded zip code to earn a discount on postage. If you use the 9 digit zip code, you will receive a 9/10 cent discount on each piece sent. You must send a minimum of 250 pieces.

Note: An additional discount of 2.6 cents per piece may be earned for presorting a mailing by zip code. However, the minimum for this discount is 500 pieces. The *Programs For Profit* programs do not presort mailings.

Clearing the Screen

Many commands allow you to display information on the screen. When you're done looking at the information, you clear the screen by pressing the carriage return.

Interrupting Processing

You may interrupt the processing of any command, including the printing of output, by pressing the [CTRL] and [C] keys, or the [BREAK] key.

To continue the program from the point of interruption, type:

CONT

To restart the program, type **RUN** and the program name, e.g.,

RUN "MAILLIST

You may cause the program to pause in the processing of a command by pressing the [CTRL] and [S] keys. To reinitiate operation, press *any* key on your keyboard.

BACKING UP DISKS

Your data, as you'll see, can be very valuable. It's possible to inadvertently lose data, or make severe mistakes in entering new data. Consequently, you should always copy your disk to another at periodically scheduled intervals. In this way you'll be able to return to the backup disk should a problem arise.

You're ready to start using the programs!

CHAPTER THREE

GETTING STARTED

On his return from the Army, Tom paid me a visit. "I couldn't believe it," Tom said. "On payday, everybody wanted to give away money. I'd be rich right now if I only could have figured out a way for them to give it to me, but I couldn't."

You may feel the same way about the money earmarked for personal computers. You suspect there's a lot of money out there that people are anxious to part with for *something* related to PCs—and if only you can figure out a way for them to give it to you, you'll be all set.

Tom's success—today he owns his own business and is well on his way to becoming financially independent by 40—started when he surveyed how other people made money, and that's how *Programs For Profit* can help you. Starting in this chapter, a look is taken at how personal computers allow money to be made today.

There are hundreds of ways, which presents a problem. It's so easy to be overwhelmed by all that can be done that you may end up doing nothing. Listing businesses, with brief descriptions, won't help because there's only so much even the most brilliant mind can grasp at one time. After you've looked at about 20 businesses, they begin to blur and it gets even harder to distinguish the right one for you. Descriptions also have to be so brief to include most opportunities that you never really learn enough about any one to get started and stay in business.

Programs For Profit takes a different approach. Just as programs share characteristics, so do businesses. These common traits are the focus of Chaps. 3, 5, and 7. Profitable opportunities are used to illustrate points. Specialized opportunities are explored in remaining chapters. So, as your understanding of the many facets of business in general expands, you'll become increasingly aware of personal computer opportunities. You'll also learn the essential business practices and options available for *your* business.

This approach also is better than a list because even though there are hundreds of opportunities today, there are countless new ones yet to be started. With this approach, you'll be ready to spot and profit from them, too.

GOING INTO BUSINESS FOR YOURSELF

Alice and Kathy both operate the same personal computer application programs. They both work the same amount of time. But Kathy makes nearly twice as much money as Alice. How can this be? The difference is that Alice works for a company and Kathy has her own business.

A business of your own means more than just some extra income. It means independence to take control of your own economic life, and freedom to work the way you want. It means an opportunity to create an enterprise that will grow with your efforts. It means direct rewards for your hard work and credit for your innovations. There's also that chance to make a lot of money.

Going into business for yourself may sound terrifying. You'll need a building for your company, and of course a company name. You'll have to hire many people, especially secretaries, accountants, and lawyers. You'll need a receptionist, and elaborate telephone equipment. You'll need to do all the things at a bank that business people do. And then there's the stock you'll have to sell. And benefit plans to attract employees, and. . . .

Nonsense! You don't need any of this to go into business. You don't even need a desk or a special room in your own home. You can work at the kitchen table or down in the cellar. Two men worked in a garage only a few years ago and built nothing less than Apple Computer, Inc.

Nor does a business have to be a full-time occupation. You can work at it part-time as many hours as you like, whenever you like, as long as you meet your commitments. In fact, it's prudent to *gradually* experience anything new. You don't need everything riding on your success to pressure you.

Going into business for yourself doesn't require backers or partners—though a partner with business experience or special skills may be helpful.

As you can see, it doesn't take much to go into business. You might not even have to do much to get customers. There are many people who hold down full-time jobs and who easily get work to do in the evening and on weekends. The real money, though, is in being able to get work for yourself.

Chuck and Bob both know how to program in BASIC and both have part-time businesses at home. Chuck uses the language far more skillfully than Bob, but Bob makes far more than Chuck, and sometimes Chuck even works for Bob. Crazy? Not really. For some people, drumming up business is fun and that's what they're good at. Bob is one of them. Chuck is the better programmer, but Bob knows how to get work so well that he gets more than he can handle—and Chuck winds up working for him and earning less.

Having a business of your own has a lot of benefits and may not require much, but since only a few people start their own businesses, you think there must be something wrong with the idea.

Not really. If you're home all day and interested in an income, business itself may seem pretty alien, and a business of your own may be simply unimaginable. *Imagine it.* In many cases, starting your own business takes less work than looking for a job and you'll also get results sooner.

If you're working for a company already, it's easy to get caught up in politics, social life, and the people around you. People devote time, including a lot of their own free time, to figuring out how to improve what they're doing. They fix on career paths, look forward to yearly increases, count on benefits, and above all want to please the people above them. There's simply no time to think about owning a business. Then, you think, there's the security of steady work compared to the risks of self-employment. These days, however, a company may not be a very secure place to work anymore.

We live in a technologically changing world. No one can predict what the results of these changes will bring. Companies lay off employees. Reputable companies close down. What's on the forefront of technology today may be washed up a decade from now. Does it make sense to invest all your time, energies, and reputation in one company? Isn't that risky? Ask laid-off workers who thought they had job security that question. Or, ask managers from the mid-seventies who worked in multi-million-dollar computer time-sharing companies. These companies found their computer technology threatened by—personal computers.

The real risk that frightens many people, whether at home or working, about going into business for themselves is a genuine fear of the unknown. Most people have never started a business before, or even known anyone who did. It's difficult to measure risks when you don't know what they are. It's difficult to plan a business when you don't know what to do.

These are legitimate fears, but ones that *Programs For Profit* will help you overcome. Your imagination will be free to envision your own business, and you'll have every right in the world to ask, "Why not me? Why shouldn't I have a business of my own?"

STARTING OUT WITH WHAT YOU KNOW

Can you program in BASIC? Or fix a personal computer? Do you know how to resolve problems that may arise in the use of a PC? Do you know what makes one computer right for one person but dead wrong for another? Do you know how to work a word processing system? Can you operate a PC?

You don't need to be doing any of these things as your full-time job. You may be operating a PC at home. Or, your curiosity may have led you to read magazines about them so you know what's available.

You may have computer-related skills. Typing on a manual typewriter provides valuable skills that will help you quickly pick up word processing. Work done on mainframe computers and minicomputers often is transferable to PCs. Are you now teaching classes to use mainframe applications? If you can enter data at a work station of a distributed data processing network, you certainly can enter data with a PC in your home.

What you're doing now well may be the basis of your own business. You already have skill and experience in the business—and that means you're on your way. But it's easy to overlook this possibility by being good at what you do and caught up in your work.

Kevin had a 9-to-5 job in a support department of a leading software company. Usually, he didn't leave work before 6:30 because he wanted to get ahead. The first goal he set was a 10 percent pay raise. But his boss was so caught up in his own career that Kevin's review was late and his extra work overlooked. Kevin also often worked with Jack, who ran his own company selling personal computer application programs. One day, Jack called and asked if Kevin was interested in doing some work for him. Kevin was amazed because he hadn't realized he had a marketable skill. But he agreed so he could earn a bit more until his raise came through. Within 3 months, Jack's business was growing so fast that he needed Kevin more than just a few evenings a week, so Jack asked Kevin to start his own business. Jack would be his first client and sign a contract for a full year's service at more than Kevin's current salary. Kevin hesitated.

Jack patiently pointed out that the increase in pay he was offering meant more real money in Kevin's pocket because as a self-employed person Kevin would gain many tax advantages. Kevin still hesitated. Jack said Kevin's services wouldn't be needed every day all the time so he would be free to take on other clients. "It's a golden opportunity," Jack said, a bit exasperated.

Kevin said, "Yes, but what about my career? I'm due for a raise."

Eventually Kevin started a new career as a self-employed person using the same skills he had used before. Then he realized there really were other people like Jack who needed his skill, so he expanded his business. Within a year he had more than doubled his salary.

Not all of us may be as fortunate as Kevin in knowing somebody with Jack's Job-like patience. It may be necessary to make yourself more aware of the world beyond your home and company. If you're working with a personal computer now, ask yourself if what you're doing is needed at a company. Do companies have all the people to do all the work that needs to get done? They usually don't.

Projects often come up that have to be delayed or canceled because people with the right skills aren't available. Work rarely flows evenly through departments. There's often enormous amounts that need to be done in a short time to seize market opportunities—and it simply doesn't make sense to hire somebody full-time who'll be idle when the rush is over. It happens in the best-run companies. Many people in many companies need your skills, and people with personal computer skills are in short supply.

If you have your own PC, your skill's value may increase. Many companies lack not only people to handle work but also equipment. If your PC is compatible with theirs, you may be able to work at home and bring your disk of work into the company for its PC.

If you have one of these skills—including the ability to operate a PC—you're ready to start your own business.

STARTING A BUSINESS

You start a business by waking up one morning with an idea, opening a window, and shouting to the world, "I'm in business!" Somebody may shout, "Go back to bed!" but don't listen.

This survey may help you get your idea. It's a bit premature to go into your choice now, but once you have your idea, you'll need to clarify the details of what you intend to offer and who you think will buy it. The methodology, too, will take a few chapters for you to pick up.

Let's focus first on starting a business built on your skills. There are advantages to such a business. You don't need a large investment, and you can start it immediately. Once you have your idea for a business, you have to let people know about it. If your idea is good and the right people hear about it, they'll contact you. The best way to begin is to tell people at work who may need your skill that you're now in business. These people already know you and the quality of your work. They also can recommend you to people they know.

Janet started her word processing business by asking department managers in her company for work she could do at home. She was surprised to get work from many managers she never suspected had *their* own part-time businesses.

You also can tell friends and relatives, and ask them to pass the news along, but take the time to explain exactly what you do. Somebody's uncle once proudly told me, "My nephew is in business for himself now." When I asked what he did, the uncle said, "He works with computers." When I asked what he did with computers, the uncle shrugged and said, "Who knows?" Today, who knows the nephew?

Word of mouth limits the growth of your business to a fairly small circle of people. You may want to introduce your business to people you don't know.

The simplest and cheapest way is to advertise in the classified section of your local paper and those in surrounding areas. Prepare one ad for all the papers. *Concisely* state your business and give your telephone number: "BASIC programming done at a reasonable rate. Call 555-5555." If there are restrictions on the time you'll be at the telephone number, be sure to include them: "Evening support for your personal computer. All makes and models. Call between 5:30 and 9 at 555-5555." Run your ad every day for a few weeks. You have to give people a chance to see it.

The chances that somebody will see your ad and call you will be increased by spending a bit more for a small ad on a nonclassified page. You don't need an advertising agency to put the ad together for you. You can do it yourself.

Most papers will lay out the ad for you so you usually just need to give information. Again, state your business and give your telephone number. This technique gives you more space so you can amplify your skill: "When Your PC Program Crashes, Call Me. Software Support. 3 Years Of Experience. 555-5555." You don't need 3 years' experience as a self-employed person to make this claim, but you do need the experience. The person who will answer the ad wouldn't care whether you received that experience working for yourself or a company. He or she will be interested in results.

Such an ad allows you to spell out the advantages your skill provides for a customer. People usually relate better to benefits than to announcements of skills that then must be interpreted. "Use Your PC To The Fullest" will attract more attention than simply announcing "PC Training—Classes In Languages And Applications." Both headlines introduce the same service but the first will attract more attention because it gives a reason why the service is valuable. In fact, these two lines should be used together in the same ad. The first line announces the service and the second gives the details.

Many skills may be advertised on standard 3 × 5 inch index cards and placed in office supply stores, at printers, and on community bulletin boards (in stores, civic centers, the public library, etc.). Create the ad yourself with a pen or Magic Marker using the techniques already presented for a newspaper ad (see Fig. 3-1).

So far, the techniques for introducing your business have been aimed at a general audience. You have no control over who will see your ad. You don't know if the people you need to reach even read the local paper.

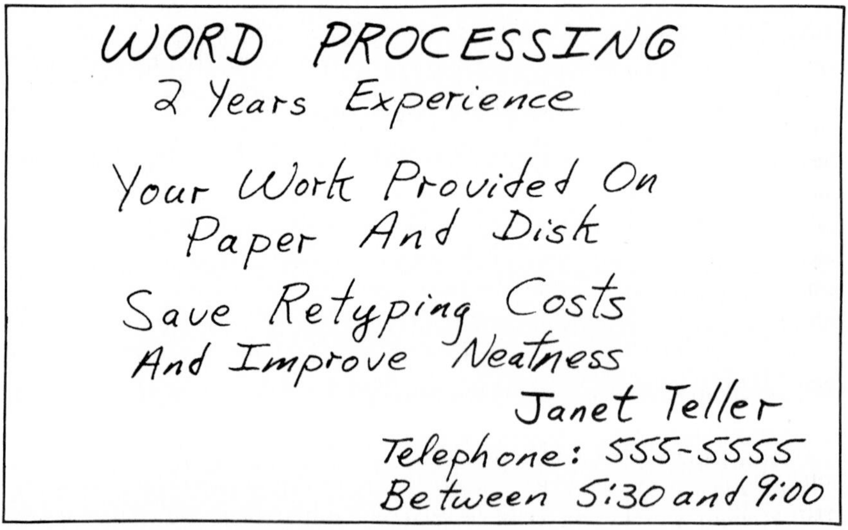

Fig. 3-1 An index card advertisement.

Your skill, also, may be valuable to only a limited number of people. You may know how to operate computer programs especially designed for insurance agencies. Placing an ad in the papers for this business means you're paying for a lot of people to look who can't possibly be customers. Instead, you can directly mail letters to all pertinent people in your general area; this will dramatically increase the likelihood that the people you want to reach will see it.

These people are listed in telephone books for your general area. Be sure to look beyond your own community. Check the Yellow Pages and white pages, but don't stop there. Look for reference books that list your potential customers ("prospects" for short). If you're a person offering programming skills, for example, look for references that list PC programs and make a list of the companies that created them. You can also look for a reference that lists software companies.

If at all possible, get a name from your source so you can direct your letter to a person, not just a company. A letter addressed to a company is sorted by a secretary or mail clerk who will decide who gets your announcement, so it very well may go to the wrong person. You always can call a company directly and simply ask who to address your letter to. If you can't get anybody else's name, address your letter to the company president. Every receptionist will know his or her name, and the president will know who to direct your letter to.

You should now have a list of people interested in your offer. Keep a copy of this list for reference. If you do more research, you'll need to know who you already have sent letters to so you won't duplicate your efforts.

Before you write your letter, think about all the things you're offering and write them down. You're probably offering more than just your original idea. If you know how to operate computer insurance programs, for instance, you offer that skill and the ability to introduce many insurance agencies to these programs. But that's not all. You also can introduce agencies to PCs because not many are using them now. Another possibility is that you also can do an agency's work on your own PC at home if they have too much other work to do on theirs. And there's still more: You can offer local support.

At this stage, you may find that your original idea isn't the best one to focus your business on after all. What's really important to offer?

To answer that, you must put yourself in your potential customer's place. What does your offer mean to him? Can you formulate a particular part of your offer as the solution to one of his major problems? What is that problem? Are you introducing him to a problem that he's not already aware of? How do you really intend to solve that problem? What benefits can he expect as a result of this particular skill? Does another one of your skills benefit him more? Will that one help him save money? Serve his customers better? Handle more customers? Add a new service to his business?

When you can answer these questions, you're ready to write your letter. Start with the prospect's problem that you're going to resolve. Tell why you're qualified to handle the solution and how you intend to do it. Introduce other things you have to offer that may be of interest to the prospect. Invite him to call you.

Figure 3-2 illustrates a direct mail letter which you may use as a model for your own. Kim Tory, the person sending it, has experience operating PC programs for the insurance agency at which she works. She now is using that experience to start her own business.

For every 20 letters you send out, you'll average one response, so you'll have to send out *at least* 60. The more letters you send out, the more chances you have that somebody will call you. It's not uncommon to send out over 200.

You don't have to type each one of those letters separately, but you want it to look as if you did. You want to develop a personal relationship with your contacts as soon as possible, and mass-produced "Dear Sir" letters won't do that. You can use a word processing system to prepare the mailing. If you don't have one, you still can quickly prepare your mailing. Type one letter on your typewriter with a black ribbon, but don't type *any* heading information (the lines from your telephone number to "Dear—"). You can print a couple of hundred of these letters very inexpensively. When the letters are printed, you only have to type in the heading information from your prospect list on each one. It will look as if you typed each letter individually. Sign the letter with a pen in *blue* ink, which enhances the illusion that the letter was specially prepared. As you type each heading, also type each envelope. Again, you will save time if you have your address printed on the upper left corner of the envelopes.

With your letter, you may wish to include a business card. A printer can prepare these cards in a couple of weeks. It won't cost much and you'll look very professional. The card shows your service, name, address, and telephone number. Your potential customer will file the card in her telephone index for future reference. These cards also can be handed out when you happen to meet somebody interested in your skill.

A response card also may be included with your letter. A response card is designed to involve your prospect with your offer by completing the card. It also puts you in the position of contacting her instead of waiting for her to call you, which is advantageous to you. Though people find many offers valu-

December 5, 1984

888 Fifth Street
St. Louis, Missouri 63103
(314) 555-5555

Mr. Philip Kish
Kish Insurance Agency
345 Jefferson Drive
St. Louis, Missouri 63103

Dear Mr. Kish,

The Beta Personal Computer Insurance Programs have helped a lot of agencies handle emergencies, but if you have a personal emergency, do you have anyone to help you operate your personal computer?

I've been operating programs specifically designed for insurance agencies for more than 2 years so I have the experience to help.

I can also come in once a week to handle your work and I'm always available to answer your questions. If your work has really backed up, I have my own IBM Personal Computer and software to help you through a crunch. If you haven't seen these programs in action, I would appreciate an opportunity to introduce them to you and show you how a personal computer can aid you.

You'll find my service highly professional and reasonably priced. Whenever you're free to discuss it, please give me a call at 555-5555.

I'm looking forward to talking with you.

Very truly,

Kim Tory

Fig. 3-2 A direct mail letter.

able, they seldom fit all of them into their schedules, so many that they're actually interested in never get a chance. Response cards, on the other hand, usually are filled out immediately. A response card also is a lot more polite than aggressively stating in your letter, "I'll call you soon."

Once again, your printer can help you with your response card. (As you can see, printers are very important to businesses, which is why it pays to leave an index card ad with as many printers as possible.) On one side of the card, ask whether or not the prospect is interested in your offer, the prospect's name, address, company, and telephone number. You also may ask, "When is the best time to call you?" Other questions can be added that can help you talk to her later on, but each new question reduces the likelihood of a response. You want to make it as simple as possible to respond.

On the other side of the response card is your address and other information required by the post office. You'll need a postage payment number, which you get at the post office. With this number, you agree to pay for response cards mailed back to you. You consequently don't pay postage for all the response cards you send out and your prospect doesn't need to put a stamp on your card. A response card is illustrated in Fig. 3-3.

That's all there is to starting your own business. You determine what you want to sell, you define who'll buy it, and decide how best to tell them about your offer. Techniques for announcing your offer, which have been presented in this chapter, are summarized in Table 3-1 for later reference.

Each time you set out to gain new customers, you'll use these techniques. On your subsequent announcements, your *previous* self-employment experience can be noted.

One question needing further clarification is how to define details of your business. You can *begin* to define them in the same way you go about preparing to write a direct mail letter to potential customers. Decide who likely candidates are for what you have to offer. Expand your original idea by listing all the things you're offering, and then put yourself in your prospects' place to look at the offer. Your understanding of your own business will gain focus in this way.

To put it all together, consider how you can start a business if your only skill is the ability to operate a personal computer. You've worked some simple application programs but you really don't have any software suitable for your own business. Here's what you'll have to do:

1. *Generally define the skills you have for making money.* In this case, that skill is the ability to operate a personal computer.
2. *Think of people who can use the skill.* Your skill can be used by people to initially enter their data. These people include small business people

☐ Yes, I'm interested
☐ I'm not interested now, but call me later

_____   _____
Name   Company

_____   _____
Telephone Number   Extension

_____   _____   _____ _____
Street   City   State Zip

The best time to call me is at _____ on _____
                               Time   Date

My personal computer is a _____.
                           Make and Model

(a)

| | | | | |

No
Postage Stamp
Necessary if
Mailed in the
United States

BUSINESS REPLY MAIL
First Class   Permit No. 000,   City,   State

POSTAGE WILL BE PAID BY
Your Name
Your Street
Your City, State, Zip

(b)

Fig. 3-3   A reply card. (a) Back of card; (b) front of card.

TABLE 3-1   TECHNIQUES FOR INTRODUCING YOUR BUSINESS

Technique	Audience/Cost
Tell friends, relatives, and people at work	Very limited, many can't use your offer; no cost.
Classified advertisement	Broader than word of mouth, but ad may be missed by people you want to reach who do not read the paper; cheap.
Small advertisement on nonclassified page	Will be seen by more people who read the paper than a classified ad—good for offer with broad appeal; costs more than classified ad, but still inexpensive.
Index card advertisement	Announces your offer to limited audience, many of whom will be interested; cheap.

Direct mail
  A. Letter alone
  B. Business card
  C. Response card
	Directs announcement to specific people and assumes that the vast majority will see it; most expensive technique and expenses increase with additions to letter.

who have personal computers. Local computer stores may be able to help you put together a list of contacts.

3. *Develop all you can offer these people and see if that sparks any new ideas, then decide if you want to change the focus of your offer.* If somebody tells you how to do it, you also can type changes in people's programs. Companies that produce programs could be clients, too. Somebody there certainly could tell you what to do. Why would a programming company need to make changes, anyhow? Companies need to have their programs tested. Most programs, today, are designed to be run by people *without* programming experience. You could test the programs.

Testing programs would really benefit a company. A person other than the programmer who wrote the code would do the testing and the results are sure to be unbiased. You also could work a lot less expensively than a programmer. As new applications are created for the home, PC programs will be aimed at people like you. Is there anyone better able to test these programs?

Program testing could be a ground-floor opportunity that might quickly lead to a position as consultant or program representative. After you test a program and get to know its capabilities better than anyone but the programmer, you would be in an excellent position to teach program operation, manage customer relations, or sell the program.

If instructions for program operation are documented, you also can help debug the documentation by seeing how accurately it reflects actual program use.

4. *Decide how best to introduce your business by studying your market.* Your market consists of companies that develop PC programs in your area, which is a relatively small audience, so you can direct your efforts to specific people. A direct mail campaign is called for. You also can put index card ads in computer stores.

5. *Does your offer sell itself or do you have to spell it out so the benefits are obvious?* The benefits may not readily be apparent.

6. *Announce your business.* All of your decision making has created a plan that now must be put into action. In this case, you now have to:

   (a) Look up people and addresses in telephone books. Go to the library and look for references that list PC software houses in your area. At your local computer stores ask for lists of local software houses— don't be afraid to explain what you're doing because your computer store quickly can become one of your first customers.

   (b) Write your letter, imitating the sample previously shown. Start with the problem you're going to resolve. Tell why you're qualified to handle the solution and how you intend to do it. Introduce other services you can offer that might be of interest to the customer. Invite the person to call you. Such a letter is illustrated in Fig. 3-4.

   (c) Decide if you want to invest in business cards or response cards. Perhaps you should see how the business goes before much money is invested in business cards.

   (d) Type your letter and take it to the printer. Have the printer also print envelopes with your return address. Use your address list to figure out how many you need and double it. You'll need extra letters for mistakes and the *next* mailing, too.

   (e) When the letters and envelopes are printed—it will take only a couple of days—type letter headings. Send out at least 10 a day for 10 days.

   (f) Make up index card ads and place them in computer stores.

   (g) After you've sent out your first batch of letters, wait a month and see what happens. You don't want to get more responses than you

February 15, 1985

716 Pier Point Lane
Morrison, MA 05501
(413) 555-5555

Mr. Barry Fields
B Software Systems, Inc.
567 Spirit Road
Andover, MA 05501

Dear Mr. Fields,

Testing personal computer software takes a totally objective person with an end user's skills, which usually don't include programming. Today, however, the same person who has done the programming does the testing. What's worse, it's completely unnecessary to pay for this high-priced skill for most of the testing.

For over a year, I've been working with a personal computer, but I don't know programming, so I don't expect to be paid like a programmer. If you tell me what your programs are supposed to do, I'll tell you if they're really doing it.

Besides aiding program testing, I also can help debug your program documentation, enter program changes, and enter data to get new users of your software up and running quickly.

I work on a free-lance basis at your office or, if my IBM PC personal computer is suitable to your needs, my home. I've also used my personal computer for conversions to IBM source code and testing programs developed for other machines.

You'll find my service highly professional, reliable, and priced far below what you pay a programmer. If you're interested in talking about it, please call me any afternoon between 1 and 5 at 555-5555.

Sincerely,

Andrea Callas

Fig. 3-4 Starting a business with personal computer skills.

can handle. If you haven't gotten any responses after a month, send out another batch of letters.

You're now in business!

CAN I QUIT MY JOB NOW?

The urge to go into business for yourself may have bitten you now that you see how easy it is—and that's great. Just don't get so excited that you don't finish *Programs For Profit*. There's still a lot you'll need to know even for a part-time business.

If you can't wait to quit your job, maybe what you're now doing all day isn't for you, after all. If you hate what you're doing, you certainly don't want to make it your own business, in which case you ought to consider another personal computer business, such as the one in the next chapter. Remember, you're not committing yourself to any business yet. You're just surveying the opportunities.

CHAPTER
FOUR
PROFITS IN
THE MAIL:
A MAIL LIST
PROGRAM

One technique presented in the last chapter for announcing an offer is to send a letter directly to the person you want to reach. Many businesses regularly send announcements to the same people, which is why a Mail List Program is valuable.

Names and addresses are typed into the program only once, stored on disk, and printed on labels as often as needed.

Your Mail List Program also may be used to respond to requests that have been prompted by newspaper or magazine ads for information brochures. In this case, you can capture names and addresses for subsequent mailings.

This chapter will show you how your Mail List Program can be valuable for your own business. You'll discover who your markets are and learn how to operate your program. The program code is also included.

WHO NEEDS DIRECT MAIL?

A Mail List Program has a surprisingly large number of applications and, when used effectively, gets remarkably profitable results.

One of the best sources of new business is old business. Someone who has bought what you offer and is satisfied will be likely to buy something else or tell somebody else about your new offer. Many businesses, consequently, want to stay in touch with customers.

Clothing stores, for example, have a continuous turnover of seasonal inventory. Everybody needs to replenish their wardrobe sooner or later, so these stores direct mailings to former customers in the hope they'll buy again. The shop where I buy my suits and sports jackets adds an incentive to its announcements by inviting me to its pre-public seasonal sales so long-standing customers get first chance at sale goods.

Direct mail benefits most retail stores, including stores that specialize in furniture, appliances, building goods, linens, jewelry, gifts, art supplies, books, musical instruments, photographic equipment, stereo equipment, computer equipment, carpeting, and gardening supplies.

Commercial companies, likewise, direct mail to other companies. A software company, for instance, lets its customers know about new programs it has. An auto parts company sends out announcements of price breaks, discounts, and special incentives to bring back customers.

Service-related companies also benefit from direct mail. Seasonal reminders are sent to everyone on a mail list by lawn care services, tire shops to remind people to change snow tires, carpet cleaning services, and income tax preparation services.

Names get on these lists in many ways. Names and addresses often are requested for receipts and the data is taken from the store's copy. A customer who pays by check gives the store the data—the customer's name and address are printed on the check. A credit card charge gives the company a name, which then can be used to find an address. A store even may put up a display that asks people to sign up for its mailing list, and many do so they will receive notices of special sales, etc.

Ads with reply cards for additional information may be placed in newspapers and magazines to generate mail lists of qualified prospects. That is, people who are interested in the product or service advertised will respond to the ad. For the people who respond, an expensive, full color, lengthy brochure will be sent. It simply would be uneconomical to send these costly brochures to a blind mailing. When a reply is received, the literature or product is promptly sent as promised.

Similarly, slick catalogs of merchandise are direct mailed to people. These catalogs serve enormous markets.

Other businesses also depend on mail lists for their very existence. A newsletter, for instance, goes only to the people who have paid for the information. There are newsletters today for thousands of different subjects and each one needs a different mail list. People pay to get on these lists.

Organizations use mail lists to keep in touch with members. There are thousands of different types of organizations: Churches, clubs (for example, a personal computer club), theater organizations, charitable organizations, unions, guilds, dance companies, writers' groups, societies, political action groups, and business associations are just a few.

Some organizations need dual-purpose mail lists. Mail may be directed to all names on the list to raise funds, but to only a selected few for special purposes. A theatrical organization, for instance, may send requests for funds to put on a show to all members on the mailing list, but only those interested in participating in the play would be sent notices for auditions.

A mail list, finally, can be used to attract new business. In this case, somebody may sell a specialized mail list. A veterinarian might sell a list of names of horse owners who come to her to the operator of a local stable. The stable operator, in turn, would send mail about the stable to these people. A computer store might sell a list of people who have bought certain makes of computers to a business specializing in developing software for those machines so announcements can be sent to these people about programs. Such a list is valuable because it pinpoints the people getting the mailing. Statistically, when pieces are blindly mailed (addressed to Resident), only 2 percent of the people contacted will respond. An unsolicited, direct mail campaign, on the other hand, can get a response rate as high as 12 percent. The savings in postage alone are significant and that means less investment for higher profits.

In another very profitable application, new business can be attracted by mailing coupons to local residents. Property books and census data available in a library contain names and addresses of residents in towns and cities. This data is used to create the mail list. Small businesses, such as ice cream shops, shoe repair shops, bakeries, bicycle shops, sporting goods stores, and drugstores, are contacted with the offer to publicize their services and products by directly mailing discount coupons. These coupons usually are designed and printed for the business. Coupons for several businesses are mailed together, which virtually assures that everybody who gets a letter will find something interesting. It also reduces the businesses' postage costs. The envelopes are printed with an announcement of the contents: "Valuable Coupons Inside." These mailings can be scheduled on a weekly basis with businesses participating in rotation, assuring you of a steady income.

HOW DIRECT MAIL CAN BENEFIT YOU

As you can see, a great many businesses and organizations benefit from using mail lists—and you can profit from this need with your Mail List Program.

Many businesses realize direct mail's advantages but don't use it because it means taking so much time away from their main business. It does take much time and many different talents to prepare a mailing. An advertising person, who may work with a designer or artist, creates an original of the piece to be mailed. This original also may be created by a typographer or a typesetting house. In the case of a newsletter, a specialist in a field creates the letter, which then may be taken to a typist. This original piece is taken to a printer or photocopyist who reproduces the pieces actually used in the mailing. The labels then must be run, each piece put in an envelope, the envelopes sealed, the labels pasted on, and the mailing taken to the post office.

To attract business, any one of the people in this chain may agree to do *all* the work. That person then will work with the other people but the mailing will be his or her responsibility. A printer, for example, may offer a client the total service of preparing an original, printing it, running labels, and doing the rest of the work, primarily to attract the printing business. Today it's not the least uncommon for a printer to take the mailing to a typist, who manually types each and every label on envelopes. Nobody in the chain, however, likes doing this work because it's not their *central* business.

Direct mail can be your specialty. You'll provide customers with the benefits of direct mail and do the work for them. What could be better?

To start a profitable business, contact people who already may handle part of the work necessary for direct mail. This market includes advertising agencies, artists, designers, copywriters, typesetters, typing services, word processing services, printers, and photocopyists. If they already handle direct mail, you'll free them to do their main business, which to them means more money and enjoyment. If they aren't presently offering the service, you'll allow them to and that will attract customers for their main business. You, in turn, will get a number of mail lists from a single source—and the time and effort you save from contacting prospects increases the profitability of your direct mail service.

A second market consists of large companies. As surprising as this sounds, relatively few large companies have an in-house direct mail service. As a result, highly paid specialists and department managers sometimes end up handling the manual end of the mailings simply because there's no one else to do it. Direct your efforts to contacting the head of the Corporate Com-

37

munications Department or Publications Department. This single source can lead to your handling mailings for many different departments.

Another market is composed of organizations that handle their direct mail internally. Many political action groups, dance companies, church groups, and clubs, for instance, personally address envelopes from lists simply because they don't have ready access to a computer.

Newsletters present another market.

To increase your own profits, you always should try to offer as complete a job as possible. An archaeological society, for example, prepares a monthly newsletter for its members. You can take a prepared draft to a typist (or type it yourself), take your original to the printer, generate the labels, stuff the newsletters in envelopes, and take them to the post office. Such a total service is very appealing to somebody with barely enough time to put the newsletter together, and you would get a fee for each additional service you perform. (Charging is more fully discussed in Chap. 7.) Of course, you actually don't have to do all the work yourself. You can farm some of it out to others.

The simplest way to reach these markets with your offer is to advertise in local papers (see Fig. 4-1 for a sample). These efforts should be supplemented with direct mail to your target markets (see Fig. 4-2 for a sample).

You can venture a step further and help the many small businesses which may be unaware of direct mail's benefits. Lowering costs of personal computers are opening this vast new market, with tremendous potential for profits. In this case, your total service will need the aid of an artist and copywriter to prepare the material to be sent.

You may want to go a step further and start a newsletter of your own, but now you'll need to do so much research to keep your newsletter competitive and informative that you'll be on the lookout for a service to handle the mailing. At that point, you'll wonder why nobody has started one because you'll be ready to do anything for more free time.

YOUR DIRECT MAIL BUSINESS

If you start a direct mail service, your basic tasks will be to maintain up-to-date mail lists and generate labels on a printer attached to a PC. Your customers will provide you with the lists of names and addresses you'll enter. From time to time, your customers may have names to add, change, and delete. That, basically, is your business. You can offer to do as much more as you like—print the pieces, stuff the envelopes, etc.

You'll use the *Programs For Profit* Mail List Program to store and update each customer's mail list, and generate the labels. This Mail List Program has

DIRECT MAIL SERVICE

— We'll Put Your Idea In The Mail —

* Computer-generated labels

* Printing

* Word processing

* Envelopes stuffed, sealed, and delivered to post office

* Help in developing lists

* Literature fulfillment

* Product fulfillment

* Ad campaigns

Total Service For Less Than You'd Guess

May Hansen, Telephone: 555-5555, 345 Main St., Pittsford

Fig. 4-1 A direct mail service advertisement.

special *additional* capabilities you can offer customers which other services cannot. It prints only names and addresses on labels, never any computer jargon. Some programs print distracting computer codes that are completely unnecessary. Your labels can include a name, a company name, a street address, city, state, and zip code. When printed, the address is always compacted to improve its appearance. This is an advantage over programs that

July 19, 1985

456 Hammerhead Road
Glendale, Mass. 05501
(415) 555-5555

Mr. Harold Jensen
Jensen Printing Co.
68 Armsford Road
Glendale, Mass. 05501

Dear Mr. Jensen,

A direct mail service attracts customers with announcements to print, but to do all the other work for a mailing yourself can cost you your printing business.

I know a lot of time and work goes into a mailing because that's my business. I pride myself on doing it so well that you'll never know just what you're missing.

I'll use my personal computer to handle the mail lists. If you're already using a computer for mail lists, I'll be happy to pick up mail list maintenance on my machine and return the updated disks to you. If you don't already offer this service, I can help you start one.

You'll find my service reliable and inexpensive. To discuss working together, please feel free to call me any weekday between 9 and 4:30 at 555-5555.

Very truly,

Your Name

Fig. 4-2   A direct mail piece targeted at printers.

allow a company name, but always leave a line on the label for the company, even when there's no company name:

FRED GRANGE

101 Second Ave.
Hillsdale, N.Y. 10021

Your Mail List Program will never print such an awkward label. If there's no company name, the space will be removed.

Many mail list programs that allow a name and a company require that you always have the name. Your program has the flexibility to allow you to enter a name and a company, or just a name, or just a company.

Your program allows you to offer your customers the ability to create multipurpose mail lists. A special *select capability* enables your customer to choose the labels from his or her list to be generated. The customer may choose to print everybody, or:

- Only people in a selected zip code
- Only people in a selected state
- Only people in a selected city
- Only people at a selected company
- Any combination of selections

The ability to combine selections is especially valuable because your Mail List Program allows two additional lines of information to be stored for each label. These lines can be anything your customer decides. A customer may record professions (e.g., doctor, lawyer, teacher), marital status (single, married, divorced), customer profitability (steady, variable), organizational function (officer, member, contributor), talents (dancer, actor, saxophonist, artist), or sex. The lines never are printed on a label, but may be used in selections.

Labels, for example, for all singles in Chicago that appear on the list can be selected. Or, special offers first can be sent only to a store's best customers. Or, notice of a meeting can be sent only to members of a special committee.

A special profitable use of this select capability is to create "spinoff" mail lists that your customers can sell themselves or make available for sale. You don't need to use this capability, but it makes your lists distinctive.

Once a selection is made, you can use the *count capability* to show you how many labels on your list meet your criteria, and how much the mailing will cost.

Before you print the labels, you may search through the labels, one at a time, just to be sure you've made the right selection. You can step through as many labels as you like.

The *Programs For Profit* Mail List Program gives you these extra features to offer your prospects that will give you an advantage over any competition you may encounter in closing deals.

OPERATING YOUR MAIL LIST PROGRAM

Your Mail List Program gives you a professional capability to keep up-to-date records for names and addresses, and to print labels for mailings.

You may store two items of your choice in addition to a name and address on each label. Once you decide what type of information to record as item 1 and item 2 (if you wish to record any), you must be consistent for all labels on that list.

You may have different customers, some with many mail lists. You should store each mail list on a separate disk. On the disk cover, write the customer's name, address, telephone number, a brief description of the mail list, and, if used, the information you're recording for item 1 and item 2. On the back of the cover, write any selection codes you're using for item 1 or item 2 (e.g., 1—approves strongly, 2—approves, 3—approves mildly, 4—disapproves mildly; such codes drastically reduce typing input and reduce errors).

You're ready to use the Mail List Program. Once you have accessed the program, you may:

- Add labels
- Change information on a label
- Remove a label from the list
- Set criteria for selecting labels
- Count labels
- Search the mail list, label by label
- Print the labels

The procedures for these activities are presented below.

ACCESSING THE MAIL LIST PROGRAM

To access the Mail List Program, type **RUN MAILLIST** in response to your system prompt:

A:RUN MAILLIST

The Mail List Program will be loaded and you will be shown the menu of mail list commands:

```
* * * * * * * * * * * * * * * * * * * * * * * * * * * * * * * * * * * * * * * * * * *
                            MAIL LIST

                    AVAILABLE COMMANDS ARE:

                    1 - ADD     2 - CHANGE
                    3 - DELETE  4 - SELECT
                    5 - COUNT   6 - SEARCH
                    7 - LABELS  8 - EXIT
* * * * * * * * * * * * * * * * * * * * * * * * * * * * * * * * * * * * * * * * * * *
            COMMAND SELECTION [ 1-8 OR ?1-?8 ]
```

The following procedures provide all you will need to know to use these commands effectively.

ADDING A LABEL

The ADD command (1) adds labels to a mail list. The command is used to create a mail list, and then to add new labels to it.

The Mail List Program prompts for each line that is to appear on the label. You respond by typing the appropriate information. The program also prompts for two items, but these lines, which are intended for recording data that later may be used to select the label, are never printed.

The procedure for adding a label is:

1. COMMAND SELECTION [Menu Level]: Type 1 for the ADD command.

2. **ENTER NAME:**   Type a person's name using 20 or less characters. If you will be entering only a company name but not a person's, press the space bar (to enter a blank space) and then the carriage return. If you do not wish to record a label once you have started the procedure, press the carriage return. You will be returned to the Menu Level where you can choose another command. Either a name for a company or a person must be entered for a label.

3. **ENTER COMPANY:**   Type the name of a company using 20 or less characters. If the label does not have a company name, press the carriage return.

4. **ENTER STREET ADDRESS:**   Type the street number and name using 30 or less characters.

5. **ENTER TOWN OR CITY:**   Type the name of a town or a city using 15 or less characters.

6. **ENTER TWO-CHARACTER STATE CODE:**   Type a state's postal code. These codes are listed in Appendix B.

7. **ENTER FIVE-DIGIT ZIP:**   Type the zip code. The zip code is not required. If you are not recording one, press the carriage return.

8. **ENTER ITEM 1:**   Type any item 1 data you want to record, using 20 or less characters. If you do not wish to record any data, press the carriage return.

9. **ENTER ITEM 2:**   Type any item 2 data using 20 or less characters. Press the carriage return if you don't wish to record the data for this label.

At this time, the label is added to the list and you are prompted to start another by ENTER NAME:. If you do not wish to add another, press the carriage return and you will be returned to the Menu Level.

The only required input for a label is the name of a person or a company. Any other information may be left incomplete by responding to the prompt with a carriage return. The label can be completed later with the CHANGE command.

The procedure for adding a label is illustrated in Fig. 4-3.

NOTE:

If your customer does not choose to use item 1 or 2, you may want to use it yourself to check your work. In the available item slot, record the date you are adding the label, e.g. 10/14. Then, at the Menu Level, choose the SELECT command (enter the number 4) and set the item equal to

* *
MAIL LIST

AVAILABLE COMMANDS ARE:

```
1 – ADD      2 – CHANGE
3 – DELETE   4 – SELECT
5 – COUNT    6 – SEARCH
7 – LABELS   8 – EXIT
```
* *
COMMAND SELECTION [1–8 OR ?1–?8] **1**   The ADD command is selected.

ENTER NAME: **HARRY WALKER**
ENTER COMPANY: **NEW HAVEN PORSCHE**
ENTER STREET ADDRESS: **202 WHALLEY**
ENTER TOWN OR CITY: **HAMDEN**   Data for the label is entered in
ENTER 2 CHARACTER STATE CODE: **CT**   response to the prompts.
ENTER 5 DIGIT ZIP: **06544**
ENTER ITEM 1: **SALESMAN**
ENTER ITEM 2: **SINGLE**

ENTER NAME: ⟨**CR**⟩   No other labels are to be added to
                                        the mail list so the carriage
                                        return is pressed in response to
                                        the prompt. At this time, you
                                        will be returned to the Menu
                                        Level.

Fig. 4-3 The ADD command.

the date. Run labels on paper and you'll have a report of all the labels you've just entered. You can proofread it and make corrections.

CHANGING INFORMATION ON A LABEL

The CHANGE command (2) is used to replace lines on a label. If a line had been left incomplete, it, too, can be entered with this procedure.

To make a change, you will identify a specific label by a name, identify a line on that label to be changed, and type the replacement. All replacement lines are restricted by the character limitations specified under the ADD command procedure.

The procedure for changing information on a label is:

1. COMMAND SELECTION: Type 2 for the CHANGE command.
2. ENTER NAME: Type the name of the person on the label that you want to change. The name must be typed *exactly* as it appears on the label. If the label does not have a person's name, press the carriage return and you will be prompted ENTER COMPANY:. Identify the label to be changed by typing the company's name; or, if after all you do not wish to change any label, press the space bar and then the carriage return and you will be returned to the Menu Level.
     The label you have identified will be displayed:

> 1.   Name: DICK JONES
> 2. Company: JONES PRINTING
> 3.   Street: 123 CHAPEL STREET
> 4.   City: NEW HAVEN
> 5.   State: CT
> 6.   Zip: 06510
> 7.   Item 1: OWNER
> 8.   Item 2: MARRIED
>
> 9. *Look for different record*

3. CHANGE WHAT?:   Look at the label and decide if it's the one you want. There may be several labels on your mail list with the same person's (or company's) name but with different addresses. If the label is *not* the one you want, type 9 and the program will return this first label to the list, take the next one with the name you entered, and display the new label. If no other label has the same name, you will be returned to step 1.
     If the label is the one you want, type the number of the line you wish to change. To change the company name, for example, type 2. You will be prompted to enter the new line by ENTER NEW COMPANY NAME: and you then type it. The revised label will be displayed and you again will be prompted CHANGE WHAT? You may change any line, including the one you just changed.
     When you have made all the changes you want, respond to CHANGE WHAT? by pressing the carriage return. Your revised label will be added to the mail list. The program then will ask you to identify another label by prompting ENTER NAME.
     When all your changes are made, respond to ENTER NAME by

pressing the carriage return. You will be prompted ENTER COM-PANY. Press the space bar and the carriage return to return to the Menu Level.

The procedure for changing a label is illustrated in Fig. 4-4.

COMMAND SELECTION [1–8 OR ?1–?8] **2**

The CHANGE command is selected.

ENTER NAME: **DICK JONES**

The label to be changed is identified by the name DICK JONES.

1.   Name: DICK JONES
2. Company: JONES PRINTING
3.   Street: 123 CHAPEL STREET
4.   City: NEW HAVEN
5.   State: CT
6.   Zip: 06510
7.   Item 1: OWNER
8.   Item 2: MARRIED

The first label on the mail list with the name DICK JONES is displayed.

9. ∗Look for different record∗

This label, however, is not the one that needs to be changed, so the program is instructed to look for another DICK JONES label.

Change What? [1–8] **9**

1.   Name: DICK JONES
2. Company: NORTHWIND REALTY
3.   Street: 2243 OAK STREET
4.   City: NEW HAVEN
5.   State: CT
6.   Zip: 06511
7.   Item 1: AGENT
8.   Item 2: SINGLE

A second label is found and displayed for verification. This is the label that needs to be changed.

9. ∗Look for different record∗

Change What? [1–8] **2**

The label line to be changed is identified.

ENTER NEW COMPANY: **SOUTHWIND REALTY**

The replacement is typed.

Fig. 4-4   The CHANGE command. (*Cont. on following page.*)

1.   Name: DICK JONES
2. Company: SOUTHWIND REALTY
3.   Street: 2243 OAK STREET ⎤
4.   City: NEW HAVEN   ⎮ ——————The revised label is displayed for
5.   State: CT   ⎮   verification
6.   Zip: 06511   ⎮
7.   Item 1: AGENT   ⎮
8.   Item 2: SINGLE   ⎦
9. *Look for different record*

                                        No other changes need to be
                                        made on this label so the
Change What? [1–8] ⟨**CR**⟩——————————carriage return is pressed.

Fig. 4-4 *(Cont.)*

REMOVING LABELS FROM A LIST

The DELETE command (3) removes labels. The procedure for deleting a label is:

1. COMMAND SELECTION: Type **3** for the DELETE command.
2. ENTER NAME: Type the name of the person on the label you want to delete. If the label has only a company name, press the carriage return (no person's name). If, after all, you do not wish to delete a label, press the space bar and the carriage return and you will be returned to the Menu Level.

The first label that matches your response will be displayed:

        Name: DICK JONES
     Company: JONES PRINTING
      Street: 123 CHAPEL STREET
        City: NEW HAVEN
       State: CT
         Zip: 06510
      Item 1: OWNER
      Item 2: MARRIED
    1. *Look For Different Record*
    2. *Delete Record Shown Above*

3. WHICH COMMAND?:   Type **1** to display the next record with the same name. If the label has no name, the number 1 causes the next label

without a name to be displayed. To delete a label with only a company name, you will have to keep looking through the list until the one you want to remove is displayed. If no new matching labels are found, you will be prompted ENTER NAME. When the label you're interested in is displayed, type 2 and the label will be flagged for removal. After you type the number 2, you will be prompted to ENTER NAME.

When you have flagged all the labels you want deleted, respond to ENTER NAME by pressing the space bar and the carriage return. The program will begin to clean the flagged labels from the mail list, as indicated by CLEANING IN PROGRESS. When the process is complete, the message CLEANING COMPLETE will be displayed and you will be returned to the Menu Level.

The procedure for deleting a label is illustrated in Fig. 4-5.

COMMAND SELECTION [1–8 OR ?1–?8] **3**   The DELETE command is selected.

ENTER NAME: **DICK JONES**   The label for Dick Jones is to be deleted.

    Name: DICK JONES
 Company: JONES PRINTING
    Street: 123 CHAPEL STREET
     City: NEW HAVEN   The first label with that name is displayed.
    State: CT
     Zip: 06510
   Item 1: OWNER
   Item 2: MARRIED

1. *Look for different record*
2. *Delete Record Shown Above*

WHICH COMMAND? [1 OR 2] : **2**   The label is flagged for deletion.
ENTER NAME: **b** ⟨CR⟩   No more labels are to be flagged now.

CLEANING IN PROGRESS . . . .   The flagged label is cleaned from the mail list.

CLEANING COMPLETE   At this time, you will be returned to the Menu Level.

Fig. 4-5   The DELETE command.

SELECTING LABELS

The SELECT command (4) is designed to be used with the COUNT, SEARCH, and LABELS commands. The SELECT command itself sets a selection criterion. Only labels that match that criterion are available for use. Once defined, the selection remains in effect until you replace it with a new selection or exit from the program. You, consequently, can count the number of labels that are selected and look at a few to be sure they're the ones you want before you print labels. There's an economy of effort and no chance of introducing selection errors due to respecification.

If you don't make any selections, all the labels on the mail list are available for printing.

The procedure for setting a selection is:

1. COMMAND SELECTION: Type **4** for the SELECT command.
2. The program will display the criteria available to make a selection:

> 1. Name
> 2. Company
> 3. Street
> 4. City
> 5. State
> 6. Zip
> 7. Item 1
> 8. Item 2

3. CHOICE FROM ABOVE: Type the number of the criterion you wish to set. If you only want to see labels for a particular state, for example, type 5. You will be prompted to set the selection, e.g.,

STATE:

Type the data (e.g., **CT**) *exactly* as it appears on the labels you want.

The program will prompt you to make another choice. Selections can be set in any order. You may set a selection for item 2 (8) and then make one for state (5), for instance. When you have made all the selections you want, press the carriage return in response to CHOICE FROM ABOVE. At this time, you will be shown the selections you have set for review.

4. ARE THESE CORRECT?:   If the settings are what you want, type **Y**

and you will be returned to the Menu Level. Your selections, then, will be defined. If you want to reset one or set a new one, type **N**.

If you again use the SELECT command, all settings are cleared so you can start over.

The procedure for setting a selection is illustrated in Fig. 4-6.

COUNTING LABELS

The COUNT command (5) counts the number of labels with data that exactly matches your selection criteria. If you have not made any selections, all labels on the list are counted. The command also calculates the projected cost for the mailing.

The procedure for counting labels is:

1. COMMAND SELECTION: Type 5 for the COUNT command.
2. WHAT DOES IT COST TO MAIL ONE PIECE?:   Type the cost. You can define the cost in many ways. You can type the cost for postage. You can include additional costs, such as the cost for an envelope, the piece itself, your labor charge for preparing a single piece. The cost will be multiplied by the label count. You do not need to specify any cost. If you want only a count, press the carriage return.

   The program will count the labels and show you the result. If you entered a cost, the mailing cost is calculated and also shown.
3. PRESS RETURN TO RETURN TO COMMAND MENU: When you are finished looking at the report, press the carriage return to clear the screen and return to the Menu Level.

The procedure for counting labels is illustrated in Fig. 4-7. The illustration assumes a selection previously has been set for the state (CT) and item 2 (SINGLE).

SEARCHING THROUGH THE MAIL LIST

The SEARCH command (6) is used to look at one label at a time. The command is intended to allow you to verify that the labels you are about to print are, in fact, the ones you want. It also can be used to search through the mail list to look for errors or duplicate labels.

The search starts with the first label you added to this list and progresses to the last. The search can be stopped at any time.

COMMAND SELECTION [1–8 OR ?1–?8] **4**   The SELECT command is
                                             selected.

1. Name ⌉
2. Company │
3. Street │
4. City   ├──────────────────────── The selections that can be set are
5. State   │   displayed.
6. Zip   │
7. Item 1 │
8. Item 2 ⌋

Choice from above [1–8] **5**   Labels are to be selected by state.
State: **CT**   The state is set. Only Connecticut
                                            labels will be used.

1. Name
2. Company
3. Street
4. City
5. State
6. Zip
7. Item 1
8. Item 2

Choice from above [1–8] **8**   Item 2 is *also* to be set.
Item 2: **SINGLE**   Item 2 is set to SINGLE; now,
                                              only Connecticut singles labels
                                              will be used.

1. Name
2. Company
3. Street
4. City
5. State
6. Zip
7. Item 1
8. Item 2

Choice from above [1–8]⟨**CR**⟩   No other selections are to be set.
THE FOLLOWING SELECTION CRITERIA HAVE
BEEN CHOSEN:

STATE: CT   ⌉   The selections that have been set
ITEM 2: SINGLE ⌋─────────────────────   are displayed for review.

ARE THESE CORRECT? **Y**   The selections are correct and you
                                              are returned to the Menu
                                              Level.

Fig. 4-6   The SELECT command.

COMMAND SELECTION [1–8 OR ?1–?8] 5   The COUNT command is selected.

What does it cost to mail one piece? .98   The cost of a single piece is typed.

There are   5   pieces to be mailed.
The mailing cost is $ 4.90   You are shown the number of labels that meet the criteria you have defined and the mailing cost.

Press RETURN to return to
   command menu⟨CR⟩   The carriage return is pressed to clear the screen and return you to the Menu Level.

Fig. 4-7   The COUNT command.

The procedure for searching through a mail list is:

1. COMMAND SELECTION: Type 6 for the SEARCH command. The present selection criteria settings, if any, will be displayed with the first label. You will be able to look at only labels that match the criteria.
2. PRESS RETURN TO CONTINUE OR X TO EXIT: When you are finished looking at a label, press the carriage return to look at another, or type **X** to return to the Menu Level.

The procedure for searching through the mail list is illustrated in Fig. 4-8.

PRINTING LABELS

Labels of your choice are printed by the procedure:

1. COMMAND SELECTION: Type 7 for the LABELS command. The presently set selection criteria, if any, will be displayed.
2. ARE THESE CORRECT?: Type **Y** if the criteria define the labels you want to print. Type **N** if they don't and you will be returned to the Menu Level so you can reset the criteria with the SELECT command.
3. PUT LABELS IN PRINTER, SET TOP OF FORM AND PRESS RETURN OR ENTER TO START PRINTING LABELS: The program pauses so you can prepare your printer. A roll of labels should be

COMMAND SELECTION [1–8 OR ?1–?8] **6** The SEARCH command is selected.

SELECTION CRITERIA:
CT   SINGLE
DICK JONES
SOUTHWIND REALTY ———————————You are shown the selection
2243 OAK STREET criteria presently in effect and
NEW HAVEN   CT   06511 the first label on the list that
AGENT meets that criteria.
SINGLE

Press RETURN to continue or X to The carriage return is pressed to
   exit⟨**CR**⟩ look at the next label that meets
  the criteria.

SELECTION CRITERIA:
CT   SINGLE
MELANIE SUMNER
THE CANDY STORE
443 MAIN STREET
WEST HAVEN   CT   06544
OWNER
SINGLE

Press RETURN to continue or X to exit **X** No more labels are to be looked at
  so X is typed to return to the
  Menu Level.

Fig. 4-8   The SEARCH command.

loaded. To generate a report of labels, insert paper instead of a roll of labels.

You can take as long as you wish to set up your printer, but it is advisable to prepare it before you begin program operation. When the printer is ready, press the carriage return (or the $\boxed{\textbf{ENTER}}$ key on the numeric pad) and the labels will be printed.

When all the labels are printed, you will be returned to the Menu Level. After printing your labels, you can print a report that shows the labels and the report.

The procedure for printing labels is illustrated in Fig. 4-9.

COMMAND SELECTION [1–8 OR ?1–?8] **7**   The LABELS command is
selected.

THE FOLLOWING SELECTION CRITERIA
    HAVE BEEN CHOSEN: You are shown the selection
STATE: CT   settings presently in effect.
ITEM 2: SINGLE

ARE THESE CORRECT? **Y**   The settings are correct.
PUT LABELS IN PRINTER, SET TOP OF   The program pauses so you can
    FORM AND PRESS RETURN OR ENTER TO   set up your printer if you
    START PRINTING LABELS . . . .⟨**CR**⟩   haven't already done so. The
NOW PRINTING LABELS . . . .   carriage return is pressed to
                                         start printing.

- -

DICK JONES   The labels are addressed.
SOUTHWIND REALTY
2243 OAK STREET
NEW HAVEN   CT
                06511
.
.
.
.
.
.

HARRY WALKER
NEW HAVEN PORSCHE
202 WHALLEY
HAMDEN   CT
                06544

                                         When the final label is printed,
                                         you are returned to the Menu
                                         Level.
- -

Fig. 4-9 The LABELS command.

ENDING PROGRAM OPERATION

When you are done with the Mail List Program, respond to COM-MAND SELECTION by typing 9 to EXIT TO SYSTEM. Any selection settings you have made will be cleared. You will be returned to your operating system level.

Remove your mail list disk and return it to its cover.

MAIL LIST PROGRAM COMMAND SUMMARY

Command Number and Name	Function
1–ADD	Adds new labels to the mail list.
2–CHANGE	Changes one or more lines on a particular label.
3–DELETE	Removes labels from the mail list.
4–SELECT	Sets selection criteria.
5–COUNT	Counts labels that meet selection criteria and calculates mail cost.
6–SEARCH	Displays labels, one at a time. Only labels that meet selection criteria are reviewed.
7–LABELS	Prints labels.
8–EXIT TO SYSTEM	Clears selection settings and returns user to operating system level.

MAIL LIST PROGRAM SOURCE CODE

```
10   REM  ROUTINE:  SET PARAMETERS FOR THE END  USER'S  PARTICULAR
20   REM  COMPUTER SCREEN.   SINCE THE PROGRAMS PRESENTED IN  THIS
30   REM  BOOK HAVE BEEN DESIGNED TO RUN ON A NUMBER OF  DIFFERENT
40   REM  MACHINES WHICH MAY DIFFER IN HEIGHT AND WIDTH  FROM  THE
50   REM  "STANDARD" 24 x 80,  THIS ROUTINE ALLOWS THE END USER  TO
60   REM  CREATE A FILE ("PARAMETER.FIL") THAT STORES THE HEIGHT AND
70   REM  WIDTH INFORMATION,  ("SCRSIZE" & "SCRHITE") AS WELL AS  A
80   REM  FLAG ("PARMSETFLAG") THAT KEEPS THE COMPUTER FROM RUNNING
90   REM  THE ROUTINE EVERY TIME THE PROGRAM IS RUN.
100   REM ********************************************************
110 DIM SELECT$(10)
120 ON ERROR GOTO 380
130 OPEN "I",#1,"PARAMTER.FIL"
140 INPUT #1,PARMSETFLAG
150 CLOSE #1
160 IF PARMSETFLAG>0 THEN 430
170 PRINT "HOW MANY CHARACTERS WIDE IS YOUR SCREEN?   ";
180 LINE INPUT SCRSIZE$
190 IF SCRSIZE$="?" THEN GOSUB 300
200 IF SCRSIZE$="?" THEN 170
210 PRINT "HOW MANY LINES LONG IS YOUR SCREEN?   ";
220 LINE INPUT SCRHITE$
230 IF SCRHITE$="?" THEN GOSUB 300
240 IF SCRHITE$="?" THEN 210
250 SCRSIZE=VAL(SCRSIZE$):SCRHITE=VAL(SCRHITE$):PARMSETFLAG=1
260 OPEN "O",#1,"PARAMTER.FIL"
270 PRINT #1,PARMSETFLAG,SCRSIZE,SCRHITE
280 CLOSE #1
290 GOTO 430
300 PRINT: PRINT  "ANSWER THIS QUESTION WITH A NUMBER.   IF  WIDTH  IS
310   PRINT  "ASKED FOR,  GENERALLY THE ANSWER WILL BE BETWEEN  40
320   PRINT  "AND 132.    IF HEIGHT IS CALLED FOR,  GENERALLY  THE
330   PRINT  "ANSWER  WILL BE BETWEEN 16  AND  66.  AFTER  YOU'VE
340   PRINT  "ANSWERED,  REMEMBER TO PRESS THE 'RETURN' OR 'ENTER'
350   PRINT  "KEY"
360 PRINT
370 RETURN
380 CLOSE:PRINT ERR,ERL
390 OPEN "O",#1,"PARAMTER.FIL"
400 PRINT #1,PARMSETFLAG,SCRSIZE,SCRHITE
410 CLOSE #1
420 RESUME 130
430 REM ******************************************************
440 REM ROUTINE: MONITORS USER'S  REQUESTS FOR PROGRAM ACTION
450 REM BY PRESENTING A MENU OF AVAILABLE CHOICES OR ACTIONS.
460 REM  THE PROGRAM WILL ALWAYS RETURN TO THIS ROUTINE AFTER
470 REM COMPLETING ANY OTHER ROUTINE IN THE PROGRAM.
480 REM ******************************************************
490 OPEN "I",#1,"PARAMTER.FIL"
500 INPUT #1,PARMSETFLAG,SCRSIZE,SCRHITE
510 CLOSE #1
520 LINE INPUT "Drive the datafile will be on: ";DRIVE$
530 FILE$=DRIVE$+":MAILLIST"
540 FOR LOOP=1 TO SCRHITE:PRINT:NEXT LOOP: REM clears the screen
550 FOR LOOP=1 TO SCRSIZE:PRINT "*";:NEXT LOOP: REM creates a border
560 CENTER=(SCRHITE/2):REM allows all screen display to be centered
    within given screen width. Used in conjunction with string lengths.
570 PRINT TAB(CENTER-4);"MAIL LIST":
    REM centers title within screen width
580 PRINT
590 PRINT TAB(CENTER-11);"AVAILABLE COMMANDS ARE:"
```

```
600 PRINT
610 PRINT TAB(CENTER-11);" 1 - ADD      2 - CHANGE
620 PRINT TAB(CENTER-11);" 3 - DELETE   4 - SELECT
630 PRINT TAB(CENTER-11);" 5 - COUNT    6 - SEARCH
640 PRINT TAB(CENTER-11);" 7 - LABELS   8 - EXIT
650 '
660 FOR LOOP=17 TO SCRHITE-3:PRINT:NEXT LOOP
670 FOR LOOP=1 TO SCRSIZE:PRINT "*";:NEXT LOOP:PRINT
680 CLOSE
690 LINE INPUT "COMMAND SELECTION  [1-8 OR ?1-?8] ";COMMAND$
700 IF LEFT$(COMMAND$,1)="?"
    THEN COMMAND=VAL(MID$(COMMAND$,2,2)) ELSE 730
710 WIDTH SCRSIZE
720 ON COMMAND GOSUB 770,790,800,840,860,880,910,920
730 COMMAND=VAL(COMMAND$)
740 ON COMMAND GOSUB 970,1670,2190,2780,3810,4170,3230,4580
750 GOTO 540
760 FOR LOOP=1 TO SCRSIZE:PRINT "*";:NEXT LOOP
770 PRINT "1- ADD:  ALLOWS YOU TO ADD NEW INFORMATION TO
    THE MAILING LIST AND
780 PRINT "PROMPTS AS IT GOES.":GOTO 930
790 PRINT "2- CHANGE: ALLOWS YOU TO EDIT ANY INFORMATION THAT
    HAS ALREADY BEEN ENTERED.":GOTO 930
800 PRINT "3- DELETE: ALLOWS YOU TO ERASE ANY INFORMATION THAT
    IS NO LONGER ACCURATE OR
810 PRINT "NEEDED.":GOTO 930
820 PRINT '
830 PRINT '
840 PRINT "4- SELECT: ALLOWS YOU TO TELL THE PROGRAM WHAT
    CRITERIA YOU WANT TO USE WHEN
850 PRINT "USING THE COUNT, SEARCH, LABELS, OR REPORTS FUNCTIONS.":
    GOTO 930
860 PRINT "5- COUNT: TELLS YOU HOW MANY RECORDS ARE IN THE
    LIST (OR MATCH YOUR SELECTION
870 PRINT "IF SELECT WAS USED) AND CALCULATES THE COST OF·
    MAILING THOSE PIECES.":GOTO 930
880 PRINT "6- SEARCH: FINDS ALL RECORDS MATCHING YOUR
    SELECTION AND SHOWS THEM TO YOU
890 PRINT "ONE AT A TIME.  IF NO CRITERIA WERE ESTABLISHED,
    THEN SEARCH SIMPLY SHOWS YOU
900 PRINT "ALL THE RECORDS IN THE LIST.":GOTO 930
910 PRINT "7- LABELS: PRINTS NAMES AND ADDRESSES ON ENVELOPE
    LABELS":GOTO 930
920 PRINT "8- EXIT: EXITS THE PROGRAM RUN, AND RETURNS TO THE
    OPERATING SYSTEM."
930 FOR LOOP=1 TO SCRSIZE:PRINT"*";:NEXT LOOP
940 LINE INPUT "PRESS 'RETURN' TO CONTINUE.....";DUMMY$
950 GOTO 540
960 ' ************** A D D   R O U T I N E ********************
970 '  This routine prompts the user for each item of mailing data.
980 '  It allows the user to add info to the list
990 ' ***********************************************************
1000 '
1010 '  VARIABLES USED:
1020 '  N$=MAILING NAME (20)
1030 '  C$=COMPANY NAME (20)
1040 '  S$=STREET ADDRESS (30)
1050 '  T$=TOWN OR CITY (15)
1060 '  ST$=STATE (2)
1070 '  Z$=ZIPCODE (7)
1080 '  I1$=FIRST ITEM (20)
1090 '  I2$=SECOND ITEM (20)
1100 '  D$=DELETE FLAG (1)
1110 '  R=CURRENT RECORD COUNTER
1120 '
```

```
1130 '   FILES USED
1140 '   MAILLIST: AN R/A FILE
1150 '
1160 '   FILE INTITIALIZATION
1170 '
1180 OPEN "R",1,FILE$
1190 OPEN "R",2,"MCOUNTER.FIL",5
1200 FIELD 2,5 AS RF$
1210 FIELD 1, 20 AS NF$,20 AS CF$,20 AS SF$,15 AS TF$,2 AS STF$,
     7 AS ZF$,20 AS I1F$,20 AS I2F$,1 AS DF$
1220 R=VAL(RF$)
1230 FOR LOOP=1 TO SCRHITE:PRINT:NEXT LOOP
1240 '   ********************************
1250 '   LOCATE LAST USED RECORD
1260 '   ********************************
1270 R=R+1
1280 '   *****************
1290 '   DATA ENTRY MODULE
1300 '   *****************
1310 LINE INPUT "ENTER NAME: ";N$
1320 IF N$="" THEN 1620
1330 LINE INPUT "ENTER COMPANY: ";C$
1340 LINE INPUT "ENTER STREET ADDRESS: ";S$
1350 LINE INPUT "ENTER TOWN OR CITY: ";T$
1360 LINE INPUT "ENTER 2 CHARACTER STATE CODE: ";ST$
1370 LINE INPUT "ENTER 5 DIGIT ZIP: ";Z$
1380 LINE INPUT "ENTER ITEM 1: ";I1$
1390 LINE INPUT "ENTER ITEM 2: ";I2$
1400 D$="L"
1410 '   *******************
1420 '   MOVE DATA TO BUFFER
1430 '   *******************
1440 LSET NF$=N$
1450 LSET CF$=C$
1460 LSET SF$=S$
1470 LSET TF$=T$
1480 LSET STF$=ST$
1490 LSET ZF$=Z$
1500 LSET I1F$=I1$
1510 LSET I2F$=I2$
1520 LSET DF$=D$
1530 '   *********************
1540 '   COPY BUFFER INTO FILE
1550 '   *********************
1560 PUT 1,R
1570 '   *********************
1580 '   MORE DATA TO ENTER?
1590 '   *********************
1600 GOTO 1230
1610 '   *********************
1620 '   CLOSE FILE
1630 '   *********************
1640 LSET RF$=STR$(R):CLOSE 2
1650 CLOSE 1
1660 GOTO 540
1670 '********** C H A N G E   R O U T I N E *************
1680 'This module allows changes to be made to the
1690 'data in the MAILLIST file.  Things like address
1700 'changes and name changes are handled here.
1710 '****************************************************
1720 FOR LOOP=1 TO SCRHITE:PRINT:NEXT LOOP
1730 LINE INPUT "ENTER NAME: ";N$:PRINT:PRINT:PRINT
1740 IF N$="" THEN LINE INPUT "ENTER COMPANY: ";C$ ELSE 1760:
     PRINT:PRINT:PRINT
1750 IF C$=" " THEN 540 ELSE C$=C$+STRING$(20-LEN(C$),32)
```

```
1760 IF N$<>"" THEN N$=N$+STRING$(20-LEN(N$),32)
1770 OPEN "R",1,FILE$
1780 FIELD 1, 20 AS NF$,20 AS CF$,20 AS SF$,15 AS TF$,2 AS STF$,
      7 AS ZF$,20 AS I1F$,20 AS I2F$,1 AS DF$
1790 R=0
1800 R=R+1:GET 1,R
1810 IF N$<>"" THEN IF NF$<>N$ OR DF$="D" THEN 1940
1820 IF C$<>"" THEN IF CF$<>C$ OR DF$="D" THEN 1940
1830 FOR LOOP=1 TO SCRHITE:PRINT:NEXT LOOP
1840 PRINT "1.    Name: ";NF$
1850 PRINT "2. Company: ";CF$
1860 PRINT "3.  Street: ";SF$
1870 PRINT "4.    City: "TF$
1880 PRINT "5.   State: ";STF$
1890 PRINT "6.     Zip: ";ZF$
1900 PRINT "7.  Item 1: ";I1F$
1910 PRINT "8.  Item 2: ";I2F$
1920 PRINT:PRINT "9. *Look for different record*"
1930 GOTO 1960
1940 IF EOF(1) THEN 1950 ELSE 1800
1950 GOTO 2010
1960 PRINT:PRINT:PRINT:INPUT "Change What? [1-8] ";C
1970 IF C=9 THEN FOR LOOP=1 TO SCRHITE:PRINT:NEXT LOOP:GOTO 1940
1980 ON C GOSUB 2030,2050,2070,2090,2110,2130,2150,2170
1990 IF C<1 OR C>9 THEN CLOSE:GOTO 1720
2000 PUT 1,R
2010 CLOSE 1
2020 GOTO 540
2030 LINE INPUT "ENTER NEW NAME: ";N$
2040 IF N$="" THEN 1830 ELSE LSET NF$=N$:GOTO 1830
2050 LINE INPUT "ENTER NEW COMPANY: ";C$
2060 IF C$="" THEN 1830 ELSE LSET CF$=C$:GOTO 1830
2070 LINE INPUT "ENTER NEW STREET: ";S$
2080 IF S$="" THEN 1830 ELSE LSET SF$=S$:GOTO 1830
2090 LINE INPUT "ENTER NEW CITY: ";T$
2100 IF T$="" THEN 1830 ELSE LSET TF$=T$:GOTO 1830
2110 LINE INPUT "ENTER NEW STATE: ";ST$
2120 IF ST$="" THEN 1830 ELSE LSET STF$=ST$:GOTO 1830
2130 LINE INPUT "ENTER NEW ZIP: ";Z$
2140 IF Z$="" THEN 1830 ELSE LSET ZF$=Z$:GOTO 1830
2150 LINE INPUT "ENTER NEW ITEM 1: ";I1$
2160 IF I1$="" THEN 1830 ELSE LSET I1F$=I1$:GOTO 1830
2170 LINE INPUT "ENTER NEW ITEM 2: ";I2$
2180 IF I2$="" THEN 1830 ELSE LSET I2F$=I2$:GOTO 1830
2190 '***** D E L E T E   R O U T I N E **************
2200 '  This routine flags an item as deleted.
2210 '  NOTE: The item is not actually deleted. It
2220 '  is simply flagged as such.
2230 '**************************************************
2240 '
2250 FOR LOOP=1 TO SCRHITE:PRINT:NEXT LOOP
2260 LINE INPUT "ENTER NAME: ";N$:PRINT:PRINT:PRINT
2270 IF N$=" " THEN 2480 ELSE N$=N$+STRING$(20-LEN(N$),32)
2280 OPEN "R",1,FILE$
2290 FIELD 1, 20 AS NF$,20 AS CF$,20 AS SF$,15 AS TF$,2 AS STF$,
      7 AS ZF$,20 AS I1F$,20 AS I2F$,1 AS DF$
2300 R=0
2310 R=R+1:GET 1,R
2320 IF NF$<>N$ OR DF$="D" THEN 2460
2330 PRINT "Name: ";NF$
2340 PRINT "Company: ";CF$
2350 PRINT "Street: ";SF$
2360 PRINT "City: "TF$
2370 PRINT "State: ";STF$
```

```
2380 PRINT "Zip: ";ZF$
2390 PRINT "Item 1: ";I1F$
2400 PRINT "Item 2: ";I2F$
2410 PRINT:PRINT "1. *Look for different record*"
2420 PRINT "2. *Delete the record shown above*"
2430 PRINT:PRINT:PRINT:INPUT "Which Command ";C
2440 IF C=1 THEN FOR LOOP=1 TO SCRHITE:PRINT:NEXT LOOP:GOTO 2460
2450 IF C=2 THEN D$="D":LSET DF$=D$:PUT 1,R:CLOSE:GOTO 2250
2460 IF EOF(1) THEN 2460 ELSE 2310
2470 CLOSE 1:GOTO 2250
2480 '****** C L E A N   R O U T I N E **************
2490 '  This routine clears out all records flagged
2500 '  as DELETED (DF$="D").  The routine does its
2510 '  job with no prompting and with no messages.
2520 '  It is designed simply to conserve disk space.
2530 '**********************************************
2540 '
2550 PRINT "CLEANING IN PROGRESS . . . . . . . ."
2560 OPEN "R",1,FILES
2570 OPEN "R",2,DRIVES+":CLEANLST"
2580 FIELD 1, 20 AS NF$,20 AS CF$,20 AS SF$,15 AS TF$,2 AS STF$,
     7 AS ZF$,20 AS I1F$,20 AS I2F$,1 AS DF$
2590 FIELD 2, 20 AS NFN$,20 AS CFN$,20 AS SFN$,15 AS TFN$,
     2 AS STFN$,7 AS ZFN$,20 AS I1FN$,20 AS I2FN$,1 AS DFN$
2600 R=0
2610 R=R+1:GET 1,R
2620 IF DF$="D" THEN 2730
2630 LSET NFN$=NF$
2640 LSET CFN$=CF$
2650 LSET SFN$=SF$
2660 LSET TFN$=TF$
2670 LSET STFN$=STF$
2680 LSET ZFN$=ZF$
2690 LSET I1FN$=I1F$
2700 LSET I2FN$=I2F$
2710 LSET DFN$=DF$
2720 PUT 2
2730 IF EOF(1) THEN 2740 ELSE 2610
2740 CLOSE 1,2
2750 KILL FILE$:NAME DRIVES+":CLEANLST" AS FILE$
2760 PRINT "CLEANING COMPLETE":FOR I=1 TO 1000:NEXT I
2770 GOTO 540
2780 '******* S E L E C T   R O U T I N E ***********
2790 '  This routine allows the user to chose those
2800 '  items by which he would like to print LABELS,
2810 '  COUNT, SEARCH, or generate REPORTS.
2820 '**********************************************
2830 S=0
2840 FOR LOOP=1 TO SCRHITE:PRINT:NEXT LOOP
2850 PRINT "1. Name"
2860 PRINT "2. Company"
2870 PRINT "3. Street"
2880 PRINT "4. City"
2890 PRINT "5. State"
2900 PRINT "6. Zip"
2910 PRINT "7. Item 1"
2920 PRINT "8. Item 2"
2930 PRINT:PRINT:PRINT: INPUT "Choice from above [1-8] ";C
2940 ON C GOTO 3140,3150,3160,3170,3180,3190,3200,3210
2950 FOR LOOP=1 TO SCRHITE:PRINT:NEXT LOOP
2960 PRINT "THE FOLLOWING SELECTION CRITERIA HAVE BEEN
2970 PRINT "CHOSEN:
2980 FOR S=1 TO 10
2990 PRINT
```

```
3000 IF SELECT$(S)="" THEN 3100
3010 ON VAL(LEFT$(SELECT$(S),1)) GOTO 3020,3030,3040,3050,
     3060,3070,3080,3090
3020 PRINT "NAME: ";MID$(SELECT$(S),2,20):GOTO 3100
3030 PRINT "COMPANY: ";MID$(SELECT$(S),2,20):GOTO 3100
3040 PRINT "STREET: ";MID$(SELECT$(S),2,20):GOTO 3100
3050 PRINT "CITY: ";MID$(SELECT$(S),2,20):GOTO 3100
3060 PRINT "STATE: ";MID$(SELECT$(S),2,20):GOTO 3100
3070 PRINT "ZIP: ";MID$(SELECT$(S),2,20):GOTO 3100
3080 PRINT "ITEM 1: ";MID$(SELECT$(S),2,20):GOTO 3100
3090 PRINT "ITEM 2: ";MID$(SELECT$(S),2,20):GOTO 3100
3100 NEXT S
3110 LINE INPUT "ARE THESE CORRECT? ";R$
3120 IF LEFT$(R$,1)<>"Y" THEN ERASE SELECT$: GOTO 2780
3130 GOTO 540
3140 LINE INPUT "Name: ";SEL$:SEL$="1"+SEL$:GOTO 3220
3150 LINE INPUT "Company: ";SEL$:SEL$="2"+SEL$:GOTO 3220
3160 LINE INPUT "Street: ";SEL$:SEL$="3"+SEL$:GOTO 3220
3170 LINE INPUT "City: ";SEL$:SEL$="4"+SEL$:GOTO 3220
3180 LINE INPUT "State: ";SEL$:SEL$="5"+SEL$:GOTO 3220
3190 LINE INPUT "Zip: ";SEL$:SEL$="6"+SEL$:GOTO 3220
3200 LINE INPUT "Item 1: ";SEL$:SEL$="7"+SEL$:GOTO 3220
3210 LINE INPUT "Item 2: ";SEL$:SEL$="8"+SEL$:GOTO 3220
3220 S=S+1:SELECT$(S)=SEL$:GOTO 2840
3230 '** L A B E L S   R O U T I N E **************
3240 '  This routine prints labels according to the
3250 '  previously chosen SELECT criteria.  If no
3260 '  choice was made under SELECT, then all data
3270 '  (except those records deleted) are printed.
3280 '*******************************************
3290 '
3300 FOR LOOP=1 TO SCRHITE:PRINT:NEXT LOOP
3310 PRINT "THE FOLLOWING SELECTION CRITERIA HAVE BEEN
3320 PRINT "CHOSEN:
3330 FOR S=1 TO 10
3340 PRINT
3350 IF SELECT$(S)="" THEN 3450
3360 ON VAL(LEFT$(SELECT$(S),1)) GOTO 3370,3380,3390,
     3400,3410,3420,3430,3440
3370 PRINT "NAME: ";MID$(SELECT$(S),2,20):GOTO 3450
3380 PRINT "COMPANY: ";MID$(SELECT$(S),2,20):GOTO 3450
3390 PRINT "STREET: ";MID$(SELECT$(S),2,20):GOTO 3450
3400 PRINT "CITY: ";MID$(SELECT$(S),2,20):GOTO 3450
3410 PRINT "STATE: ";MID$(SELECT$(S),2,20):GOTO 3450
3420 PRINT "ZIP: ";MID$(SELECT$(S),2,20):GOTO 3450
3430 PRINT "ITEM 1: ";MID$(SELECT$(S),2,20):GOTO 3450
3440 PRINT "ITEM 2: ";MID$(SELECT$(S),2,20):GOTO 3450
3450 NEXT S
3460 LINE INPUT "ARE THESE CORRECT? ";R$
3470 IF LEFT$(R$,1)<>"Y" THEN 540
3480 FOR LOOP=1 TO SCRHITE:PRINT:NEXT LOOP
3490 PRINT "PUT LABELS IN PRINTER, SET TOP OF FORM AND PRESS"
3500 LINE INPUT "RETURN OR ENTER TO START PRINTING LABELS........";
     START$
3510 PRINT "NOW PRINTING LABELS........"
3520 FOR LOOP=1 TO SCRHITE/2:PRINT:NEXT LOOP
3530 OPEN "R",1,FILE$
3540 FIELD 1, 20 AS NF$,20 AS CF$,20 AS SF$,15 AS TF$,2 AS STF$,
     7 AS ZF$,20 AS I1F$,20 AS I2F$,1 AS DF$
3550 R=0
3560 R=R+1:GET 1,R
3570 IF DF$="D" THEN 3780
3580     FOR S=1 TO 10
3590             L=VAL(LEFT$(SELECT$(S),1))
```

```
3600            S1$=MID$(SELECT$(S),2,20)
3610     IF L<1 THEN 3720
3620 ON L GOTO 3630,3640,3650,3660,3670,3680,3690,3700
3630       IF S1$+STRING$(20-LEN(S1$),32)<>NF$ THEN 3780 ELSE 3710
3640       IF S1$+STRING$(20-LEN(S1$),32)<>CF$ THEN 3780 ELSE 3710
3650       IF S1$+STRING$(20-LEN(S1$),32)<>SF$ THEN 3780 ELSE 3710
3660       IF S1$+STRING$(15-LEN(S1$),32)<>TF$ THEN 3780 ELSE 3710
3670       IF S1$+STRING$(2-LEN(S1$),32)<>STF$ THEN 3780 ELSE 3710
3680       IF S1$+STRING$(7-LEN(S1$),32)<>ZF$ THEN 3780 ELSE 3710
3690       IF S1$+STRING$(20-LEN(S1$),32)<>I1F$ THEN 3780 ELSE 3710
3700       IF S1$+STRING$(20-LEN(S1$),32)<>I2F$ THEN 3780 ELSE 3710
3710     NEXT S
3720     IF NF$<>"" THEN LPRINT NF$
3730     IF LEFT$(CF$,1)<>CHR$(32) THEN LPRINT CF$
3740     IF SF$<>"" THEN LPRINT SF$
3750 LPRINT TF$;STF$
3760 LPRINT TAB(20);ZF$
3770 LPRINT:LPRINT:IF LEFT$(CF$,1)<>CHR$(32) THEN LPRINT
3780 IF EOF(1) THEN 3790 ELSE 3560
3790 CLOSE 1:GOTO 540
3800 '
3810 '****** C O U N T   R O U T I N E ***************
3820 '  This routine counts records and computes mail-
3830 '  ing costs.  If there are select criteria in
3840 '  effect, it calcutes only the cost of mailing
3850 '  those pieces that meet the criteria.
3860 '**********************************************
3870 '
3880 FOR LOOP=1 TO SCRHITE:PRINT:NEXT LOOP
3890 COUNT=0:COST=0
3900 INPUT "What does it cost to mail one piece ";COST
3910 OPEN "R",1,FILE$
3920 FIELD 1, 20 AS NF$,20 AS CF$,20 AS SF$,15 AS TF$,2 AS STF$,
     7 AS ZF$,20 AS I1F$,20 AS I2F$,1 AS DF$
3930 R=0
3940 R=R+1:GET 1,R
3950 IF DF$="D" THEN 4110
3960     FOR S=1 TO 10
3970            L=VAL(LEFT$(SELECT$(S),1))
3980            S1$=MID$(SELECT$(S),2,20)
3990     IF L<1 THEN 4100
4000 ON L GOTO 4010,4020,4030,4040,4050,4060,4070,4080
4010       IF S1$+STRING$(20-LEN(S1$),32)<>NF$ THEN 4110 ELSE 4090
4020       IF S1$+STRING$(20-LEN(S1$),32)<>CF$ THEN 4110 ELSE 4090
4030       IF S1$+STRING$(20-LEN(S1$),32)<>SF$ THEN 4110 ELSE 4090
4040       IF S1$+STRING$(15-LEN(S1$),32)<>TF$ THEN 4110 ELSE 4090
4050       IF S1$+STRING$(2-LEN(S1$),32)<>STF$ THEN 4110 ELSE 4090
4060       IF S1$+STRING$(7-LEN(S1$),32)<>ZF$ THEN 4110 ELSE 4090
4070       IF S1$+STRING$(20-LEN(S1$),32)<>I1F$ THEN 4110 ELSE 4090
4080       IF S1$+STRING$(20-LEN(S1$),32)<>I2F$ THEN 4110 ELSE 4090
4090     NEXT S
4100 COUNT=COUNT+1
4110 IF EOF(1) THEN 4120 ELSE 3940
4120 PRINT:PRINT:PRINT "There are ";COUNT;" pieces to be mailed."
4130 PRINT USING "The mailing cost is $###.##";COUNT*COST
4140 PRINT:PRINT:PRINT:
     LINE INPUT "Press RETURN to return to command menu";X$
4150 CLOSE 1:GOTO 540
4160 '
4170 '******* S E A R C H   R O U T I N E ************
4180 '  This routine allows the user to step through
4190 '  the records in the mailling list.  If se-
4200 '  lect criteria are in effect, then only
4210 '  those records meeting the criteria are shown.
```

```
4220 '***********************************************
4230 '
4240 FOR LOOP=1 TO SCRHITE:PRINT:NEXT LOOP
4250 OPEN "R",1,FILE$
4260 FIELD 1, 20 AS NF$,20 AS CF$,20 AS SF$,15 AS TF$,2 AS STF$,
     7 AS ZF$,20 AS I1F$,20 AS I2F$,1 AS DF$
4270 R=0
4280 R=R+1:GET 1,R
4290 IF DF$="D" THEN 4550
4300    FOR S=1 TO 10
4310          L=VAL(LEFT$(SELECT$(S),1))
4320          S1$=MID$(SELECT$(S),2,20)
4330    IF L<1 THEN 4430
4340 ON L GOTO 4350,4360,4370,4380,4390,4400,4410,4420
4350       IF S1$+STRING$(20-LEN(S1$),32)<>NF$ THEN 4550 ELSE 4430
4360       IF S1$+STRING$(20-LEN(S1$),32)<>CF$ THEN 4550 ELSE 4430
4370       IF S1$+STRING$(20-LEN(S1$),32)<>SF$ THEN 4550 ELSE 4430
4380       IF S1$+STRING$(15-LEN(S1$),32)<>TF$ THEN 4550 ELSE 4430
4390       IF S1$+STRING$(2-LEN(S1$),32)<>STF$ THEN 4550 ELSE 4430
4400       IF S1$+STRING$(7-LEN(S1$),32)<>ZF$ THEN 4550 ELSE 4430
4410       IF S1$+STRING$(20-LEN(S1$),32)<>I1F$ THEN 4550 ELSE 4430
4420       IF S1$+STRING$(20-LEN(S1$),32)<>I2F$ THEN 4550 ELSE 4430
4430    NEXT S
4440 PRINT "SELECTION CRITERIA: ":FOR X=1 TO 10:
     IF SELECT$(X)<>"" THEN PRINT MID$(SELECT$(X),2,30);"    ";:
     NEXT X
4450 PRINT:PRINT:PRINT
4460 PRINT NF$
4470 PRINT CF$
4480 PRINT SF$
4490 PRINT TF$;" ";STF$;"   ";ZF$
4500 PRINT I1F$
4510 PRINT I2F$
4520 PRINT:LINE INPUT "Press RETURN to continue or X to exit   ";X$
4530 IF X$="X" THEN 4560
4540 FOR LOOP=1 TO SCRHITE:PRINT:NEXT LOOP
4550 IF EOF(1) THEN 4560 ELSE 4280
4560 CLOSE 1:GOTO 540
4570 '
4580 '***** E X I T   R O U T I N E *********
4590 RESET:SYSTEM
```

CHAPTER FIVE

WHEN A PROSPECT CALLS . . .

Your telephone rings. You answer it and hear somebody asking about your business. You giggle. "Holy cow! I really didn't think anybody would call!"

That's not the right way to handle a potential customer's call. Taken properly, the call will begin a chain of events, which you'll read about in this chapter, that can end in a very profitable agreement for you.

TAKING A PROSPECT'S CALL

When you run advertisements and send out direct mail about your business, be prepared to get telephone calls from people interested in your offer. Sometimes a person will call you simply for more information. Answer his questions, but ask your own to discover how you *profitably* can help him:

Prospect: "Your ad interested me, but I'm not sure how we can use your service. Can you tell me some more about what you do?"

You: "I test personal computer programs as an end user. I work out of my home on a part-time basis. I can come to your office during my lunch hour or in the evening. *I probably can tell you something more relevant if you tell me a bit about what you do.*"

Prospect: "Sure. We develop software for home computers. Right now, we've got some in the testing stage and . . ."

As your prospect talks, you will focus an offer on what he's saying. It may not be the offer you advertised. Businesses may suddenly and unexpectedly expand during these conversations:

Prospect: "Our growth has slowed a bit because we keep getting calls about the systems we installed and that's a real drag on the business. I'm looking for someone like you to field those calls so we can install more systems."
(Inspiration! You boldly expand your business!)

You: "Have you ever considered that your real problem may be training people in how to use your systems? If they really knew what they were doing, I bet you wouldn't be pestered by so many troublesome calls." ·

Prospect: "I hadn't considered that. Maybe you're right, but how can you help me?"

You: "Teaching them correctly in the first place could be your answer. In my full-time job, I teach high school students. I think I can help."

Prospect: "You just might be able to. Come in and let's talk."

If you can't think of anything relevant, ask for permission to call back in a few months. Circumstances change and the company at a later time may need your offer, or you may be offering something new. You have a contact at this company—try not to lose it.

When a prospect wants to talk, set up a face-to-face meeting. Your real objective in taking a call is to set up a meeting. A meeting gives you more time to probe a prospect to see what you can offer him or her. You can learn a lot by looking around the business. Materials you have can be presented. Above all, you'll be able to size up your prospect.

After a few brief questions, many prospects will try to arrange a meeting. If you have something that they're interested in, potential customers know that a meeting quickly will show if your offer really is what they need.

When you realize it's time to set up a meeting, keep your side of the conversation short and ask questions that close in on a mutually convenient time to meet. A typical conversation will go:

Prospect: "I was intrigued by your letter and would like to get together to discuss it."

You: "That's great! What's better for you, mornings or afternoons?"

Prospect: "I'm booked solid throughout the day. Would you mind stopping over after work, say about 6 p.m.?"

You: "That's fine. I'm busy Tuesday. What's your schedule look like?"

Prospect: "Thursday's open."

You: "Great. I'll see you Thursday at 6 p.m. Thanks for calling."

Do you see how quickly you can determine a specific meeting time? A broad question ("What's better, morning or afternoon?") is first asked to eliminate possibilities, and then a specific day is pinpointed.

As you can see, you don't say much to set the meeting up. You'll do your talking at the meeting.

A prospective customer, finally, may call you with a proposal for work. She may tell you exactly what she needs done, how much she can afford to pay, and how soon she needs the work.

As your reputation grows, you can expect these offers, even without advertising. Such offers usually come from people knowledgeable about PCs, who may be preparing proposals to present to one of their potential customers.

When you receive an offer, you have to decide if:

1. You have the skills to do the work.
2. You have the time.
3. The price being offered is acceptable.
4. You want to do the work.

Unless you've worked with the person before, you should take a few days to examine the offer and develop your own estimates for how much work you'll be doing. You may find more work than first indicated. Bring these discrepancies to your prospect's attention. She may be willing to pay you more.

If you do decide to do the work, *always* put your agreement in writing so there will be no misunderstanding about who owes who what and when.

If your prospect has prepared the agreement, read it over very carefully before signing.

When a prospective customer calls, you *don't* say a lot of things:

1. When he introduces himself, don't sound surprised. Never say: "You're the first person I've ever dealt with and I'm new at it so you may have to bear with a few mistakes." It won't make you sound like a professional.

    Get in the habit of answering your telephone with a professional "Hello," and the name of your business. Develop an even business tone. Doris is a wonder at this. The first time I called to use her word processing service, I was sure I was dealing with a person in a large office. I pictured her carefully scheduling work for a wealth of employees. I wondered who would be assigned to work with me. One day I dropped a manuscript off instead of waiting for her to pick it up. What a shock! Where was the large, corporate building? Her address led me to a simple home. When I went in, I found a cat stepping over somebody's manuscript, a dog in the back yard barking at a squirrel, and two children fighting. Corporate America took on a whole new image. The telephone rang. Doris nudged the door to her work area closed and, in a highly professional voice, said, "Word Processing Services. May I help you?" What images that voice could conjure up.

2. Don't make small talk. Your prospect isn't calling to strike up a friendship.

3. Don't gush on about your offer or try to force a sale. Commitments rarely are made over the telephone.

4. Never claim to have a skill you lack. Never present yourself as running a full-time business if you're only a part-timer. Never lie about the equipment you have or your level of expertise. On the other hand, never shy away from promoting what you can do if the opportunity arises.

Above all, *always* be honest, but present your honesty in a positive way:

Prospect: "Has anybody else used your service to select PC equipment before?"

You: "Quite frankly, no, *which is why I'm willing to work inexpensively for this opportunity.*"

Prospect: "Now that's something to consider!"

Finally, *never, ever* be rude. If you're in the middle of a family argument, answer the telephone with a business tone. Even if the caller says he's not interested, politely thank him for calling. Hang up, open your door, and with any luck the argument will have blown over.

It pays, in many ways, to act professionally at all times.

PREPARING FOR A MEETING

You should prepare to meet your prospect by anticipating what you will encounter.

You will have to explain your offer. It will help to bring along samples. You can talk around a sample and use it to point out features of your offer. If you're offering a direct mail service using the *Programs For Profit* Mail List Program, for example, you can bring along a sample sheet of labels and point out your advantages: You don't leave a blank line if there's no company name on the label, you don't show distracting computer code, etc. You also can type up a page, which you can leave behind, that shows data input so you can discuss your SELECT capability and its many applications.

Do you have any references? If so, bring along copies. Have you done work for others? If so, type up a list showing specific jobs and companies for which you've worked. Your potential customer may not wish to see any of these materials, but if she does, you'll be ready and that, in itself, will make a positive impression.

PREPARING AN AGREEMENT

You may be able to prepare an agreement so that you can sign up a customer at your first meeting. The agreement may prove to be a handy sales tool. It is simply a statement of what you and somebody else agree to, and you don't need a lawyer to draw one up. It can take the form of a letter that you *and* your customer sign. Such a letter states what you intend to do, how you'll charge, and the cost (these topics are explored in Chap. 7), and anything else you feel is appropriate. Leave out sales talk. At the bottom, type a space for your name and the date, and the customer's name and a date. Copy the letter and bring both copies to your meeting. After the agreements are signed, your customer (no longer your prospect) will get one copy and you'll take the other.

Bruce offers a service to test software. He has prepared a simple agreement by stating:

1. Exactly what he intends to do. He will run software according to a company's specifications. He will note any problems he encounters.
2. Information he thinks is relevant. He will maintain the confidentiality of material.
3. How he charges for the service and how much those costs are. He has decided to charge by the hour, with an additional fee for the use of his equipment. Realizing many business people don't like open-ended agreements, Bruce has inserted space for a limit he may charge for a trial period. Both the amount and the duration of the trial period will be filled in at the meeting.

Bruce has left space for both his and the customer's signatures. This agreement, shown in Fig. 5-1, may be used as a model for your own.

An agreement also may be prepared in advance when there are only a limited number of foreseeable options for a job. This agreement lists all the options. In your meeting, you will explain the options and costs. The prospective customer will gain an understanding of the work involved. As he begins to select options, you can begin to close in on your sale:

You: "Let's customize a computerized bookkeeping system just for you. I offer accounts payable, accounts receivable, payroll, and general ledger. What do you have the most problems with today?"

Prospect: "People owe me a lot of money, but I just don't have time to sort it all out. I guess that's accounts receivable."

You: "I offer open item and balance forward bookkeeping. Which would you prefer?"

Prospect: "I would love to have all the items shown that I've worked on. What's that one?"

You: "Open item. Let me show you an example. . . ."

As he begins to define how you can help him, he also begins to sell himself on the service:

You: "So that's what the whole computerized accounts receivable service looks like—exactly what you've told me you want."

Prospect: "That is everything I want and I like it. Where do I sign?"

March 3, 1985

678 Burgress Drive
Palo Alto, CA 94303
(415) 555-5555

Mr. Jeffery Philips
923 Lawndale Road
Palo Alto, CA 94303

Dear Mr. Philips,

   I will be happy to test your personal computer software. I will
run your programs according to your specifications. Any errors or
problems that I find will be clearly noted and provided to you.
   I agree to maintain the confidentiality of any materials so
designated by you.
   The cost for this service is $_____ per hour, to be paid
within 30 days of invoice submission. An additional hourly charge
of $_____ will be added for the use of my IBM PC and
peripherals. The total amount is not to exceed _____ for an
initial trial period of _____. If this is acceptable to you, please
sign below.

                              Very truly,

                              Your Name

Accepted by:

_____   _____
(name and title)   (date)

Fig. 5-1   A simple agreement.

This approach also lets you compute costs as you check off tasks that need to be done so you can present the total cost and sign your customer up at the first meeting.

To prepare such an agreement, you must know all the options. The agreement, again, may take the form of a letter. You list options and costs. Don't put in anything about how great an option is; just list it. At the meeting, you will go down your list, checking off what interests your prospect. You then can quickly compute the total cost and present that figure. If it all looks good, you both sign.

Maxine offers a direct mail service. She has prepared an agreement stating:

1. All the options she offers. In her meeting she will explain each option and check the service desired. The prospect will see exactly what's involved in the service, understand how charges are figured, and know what the total service will cost.
2. Information she considers relevant. This information includes payment terms, mailing authorization, agreement termination terms, and confidentiality.

Her agreement is shown in Fig. 5-2. This is a lengthy agreement, so Maxine has typed one copy and printed 100 copies to eliminate the retyping time. Before a meeting, she types in the company name and makes a copy. She looks professionally prepared going into the meeting with an agreement for the prospect to sign.

If you have a word processing system, you can store a master agreement on disk and type in the company name before running off two copies. This technique will save printing costs.

You may be able to prepare an agreement like Maxine's. But before you print copies, make sure you have *all* the bugs out. Have you completely and accurately defined what you offer? Do you find yourself often making changes or exceptions? Have you left out an important piece of relevant information? If so, improve your agreement and try it out again.

MEETING YOUR PROSPECT

Your goals in meeting a prospect are to define a *specific* project or area for work, and, if possible, sign an agreement to do it. It's to everybody's benefit to sign the agreement as quickly as possible. Nobody makes money in these meetings. These meetings only allow money to be made.

DIRECT MAIL AGREEMENT

Dear Sir,

I agree to provide the following services for
_____:
(company name)

☐ Collect Addresses. Addresses will be submitted for approval, which must occur 5 days after submission. Cost: $_____ per 100 labels.

☐ Completely handle all data for mailings, as provided by
_____. This service includes entering and
(company name)
maintaining the labels. A report of labels, as entered, will be
provided to _____. Any corrections required
(company name)
because I made an error will be made free of charge. Address changes and deletions, otherwise, will be charged at a cost of $_____ per label. New labels will be added at a cost of $_____ per label.

☐ Print labels on the following basis:
   ☐ Daily, at a cost of $_____ per label.
   ☐ Weekly, at a cost of $_____ per label.
   ☐ Monthly, at a cost of $_____ per label.
   ☐ As required, at a cost of $_____ per label.
   ☐ Other, at a cost of $_____ per label.
Any selections made by_____will be done
(company name)
free of charge. These selections must be specified within 24 hours of a scheduled mailing.

☐ Prepare the mailing on the following basis:
   ☐ Provide all envelopes, at cost plus 15%.
   ☐ Envelopes will be provided by _____ at
                         (company name)
   least 24 hours before a scheduled mailing.

Fig. 5-2 A complex agreement. (*Cont. on following page.*)

☐ Prepare copies of pieces to be mailed for the cost of printing (or copying) plus 15%.

☐ Material to be sent will be provided by _____
(company name)
at least 24 hours before the scheduled mailing.

☐ Develop original piece to be mailed. The price of the piece will be quoted for each piece.

☐ Handle postage, at cost of postage plus 15%. Projected postage costs for a mailing will be provided free of charge at any time.

☐ Deliver mailing to you for postage handling.

☐ Prepare reports of labels or stored data at a cost of $_____ per report.

In exchange for these services, _____ agrees
(company name)
to all charges specified above. Postage cost (less service charge) is to be paid prior to the mailing, in accordance with the projected amount. All other charges are to be paid within 15 days of the mailing or invoice submission, whichever occurs later. Authorization for a mailing must be made in writing by

_____ and received at least 24 hours before a
(person's name)
mailing. Once authorized, _____ agrees to pay
(company name)
all mailing costs.

Written notification is required at least 30 days in advance for either party to terminate this agreement.

I agree to maintain the confidentiality of any materials so designated.

The following parties have executed this agreement.

Accepted by:

_____   _____   _____
(name)   (name)   (title)

_____   For: _____
(date)   (company name)

                         _____
                         (date)

Fig. 5-2   (Cont.)

You should dress *neatly*, *professionally*, and *conservatively*. Don't show up in jeans and a T-shirt at your first meeting. Men should wear jackets and ties; women, skirts.

Joe worked in the communications department of a major software company. He was great at putting together successful ad campaigns to build up his company's image, but he didn't care at all about his own image. Old clothes were fine for him, and as long as he worked for the company where he had established his reputation, all was fine. But Joe decided to set up his own part-time business. He sent out letters announcing his service and soon received a call. All went well over the telephone and a meeting was arranged. That was when trouble started. For Joe, it was business as usual. He arrived wearing wrinkled pants and a shirt covered in fuzz balls and confidently said, "I would like to present your image to the world." Joe left, puzzled by why he wasn't asked to do the work.

Today, a few executives may not care how you look as long as what you're offering looks good. Most do care, however, so why take a chance? Look your best.

Arrive for your appointment on time, if not a bit early. That means you'll have to leave home giving yourself enough time for traffic jams or other possible calamities. If you're early, tell the receptionist you will be happy to wait. Take the extra time to relax and acclimate yourself to the surroundings. Look for company literature that you can read to learn about its business. No matter how long you have to wait be patient and cheerful. Remember, though you'll be helping your prospect, he doesn't have to see you at all.

Ideally, your potential customer will be having a wonderful day and be in good spirits when you meet him. He will ask if you had any problems finding the company. Even if you did, you'll say you didn't, to keep *his* day free of problems. Your prospect will present a brief overview of his business. He may ask to see something about your business to validate your ad. You'll show samples or other pertinent materials you have brought along. He will tell you about the project for which he thinks your skills are applicable. When he has finished, you'll ask questions that will help you define exactly how much work must be done. If it's a large project, you probably will have to take notes, go home, and work up a proposal. You'll tell him about how long it will take to prepare the proposal. It should never take more than a few days. He will invite you to call if you need more information and take your business card, if you have one. Then you will leave, go home, and work on the proposal.

On the other hand, if you can figure the cost for the work with the agreement you prepared for the meeting, you will be able to carefully spell out exactly what you will do at this meeting and tell how much it will cost. Your prospect will say, "That sounds reasonable," and will sign both copies of your agreement. You will thank your new customer for the business, give him a copy of the agreement, leave, and, once outside, celebrate!

PREPARING A PROPOSAL

Proposals can be 5-inch-thick documents prepared by Fortune 500 companies for big projects. A proposal also can be a letter. (In fact, those hefty proposals are just very long letters.) This letter states, in very detailed form, exactly what you intend to do to fulfill a prospect's need and how much it will cost. You also may craftily sneak in sales plugs from time to time.

A proposal is used when you have to estimate time and costs. Once these are agreed to, you're bound to stick to your projections so you need to be careful in your preparations.

At your meeting, your prospective customer will present a need related to what you have to offer. She may need an application program developed for a particular personal computer so that special features of that model can be used. You will take extensive and very accurate, detailed, and readable notes about exactly what she wants.

You need to find out how much material and equipment she can provide to get the job done. Looking at that question another way, ask yourself how much do you have to do from scratch? If a program is to be developed, for example, will specifications be provided? Flow charts? Machine time? You need to find out exactly how much work she wants done. If you write a program, are you also supposed to be responsible for testing? Does the client want end user documentation? REMARK statements in the code? program documentation? You also need to determine if she has unrealistic expectations—it's best to handle these early.

After the program is delivered, are you expected to be available free of charge to answer anybody's questions about it? Will you teach people how to use the program? Each of these questions helps define how long the project will take and how much it will cost. If possible, find out how long and how much the client thinks it will cost.

Take your notes home and start thinking. Do you have all the skills required to handle the job? To take advantage of special personal computer features, you may have to program in machine language. Can you do it? If not, do you know somebody with the skills? How much will that cost? Do you have the time to tackle the job? Does it sound too big for you? If you have these basic answers, then, you can ask yourself the most interesting question of all: Exactly how will the job be done?

First, you will have to define your approach to the project. It may be completely different from what you and the client discussed. Your prospect may have wanted you to enhance a program, but after you have a chance to look at what the customer calls code, you realize it will be far more economical to write a new program. Do you call or go ahead and work out a proposal for the new approach?

You should work out the proposal. Verify your facts, and get down to details. Will it be cheaper to take a new approach? Will it save time? Collect facts and figures to support your view, and then return professionally ready to present your proposal and justify your approach.

You may have to do research to decide how much work must be done. A prospective customer may want you to teach people to run his inventory program. Before you can estimate how long it will take to develop the course, you will need to learn to operate the program yourself. The owner of a delicatessen may want a payroll program, but before you can design the software, you'll need to research the types of deductions his personnel may take, what reports and forms he will need to print, the number of employees usually on the payroll, and how checks are to be made out. This research, also, will make you aware of the details that show how other people spend their lives.

Based on your research, you will sketch in your approach more fully and start defining your plan for doing the work. Break the job down into tasks and figure out how long each task will take. Detail the project and look at your time estimates for doing each component task. Is the work that has to be done realistically reflected in your estimates?

Can any of the tasks be done simultaneously? Can somebody do program documentation, for example, while you do final testing? Move together all the overlapping time periods, and then add the time actually necessary to get the job done.

Keep all your notes. If your client has questions, you may need them to justify your bid. Your notes also may be important if you need to modify your proposal.

You now have all you need to prepare the actual proposal. The proposal will consist of three parts: a statement of work, price, and terms.

The statement of work rigorously details *exactly* what you will provide. A complete statement of work should show your prospect that you understand his project very well. It will leave no doubt about what he will be getting or what you will be expected to do. At the end, state your estimate for how long it will take to do all the work.

The price presentation shows your cost estimate and how you wish to be paid. Chapter 7 presents a full discussion of these topics.

Terms presents qualifications and restrictions you wish to impose or which you feel your prospect would like to impose. Be fair in imposing terms. Put yourself in your client's place and see how you would react to the terms. Ask yourself what terms your prospect would impose were he to draw up an agreement, and if these are fair and valid to you, add them to your proposal.

The following paragraphs show you how a proposal actually is prepared.

In their first meeting, Janet has learned that the owner of a laundry wants to put his payroll on his personal computer. He is unable to find application software he likes, so he wants a program customized to his needs. Janet is unable to use any of the standard agreements she has brought along because she just doesn't know what's involved in the job.

Janet: "May I take a look at the work so I can see what has to be done?"

Owner: "I would have been surprised if you wanted to do anything else."

Janet: "I'll need to come back to collect data, and I probably will have to talk to you about exactly what you want."

Owner: "Feel free to come by whenever you like."

Janet spends a few days collecting data and researching payroll programs to see what's already been done. She then designs her own payroll program customized to the laundry owner's needs. She prepares a plan for working on the program and uses that plan to figure her cost and time estimates.

Janet writes her proposal. So that there will be no misunderstanding about what will be delivered, she details the finished program (listing all its capabilities), states what she will do (create and debug, provide a source code listing and the program on two disks), and tells how long she estimates the work will take. She presents her price for doing the work. She has thought about terms she wants (the laundry will supply test data and someone on the laundry staff will do the testing), and has put herself in the laundry owner's place to create terms he might want (all program rights go to the laundry). The proposal ends by stating when the work will begin and asks for the prospect's signature. Figure 5-3 shows the complete proposal, which you can use as a model for your own.

When the proposal is typed and a copy made, Janet calls the owner of the laundry and says, "I've just completed your proposal. When can I come by and present it to you?"

August 24, 1985

123 Dawnes Lane
Greenwich, Rhode Island 02886
(401) 555-5555

Mr. Daniel Folgi
Folgi's Laundry
345 Bennet Place
Warwick, Rhode Island 02886

Dear Mr. Folgi,

I am pleased to provide this proposal for the Payroll Program project you presented at our 15 August 1985 meeting.

STATEMENT OF WORK

I will prepare a Payroll Program in BASIC for an IBM Personal Computer. The program will perform the following functions:

1. Compute wages for hourly employees. Overtime rates will be included in the computations.
2. Record Year-To-Date wages, salary, and deductions by employee in a master file. Up to 20 employees (which is well beyond your present staff) will be allowed. Weekly details will be stored in a detailed transaction file.
3. Compute and record the following deductions: social security tax, U.S. withholding tax, pension plan, credit union savings plan, credit union loan payments, and state tax.
4. Record the following for each employee: name, address, telephone number, social security number, exemptions, next of kin, deductions, available and used sick days, vacation time, holidays, and payment check numbers.
5. Provide the following functional capabilities for employee records: ADD, CHANGE, DELETE.
6. Fully prompt the user through all procedures.
7. Print checks according to your check format.
8. Print a payroll register.
9. Print a check register.
10. Print a state tax report.
11. Print 941 forms.
12. Print W-2 forms.

Fig. 5-3   A proposal. *(Cont. on following page.)*

13. Print reports for: available time off by employee; sick days taken; vacation time taken.
14. Print a monthly report of deductions by employee.
15. Print a monthly report of deduction amounts by deduction.

Work will include program design, development, and debugging. At the conclusion of work, you will be provided with a source code listing and two disks on which the code is written. The program will take approximately 6 weeks to deliver.

PRICE
  [*Discussed in Chapter 7*]

TERMS
1. You will supply test data and someone to do the testing. Testing is to be completed within 10 days of program submission. Problems found are to be clearly listed and given to me.
2. You will make available an IBM PC, disks (as necessary), and a printer.
3. You will have all rights to the program.
4. I agree to work with a person of your choice on documentation, who you will pay separately.
5. Acceptance of the program must be made within 10 days of final program submission by Daniel Folgi, or a list of problems to be resolved will be given to me. Acceptance testing will be performed by Daniel Folgi preparing his actual payroll.
6. Check formats are to be provided by August 30, 1985.

If this proposal is acceptable to you, please sign below and I will begin the project on 24 August 1985.

Very truly,

Janet Slade

Accepted by:

_____   _____
(name)   (title)

_____
(date)

Fig. 5-3 (*Cont.*)

The client may want details over the telephone. If possible, avoid giving any details. A person can easily get the wrong idea by focusing on one or only a few facts. It will be better to present the complete proposal with all details in perspective in person.

PRESENTING YOUR PROPOSAL

The presentation of a proposal never should take too long, but remember that this presentation is part of selling your offer. Start your presentation by *briefly* reviewing the advantages of your offer, focusing on the problem you will overcome. "My service will take your mind off supporting your billing programs and let you concentrate on getting new customers." "By properly training users to work your programs, you'll have less calls for help and that means more time to do your own work." "This program will make doing your payroll a lot easier each week."

Explain what you intend to do. Show your potential customer all the details of the work you will do. Show any illustrations you have brought along (e.g., illustrations of proposed program-user dialogues, sample handouts you intend to use as teaching aids). After you have given your client a clear picture of what he or she will get, present your price.

Then, hand over a copy of your proposal. Never hand over your proposal before you finish talking or you may never get a chance to finish. A client always will read any document he's asked to sign, and while he's reading, he simply won't listen to you.

Answer any questions asked. You may need to consult the notes you used for your estimates.

Your client may ask for a few days to think the proposal over. If she does, suggest a time limit. Other problems will come up and distract her from your proposal—which is not something you want to happen. So, politely ask, "May I call you on Thursday for a decision?" Then, make sure you call, and keep calling until you get through.

When you get through, ask, "Have you reached a decision on my proposal yet?" When she says yes, get over there as soon as possible to turn your proposal into an agreement by signing it.

Your prospect may not need time to think your proposal over. That's okay, too. If she wants to sign when you present the proposal, by all means let her. Then all you have to do is the work you promised—and collect your money.

WHEN THINGS GO WRONG

Things may not always work out as ideally as presented in this chapter. Let's take a look at things that may go wrong, how to handle the situation, and how to detect if you're heading for trouble.

The first thing that can go wrong is that there's a misunderstanding between you and your client about what you have to offer. In fact, there's no way that the person can possibly use what you have to offer. If you set up a software testing service, for instance, someone may call and sound eager, but when you meet, you discover the programs are designed to be used for microscopic cell research—and you barely eked out a D in high school biology. You simply can't help because you lack the necessary experience. In such cases, you should clarify the situation as soon as possible ("I'm sorry, but I simply don't have the experience to do the job"), thank him for his time, and ask him to think of you if he ever has something more suitable. You'll be disappointed, and you'll lose the time and expense it took to meet the person, but you really haven't lost much. You should anticipate such disappointments. On average, only one out of five meetings results in an agreement.

Similarly, in your first meeting the person may decide that, after all, she's really not interested. Once again, you'll be disappointed and at a small loss. But, before you leave this situation, try to determine what caused her to lose interest. Is it your price? If so, are you willing to reduce your price? Do you lack a particular type of service in which the person is interested? For example, you only may print mailing labels, but your client wants the entire mailing handled. If so, do you want to expand your service? Has the prospect simply not thought through all that's involved in getting the job done? If so, can you spend a few minutes educating her and showing her how valuable the undertaking is?

You may find yourself in a situation in which someone likes your offer, but looks at your prepared agreement or proposal and wants to negotiate a few points. The terms are reasonable and you readily agree to the suggestions. Do you need to go home, retype your agreement or proposal, and return for a signing? Not at all—lines on a prepared form can be crossed off or changed, and new ones added as long as you both initial and date each change on every copy.

There are, unfortunately, a very small number of people who do some really awful things, especially to someone new in business. Most people you'll deal with are fine, honest, and concerned about you. They know that the basis of any good business relationship must be mutually beneficial and so they'll look out for your interests as well as their own. But there are those few you should stay away from at all costs.

How do they operate? How can you tell if you're dealing with one? There are warning signs.

If you start an innovative business, you may find yourself called by someone whose only interest is finding out enough to imitate your offer. He hasn't the slightest interest in using your service or buying your product. He'll tell you little, if anything, about the project he has in mind for you. Mostly, he'll ask you a lot of questions. He'll be especially interested in how you charge and what you charge. As incredible as it sounds, he may even offer you a partnership: "Your offer sounds really good and it's exactly what I've been looking to get into. If we do it together. . . ." You don't need a partner like this.

If a caller is evasive about the work she has, try to pin her down by saying: "I really can't tell you much about what I do unless I know what you have in mind. Can you detail what you want done?" Avoid talking about prices over the telephone. If you sense you're only being pumped for information, politely excuse yourself: "I'm sorry, but this sounds like one of those cases where neither one of us has clearly thought about what we should be discussing. I really appreciate your time. If you can spell out a specific project, please give me a call and let's get together."

You may encounter somebody who really does need help, but not exactly the help you're offering. You're at a meeting to discuss your software testing service. This potential customer actually does have a program that needs testing, and you think you can handle it. Then, he says he has more programs, and you begin to think you've uncovered a golden opportunity. He says he would use your service *if only he knew how to market programs.* Can you help? You've obviously marketed your own service. He can't pay you right now, but once things take off. . . . At this point, *you* should take off. Simply say, "I'm sorry, but what you want isn't in my line of business." But don't leave *too quickly.* You actually may have uncovered a very interesting and lucrative opportunity. Do a bit of probing. Does the prospect have a good product or service? Do you have the skills to help? Can you make money by helping? What exactly is being offered?

The worst thing a person can do is intentionally lead you on, getting as much as possible from you, and paying you nothing. How can any sensible person be foolish enough to let such a thing happen? Let me explain how it happened to me. When I first started out in my own business, I was eager to sign up as many customers as I could. One of my first customers offered me a lot of work, but he wasn't sure I could handle it. After all, I was new in the business. How could he trust me? I was puzzled. What did he want me to do? He suggested we work together for awhile to see how things went. I was so confident that he would like my work that I readily agreed. I started one project. Just before it was finished, he told me he liked what I had done so far, but the project was put on hold. He couldn't judge the *finished* quality of my work. Could I finish another project that someone else had started? "Sure," I said. "No problem. Just watch me." When that was done, he still didn't know. I finally began to suspect that something was amiss. I told him I had done a lot of work already and now it was only fair to pay me. He nodded, and told me to send him an invoice. He gave me more work. What a wonderful man! How wrong I had been about him. I sent my invoice, started his new work, and waited for my money before I submitted anything new. I waited. He never called to ask for the materials he gave me for his "new" job back, and I'm still waiting for my money.

A client may not be satisfied with your proposal. If you're proposing to develop a program, he may want to see detailed specifications. Once you've worked on that difficult task, he may take your specifications, tell you what you did really wasn't what he had in mind, turn around and invite somebody else in to make a proposal on preparing a program from *your* specifications—and, of course, he would like to see some code from him.

You should never feel you have to undergo "testing." If somebody wants to try you out, you should accept the test only when an agreement is signed stating that you will be paid at a reduced price during the testing period on a scheduled basis. It's only fair that *both* parties to the agreement accept part of the risk.

As I've said, most people are honest. You can't become paranoid, or you'll lose business. A person can turn down your offer for any number of valid reasons. He may have set up a competitive bidding situation and liked someone else's proposal better than yours. She may need the work before you can get it done. He may not like your plan. If, after reviewing your proposal, your potential customer says he isn't interested, politely thank him for his time and consideration and ask for permission to call in a few months.

A prospect may tell you she likes your offer, but isn't ready to go ahead right now. In most cases, she'll be speaking honestly to you. Thank her for her time. You may find that 6 months or a year later—usually when you're overloaded with work—she'll call and say, "Remember that proposal you did for me? I'd like to go ahead and start it next week." Under these circumstances, it is perfectly acceptable to review your own proposal and make whatever time and cost changes you feel are necessary.

Finally, you and your customer may sign a proposal, but after you begin, you realize with horror that your estimates were much too low. The job will cost you a lot more than what you figured. You shouldn't have to "eat" the mistake and do the work at a loss. To simply go ahead will mislead your customer so that when you next do a job, he'll feel suspicious: "The last time we worked together you charged so much less, but now when you think you're in solid, your prices go up. You're not in as solid as you think." If you take a loss, you also will feel anger toward your customer and it will show. Consequently, the minute you realize you've made a gross mistake estimating work, you should call your customer and explain the situation. You should apologize. You may lose the job, but in most cases, the customer will ask you to come in and renegotiate a fair agreement. Don't make a habit of underestimating.

When things go wrong, don't despair. It happens to everybody. The president of a Boston software company asked me in our first meeting to tell him about my greatest disaster because he knew that the way a crisis is handled tells a lot about a person. And remember, most business relationships are very rewarding. You'll not only make money, but also meet many interesting, successful, and concerned people.

CHAPTER
SIX
PROFITS FROM EXPENSES: AN ACCOUNTS PAYABLE PROGRAM

As soon as you start your business—even before you sign up your first customer—you incur something that's very valuable: expenses. It may seem paradoxical that an expense can be valuable, but it is.

WHY YOU NEED AN ACCOUNTS PAYABLE PROGRAM

Assume you earned $25,000.00 in 1982. If you're single, you would have owed taxes of $5371.00. Your income, however, really wasn't $25,000.00. You had to pay expenses to make that amount and these expenses reduce your taxable income. If your expenses were $10,000.00, the actual income that you report is only $15,000.00, which means you had to pay in taxes only $2337.00—a difference in your favor of $3034.00!

You should record every penny you spend for your business because comprehensive records save you money on your federal, state, and city taxes.

Expense records also are important so you can see where the money in your business is going. Since you spend money at a different time than you collect it, accurate records are necessary to show if you're making any money at all. Such records may help you price your offer. When you first price an offer, you may be unaware of hidden costs, but the records will give you the facts necessary to adjust your price so you profit from your work. Your expense records also can call to your attention areas where you are spending a large proportion of money, so you can seek alternative ways to do business.

As you can see, business expenses can be tricky. On the one hand, you want to minimize your expenses to make as much as you can in your business. On the other hand, you want to spend as much as you can to reduce your taxes. To steer a profitable course for your business, you need accurate, up-to-date information about your expenses—and that, unfortunately, is what most businesses don't have.

It's a difficult chore to keep records manually. By the end of a busy day, pockets can be full of receipts which should be recorded, but usually aren't. Preparing reports by hand is unthinkable. Business people, as a result, have been penalized by unnecessary taxes and lower profits.

Your Accounts Payable (or A/P) Program will enable you to avoid these unnecessary losses. You'll have up-to-date information about expenses so you can make decisions to maximize profits.

You may be able to save money in another way, too. Many accountants will reduce their rates if you bring them clear, well-organized reports of your expenses, instead of a clutter of receipts that must be pieced together. Your A/P Program will print these reports in minutes.

Without question, you'll save time just by having all your records organized at tax time. Usually, locating and organizing records for tax forms takes days or weeks away from a business. You can't make money while you're tracking down receipts. You won't have that problem anymore when you use your A/P Program.

You can use the A/P Program to handle expenses for other businesses, too. Many of these businesses don't have personal computers to handle their records. Many people don't want the expense of buying computers, but they want the information computers can provide. But as more businesses buy computers, their computerless competitors will need such a service to survive.

Your A/P Program provides one-half the capabilities you need to start a bookkeeping service. The other half is an Accounts Receivable (or A/R) Program, which is presented in Chap. 8. Markets for this service and techniques for entering them are described in Chap. 8. Together these programs give you a complete and professional bookkeeping capability.

By the way, a bookkeeping service is tax-deductible.

HOW YOUR A/P PROGRAM HELPS YOU

Your A/P Program is intended to make it as simple as possible to record and use expense information. The program is suitable for single-person businesses, small businesses, and fairly substantial businesses. Over 3500 bills can be stored on a single disk.

If you're offering a bookkeeping service, you have a lot to offer your customers:

- Help for a client making payments by calling to his or her attention all unpaid bills. In this display, all bills for a single company are together, so your client can consolidate them all with a single check. Looking at the list, your client will see the total owed and can decide who and how much to pay.
- A neat, well-organized Month End Report, which lists all money spent in the month.
- A Report of Year-To-Date Totals by expense category. The report shows how much has been spent so far on each of 36 possible expenses. The last report for the year provides tax information.
- A Breakdown Report, which shows the percentage each expense represents to the total. This report focuses attention on the area where the most is spent.
- A Past Due Report, which brings all overdue bills to a client's attention, assuring that he or she won't lose a high credit rating because of an oversight.
- A Cash Requirements Report, which shows commitments for the coming months, and helps keep your client from overcommitting cash.
- The ability to look at expenses and income (with your A/R Program) to

see if upcoming expenses for the following year can be paid early to move the client into a lower tax bracket.

Since tax laws change, a flexible computation capability has been built into your A/P Program to allow you to combine yearly expense totals. Using this capability, you can combine only deductible expenses, for example, which will help you complete your tax forms. You also can combine the categories heat, electricity, and water under Utilities, which is the expense category used on federal income tax forms.

A great deal has been computerized to save you time when you enter these expenses. Your A/P Program is able to record automatically:

- The correct date for payments
- Payment amounts that match the invoice amount
- A sequence of check numbers for payment so you will not have to keep entering them
- Travel expenses to a destination, so you will not have to remember mileage and tolls

Your A/P Program's flexibility makes it adaptable to different businesses. You can record:

- Expenses only when they are paid, a technique suitable for most small businesses.
- Invoices; and, at a later time, you can apply full or partial payments to invoices.

Your program also can print a travel journal that logs business trips in accordance with IRS requirements. Inquiries into expenses also can be made at any time to answer your client's questions.

WHAT ARE EXPENSES?

When Stan started his consulting business from his home, he carefully recorded in a ledger book every penny he spent on his business—or so he thought.

Eight months into his business, Stan happened to read an article that mentioned, in passing, that the cost for utilities for that proportion of a house used for business is tax-deductible. Stan hadn't kept any of *those* records. He had figured that since he wasn't renting an office, he really didn't have any of these expenses. After that, he wondered about the other expenses he should have been recording all along.

Simply knowing what expenses to record is a major problem when you first start out in business. One of the most overlooked of the many hidden expenses of business is travel, which usually is thought of in long-distance terms. But, *any* trip you make for business is a travel expense. Going to the post office to mail a business letter, or to a company to call on a prospect (even if the prospect never becomes a customer), or to a store to buy paper for your printer are all examples of travel expenses that generally are overlooked. Over a year, the cost for travel amounts to a considerable sum. Laundry and cleaning of your business wardrobe is another, often overlooked, deduction, also.

If a space in your home is consistently and exclusively used either as a place to meet or deal with customers or clients, or as your principal place of business, you can take home office deductions for mortgage interest, taxes, operating expenses (heat, water, electricity, rent) and depreciation attributable to that space. You do not need an entire room devoted to your business to take these deductions, but a screen or other partition is highly recommended as an area separator.

These home business deductions allow you to have an income for tax purposes less than your actual business income. You would pay for the home expenses whether or not you had the business. Many people conduct part-time businesses from their homes simply to gain these deductions.

If you use your personal computer for business, it's a tax deduction. In the year when you purchase any piece of equipment, you can claim a deduction for the entire purchase price (up to $5000) or depreciate it over 5 years. If you use your PC for other activities, only the percentage used for business is deductible. With tax laws like this, it makes a lot of sense to start a business when you buy a PC!

Software that you buy also is deductible, but you must apportion the expense over 5 years, or (if you can show that it will no longer be useful in less time) less. You cannot deduct the full expense of a program in the year you bought it—unless the program will be good for that year only.

If you start or already have a business, the cost of this book is a tax deduction.

Your A/P Program is designed to track 36 expenses, of which you can define two items of your choice. The remaining 34 expenses are listed and explained in Table 6-1. In the table, federal income tax deductions are shown

TABLE 6-1 EXPENSES

Expense	Explanation
1. Accounting	Accounting, bookkeeping, and auditing expenses, including books, and costs for preparing *any* tax returns. All deductible.
2. Advertising	Costs for magazine, newspaper, radio and television advertising; costs for preparing materials, including ads, posters, and displays; premiums and coupons given to attract customers; cost of prizes; Christmas presents given to prospects or customers to attract new business. All deductible.
3. Bad debts	Previously reported income which actually is nonrecoverable. Deductible. Most small businesses will use the CASH method of accounting so this deduction will be used "to legitimize" out-of-pocket expenses for nonrecoverable debts. If you handle a mailing, for example, and send out an invoice but aren't paid, you will record all expenses for the mailing (e.g., envelopes, postage), enter on your tax form the uncollected invoice amount as income, and also enter the same amount as a bad debt. The income and bad debt will cancel one another, but you will have documented the reason for uncollected, out-of-pocket expenses.
4. Bank service charges	Charges for checking accounts, etc. Deductible.
5. Car/truck expense	Actual expenses for car/truck use, including cost of gasoline, oil, license plates, driver's fee, garage rent, washing and waxing, insurance premiums, repairs, damage not covered by insurance. All deductible. Only that percentage of vehicle business use should be recorded. Alternatively, you can compute this deduction using expense 6. If two or more vehicles are used in a business, this method (5) must be used.

TABLE 6-1   EXPENSES   *(Cont.)*

Expense	Explanation
6. Car/truck travel	Expenses based on fixed mileage rate. Parking fees and tolls also may be included. Deductible. Use *either* this expense or 5 to record car expenses. Note: You may record both expense 5 and 6 for yourself, and, at the end of the year, use the larger figure for your taxes.
7. Commissions	Commissions paid to employees, agents, and salespersons. Deductible.
8. Contributions	To religious, charitable, scientific, literary, and educational organizations if it's provable that the expense helps your business. Deductible.
9. Dues and publications	Dues for professional organizations and clubs, e.g., chamber of commerce. Business-related trade journals, papers, and magazine subscriptions. Deductible.
10. Electricity	Percentage chargeable to business. Deductible.
11. Employee benefit program	Your contribution. Deductible.
12. Entertainment	Expenses for entertaining prospects and clients, keeping old customers, maintaining employee welfare. Deductible.
13. Freight	Expenses for delivery of merchandise bought and sold. Deductible.
14. Heat	Percentage chargeable to business. Deductible.
15. Insurance	Insurance premiums for business. Deductible.
16. Interest on business debt	Includes life insurance, bank, and personal loans; mortgage tax penalty payments; installment payments;

TABLE 6-1   EXPENSES   *(Cont.)*

Expense	Explanation
	margin accounts with stock brokers. Deductible.
17. Inventory	Material purchased for resale. Deductible.
18. Laundry and cleaning	Expenses for business clothing. Deductible.
19. Legal and professional fees	For agents, accountants, lawyers, investment counselors, technicians, brokers, etc. Deductible.
20. Loans	Principle repayment amounts. Nondeductible.
21. Notes	Notes payable cash payments. Nondeductible.
22. Office supplies	Costs of paper, printer ribbons, pencils, pens, etc. Also costs for services; printing, copying, etc. Deductible.
23. Pension and profit sharing plans	Contributions for your employees. Deductible. Contributions for your own plan are entered on Form 1040.
24. Postage	For business purposes only. Deductible.
25. Rent on business property	Including office space, safe deposit boxes, and parking facilities. Deductible.
26. Tax, city	Sales tax, income tax. Deductible.
27. Tax, federal	Federal income tax payments. Nondeductible.
28. Tax, social security	For payments to employees' accounts. Deductible.
29. Tax, state	State unemployment insurance tax, state unincorporated business tax, state sales tax, state income tax, state gross receipts tax. Deductible.
30. Telephone	Percentage used for business. Deductible.

TABLE 6-1 EXPENSES (*Cont.*)

Expense	Explanation
31. Travel	Expenses for rail fare, airline fare, taxi fare, meals, room, tips, telephone, baggage charges, laundry, and cleaning. Deductible.
32. Wages	Amounts paid to employees. Deductible.
33. Water	Percentage used for business. Deductible.
34. Miscellaneous	Use this expense, item 1, and item 2 to record expenses appropriate to a business that are not entered elsewhere. These expenses can include the following tax deductions: 1. Cost of repairs 2. Depletions 3. Depreciation 4. Expenses of a building used for business, including painting, repair, rubbish removal, janitor service, and landscaping 5. Damages not covered by insurance. 6. Rental and investment real estate expenses 7. Gifts for customers—$25.00 limit 8. Research expenses 9. Cost of financial data for own business Note: If you use expense 5 (car/truck expense), be sure to record vehicle depreciation.

for 1983. Tax laws for specific years determine which ones are and which ones aren't deductible. For a bookkeeping service, you will not need to distinguish between deductible and nondeductible expenses for your clients. Your books can be turned over to an accountant for that job.

NOTE:

To complete your own IRS returns, you will need Schedule C [Profit (or Loss) From Business Or Profession], Schedule SE (Social Security Self-

Employment Tax), and Form 1040-ES (for estimated tax payments). You also should check on tax reporting requirements for your state and city.

The expenses in Table 6-1 are intended to be extensive enough to handle most business situations. In your own business you probably won't record information for all of them.

HOW YOUR A/P PROGRAM WORKS

To use your A/P Program to the fullest, you will need to know a bit about how it works internally.

Your A/P Program works with two files (illustrated in Fig. 6-1), which may be thought of as folders which hold records (or forms). The files are called the Transaction File and the Totals File.

All your records for both paid and unpaid bills will be stored in the Transaction File. Specifically, for each bill, you will complete the record shown in Fig. 6-2. To help you, the program will prompt you to complete each line. You're not required to complete the whole record when you first add it. You may record only the invoice part and add payments and check numbers later.

The program will help you complete a record, too. When you want to pay bills, the program will go to the Transaction File and pick out *all* your unpaid bills. It will list the bills by companies, so that you see all the ones you owe a company. You then decide which bills you want to pay. As you might expect, the program will prompt you for this information, too. Any record stored in this file can be taken out and changed or deleted.

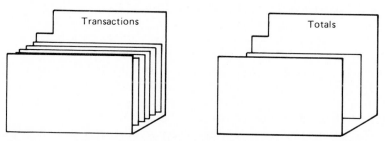

Fig. 6-1 The Transaction File and the Totals File can be thought of as two folders that hold records and forms.

```
EXPENSE SELECTION: _____

PAY WHO? _____

BILL AMOUNT: _____

DUE DATE: _____

COMMENT: _____

PAYMENT DATE: _____

CHECK NUMBER: _____
```

Fig. 6-2 Record card for Transaction File.

The Totals File, on the other hand, contains a *single*, but very important form that lists all 36 expenses and how much has been spent for each one. This is illustrated in Fig. 6-3. You don't have to type *any* information to complete *this* form. It'll be taken from the Transaction File.

Here's how your A/P Program uses these two files to save you time and improve accuracy.

You'll keep the books for expense records by printing reports for each month. These reports show exactly how much has been spent in 1 month. They're called Month End Reports.

The program prints a Month End Report by going to your Transaction File and picking out all the bills that have been paid during a month. It moves these records into a work area inside the computer. The program begins to work on the records. It puts the records of what you spent on each expense together. The amount you spent during the month for an expense is added up, and then the amount for another expense is totaled, and so on, until the program adds up how much you spent for *everything* during the month. At this time, the program is ready to print your month end report (see Fig. 6-4).

The detailed Month End Report shows actual data about the paid bills. For each expense, the report lists the person (or company) paid, how much was paid, the date the bill was due, and the date it was paid.

The program isn't finished yet. It keeps all the work done in the work area, even after the report is printed. The program then takes each expense,

EXPENSE	TOTAL
1–ACCOUNTING	92.00
2–ADVERTISING	345.00
3–BAD DEBTS	0.00
.	
.	
.	
36–ITEM 2	51.25

Fig. 6-3   The Totals File.

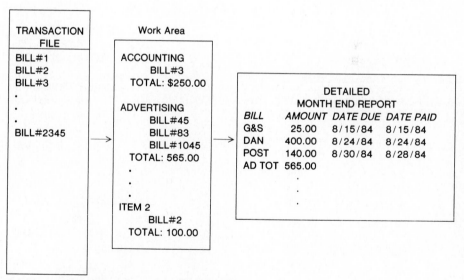

Fig. 6-4   The detailed Month End Report.

one at a time, and uses it to update the record in the Totals File (see Fig. 6-5).

As you can see, you don't have to spend hours adding up all the expenses. It will be done in minutes for you *automatically*.

Expenses accrue in the Totals File throughout the year in this same way. At year's end, the Totals File contains all you spent on each expense. You print a report of these totals, which contains your tax information, and close the book for the year.

Internal safeguards ensure that your records and reports are accurate. All records that are used to update the Totals File are flagged so they won't be used again. You may want to increase your totals for tax purposes by adding the same expense into the Totals File twice, but the IRS doesn't allow it and neither does your A/P Program!

To keep your printed reports and internally stored records synchronized, the program will not allow "on the fly" changes to the Totals File. Amounts in the Totals File are changed only by updating with Month End Totals, or closing the book for a year (which clears the amounts so expenses for a new year can be accumulated).

Since all the details about paid bills are printed in the Month End Report

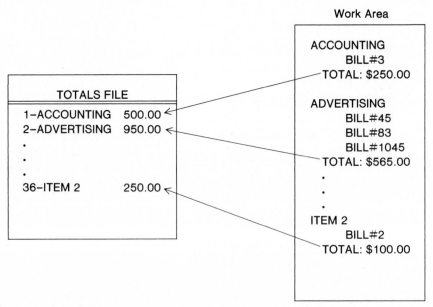

Fig. 6-5 Updating the Totals File.

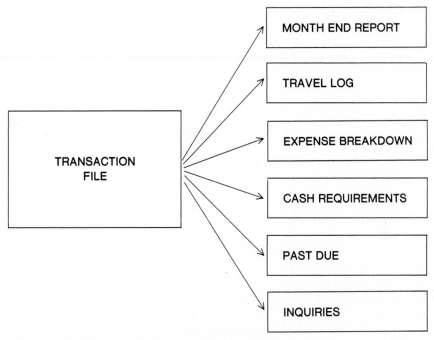

Fig. 6-6 Reports generated from the Transaction File.

and incorporated into the Totals File, you really don't need to keep these records anymore. The program quickly can clean them from your disk, freeing space for new records.

Finally, it will be helpful to know where information for a report is coming from. The reports shown in Fig. 6-6 are generated from the Transaction File. The Totals File is used to generate the reports shown in Fig. 6-7.

You're now ready to start operating your A/P Program.

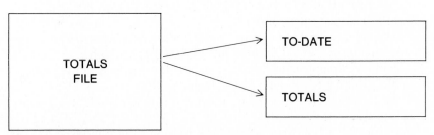

Fig. 6-7 Reports generated from the Totals File.

OPERATING YOUR A/P PROGRAM

The A/P Program uses 13 commands:

* *
PAYMENTS PROGRAM

AVAILABLE COMMANDS ARE:

1 – ADD	2 – PAID
3 – CHANGE	4 – DELETE
5 – MONTHLY	6 – TRAVEL
7 – TO DATE	8 – TOTALS
9 – BREAKDOWN	10 – PAST DUE
11 – CASH	12 – INQUIRY
13 – EXIT	

* *
COMMAND SELECTION [1-13 or ?1-?13]:

Complete expense records may be maintained by using just three of these commands: ADD, MONTHLY, and TO DATE. The ADD command lets you add bills and record payments. The MONTHLY command prints a report of the month's activity that really constitutes "your books." The To-Date Report will provide you with yearly totals of your expenses that you'll use to figure your taxes.

If you want to use the fixed rate method instead of recording all costs for your vehicles, you also will use the TRAVEL command, which will generate a travel journal for the year.

If you want to see unpaid bills and your cash requirements for the coming months, you also will use the PAID command to record payments, the PAST DUE and CASH commands to print reports of commitments.

If you want help in combining expenses for taxes, you will use the TOTALS command.

The BREAKDOWN and INQUIRY commands may be used at any time to gain insight into a business.

For your own books, try to use your A/P Program to record expenses on the day you incur them. That way you'll be less likely to forget an expense. You'll find recording will take only a few minutes. Try to get in the habit of recording your expenses just before you quit for the day.

On the cover of your data disk, make a note of how you'll be using item 1 and item 2, if you'll be using them at all—you don't have to. For convenience, you also should keep a list of the program's 34 other expenses and identification numbers handy.

If you'll be using your A/P Program for a bookkeeping service, prepare to meet prospective customers by printing sample reports. Make your reports realistic and extensive. In your meeting, explain how each report can be used for your prospect's benefit.

When you sign up a customer, include on your data disk cover the reports the customer wants. *Store each customer's data* on a separate disk. Label the disk cover with the customer's name and telephone number.

As you prepare to convert your customer from a manual system to your service, ask the client to spend some time with you explaining the records he normally keeps. Make suggestions about other records he can keep, e.g., for tax deductions. Find out how he wants vehicle expenses kept. Agree on the categories for his expenses until you know his business well enough to do it on your own. You usually will go to each customer's place of business once a month to record expenses and print reports.

Whether you're keeping books for yourself or for somebody else, *always keep receipts for all expenses!* You will need them if you're audited. Keep invoices for future references. If you don't have a receipt for an expense, keep the payment check.

Keep each customer's Month End Reports together. Buy a folder for each customer and insert his or her reports. At minimum, also include the December To-Date Report, which will provide tax information.

Your A/P Program allows you to store over 3500 expense records on a single data disk. Since payments automatically may be removed after the Month End Report is printed, you should be able to use a single disk for each customer for the duration of your relationship.

NOTE:

Remember to save all receipts!

Your A/P Program command procedures and uses are described below.

ACCESSING THE A/P PROGRAM

To access the A/P Program, type **RUN PAYMENT** in response to your system prompt:

A: **RUN PAYMENT**

The program will be loaded and you will be prompted for your data file disk drive. The first time you access the program, you will be prompted to enter the mileage rate for computing fixed rate travel expenses:

ENTER RATE PER MILE:

Type the mileage rate allowed by the U.S. government for the year. In 1982, this rate was 20¢ per mile, so you would type .20. The number is entered as a decimal. This number can be reset whenever you want, using the TO-DATE command.

Each time you access the program, you also will be prompted for the correct date and you'll type it. At this time, the command menu will be displayed so you can use the command of your choice.

NOTE:

Your A/P Program is too large to be loaded as a single unit. Consequently, the program has been split into six programs (see the program list under "Accounts Payable Program Source Code" at the end of this chapter). When you first request (access) a command, the appropriate program will be loaded. If, for example, you first use command 7, the PAYMENT4.BAS program is loaded. If you should then use command 1, the PAYMENT1.BAS program automatically will be loaded as a replacement. The replacements are handled so quickly that you should not experience *any* delay.

This separation of programs is organized around functions for programming clarity. Each of the PAYMENT programs includes all of the functions needed to perform all aspects of its corresponding command(s).

RECORDING AN EXPENSE

The ADD command (1) is used to record bills and payments. Recording of a payment is optional and may be done later with the PAID command.

You'll use the ADD command with invoices, receipts, and checkbook in hand. First, enter expenses that you paid by cash. All required information can be read from each receipt. Second, enter expenses you paid by check. Go through the checkbook starting with the smallest check number. The program automatically will increment check numbers so you won't have to keep typing them. Finally, enter invoices, if you wish to record this information—you don't have to. You simply can record expenses that are paid. If you do not enter invoices you will have no need to use the PAID (for paying an invoice), PAST DUE (for the overdue bills report), or CASH (for the cash commitments report) commands.

NOTE:

Retain all receipts and canceled checks. In case of an audit, you will need them to support your figures.

The procedure for recording all expenses except car/truck travel (expense 6) is:

1. COMMAND SELECTION: Type 1 for the ADD command.
2. EXPENSE SELECTION (1-36 or ?): Type the number for an expense category. You will type 1, for example, to record an accounting expense. Type ? if you want to see the list of expenses. You'll find it easiest to work from a printed list of expenses and numbers. The program will display the name of the expense you have selected.
3. PAY WHO? Type the name of the person, company, agency, etc. that has charged you. You can use 25 or less characters. You type **JAKE'S OFFICE SUPPLIES**, for example, if you just bought paper from that store. If the expense is paid by check, this will be who you make the check out to.
4. AMOUNT?: Type the amount of the expense. Do not type a $ or comma. The amount may be negative, in which case, it must be prefaced with a minus sign, e.g., −400.00. A plus sign is *not* allowed for positive amounts. The ability to enter a negative amount is intended specifically to account for bad checks that are returned *after* the transaction has been updated into the Totals File. The negative amount will reduce the expense total when the file next is updated. To reduce the amount, create your own bill for a negative amount and pay it in full (type C in response to PAYMENT DATE). *Do not use "negative bills" to account for rebates, returns, or refunds; these amounts are income.* Do not use this technique to account for a bad check returned *before* you close your transactions for a month; in this case, use the CHANGE command to remove the payment information.

5. DUE DATE: Type the date payment is due or press the carriage return and the current date will be recorded. If you will be recording a payment, you can use the payment date as the due date in most cases. It will save you time. Ask your clients if they want the actual due date recorded for expenses that already have been paid.

6. COMMENT: Type any reminder you wish to record for this bill using 50 or less characters. You can record a purchase order number, for example.

7. PAYMENT DATE: You can respond in four ways:

    a. Press the carriage return if you have not yet paid this bill and it will be recorded as an open invoice. You will be prompted PAY WHO? enabling you to record another bill.

    b. Type C if you paid the bill in full on the current day.

    c. Type the date of another day in the month when you paid the bill in full.

    d. Type P if you paid only a partial amount of the whole bill.

If you paid the bill in full or only partially you will be prompted CHECK NUMBER. Type the number of the check used to pay the bills, CASH (if no check was used for payment), or press the carriage return to automatically enter a check number. This automatic capability is designed to be used when all expenses are paid from the same checkbook and you either write out checks as you record expenses, or record expenses in the same order that you wrote out the checks. Entering CASH between checks will not disrupt the sequence. When you enter a new check number, all subsequent check numbers are generated from it.

If you make only a partial payment, you also will be prompted for the amount you paid, PARTIAL PAYMENT AMOUNT, the date you made the payment (which is recorded by typing either C for the current day or the date of another day in the month), and a comment. A partial payment will result in two *new* records, one for the paid amount, and one for the unpaid balance.

The way the program handles partial payments best can be seen by the illustration in Fig. 6-8a. A bill of $400.00 is owed to Tim Winsten for advertising (expense 2). On August 15, Tim Winsten is paid only $200.00. The program "splits" the record into one that is fully paid and another that has an unpaid balance (see Fig. 6-8b).

All information automatically is copied to the new record. If you want to change or delete this unpaid bill, you will look for Tim Winsten's bill of $200.00 (*not* $400.00). If you try to retrieve the original record of a $400.00 bill you won't find it because it will have been erased.

```
EXPENSE SELECTION: 2
PAY WHO? TIM WINSTEN
BILL AMOUNT: 400.00
DUE DATE: 8 / 15 / 83
COMMENT: RADIO CAMPAIGN
PAYMENT DATE: _____
CHECK NUMBER: _____
```

Fig. 6-8a Original A/P bill record.

Paid Record | Unpaid Record

```
EXPENSE SELECTION: 2
PAY WHO? TIM WINSTEN
BILL AMOUNT: 200.00
DUE DATE: 8 / 15 / 83
COMMENT: RADIO CAMPAIGN
PAYMENT DATE: 8 / 15 / 83
CHECK NUMBER: 753
```

```
EXPENSE SELECTION: 2
PAY WHO? TIM WINSTEN
BILL AMOUNT: 200.00
DUE DATE: 8 / 15 / 83
COMMENT: _____
PAYMENT DATE: _____
CHECK NUMBER: _____
```

Fig. 6-8b Two new A/P records resulting from partial payment of original bill.

When all information is specified, the expense record will be added to the Transaction File. The program will prompt PAY WHO? and you will type the name for another bill in this expense category or press the carriage return to select another category. When you have added all payments and invoices (if you are recording them), respond to EXPENSE SELECTION by pressing the carriage return and you will be returned to the Menu Level.

The procedure for adding records for all expenses except car/truck travel is illustrated in Fig. 6-9.

If you use the fixed mileage rate to compute vehicle expenses, you want to keep track of mileage, tolls, dates, and destination. The above procedure is inappropriate for this record keeping, so another procedure is used which simplifies bookkeeping:

1. EXPENSE SELECTION: Type 6 for car/truck travel.
2. WHERE TO: Type your destination using 25 or less characters. You can type a person's or a company's name, or anything meaningful to you.
3. MILES: Type the *total, round* trip miles between your home (or business) and your destination. The figure is entered as a decimal, e.g., 25.6.
4. TOLLS: Type the toll cost for all tolls you had to pay and any parking fees. If you didn't have to pay anything, press the carriage return.
5. DATE: Press the carriage return for the current date or type the date of your trip.
6. COMMENT: Type any comment you wish, using 50 or less characters.

At this time this record will be added to the Transaction File and you can specify another trip, or press the carriage return in response to WHERE TO? and you'll be able to request another expense.

Once you have a travel record for a person, you only need to enter the person's name and the date of the trip. You will not have to bother with miles or tolls because the program "remembers" them for you. This will make keeping a travel log *much* simpler than manually possible. To use this automatic capability, press the carriage return in response to MILES. Both miles and tolls will be copied from your last record for this destination. Anytime you wish, you can reset miles or tolls by typing a number in response to MILES.

NOTES:

1. The car/truck travel expense is computed by:

    (Miles × fixed mileage rate) + (tolls + parking fees) = expense

    The fixed mileage rate is the rate you set for the program.

Payments Program

Available commands are:

1–Add	2–Paid
3–Change	4–Delete
5–Monthly	6–Travel
7–To date	8–Totals
9–Breakdown	10–Past due
11–Cash	12–Inquiry
13–Exit	

Command selection [1–13 or ?1–?13] :**1**   The ADD command is selected.

Expense selection (1–36 or ?) :**?**
  1 –Accounting
  2 –Advertising
  3 –Bad Debts
  4 –Bank Service Charges
  5 –Car / Truck Expense
  6 –Car / Truck Travel
  7 –Commissions
  8 –Contributions
  9 –Dues and Publications
10–Electricity
11–Employee Benefit Program
12–Entertainment   For reference, expenses are listed.
13–Freight
14–Heat
15–Insurance
16–Interest on Business Debt
17–Inventory
18–Laundry and Cleaning
19–Legal and Professional Services
20–Loans
21–Notes
22–Office Supplies
23–Pension and Profit Sharing Plans
Enter return to continue :⟨**CR**⟩   The above expenses are all that
will fit on a standard screen at a
time. The carriage return clears
the screen and allows the
remaining expenses to be
displayed.

Fig. 6-9   Adding expense records. (*Cont. on following page.*)

24–Postage
25–Rent on Business Property
26–Tax–City
27–Tax–Federal
28–Tax–Social Security
29–Tax–State
30–Telephone
31–Travel
32–Wages
33–Water
34–Miscellaneous
35–Item–1
36–Item–2

Expense selection (1–36 or ?) :**24**   A payment for postage will be
                                                          recorded (expense 24).

Postage
Pay who ? :**POST OFFICE**
Amount ? :**3.45**   Data for the record is entered.
Due date : **082084**   The "bill" and the payment are
Comment :⟨**CR**⟩   recorded together.
Payment date :**082084**
Check number :**CASH**   Cash was used to pay for the
                                                          postage.

Billing record has been recorded!
  ..Amount = 3.45
Pay who ? :⟨**CR**⟩   No other payments for postage
                                                          will be recorded now.

Expense selection (1–36 or ?) :**5**   A payment for a car expense will
                                                          be recorded.

Car / Truck Expense
Pay who ? :**AL'S SERVICE**
Amount ? :**128.67**   Data for the record is entered.
Due date : **040483**
Comment :**TUNE-UP**
Payment date :**C**   The current date will be recorded.
Check number :**231**   A check number is entered.
Billing record has been recorded!
  ..Amount = 128.67
Pay who ? :**YATES TIRE**
Amount ? :**167.89**
Due date : **081784**   A record for another car expense
Comment :**TIRE NEW TIRES**   is added.
Payment date :**081784**

Fig. 6-9 *Cont.*

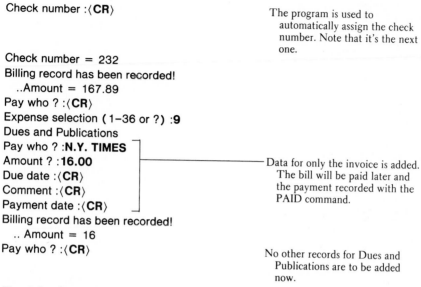

Check number :⟨**CR**⟩

The program is used to automatically assign the check number. Note that it's the next one.

Check number = 232
Billing record has been recorded!
..Amount = 167.89
Pay who ? :⟨**CR**⟩
Expense selection (1–36 or ?) :**9**
Dues and Publications
Pay who ? :**N.Y. TIMES**
Amount ? :**16.00**
Due date :⟨**CR**⟩
Comment :⟨**CR**⟩
Payment date :⟨**CR**⟩
Billing record has been recorded!
.. Amount = 16
Pay who ? :⟨**CR**⟩

Data for only the invoice is added. The bill will be paid later and the payment recorded with the PAID command.

No other records for Dues and Publications are to be added now.

Fig. 6-9 *Cont.*

2. Car/truck travel records are treated differently than other expense records. At year's end, you'll print a travel log, so you need travel records kept on disk until the journal is printed. You can print a log whenever you want, but you only save the one for the whole year. After you have printed it, the program allows you to update the Totals File with your car/truck travel expenses. The total for this expense, alone, *replaces* the previous total. (With all other expenses, *monthly* totals are added to the ones already there.)

The procedure for recording a car/truck travel expense is illustrated in Fig. 6-10.

RECORDING BILL PAYMENTS

The PAID command (2) is used to record payment of a bill. The procedure makes recording these payments very easy:

1. COMMAND SELECTION: Type **2** for the PAID command. The program will display *all* unpaid bills for past and future dates. The report

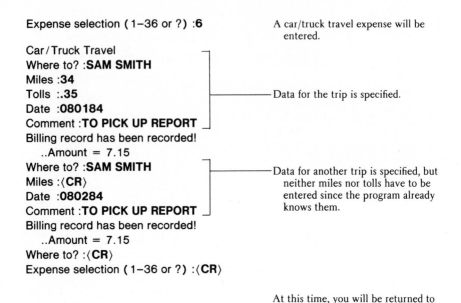

Expense selection (1–36 or ?) :**6**   A car/truck travel expense will be
                                                      entered.

Car/Truck Travel
Where to? :**SAM SMITH**
Miles :**34**
Tolls :.**35**   ─────────── Data for the trip is specified.
Date :**080184**
Comment :**TO PICK UP REPORT**
Billing record has been recorded!
   ..Amount = 7.15
Where to? :**SAM SMITH**   ─────────── Data for another trip is specified, but
Miles :⟨**CR**⟩   neither miles nor tolls have to be
Date :**080284**   entered since the program already
Comment :**TO PICK UP REPORT**   knows them.
Billing record has been recorded!
   ..Amount = 7.15
Where to? :⟨**CR**⟩
Expense selection (1–36 or ?) :⟨**CR**⟩

                                     At this time, you will be returned to
                                     the Menu Level.

Fig. 6-10 Adding a car/truck travel record.

is organized so all bills for a certain company are shown together. For a
company with multiple bills, the oldest is shown first. Each line is
numbered.

2.   PAY WHAT?:   Type the number of the line that shows the bill you
     want to pay, or a **?** to see the list of unpaid bills again.
3.   DATE PAID: You can respond in three ways:
     a.   Type **C** if you paid the bill in full on the current day.
     b.   Type the date of another day when you paid the bill. Do not enter
          a date for a month for which you already have cleared records.
     c.   Type **P** if you paid only a partial amount of the whole bill.

   These responses are treated in exactly the same way as responses to
PAYMENT DATE when you record an expense with the ADD command.
   When you have recorded all your payments, respond to PAY WHAT?
by pressing the carriage return and a total of the amount you have recorded
as paid will be displayed. Add up the amount on your checks. The totals
should be exactly the same. If there is a difference, review the records you
just entered and make your corrections with the CHANGE command.

When you are finished looking at the paid total, press the carriage return and you will be returned to the Menu Level.

The procedure for recording a payment is illustrated in Fig. 6-11.

CHANGING A RECORD

The CHANGE command (3) is used to change one or more lines of a record. The record can be for a paid or unpaid bill.

NOTE:

Changes to paid bills that already have been used to update the Totals File *will not* be reflected in *any* Month End Report or in your expense totals.

Any information on the record can be changed. You have to identify the record, and the line on that record you want to change. You then can type the replacement.

The procedure for changing a record is:

1. COMMAND SELECTION: Type 3 for the CHANGE command.
2. EXPENSE SELECTION: Type the number (1-36) of the expense you want to change or type a ? to print the list of expenses.
3. PAY WHO?: Type the name on the bill *exactly* as you entered it. At this time, the first bill that you entered with the name will be displayed.
4. CHANGE WHAT?: If the record is *not* the one you want to change, type 8 and the next bill with the name will be displayed. When the record you want is displayed, type the number of the line you want to change. You will be prompted to enter the replacement line. Type it. As many lines as you want can be changed in this way. When you are done with this record, press the carriage return in response to CHANGE WHAT? and you will be able to select another expense. When you are done making changes, press the carriage return in response to EXPENSE SELECTION and you will be returned to the Menu Level.

The procedure for changing a record is illustrated in Fig. 6-12.

Command selection [1–13 or ?1–?13] :**2**   The PAID command is selected.

All open invoices are displayed.

Bill	Amount	Due Date	Comment
(1) GAS CO.	$29.59	05/17/84	
(2) KERLAND CO.	$345.67	06/15/84	PARTNER INSURANCE
(3) N.Y. TIMES	$16.00	04/17/84	
(4) N.Y. TIMES	$16.00	08/26/84	

Pay what? :**3**   The invoice on line 3 will be paid first.

Date paid :**090184**
Comment :**COMBINED CHECK**   Both payments to the *New York Times* are to be made with one check.
Check number :**246**
Record has been updated
Pay what? :**4**
Date paid :**090184**
Comment :**COMBINED CHECK**
Check number :**246**   The same check number is entered as for the first payment.

Record has been updated
Pay what? :**2**
Date paid :**090184**
Comment :⟨**CR**⟩
Check number :⟨**CR**⟩   Payment is made for another company and this time, the program is used to generate the check number.

Check number = 247
Record has been updated
Pay what? :**1**
Date paid :**090184**
Comment :⟨**CR**⟩   The final invoice is paid.
Check number :⟨**CR**⟩
Check number = 248
Record has been updated
Pay what? :⟨**CR**⟩
Total paid = 407.26   The total for all payments is shown.

Enter return to continue ⟨**CR**⟩   When the carriage return is pressed, the display is cleared and you will be returned to the Menu Level.

Fig. 6-11 Paying a bill.

Command selection [1–13 or ?1–?13] :**3**   The CHANGE command is
                                                selected.

Expense selection (1–36 or ?) :**9**   A Publications and Dues expense
                                                is to be changed.

Pay Who ?:**COMTRIX NEWS**   The payee for whom a record is
                                                to be changed is identified.

                                                The first record is displayed.

       (1) Expense Selection = 9 – Dues and Publications
       (2) Payee   = COMTRIX NEWS
       (3) Due date   = 09 / 23 / 84
       (4) Amount   = 24
       (5) Date paid   =
       (6) Check number   =
       (7) Comment   = YEARLY SUBSCRIPTION
       (8) Look for different record

Change What ?:**4**   The line to be changed is
                                                identified.

Enter new amount :**32**   The replacement line is entered.
Change What ?:⟨**CR**⟩   No other changes to this record
                                                are to be made now.

Record updated
Expense selection (1–36 or ?) :⟨**CR**⟩   No other changes are to be made.
                                                At this time, you will be
                                                returned to the Menu Level.

Fig. 6-12 Changing an expense record.

DELETING A RECORD

The DELETE command (4) is used to delete a record. Records for paid and unpaid bills may be deleted.

NOTE:

Deleting a paid bill that already has been used to update the Totals File *will not* be reflected in any Month End Report or in your expense totals.

The command usually will be used to remove invoices that you have decided not to pay. You may have entered an invoice for renewal of a magazine, for example, and later decided you no longer wish to subscribe.

The procedure for deleting a record is:

1. COMMAND SELECTION: Type **4** for the DELETE command.
2. EXPENSE SELECTION: Type the number (1–36) of the expense for which you want to delete a record, or a **?** to print the list of expenses.
3. PAY WHO?:   Type the name on the bill *exactly* as you entered it. At this time, the first bill that you entered with the name will be displayed.
4. OK TO DELETE: Type **Y** and the record displayed will be flagged for deletion. Type **NO**, no flag will be set for this record, and you will be prompted LOOK FOR DIFFERENT RECORD (Y/N). Type **Y** to display the next bill with the person's name and you again will be asked OK TO DELETE. Type **N**, and you will be able to select an expense again.

When you have flagged all records you want deleted, press the carriage return in response to EXPENSE SELECTION and all your flagged records will be cleared from your disk.

The deletion procedure is illustrated in Fig. 6-13.

PREPARING A MONTH END REPORT

A Month End Report provides detailed documentation of expenses paid during the month.

The report groups all bills that you paid by expenses. You will see, for example, all office expenses for the month listed together. The expenses are listed in alphabetical order (which also is the order in which they're numbered). The total amount you spent during the month for each expense is shown, as well as the total amount you spent on *all* expenses. As such, the report provides valuable, easy-to-use information for you—and for an accountant.

Keep reports for a single year together. Buy a folder, label it with:

EXPENSES

Person's (or company's) name

Year for which records are kept

Address

City, state, zip code

Command selection [1–13 or ?1–?13] :**4**   The DELETE command is
selected.

Expense selection (1–36 or ?) :**9**   A Dues and Publications bill is to
be deleted.

Pay Who ?:**COMTRIX NEWS**   The record is identified, and then
displayed.

        Expense Selection = 9 – Dues and Publications
        Payee   = COMTRIX NEWS
        Due date   = 09/23/84
        Amount   = 32
        Date paid   =
        Check number =
        Comment   = YEARLY SUBSCRIPTION

OK to delete?:**Y**   The deletion is verified.
Expense selection (1–36 or ?) :⟨**CR**⟩
Old file had 13 bills. New file has   No other records are to be deleted
  12 bills.   so cleaning is begun. Note that
you are shown the Transaction
File had 13 bills when you
began but has 12 now—one has
been deleted.

Fig. 6-13 Deleting a bill.

Telephone number

PREPARED BY: Your name

Your telephone number

    Once you have printed a Month End Report, you can update the Totals
File and prepare reports that use these totals.
    The MONTHLY command (5) generates the Month End Report. The
Month End Report procedure is:

1. COMMAND SELECTION: Type 5 for the MONTHLY command.
2. OUTPUT TO SCREEN (1) OR PRINTER (2): Type 1 to see a display of the report and type 2 to print it. You may want to look at a display
to preview the report, or see how expenses are accruing during a month.
3. ENTER MONTH NAME: Type the name of the month and the year

for which the report is to be generated. This date will appear on the report title. If you are preparing the report for a period different than a month, type its description, e.g., **1ST QTR**.

4. ENTER STARTING DATE: The Month End Report is generated for a period you specify. Usually, this period will be a month, so you type the date of the first day in the month. The period, however, can be for as long as you wish, in which case you type the first day of the period.

5. ENTER ENDING DATE: Type the date of the last day in the period. Usually, you type the date of the last day in the month. At this time, the Month End Report is generated and printed or displayed as you requested.

   If you have entered for a client all payments for the month with the ADD command, total up your receipts and compare your total to the report's expense total. The totals should be *exactly* the same. If not, respond to the remaining prompts with **N**, which will end this procedure. You then can use the CHANGE command to reconcile the differences. Also, look at your report for misspelled names, incorrect dates, or comments you no longer need. Use the CHANGE command to make changes. When all changes are made, generate a final Month End Report.

6. OK TO UPDATE EXPENSE TOTALS (Y/N):   Type **Y** to move expenses shown in the report to the Totals File. Typing **Y** also causes the records in the Month End Report to be flagged so they will *not* appear again in any subsequent Month End Report, including one generated for this same month. You will have access to these records only with the INQUIRY and BREAKDOWN commands. Type **N** if you don't want the records flagged and you will be returned to the Menu Level.

7. DO YOU WANT THE MONTHLY BREAKDOWN REPORT (Y/ N)?:   A Breakdown Report shows revealing statistics about a business. The report highlights where money is going. Type **Y** if you wish to print this report for the month. Type **N** if you don't want it. A Breakdown Report for any period (including year-to-date) also can be printed (with the BREAKDOWN command). By comparing reports, you can explore business expenditures. You can focus on expenses that take most of the cash and seek to reduce them to improve profitability. An example of a Breakdown Report is shown with the BREAKDOWN command.

8. OK TO CLEAR EXPENSE TRANSACTIONS (Y/N):   Type **Y** to clear the flagged records from your Transaction File. Type **N** to retain them for inquiries.

At this time the flagged records will be removed, if you requested it. You then will be returned to the Menu Level.

NOTE:

In a Month End Report, partial payment amounts are indicated by "P". See Robinson, Expense Code 22, in Fig. 6-15.

The procedure for generating a Month End Report and updating the Totals File is illustrated in Fig. 6-14. The resultant Month End Report is shown in Fig. 6-15.

Command selection [1–13 or ?1–?13] :**5** — The MONTHLY command is selected.

Output to screen (1) or printer (2)**2** — The report is to be printed.
Enter month name :**AUGUST 1984** — August 1984 is to appear in the title.

Enter starting date :**080184** ⌐———————— Starting and ending days are
Enter ending date :**083184** ⌐ specified.

At this time, the report is printed.

Ok to update expense totals (Y / N) :**Y** — Permission is given to move the figures shown in the report to the Totals File and flag the records so they won't be used again.

Totals updated
Records flagged as used in totals
Do you want the monthly breakdown
  report (Y / N) :**N**
Ok to clear expense transactions
  (Y / N) :**Y** — Permission is given to remove the August records from the Transaction File. Thirteen records are deleted, leaving 10 unpaid bills and/or travel records.

Old file had 23 bills. New file
  has 10 bills

Fig. 6-14 Printing the Month End Report and updating the Totals File.

Month End Report for AUGUST 1984				
Bill	Amount	Due Date	Date Paid	Expense Cd.
G & S DESIGN	$1,543.98	08/15/84	08/24/84	2
Total Advertising	$1,543.98			
YATES TIRE	$167.89	08/17/84	08/17/84	5
AL'S SERVICE	$128.67	08/19/84	08/26/84	5
Total Car/Truck Expense	$296.56			
N.Y. TIMES	$16.00	08/26/84	08/26/84	9
Total Dues and Publication	$16.00			
U.I.	$48.65	08/15/84	08/15/84	10
Total Electricity	$48.65			
S.C. GAS	$67.82	08/15/84	08/15/84	14
Total Heat	$67.82			
CLEAN–RITE	$7.56	08/24/84	08/24/84	18
Total Laundry and Cleaning	$7.56			
ROBINSON	$200.00P	08/25/84	08/25/84	22
Total Office Supplies	$200.00			
POST OFFICE	$2.34	08/01/84	08/01/84	24
POST OFFICE	$3.45	08/20/84	08/20/84	24
Total Postage	$5.79			
U.S. GOV'T	$954.98	07/15/84	08/01/84	27
Total Tax–Federal	$954.98			
BELL	$84.24	08/15/84	08/15/84	30
Total Telephone	$84.24			
ERIN'S TRAV.	$548.27	08/20/84	08/20/84	31
Total Travel	$548.27			
Total Expenses =	$3,773.85			

Fig. 6-15 A Month End Report.

USING CAR/TRUCK TRAVEL EXPENSE INFORMATION

Car/truck travel records (expense 6) are handled differently than all other expense records. The amount accrued for car/truck travel in a month is not shown on the Month End Report, and is not used to update the Totals File with the other records. Unlike other records, these must be saved so that a travel log can be printed at the end of a year.

The fixed mileage rate really isn't as fixed as its name implies. After a set amount of miles (usually 15,000) the rate allowable as a tax deduction declines. When you have logged these miles, the rate has to be changed.

The TRAVEL command (6) allows you to print the Travel Log, monitor your mileage, and keep your Totals File up to date.

If you are keeping car/truck travel records, you should use this command each month *before* you prepare *any* Totals report.

NOTE:

The mileage rate is changed with the TO-DATE command (7).

The procedure for using the TRAVEL command is:

1. COMMAND SELECTION: Type 6 for the TRAVEL command.
2. OUTPUT TO SCREEN (1) OR PRINTER (2):   Type 1 to display the travel log and type 2 to print it. You generally will print it only at the end of the year. You will see a display at the end of most months to check on the total number of miles logged. When the mileage approaches the fixed rate limit, you have to closely monitor trips to change the rate at the right time.

   At this time the Travel Log is prepared, the car/truck travel expense is recomputed, and the Year-To-Date Total (in the Totals File) replaced. You then will be returned to the Menu Level.

An example of a Travel Log Report is shown in Fig. 6-16.

USING INFORMATION ABOUT TOTALS

Your A/P Program provides capabilities so you effectively can use the Totals File. Specifically, the program enables you to:

1. Generate a To-Date Report, using the TO-DATE command (7). The report shows the up-to-date total you have spent on each one of the 36 expenses. The report for the end of the year provides tax information.
2. Combine expense totals and look at the result, using the TOTALS command (8). Essentially, the program acts as an "intelligent calculator." You can use this capability to combine expenses to meet tax specifications.

Travel Log Report

Location	Date	Miles	Tolls	Amount	Comment
TOM JOHNSON	01/23/84	29	0.00	$5.70	
TOM JOHNSON	01/28/84	29	0.00	$5.70	
TOM JOHNSON	02/03/84	29	0.00	$5.70	
SID BLAKEMAN	02/04/84	46	4.50	$13.66	
FRED DELFORD	02/05/84	32	0.50	$6.90	
SID BLAKEMAN	02/07/84	46	4.50	$13.66	
TOM JOHNSON	02/09/84	29	0.00	$5.70	
FRED DELFORD	02/24/84	32	0.50	$6.90	
JAKE MCGRATH	03/01/84	46	1.00	$10.18	
FRED DELFORD	03/12/84	32	0.50	$6.90	
JAKE MCGRATH	03/16/84	46	1.00	$10.18	
SAM SMITH	08/01/84	34	0.35	$7.15	REPORT
SAM SMITH	08/02/84	34	0.35	$7.15	REPORT
TOM JOHNSON	12/02/84	29	0.00	$5.70	
JAKE MCGRATH	12/15/84	46	1.00	$10.18	

Total miles = 539

Fig. 6-16 A Travel Log Report.

3. Generate a Breakdown Report, using the BREAKDOWN command (9). This report shows for a period of your choice the percentage breakdown of expenses. The report highlights those expenses on which you're spending the most.

The procedure you'll use for each of these capabilities is presented below.

The procedure for generating a To-Date Report is:

1. COMMAND SELECTION: Type 7 for the TO-DATE command.
2. OUTPUT TO SCREEN (1) OR PRINTER (2): Type the number for where you want to see the report and it will be produced.
3. DELETE EXISTING TRAVEL RECORDS (Y/N): Type **Y** *only after you have printed your Travel Log at the end of the year.* This clearing allows records to be kept for the new year. Type **N** at all other times and the records will be retained.
4. DELETE EXISTING TOTALS (Y/N): Type **Y** *only after you have printed your Year End To-Date Report and used the totaling capability;* the Totals File will be cleared so records for the new year can be kept. Type **N** at all other times and the records will be retained.

5. CHANGE MILEAGE RATE (Y/N): Type **Y** to change the fixed mileage rate and you will be prompted for the new rate, which will be typed as a decimal, e.g., .11. Type **N** if the mileage rate does not need to be changed.

At this time, you will be returned to the Menu Level.

An example of a To-Date Report is shown in Fig. 6-17.

You should include at minimum a To-Date Report for the end of the year in your Month End Reports folder. If you wish, you can include a To-Date Report for each month.

The procedure for using the totaling capability is:

1. COMMAND SELECTION: Type 8 for the TOTALS command.
2. EXPENSE SELECTION: Type a number (1–36) for the first expense you want used in the calculation. The program, again, will prompt for a selection and you will type the number of the next expense you want. When you have specified all expenses in this way, respond to EXPENSE SELECTION by pressing the carriage return, the total will be computed and displayed. You then can begin selection for another total. When you are finished, press the carriage return in response to EXPENSE SELECTION after a total and you will be returned to the Menu Level.

The procedure for using the totaling capability is illustrated in Fig. 6-18.

The Breakdown Report shows expenses listed in descending order, so the expense you spent the most on is at the top and the one you spent the least on at the bottom. Expenses for which you paid nothing are not shown. The percentage the expense represents to the total of all expenses in the period also is shown.

The report can be generated from figures in the Totals or Transaction File. If the Totals File is used, you will see Year-To-Date expenses broken down. If the Transaction File is used, a breakdown for any period of your choice can be specified and all records in the file (whether or not updated in the Totals File) will be used for this report.

NOTE:

If you wish to see breakdowns for periods other than the current month (for example, a quarter), *do not* clear records from the Transaction File after you update the Totals File. Clear the records only at the end of the period.

1–Accounting	$4,545.60
2–Advertising	$2,278.85
3–Bad Debts	$0.00
4–Bank Service Charges	$51.98
5–Car/Truck Expense	$1,151.54
6–Car/Truck Travel	$0.00
7–Commissions	$0.00
8–Contributions	$0.00
9–Dues and Publications	$796.36
10–Electricity	$436.14
11–Employee Benefit Program	$0.00
12–Entertainment	$0.00
13–Freight	$0.00
14–Heat	$1,124.60
15–Insurance	$0.00
16–Interest on Business Debt	$0.00
17–Inventory	$0.00
18–Laundry and Cleaning	$164.43
19–Legal and Professional Services	$0.00
20–Loans	$0.00
21–Notes	$0.00
22–Office Supplies	$1,632.65
23–Pension and Profit Sharing Plans	$0.00
24–Postage	$549.24
25–Rent on Business Property	$0.00
26–Tax–City	$0.00
27–Tax–Federal	$3,519.96
28–Tax–Social Security	$0.00
29–Tax–State	$674.92
30–Telephone	1,722.56
31–Travel	$7,339.74
32–Wages	$0.00
33–Water	$143.87
34–Miscellaneous	$0.00
35–Item–1	$0.00
36–Item–2	$0.00

Fig. 6-17 A To-Date Report of expenses.

The procedure for generating a Breakdown Report is:

1. COMMAND SELECTION: Type 9 for the BREAKDOWN command.
2. REPORT FROM TOTALS FILE (1) OR TRANSACTION FILE

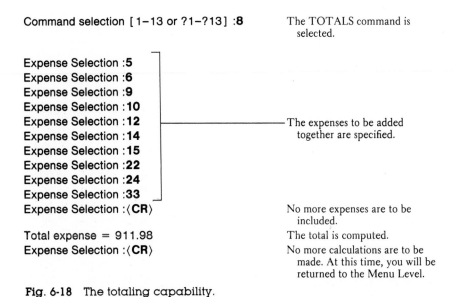

Command selection [1–13 or ?1–?13] :**8**   The TOTALS command is
                                                     selected.

Expense Selection :**5**
Expense Selection :**6**
Expense Selection :**9**
Expense Selection :**10**
Expense Selection :**12**   The expenses to be added
Expense Selection :**14**   together are specified.
Expense Selection :**15**
Expense Selection :**22**
Expense Selection :**24**
Expense Selection :**33**
Expense Selection :⟨**CR**⟩   No more expenses are to be
                                                     included.
Total expense = 911.98   The total is computed.
Expense Selection :⟨**CR**⟩   No more calculations are to be
                                                     made. At this time, you will be
                                                     returned to the Menu Level.

Fig. 6-18   The totaling capability.

(2):   Type the number from which figures for the report should be taken.
If you type 2 (for the Transaction File), you will be prompted START-
ING DATE and ENDING DATE for the period you want to see. Records on your Transaction File (flagged or not) that fall within the period
will be selected. Any records you may have cleared from the file, naturally, won't be included.
3.   OUTPUT TO SCREEN (1) OR PRINTER (2):   Type the number
determining the form of the report—displayed or printed.
4.   EXCLUDE ANY EXPENSES (Y/N):   You may not want all expenses
included in the calculations. In April, for example, you may wish to
exclude "tax—federal" after paying your income tax because the figure
will give a "bulge" to the report. Type **Y** to exclude expenses and you
will be prompted for those to exclude; type one number in response to
each expense selection and press the carriage return when you're
through. Type **N** and all expenses will be used.

At this time, the report will be generated and you'll be returned to the
Menu Level.

The procedure and an example of a Breakdown Report are shown in Fig.
6-19.

The value of reports can be seen from this discussion. Accounting has

Command selection [1–13 or ?1–?13] :**9**   The BREAKDOWN command is
selected.

Report from Totals File (1) or   Figures are to be taken from the
    Transaction file (2) :**1**   Totals File.
Output to screen (1) or printer (2):**1**   The report will be displayed.
Exclude any expenses (Y /N) :**Y**   Only ACCOUNTING (expense
Exclude which (1–36) :**1**   1) is excluded.
Exclude which (1–36) :⟨**CR**⟩   At this time, the report is
displayed.

Travel	Total expense :	$7,339.74 % of total : 34.00
Tax–Federal	Total expense :	$3,519.96 % of total : 16.31
Advertising	Total expense :	$2.278.85 % of total : 10.56
Telephone	Total expense :	$1,722.56 % of total : 7.98
Office Supplies	Total expense :	$1,632.65 % of total : 7.56
Car / Truck Expense	Total expense :	$1,151.54 % of total : 5.33
Heat	Total expense :	$1,124.60 % of total : 5.21
Dues and Publications	Total expense :	$796.36 % of total : 3.69
Tax–State	Total expense :	$674.92 % of total : 3.13
Postage	Total expense :	$549.24 % of total : 2.54
Electricity	Total expense :	$436.14 % of total : 2.02
Laundry and Cleaning	Total expense :	$164.43 % of total : 0.76
Water	Total expense :	$143.87 % of total : 0.67
Bank Service Charges	Total expense :	$51.98 % of total : 0.24

Enter return to continue ⟨**CR**⟩   The screen is cleared and you will
be returned to the Menu Level.

Fig. 6-19   An Expense Breakdown Report.

been excluded from the calculations—there was an expensive one-time audit
that gives the figures an unnatural bulge. As you can see in the report, more
than one-quarter of all Year-To-Date expenses have gone to travel. Consequently, the greatest opportunities for increasing profitability are in cutting
travel expenses by reducing airfare and costs for hotels and meals.

PREPARING INVOICE REPORTS

Two types of invoice reports can be prepared:

- A Past Due Report, which shows invoices that have not been paid by their
due date

■ A Cash Requirements Report, which lists invoices that will come due in the future

The invoices in both reports will be listed from the oldest to the newest. It is assumed the oldest will be paid first for past due invoices, and the most recent first for cash requirements. A "P" will be placed next to any amount for which a partial payment has been made. Each report also will show you the total due.

These reports can be prepared only if you're keeping invoice records (i.e., unpaid bills).

The PAST DUE command (10) generates the Past Due Report, and the CASH command (11) generates the Cash Requirements Report.

The procedure for generating these reports is exactly the same:

1. COMMAND SELECTION: Type the number of the command that will generate the report you want.
2. OUTPUT TO SCREEN (1) OR PRINTER (2): Type 1 if you want the report displayed or 2 if you want a hard copy printed.
3. ENTER DUE DATE: Type the due date in which you're interested. For the Past Due Report, invoices with due dates on or before your specification will be listed. For the Cash Requirements Report, invoices with due dates on or after your specification will be printed.

An example of a Past Due Report is shown in Fig. 6-20 and a Cash Requirements Report in Fig. 6-21. The due date for both reports is 5/1/83.

Bill	Amount	Due Date	Comment
N.Y. TIMES	$16.00	04/17/83	
Total past due =	$16.00		

Fig. 6-20 A Past Due Report.

Bill	Amount	Due Date	Comment
N.Y. TIMES	$16.00	05/17/83	
GAS CO.	$29.59	05/17/83	
Total cash required =	$45.59		

Fig. 6-21 A Cash Requirements Report.

MAKING INQUIRIES

The INQUIRY command (12) lets you inspect any Transaction File record.

You see records for each one of the 36 expense categories at a time, or you can look at all records. You can look at records for a single day or for a period, which may be a month, a quarter, the year, or anything you like.

This command usually will be used to answer questions about an expense very quickly, and to see exactly how information is stored so you can select records for changes or deletion.

The procedure for making an inquiry is:

1. COMMAND SELECTION: Type 12 for the INQUIRY command.
2. ENTER START DATE: Type the date of the first day in the period at which you want to look.
3. ENTER END DATE: Press the carriage return if you want to look only at one day, or type the date of the last day in the period.
4. EXPENSE SELECTION: Type the number (1–36) of the expense in which you're interested, or press the carriage return to see *all* expenses.

The program will show you all bills (paid and unpaid) with a due date in the specified period that are stored on the disk.

When the last record has been displayed, you will be able to request another expense for this same period.

When you are done, type **DONE** in response to EXPENSE SELECTION, and you will be able to specify a new period.

NOTE:

Do not press the carriage return in response to EXPENSE SELECTION when you're done looking at expenses for the period or you will have to look at *all* expenses for the period. Type **DONE** when you're finished.

If you do not want to look at another period, press the carriage return in response to ENTER START DATE and you will be returned to the Menu Level.

The inquiry capability is illustrated in Fig. 6-22.

Command selection [1–13 or ?1–?13] :**12**   The INQUIRY command is selected.

Enter start date :**040183** ⎤──────────── The period in question is
Enter end date :**043083** ⎦   specified.
Enter expense code :**24**   The expense to be looked at is entered. In this case, records for postage (expense 24) are to be looked at.

The records are displayed.

Expense Selection = 24 – Postage
Payee   = POST OFFICE
Due date   = 04 / 11 / 83
Amount   = 23.8
Date paid   = 04 / 11 / 83
Check number   = CASH
Comment   =

Expense Selection = 24 – Postage
Payee   = POST OFFICE
Due date   = 04 / 12 / 83
Amount   = 3.45
Date paid   = 04 / 12 / 83
Check number   = CASH
Comment   =

Expense Selection = 24 – Postage
Payee   = POST OFFICE
Due date   = 04 / 15 / 83
Amount   = 9.78
Date paid   = 04 / 15 / 83
Check number   = CASH
Comment   =

Enter expense code :**DONE**
Enter start date :⟨**CR**⟩

Fig. 6-22 Making an inquiry.

ENDING PROGRAM OPERATION

The END command (13) ends A/P Program operation and returns you to the operating system level. At this time you should remove your data disk and return it to its cover.

SCHEDULE OF ACTIVITIES

Time	Action
Every day (your business)	1. Record all payments you made during the day. 2. Record all invoices you receive during the day (optional).
First day of month (your business)	1. Print Month End Report for last month. 2. Run Travel Log, if using fixed rate method. 3. Print Year-To-Date Report. 4. Print any other reports in which you're interested.
Early in month (client's business)	1. Record all payments made since you last entered them. 2. Record all invoices received since you last entered them (optional). 3. Print Month End Report for last month. 4. Run Travel Log, if client uses fixed rate method. 5. Print Year-To-Date Report. 6. Print other reports for client. 7. Sit down with client and make payments, showing client open invoices with PAID command (optional).

Time	Action
Early in new year	1. Print Travel Log and clear records.
	2. Print December Month End Report.
	3. Print Year-To-Date Report and other reports for the last year.
	4. Use the TOTALS capability to figure taxes.*
	5. Clear Totals File.*

*Do not update the Totals File with January payments until *after* you have computed taxes and cleared the Totals File. Payments can be recorded on the Transaction File before the Totals File is cleared.

ACCOUNTS PAYABLE PROGRAM COMMAND SUMMARY

Command Numbers and Name	Function
1–ADD	Records invoices and payments.
2–PAID	Records payments for previously stored invoices.
3–CHANGE	Changes information for any record in the Transaction File.
4–DELETE	Deletes any record from the Transaction File.
5–MONTHLY	Generates the Month End Report and updates the Totals File.
6–TRAVEL	Generates Travel Log, and updates Totals File.
7–TO DATE	Generates To-Date Report of expenses.
8–TOTALS	Provides ability to total specific expenses.
9–BREAKDOWN	Provides statistics on composition of expenses.
10–PAST DUE	Lists all overdue bills.
11–CASH	Lists bills due in coming months.
12–INQUIRY	Enables you to look at any record on the Transaction File.
13–EXIT	Ends program operation.

ACCOUNTS PAYABLE PROGRAM SOURCE CODE

The A/P Program consists of six programs:

1. PAYMENT.BAS acts as a monitor and comprises the functions common to the entire A/P Program set, including the EXIT request (no. 13) from the main menu.
2. PAYMENT1.BAS handles the ADD request (no. 1) from the main menu.
3. PAYMENT2.BAS handles the PAID (no. 2) and CHANGE (no. 3) requests from the main menu.
4. PAYMENT3.BAS handles the DELETE (no. 4) and MONTHLY (no. 5) requests from the main menu.
5. PAYMENT4.BAS handles the TRAVEL (no. 6), TO DATE (no. 7), and TOTALS (no. 8) requests from the main menu.
6. PAYMENT5.BAS handles the BREAKDOWN (no. 9), PAST DUE (no. 10), CASH (no. 11), and INQUIRY (no. 12) requests from the main menu.

You should type in all six programs in the order of their corresponding names, assigning each program its respective name. **All six programs must be stored on the same disk.**

PAYMENT.BAS

```
10 REM *************************************************************************
20 REM THIS PROGRAM WILL PROVIDE THE FOLLOWING FUNCTIONS OF AN ACCOUNTS    *
30 REM PAYABLE SYSTEM:                                                     *
40 REM     ADD : CREATE AND OPTIONALLY PAY A BILL                          *
50 REM     PAID : PAY OUTSTANDING BILLS                                    *
60 REM     CHANGE : TO UPDATE A BILL OR PAYMENT                            *
70 REM     DELETE : TO DELETE A BILL FROM THE SYSTEM                       *
80 REM     INQUIRY : A REPORT SHOWING RECORDS IN THE TRANSACTION FILE      *
90 REM     PAST DUE : A REPORT SHOWING BILLS THAT ARE PAST DUE             *
100 REM    CASH REQUIREMENTS : PROJECTED CASH REQUIRED TO PAY BILLS        *
110 REM    MONTH END : TRIAL BALANCE AND MONTHLY PAYABLES JOURNAL          *
120 REM    BREAKDOWN : REPORT SHOWING TOTAL EXPENSES BY EXPENSE CODE       *
130 REM    TRAVEL LOG : TRAVEL JOURNAL                                     *
140 REM    TOTALS : REPORT SHOWING EXPENSES COMBINED AS SPECIFIED BY THE USER *
150 REM    TO DATE : A REPORT SHOWING THE CURRENT CONTENTS OF THE TOTALS FILE *
160 REM *************************************************************************
170 REM *************************************************************************
180 REM THIS SECTION WILL PROMPT FOR THE DISK DRIVE DESIGNATOR             *
190 REM *************************************************************************
200 LINE INPUT "Drive the datafile will be on :";TDISK$
210 IF TDISK$ = "" THEN PRINT "The default drive will be used": GOTO 240
220 IF MID$(TDISK$,1,1) < "A" OR MID$(TDISK$,1,1) > "P" THEN GOTO 200
230 DISK$ = SPACE$(2) : LSET DISK$ = MID$(TDISK$,1,1) +":"
```

```
240 REM ****************************************************************
250 REM THIS SECTION WILL READ THE SCREEN HEIGHT AND WIDTH SIZES FROM THE *
260 REM PARAMETER FILE .. IF NO PARAMETER FILE EXISTS PROMPT FOR THE      *
270 REM VALUES AND CREATE ONE FOR NEXT TIME .. IN ANY CASE SET THE VARS.  *
280 REM SCREENHEIGHT AND SCREENWIDTH                                      *
290 REM ****************************************************************
300 OPEN "R",#1,DISK$+"PARAMTER.FIL",8
310 FIELD #1,4 AS SCREENHEIGHT$,4 AS SCREENWIDTH$
330 I = 1 : GET #1,I
340 SCREENHEIGHT = CVI(SCREENHEIGHT$)
350 SCREENWIDTH  = CVI(SCREENWIDTH$)
360 IF SCREENWIDTH > 0 AND SCREENWIDTH > 0 THEN GOTO 470
370 LINE INPUT "Enter screen height value (1-24) :"; SCREENPARM$
380 SCREENHEIGHT = VAL(SCREENPARM$)
390 IF SCREENHEIGHT < 1 OR SCREENHEIGHT > 24 THEN GOTO 370
400 LINE INPUT "Enter screen width value (1-80) :"; SCREENPARM$
410 SCREENWIDTH = VAL(SCREENPARM$)
420 IF SCREENWIDTH < 1 OR SCREENWIDTH > 80 THEN GOTO 400
430 LSET SCREENHEIGHT$ = MKI$(SCREENHEIGHT)
440 LSET SCREENWIDTH$  = MKI$(SCREENWIDTH)
450 I = 1 ;
460 PUT #1,I
470 CLOSE
480 GOSUB 1800                            ' GO GET MILEAGE RATE
490 REM *****************************************************************
500 REM NOW GET THE LAST CHECK NUMBER FROM THE CHECK FILE ON DISK         *
510 REM *****************************************************************
520 OPEN "R",#1,DISK$+"CHECK.FIL",4
530 FIELD #1,4 AS LASTCHECK$
550 I = 1 : GET #1,I
560 LASTCHECK = CVS(LASTCHECK$)
570 CLOSE #1
580 DIM SORTKEY$(200)
590 DIM SORTKEY(200)
600 DIM SORTREC(200)
610 DIM MNTHTOT(36)
620 DIM WORKTOT(36)
630 DIM PCTTOT(36)
635 MERGEDFILE$ = " "
640 LINE INPUT "Enter current date";CDATE$
650 IF CDATE$ = "" THEN GOTO 640
660 PRINT "Current system date :"
MID$(CDATE$,1,2) "/" MID$(CDATE$,3,2) "/" MID$(CDATE$,5,2)
670 SCREENCNTR  = SCREENWIDTH/2
680 LEFTMARG    = SCREENCNTR - 20
690 REM *****************************************************************
700 REM NOW SET UP THE EXPENSE DESCRIPTION TABLE                          *
710 REM *****************************************************************
720 DIM EXPDESC$(36)
730 FOR I = 1 TO 36 : READ EXPDESC$(I) : NEXT I : GOTO 2000
740 DATA "Accounting","Advertising","Bad Debts","Bank Service Charges"
750 DATA "Car/Truck Expense","Car/Truck Travel","Commissions","Contributions"
760 DATA "Dues and Publications","Electricity","Employee Benefit Program"
770 DATA "Entertainment","Freight",
"Heat","Insurance","Interest on Business Debt"
780 DATA "Inventory","Laundry and Cleaning","Legal and Professional Services"
790 DATA "Loans","Notes","Office Supplies","Pension and Profit Sharing Plans"
800 DATA "Postage","Rent on Business Property","Tax-City","Tax-Federal"
810 DATA "Tax-Social Security","Tax-State","Telephone","Travel","Wages"
820 DATA "Water","Miscellaneous","Item-1","Item-2"
830 REM *****************************************************************
840 REM THIS SUBROUTINE WILL SORT SELECTED RECORDS BY SORTKEY$ (ASCENDING)*
850 REM RECCNT = NBR OF RECORDS TO SORT: SORTKEY$ = KEYS TO SORT :        *
860 REM SORTREC = RECORD NBRS OF KEYS BEING SORTED                        *
```

```
870 REM ****************************************************************
880 SWITCHED = 0
890 FOR I = 1 TO RECCNT-1
900 IF SORTKEY$(I+1) > SORTKEY$(I) THEN GOTO 950
910 IF SORTKEY$(I+1) = SORTKEY$(I) THEN GOTO 950
920 HOLDREC = SORTREC(I) : SORTREC(I) = SORTREC(I+1) : SORTREC(I+1) = HOLDREC
930 HOLDKEY$ = SORTKEY$(I) : SORTKEY$(I) = SORTKEY$(I+1) :
SORTKEY$(I+1) = HOLDKEY$
940 SWITCHED = 1
950 NEXT I
960 IF SWITCHED = 1 THEN GOTO 880
970 RETURN
980 REM ****************************************************************
990 REM THIS SUBROUTINE WILL PRODUCE THE MONTHLY BREAKDOWN REPORT FOR   *
1000 REM FOR PREVIOUSLY SELECTED AND TOTALED EXPENSES                   *
1010 REM ****************************************************************
1020 FOR I = 1 TO 36 : WORKTOT(I) = MNTHTOT(I) :PCTTOT(I) = 0 : NEXT I
1030 LINE INPUT "Exclude any expenses (Y/N) :";CHGFIELD$
1040 IF CHGFIELD$ <> "Y" AND CHGFIELD$ <> "N" THEN GOTO 1030
1050 IF CHGFIELD$ <> "Y" THEN GOTO 1120
1060 LINE INPUT "Exclude which (1-36) :"; CHGFIELD$
1070 IF CHGFIELD$ = "" THEN GOTO 1120
1080 CHGFIELD = VAL(CHGFIELD$)
1090 IF CHGFIELD < 1 OR CHGFIELD > 36 THEN
PRINT "Invalid expense code" : GOTO 1060
1100 WORKTOT(CHGFIELD) = 0
1110 GOTO 1060
1120 TOTDUE = 0  : FOR I = 1 TO 36 : TOTDUE = TOTDUE + WORKTOT(I) : NEXT I
1130 IF TOTDUE < .01 THEN PRINT "No remaining expenses" : CLOSE :RETURN
1140 RECCNT = 0
1150 FOR I = 1 TO 36
1160 IF WORKTOT(I) <=0 THEN GOTO 1210
1170 PCTTOT(I) = WORKTOT(I)/TOTDUE * 100
1180 RECCNT = RECCNT + 1
1190 SORTKEY(RECCNT) = WORKTOT(I)
1200 SORTREC(RECCNT) = I
1210 NEXT I
1220 SWITCHED = 0
1230 FOR I = 1 TO RECCNT - 1
1240 IF SORTKEY(I+1) <= SORTKEY(I) THEN GOTO 1280
1250 HOLDREC = SORTKEY(I) : SORTKEY(I) = SORTKEY(I+1) : SORTKEY(I+1) = HOLDREC
1260 HOLDKEY = SORTREC(I) : SORTREC(I) = SORTREC(I+1) : SORTREC(I+1) = HOLDKEY
1270 SWITCHED = 1
1280 NEXT I
1290 IF SWITCHED = 1 THEN GOTO 1220
1300 J = 0
1310 FOR I = 1 TO RECCNT
1320 PRINT #2,
USING "\                         \";MID$(EXPDESC$(SORTREC(I)),1,25);
1330 PRINT #2," Total expense :";:PRINT #2,USING "$$##,###.##";SORTKEY(I);
1340 PRINT #2," % of total :";: PRINT #2,USING "###.##";PCTTOT(SORTREC(I))
1350 J = J + 1
1380 NEXT I
1390 PRINT #2," " : PRINT #2," "  : CLOSE : GOSUB 2300
1395 LINE INPUT "Enter return to continue"; CHGFIELD$ : RETURN
1400 REM ****************************************************************
1410 REM THIS SECTION WILL HANDLE THE HELP REQUEST FROM THE MAIN MENU   *
1420 REM ****************************************************************
1430 CHGFIELD$ = MID$(CHGFIELD$,2,2)
1440 CHGFIELD = VAL(CHGFIELD$)
1450 IF CHGFIELD < 1 OR CHGFIELD > 13 THEN
PRINT "Help is available for all commands by typing ?xx
where xx = 1 to 13" : RETURN
```

```
1460 ON CHGFIELD GOSUB 1480,1500,1520,1550,1670,1710,1780,
1740,1690,1610,1640,1580,1790
1470 RETURN
1480 PRINT "This command is used to enter information about a bill."
1490 RETURN
1500 PRINT "This command is used to record payments against outstanding bills"
1510 RETURN
1520 PRINT "This command is used to change any field in a record that has not"
1530 PRINT "been used yet to update the year to date totals."
1540 RETURN
1550 PRINT "This command is used to delete a bill that has not
been used yet to"
1560 PRINT "update the year to date totals."
1570 RETURN
1580 PRINT "This command is used to review the transaction file by date and,"
1590 PRINT "if desired, expense code."
1600 RETURN
1610 PRINT "This command will produce a report showing bills that must be paid"
1620 PRINT "as of a specified date"
1630 RETURN
1640 PRINT "This command will produce a report showing bills that will be due"
1650 PRINT "in the future."
1660 RETURN
1670 PRINT "This command will produce a Monthly Payables Journal"
1680 RETURN
1690 PRINT "This command shows expenses ranked by size for a specified period"
1700 RETURN
1710 PRINT "This command produces a report which may be used as a journal for"
1720 PRINT "the IRS to show a years travel."
1730 RETURN
1740 PRINT "This command allows the user to combine year to date expenses in"
1750 PRINT "any way desired.  The command can be usefull in preparing income"
1760 PRINT "taxes."
1770 RETURN
1780 PRINT "This command is used to print the contents of the TOTALS file."
1785 RETURN
1790 PRINT "This command is used to leave the program."
1795 RETURN
1800 REM *******************************************************************
1810 REM THIS SUBROUTINE WILL GET THE MILEAGE RATE FROM DISK AND IF NOT    *
1820 REM FOUND THERE WILL PROMPT THE USER FOR IT AND SAVE IT ON DISK       *
1830 REM *******************************************************************
1840 OPEN "R",#1,DISK$+"RATE.FIL",4
1850 FIELD #1,4 AS MILERATE$
1855 GET #1,1
1860 MILERATE = CVS(MILERATE$)
1865 IF MILERATE > 0 THEN GOTO 1920
1870 LINE INPUT "Enter rate per mile :" ; TMILERATE$
1880 MILERATE = VAL(TMILERATE$)
1890 IF MILERATE = 0 THEN GOTO 1870
1900 LSET MILERATE$ = MKS$(MILERATE)
1910 I = 1 : PUT #1,I
1920 CLOSE #1
1930 RETURN
2000 REM *******************************************************************
2001 REM THIS WILL OPEN THE COUNT FILE AND GET THE RECORD COUNTS           *
2002 REM *******************************************************************
2005 OPEN "R",#1,DISK$+"PAYFILES.CNT",8
2010 FIELD #1,4 AS BILLCNT$,4 AS TOTLCNT$
2020 GET #1,1
2030 BILLCNT = CVS(BILLCNT$)
2040 TOTLCNT = CVS(TOTLCNT$)
2050 CLOSE #1 : GOTO 2500
```

133

```
2100 REM *********************************************************************
2101 REM THIS SUBROUTINE WILL SAVE THE RECORD COUNTS IN THE COUNT FILE    *
2102 REM *********************************************************************
2105 OPEN "R",#1,DISK$+"PAYFILES.CNT",8
2110 FIELD #1,4 AS BILLCNT$,4 AS TOTLCNT$
2120 LSET BILLCNT$ = MKS$(BILLCNT)
2130 LSET TOTLCNT$ = MKS$(TOTLCNT)
2140 PUT #1,1
2150 CLOSE #1 : RETURN
2300 REM *********************************************************************
2301 REM THIS SUBROUTINE WILL PRINT THE REPORT FILE ON THE REQUESTED DEV. *
2302 REM *********************************************************************
2305 OPEN "I",#1,DISK$+"REPORT.FIL"
2310 J = 0
2320 IF EOF(1) THEN GOTO 2380
2330 LINE INPUT #1,A$
2340 J = J + 1
2350 IF OUTTYPE$ = "2" THEN LPRINT A$ : GOTO 2320
2360 IF J MOD (SCREENHEIGHT - 1) = 0 THEN
LINE INPUT "Enter return to continue :";CHGFIELD$
2370 PRINT A$ : GOTO 2320
2380 CLOSE #1 : FOR I = 1 TO 4 : PRINT : NEXT I : RETURN
2500 REM *********************************************************************
2510 REM THIS IS THE MAIN PROCESSING PART OF THE PROGRAM                    *
2520 REM *********************************************************************
2530 FOR I = 1 TO SCREENHEIGHT : PRINT : NEXT I   ' SCROLL THE SCREEN CLEAR
2540 PRINT TAB(LEFTMARG) ; "             Payments Program               "
2550 PRINT
2560 PRINT TAB(LEFTMARG) ; "          Available commands are:"
2570 PRINT TAB(LEFTMARG) ; " 1-Add                    2-Paid          "
2580 PRINT TAB(LEFTMARG) ; " 3-Change                 4-Delete        "
2590 PRINT TAB(LEFTMARG) ; " 5-Monthly                6-Travel        "
2600 PRINT TAB(LEFTMARG) ; " 7-To date                8-Totals        "
2610 PRINT TAB(LEFTMARG) ; " 9-Breakdown             10-Past due       "
2620 PRINT TAB(LEFTMARG) ; "11-Cash                  12-Inquiry        "
2630 PRINT TAB(LEFTMARG) ; "13-Exit                                    "
2635 PRINT : PRINT : PRINT : PRINT
2640 PRINT TAB(LEFTMARG) ; "  " ; :
LINE INPUT "Command selection [1-13 or ?1-?13] :" ; CHGFIELD$
2650 IF CHGFIELD$ = "" THEN GOTO 2640
2660 IF MID$(CHGFIELD$,1,1) = "?" THEN GOSUB 1400 : GOTO 2640
2670 CHGFIELD = VAL(CHGFIELD$)
2680 IF CHGFIELD < 1 OR CHGFIELD > 13 THEN GOTO 2640
2690 FOR I = 1 TO SCREENHEIGHT : PRINT : NEXT I
2691 IF CHGFIELD <> 13 THEN GOTO 2700
2692 OPEN "R",#1,DISK$+"CHECK.FIL",4
2693 FIELD #1,4 AS LASTCHECK$
2694 LSET LASTCHECK$ = MKS$(LASTCHECK) : I = 1 : PUT #1,I : CLOSE : END
2700 IF CHGFIELD > 1 THEN GOTO 2716
2710 IF MERGEDFILE$ <> "1" THEN
MERGEDFILE$ = "1" : CHAIN MERGE
"PAYMENT1.BAS",3000,ALL,DELETE 3000-10000 : GOTO 2030
2715 GOTO 3000
2716 IF CHGFIELD > 3 THEN GOTO 2720
2717 IF MERGEDFILE$ <> "2" THEN MERGEDFILE$ = "2" :
CHAIN MERGE "PAYMENT2.BAS",3000,ALL,DELETE 3000-10000 : GOTO 2030
2718 GOTO 3000
2720 IF CHGFIELD > 5 THEN GOTO 2740
2722 IF MERGEDFILE$ <> "3" THEN MERGEDFILE$ = "3" :
CHAIN MERGE "PAYMENT3.BAS",3000,ALL,DELETE 3000-10000 : GOTO 2030
2730 GOTO 3000
2740 IF CHGFIELD > 8 THEN GOTO 2760
2742 IF MERGEDFILE$ <> "4" THEN MERGEDFILE$ = "4" :
CHAIN MERGE "PAYMENT4.BAS",3000,ALL,DELETE 3000-10000 : GOTO 2030
```

```
2750 GOTO 3000
2760 IF MERGEDFILE$ <> "5" THEN MERGEDFILE$ = "5" :
CHAIN MERGE "PAYMENT5.BAS",3000,ALL,DELETE 3000-10000 : GOTO 2030
3000 ON CHGFIELD GOSUB 3050,4010,4690,5540,7040,8710,9310,
9090,8300,6540,6540,6070,2692
3010 GOTO 2530
10000 REM THIS LINE IS HERE FOR A COMMON DELETE-THRU LINE NUMBER FOR CHAIN
```

PAYMENT1.BAS

```
3000 ON CHGFIELD GOSUB 3050,4010,4690,5540,7040,
2530,2530,2530,2530,2530,2530,2530,3020
3010 GOTO 2530
3020 OPEN "R",#1,DISK$+"CHECK.FIL",4
3030 FIELD #1,4 AS LASTCHECK$
3040 LSET LASTCHECK$ = MKS$(LASTCHECK) : I = 1 : PUT #1,I : CLOSE : END
3050 REM ***************************************************************
3060 REM THIS SECTION WILL HANDLE THE ADD COMMAND FROM THE MAIN MENU      *
3070 REM ***************************************************************
3080 OPEN "R",#1,DISK$+"BILLS.DAT",107
3090 FIELD #1,4 AS EXPCDF$,25 AS PAYEEF$,6 AS DDATEF$,
6 AS PDATEF$,4 AS AMTF$,4 AS PFLAGF$,4 AS TFLAGF$,4 AS CHKNBRF$,50 AS COMMF$
3100 PRINT : PRINT : PRINT :
LINE INPUT "Expense selection (1-36 or ?) :" ;EXPCD$
3110 IF EXPCD$ = "" THEN CLOSE :GOSUB 2100 : RETURN
3120 IF EXPCD$ <> "?" THEN GOTO 3170
3130 FOR I = 1 TO 36
3140 PRINT I "-" EXPDESC$(I)
3150 IF (I+1) MOD SCREENHEIGHT = 0 THEN
LINE INPUT "Enter return to continue :";DUMM$
3160 NEXT I : GOTO 3100
3170 EXPCD = VAL(EXPCD$)
3180 IF EXPCD < 1 OR EXPCD > 36 THEN PRINT "Invalid expense code!": GOTO 3100
3190 COPYFLG$ = "N"
3200 PRINT EXPDESC$(EXPCD)
3210 IF EXPCD <> 6 THEN GOTO 3450
3220 LINE INPUT "Where to? :" ; WHERE$
3230 IF WHERE$ = "" THEN GOTO 3100
3240 PAYEE$ = SPACE$(25)
3250 LSET PAYEE$ = WHERE$
3260 SAVEREC = 0
3270 FOR I = 1 TO BILLCNT
3280 GET #1,I
3290 IF CVS(EXPCDF$) <> 6 THEN GOTO 3320
3300 IF PAYEE$ <> PAYEEF$ THEN GOTO 3320
3310 SAVEREC = I
3320 NEXT I
3330 LINE INPUT "Miles :"; MILES$
3340 IF MILES$ = "" AND SAVEREC <> 0 THEN
GET #1,SAVEREC:MILES = CVS(CHKNBRF$) : TOLL = CVS(PFLAGF$) :
AMT = CVS(AMTF$) : GOTO 3410
3350 MILES = VAL(MILES$)
3360 IF MILES = 0 THEN PRINT "Invalid mileage amount" : GOTO 3330
3370 CHKNBR = MILES
3380 LINE INPUT "Tolls :";TOLL$
3390 TOLL = VAL(TOLL$)
3400 AMT = (MILERATE * MILES) + TOLL
```

```
3410 LINE INPUT "Date   :"; DDATE$
3420 IF DDATE$ = "" THEN DDATE$ = CDATE$           ' DEFAULT TO CURRENT DATE
3430 LINE INPUT "Comment :";COMM$
3440 GOTO 3710
3450 LINE INPUT "Pay who ? :" ;PAYEE$
3460 IF PAYEE$ = "" THEN GOTO 3100
3470 LINE INPUT "Amount ? :" ; AMT$
3480 IF AMT$ = "" THEN GOTO 3100
3490 AMT = VAL(AMT$)
3500 IF AMT = 0 THEN PRINT "Amount must NOT be zero!" :GOTO 3470  'neg is ok
3510 LINE INPUT "Due date : "; DDATE$
3520 IF DDATE$ = "" THEN DDATE$ = CDATE$    ' FILL IN THE CURRENT DATE
3530 LINE INPUT "Comment :" ; COMM$
3540 PPFLG$ = "N"
3550 LINE INPUT "Payment date :" ; PDATE$
3560 IF PDATE$ = "" THEN GOTO 3710
3570 IF PDATE$ = "C" THEN PDATE$ = CDATE$   ' FILL IN THE CURRENT DATE
3580 IF PDATE$ <> "P" THEN GOTO 3660        ' PARTIAL PAYMENT PROCESSING
3590 LINE INPUT "Partial payment date :"; PDATE$
3600 IF PDATE$ = "" THEN PDATE$ = CDATE$
3610 LINE INPUT "Partial payment amount :";PPAMT$
3620 PPAMT = VAL(PPAMT$)
3630 IF PPAMT = < .01 THEN GOTO 3610
3640 IF PPAMT > AMT OR PPAMT = AMT THEN
PRINT "Partial payment amount must be less than bill amount":GOTO 3610  '
3650 PPFLG$ = "Y"
3660 LINE INPUT "Check number :" ; CHKNBR$
3670 CHKNBR = VAL(CHKNBR$)
3680 IF CHKNBR > 0 THEN LASTCHECK = CHKNBR : GOTO 3710
3690 IF CHKNBR$ = "$" THEN CHKNBR$ = "CASH" : GOTO 3710
3700 IF CHKNBR$ = "" THEN LASTCHECK = LASTCHECK + 1 :
CHKNBR = LASTCHECK : PRINT "Check number = " CHKNBR
3710 REM ****************************************************************
3720 REM OK .. WE HAVE ALL THE INFO .. MOVE IT TO THE RECORD AND WRITE IT OUT *
3730 REM ****************************************************************
3740 LSET EXPCDF$ = MKS$(EXPCD)
3750 LSET PAYEEF$ = PAYEE$
3760 LSET AMTF$  = MKS$(AMT)
3770 IF PPFLG$ = "Y" THEN LSET AMTF$ = MKS$(AMT - PPAMT)
3780 LSET DDATEF$ = DDATE$
3790 LSET COMMF$  = COMM$
3800 LSET PDATEF$ = PDATE$
3810 IF PPFLG$ = "Y" THEN LSET PDATEF$ = "       "
3820 IF CHKNBR$ <> "CASH" THEN LSET CHKNBRF$ = MKS$(CHKNBR)
3830 IF CHKNBR$ = "CASH" THEN LSET CHKNBRF$ = CHKNBR$
3840 IF PDATEF$ = "       " THEN LSET CHKNBRF$ = "     "
3850 IF EXPCD = 6 THEN LSET CHKNBRF$ = MKS$(MILES)
3860 LSET TFLAGF$ = "     "
3870 LSET PFLAGF$ = "     "
3880 IF PPFLG$ = "Y" THEN LSET PFLAGF$ ="P"
3890 IF EXPCD = 6 THEN LSET PFLAGF$ = MKS$(TOLL)
3900 BILLCNT = BILLCNT + 1
3910 PUT #1,BILLCNT
3920 PRINT "Billing record has been recorded! ..Amount = " CVS(AMTF$)
3930 IF PPFLG$ <> "Y" THEN GOTO 3990
3940 LSET AMTF$ = MKS$(PPAMT)
3950 LSET PDATEF$ = PDATE$
3960 I = (LOF(1)/107) + 1
3970 PUT #1,I
3980 PRINT "Partial payment record has been recorded! ..
Amount = ";:PRINT USING "$$##,###.##";CVS(AMTF$)
3990 IF EXPCD = 6 THEN GOTO 3220
4000 GOTO 3450
10000 REM THIS LINE IS HERE TO PROVIDE A COMMON
DELETE-THRU LINE-NBR FOR CHAIN
```

PAYMENT2.BAS

```
3000 ON CHGFIELD GOSUB 3050,4010,4690,5540,7040,2530,2530,
2530,2530,2530,2530,2530,3020
3010 GOTO 2530
3020 OPEN "R",#1,DISK$+"CHECK.FIL",4
3030 FIELD #1,4 AS LASTCHECK$
3040 LSET LASTCHECK$ = MKS$(LASTCHECK) : I = 1 :
PUT #1,I : CLOSE :GOSUB 2100 : END
4010 REM ********************************************************************
4020 REM THIS SECTION WILL TAKE CARE OF THE PAID COMMAND FROM THE MAIN MENU *
4030 REM ********************************************************************
4040 OPEN "R",#1,DISK$+"BILLS.DAT",107
4050 FIELD #1,4 AS EXPCD$,25 AS PAYEE$,6 AS DDATEF$,
6 AS PDATEF$,4 AS AMTF$,4 AS PFLAGF$,4 AS TFLAGF$,4 AS CHKNBRF$,50 AS COMMF$
4060 J = 0
4070 FOR I = 1 TO BILLCNT
4080 GET #1,I
4090 IF PDATEF$ <> "      " THEN GOTO 4140    ' ONLY DO UNPAID BILLS
4100 IF CVS(EXPCD$) = 6 THEN GOTO 4140        ' IGNORE TRAVEL EXPENSES
4110 J = J + 1
4120 SORTKEY$(J) = PAYEE$+DDATEF$
4130 SORTREC(J) = I
4140 NEXT I
4150 IF J < 1 THEN
PRINT "No outstanding bills at this time ":
LINE INPUT "Enter return to continue"; CHGFIELD$ :
CLOSE :GOSUB 2100 : RETURN
4160 SWITCHED = 0
4170 FOR I = 1 TO J-1
4180 IF SORTKEY$(I+1) > SORTKEY$(I) THEN GOTO 4230    -
4190 IF SORTKEY$(I+1) = SORTKEY$(I) THEN GOTO 4230
4200 HOLDREC = SORTREC(I)   : SORTREC(I) = SORTREC(I+1) :
SORTREC(I+1) = HOLDREC
4210 HOLDKEY$ = SORTKEY$(I):SORTKEY$(I) = SORTKEY$(I+1):
SORTKEY$(I+1) = HOLDKEY$
4220 SWITCHED = 1
4230 NEXT I
4240 IF SWITCHED <> 0 THEN GOTO 4160
4250 FOR I = 1 TO J
4260 IF I = 1 OR I MOD 60 = 0 THEN PRINT
"          Bill             Amount    Due Date           Comment       "
4270 IF I = 1 OR I MOD 60 = 0 THEN PRINT
"   ---------------------   --------  --------  ------------------------"
4280 GET #1,SORTREC(I)
4290 PRINT "(";:PRINT USING"##";I;: PRINT ") " PAYEE$ " ";
4300 PRINT USING "$$##,###.##";CVS(AMTF$);
4310 PRINT "  " MID$(DDATEF$,1,2) "/" MID$(DDATEF$,3,2) "/" MID$(DDATEF$,5,2);
4320 PRINT "  ";: PRINT USING "\                        \";COMMF$
4330 IF I MOD SCREENHEIGHT = 0 THEN
LINE INPUT "Enter return to continue :";CHGFIELD$
4340 NEXT I
4350 TOTPAID = 0
4360 LINE INPUT "Pay what? :"; RECNO$
4370 IF RECNO$ = "" THEN PRINT "Total paid = " TOTPAID :
LINE INPUT "Enter return to continue";CHGFIELD$ :
CLOSE : GOSUB 2100 :RETURN
4380 IF RECNO$ = "?" THEN GOTO 4060
4390 RECNO = VAL(RECNO$)
4400 IF RECNO < 1 OR RECNO > J THEN PRINT "Invalid selection":GOTO 4360
4410 GET #1,SORTREC(RECNO)
4420 LINE INPUT "Date paid :"; PDATE$
4430 IF PDATE$ = "" THEN PDATE$ = CDATE$      ' DEFAULT TO CURRENT DATE
4440 IF PDATE$ <> "P" THEN GOTO 4540
4450 LSET PFLAGF$ = "P"
```

```
4460 LINE INPUT "Partial payment amount :";PPAMT$
4470 PPAMT = VAL(PPAMT$)
4480 IF PPAMT = 0 OR PPAMT > CVS(AMTF$) THEN PRINT
"Partial payment amount must be less then billing amount":GOTO 4460
4490 LSET AMTF$ = MKS$(CVS(AMTF$) - PPAMT)
4500 BILLCNT = BILLCNT + 1 : PUT #1,BILLCNT: PRINT
"Partial payment record created"
4510 LSET AMTF$ = MKS$(PPAMT)
4520 LINE INPUT "Partial payment date :"; PDATE$
4530 IF PDATE$ = "" THEN PDATE$ = CDATE$        ' DEFAULT TO CURRENT DATE
4540 LSET PDATEF$ = PDATE$
4550 LINE INPUT "Comment :";COMM$
4560 LSET COMMF$ = COMM$
4570 LINE INPUT "Check number :" ; CHKNBR$
4580 CHKNBR = VAL(CHKNBR$)
4590 IF CHKNBR > 0 THEN LASTCHECK = CHKNBR : GOTO 4620
4600 IF CHKNBR$ = "$" THEN CHKNBR$ = "CASH" : GOTO 4620
4610 IF CHKNBR$ = "" THEN LASTCHECK = LASTCHECK + 1 :
CHKNBR = LASTCHECK : PRINT "Check number = " CHKNBR
4620 IF CHKNBR$ = "CASH" THEN LSET CHKNBRF$ = CHKNBR$ GOTO 4640
4630 LSET CHKNBRF$ = MKS$(CHKNBR)
4640 PUT #1,SORTREC(RECNO)
4650 IF PFLAGF$ = "P  " THEN TOTPAID = TOTPAID + PPAMT : GOTO 4670
4660 TOTPAID = TOTPAID + CVS(AMTF$)
4670 PRINT "Record has been updated"
4680 GOTO 4360
4690 REM ********************************************************************
4700 REM THIS SECTION WILL HANDLE THE CHANGE REQUEST FROM THE MAIN MENU    *
4710 REM ********************************************************************
4720 OPEN "R",#1,DISK$+"BILLS.DAT",107
4730 FIELD #1,4 AS EXPCDF$,25 AS PAYEEF$,6 AS DDATEF$,
6 AS PDATEF$,4 AS AMTF$,4 AS PFLAGF$,4 AS TFLAGF$,4 AS CHKNBRF$,50 AS COMMF$
4740 RECNO = 0
4750 GOSUB 5280                                      ' FIND DESIRED RECORD
4760 IF FOUND$ = "Q" THEN CLOSE : RETURN
4770 FOR J = 1 TO 5 : PRINT : NEXT J
4780 PRINT "(1) Expense Selection = " CVS(EXPCDF$) "- " EXPDESC$(CVS(EXPCDF$))
4790 IF EXPCD = 6 THEN PRINT "(2) To where        = " PAYEEF$ : GOTO 4810
4800 PRINT "(2) Payee              = " PAYEEF$
4810 PRINT "(3) Due date           = " MID$(DDATEF$,1,2)
"/" MID$(DDATEF$,3,2) "/" MID$(DDATEF$,5,2)
4820 PRINT "(4) Amount             = " CVS(AMTF$)
4830 IF EXPCD = 6 THEN PRINT "(5) Tolls          = "
CVS(PFLAGF$) : GOTO 4850
4840 PRINT "(5) Date paid          = " MID$(PDATEF$,1,2)
"/" MID$(PDATEF$,3,2) "/" MID$(PDATEF$,5,2)
4850 IF EXPCD = 6 THEN
PRINT "(6) Miles          = " CVS(CHKNBRF$) : GOTO 4890
4860 IF CHKNBRF$ = "CASH" THEN
PRINT "(6) Check number   = " CHKNBRF$ : GOTO 4890
4870 IF CHKNBRF$ = "   " THEN
PRINT "(6) Check number   = " : GOTO 4890
4880 PRINT "(6) Check number       = " CVS(CHKNBRF$)
4890 PRINT "(7) Comment            = " COMMF$
4900 PRINT "(8) Look for different record "
4910 PRINT : PRINT : LINE INPUT "Change What ?:"; CHGFIELD$
4920 IF CHGFIELD$ = "" THEN PUT #1,I : PRINT "Record updated" : GOTO 4740
4930 IF CHGFIELD$ = "8" THEN PUT #1,I : PRINT "Record updated" : GOTO 4750
4940 CHGFIELD = VAL(CHGFIELD$)
4950 IF CHGFIELD < 1 OR CHGFIELD > 7 THEN GOTO 4910
4960 ON CHGFIELD GOSUB 4980,5040,5080,5110,5140,5200,5270
4970 GOTO 4910
4980 IF CVS(EXPCDF$) = 6 THEN
PRINT "Travel expense code cannot be changed":RETURN
```

138

```
4990 LINE INPUT "Enter new selection code :"; TEXPCD$
5000 TEXPCD = VAL(TEXPCD$)
5010 IF TEXPCD < 1 OR TEXPCD > 36 THEN
PRINT "Invalid selection code" : GOTO 4980
5020 IF TEXPCD = 6 THEN
PRINT "Expense code cannot be changed to 6" : GOTO 4980
5030 LSET EXPCDF$ = MKS$(TEXPCD) : RETURN
5040 IF EXPCD = 6 THEN
LINE INPUT "Enter new destination :"; PAYEE$ : GOTO 5060
5050 LINE INPUT "Enter new payee :"; PAYEE$
5060 IF PAYEE$ = "" THEN GOTO 5040
5070 LSET PAYEEF$ = PAYEE$ : RETURN
5080 LINE INPUT "Enter new due date :"; DDATE$
5090 IF DDATE$ = "" THEN DDATE$ = CDATE$    ' DEFAULT TO CURRENT DATE
5100 LSET DDATEF$ = DDATE$ : RETURN
5110 LINE INPUT "Enter new amount :"; AMT$
5120 AMT = VAL(AMT$) : IF AMT = 0 THEN
PRINT "Amount must NOT be zero": GOTO 5110
5130 LSET AMTF$ = MKS$(AMT) : RETURN
5140 IF EXPCD <> 6 THEN GOTO 5170
5150 LINE INPUT "Enter new tolls amount :"; TOLLS$
5160 LSET PFLAGF$ = MKS$(VAL(TOLLS$)) : RETURN
5170 LINE INPUT "Enter new date paid :"; PDATE$
5180 IF PDATE$ = "" THEN PDATE$ = ""         ' DEFAULT TO CURRENT DATE
5190 LSET PDATEF$ = PDATE$ : RETURN
5200 IF EXPCD = 6 THEN
LINE INPUT "Enter new number of miles :"; CHKNBR$ : GOTO 5220
5210 LINE INPUT "Enter new check number :";CHKNBR$
5220 IF CHKNBR$ = "" THEN GOTO 5200
5230 IF CHKNBR$ = "CASH" THEN LSET CHKNBRF$ = CHKNBR$ : RETURN
5240 CHKNBR = VAL(CHKNBR$)
5250 IF CHKNBR < 1 AND EXPCD <> 6 THEN GOTO 5200
5260 LSET CHKNBRF$ = MKS$(CHKNBR) : RETURN
5270 LINE INPUT "Enter new comments :"; COMM$ : LSET COMMF$ = COMM$ : RETURN
5280 REM *******************************************************************
5290 REM THIS SUBROUTINE WILL PROMPT FOR THE KEY VALUES AND LOCATE THE RECORD *
5300 REM *******************************************************************
5310 IF RECNO <> 0 THEN GOTO 5450
5320 LINE INPUT "Expense selection (1-36 or ?) :" ;EXPCD$
5330 IF EXPCD$ = "" THEN FOUND$ = "Q" : RETURN
5340 IF EXPCD$ <> "?" THEN GOTO 5390
5350 FOR I = 1 TO 36
5360 PRINT I "-" EXPDESC$(I)
5370 IF (I+1) MOD SCREENHEIGHT = 0 THEN
LINE INPUT "Enter return to continue :";DUMM$
5380 NEXT I:GOTO 5320
5390 EXPCD = VAL(EXPCD$)
5400 IF EXPCD < 1 OR EXPCD > 36 THEN PRINT "Invalid expense code!": GOTO 5320
5410 IF EXPCD = 6 THEN LINE INPUT "Where to ?:";TPAYEE$ : GOTO 5430
5420 LINE INPUT  "Pay Who ?:"; TPAYEE$
5430 IF TPAYEE$ = "" THEN GOTO 5320
5440 PAYEE$ = SPACE$(25) : LSET PAYEE$ = TPAYEE$
5450 I = RECNO
5460 I = I + 1
5470 IF I > BILLCNT THEN PRINT "Record not found" : RECNO = 0 : GOTO 5320
5480 GET #1,I
5490 IF (EXPCD = CVS(EXPCDF$)) AND (PAYEE$ = PAYEEF$) THEN GOTO 5510
5500 GOTO 5460
5510 IF TFLAGF$ <> "    " THEN
PRINT "Bill cannot be changed.  Already used in totals" : GOTO 5320
5520 FOUND$ = "Y" : RECNO = I
5530 RETURN
10000 REM THIS LINE IS HERE TO PROVIDE A COMMON
DELETE-THRU LINE-NBR FOR CHAIN
```

PAYMENT3.BAS

```
3000 ON CHGFIELD GOSUB 3050,4010,4690,5540,7040,2530,
2530,2530,2530,2530,2530,2530,3020
3010 GOTO 2530
3020 OPEN "R",#1,DISK$+"CHECK.FIL",4
3030 FIELD #1,4 AS LASTCHECK$
3040 LSET LASTCHECK$ = MKS$(LASTCHECK) : I = 1 :
PUT #1,I : CLOSE :GOSUB 2100: END
5280 REM ********************************************************************
5290 REM THIS SUBROUTINE WILL PROMPT FOR THE KEY VALUES AND LOCATE THE RECORD *
5300 REM ********************************************************************
5310 IF RECNO <> 0 THEN GOTO 5450
5320 LINE INPUT "Expense selection (1-36 or ?) :" ;EXPCD$
5330 IF EXPCD$ = "" THEN FOUND$ = "Q" : RETURN
5340 IF EXPCD$ <> "?" THEN GOTO 5390
5350 FOR I = 1 TO 36
5360 PRINT I "-" EXPDESC$(I)
5370 IF (I+1) MOD SCREENHEIGHT = 0 THEN
LINE INPUT "Enter return to continue :";DUMM$
5380 NEXT I:GOTO 5320
5390 EXPCD = VAL(EXPCD$)
5400 IF EXPCD < 1 OR EXPCD > 36 THEN PRINT "Invalid expense code!": GOTO 5320
5410 IF EXPCD = 6 THEN LINE INPUT "Where to ?:";TPAYEE$ : GOTO 5430
5420 LINE INPUT  "Pay Who ?:"; TPAYEE$
5430 IF TPAYEE$ = "" THEN GOTO 5320
5440 PAYEE$ = SPACE$(25) : LSET PAYEE$ = TPAYEE$
5450 I = RECNO
5460 I = I + 1
5470 IF I > BILLCNT THEN PRINT "Record not found" : RECNO = 0 : GOTO 5320
5480 GET #1,I
5490 IF (EXPCD = CVS(EXPCDF$)) AND (PAYEE$ = PAYEEF$) THEN GOTO 5510
5500 GOTO 5460
5510 IF TFLAGF$ <> "    " THEN PRINT
"Bill cannot be changed.  Already used in totals" : GOTO 5320
5520 FOUND$ = "Y" : RECNO = I
5530 RETURN
5540 REM ********************************************************************
5550 REM THIS SECTION WILL HANDLE THE DELETE REQUEST FROM THE MAIN MENU     *
5560 REM ********************************************************************
5570 OPEN "R",#1,DISK$+"BILLS.DAT",107
5580 FIELD #1,4 AS EXPCDF$,25 AS PAYEEF$,
6 AS DDATEF$,6 AS PDATEF$,4 AS AMTF$,4 AS PFLAGF$,
4 AS TFLAGF$,4 AS CHKNBRF$,50 AS COMMF$
5590 RECNO = 0
5600 GOSUB 5280                                      ' FIND DESIRED RECORD
5610 IF FOUND$ = "Q" THEN GOTO 5850                  ' GO REORG THE FILE
5620 FOR J = 1 TO 5 : PRINT : NEXT J
5630 PRINT "Expense Selection = " CVS(EXPCDF$) "- " EXPDESC$(CVS(EXPCDF$))
5640 IF EXPCD = 6 THEN PRINT "To where        = " PAYEEF$ : GOTO 5660
5650 PRINT "Payee              = " PAYEEF$
5660 PRINT "Due date           = " MID$(DDATEF$,1,2)
"/" MID$(DDATEF$,3,2) "/" MID$(DDATEF$,5,2)
5670 PRINT "Amount             = " CVS(AMTF$)
5680 IF EXPCD = 6 THEN PRINT "Tolls            = " CVS(PFLAGF$) : GOTO 5700
5690 PRINT "Date paid          = " MID$(PDATEF$,1,2)
"/" MID$(PDATEF$,3,2) "/" MID$(PDATEF$,5,2)
5700 IF EXPCD = 6 THEN PRINT "Miles            = " CVS(CHKNBRF$) : GOTO 5740
5710 IF CHKNBRF$ = "CASH" THEN PRINT
"Check number     = " CHKNBRF$ : GOTO 5740
5720 IF CHKNBRF$ = "    " THEN PRINT "Check number        = " : GOTO 5740
5730 PRINT "Check number       = " CVS(CHKNBRF$)
5740 PRINT "Comment            = " COMMF$
5750 PRINT : PRINT
```

```
5760 LINE INPUT "OK to delete?:"; CHGFIELD$
5770 IF CHGFIELD$ <> "Y" AND CHGFIELD$ <> "N" THEN GOTO 5760
5780 IF CHGFIELD$ <> "Y" THEN GOTO 5810
5790 LSET EXPCDF$ = MKS$(0)
5800 PUT #1,I
5810 LINE INPUT "Look for different record (Y/N) :";CHGFIELD$
5820 IF CHGFIELD$ <> "Y" AND CHGFIELD$ <> "N" THEN GOTO 5810
5830 IF CHGFIELD$ <> "Y" THEN GOTO 5590
5840 GOTO 5600
5850 REM ****************************************************************
5860 REM THIS SECTION WILL RE-ORGANIZE THE BILLS FILE AND ELIMINATE ALL  *
5870 REM RECORDS WITH AN EXPENSE CODE OF ZERO                            *
5880 REM ****************************************************************
5890 CLOSE : PRINT "File reorginization in progress"
5900 OPEN "R",#1,DISK$+"BILLS.DAT",107
5910 FIELD #1,4 AS EXPCDF$,103 AS DUMMY1$
5920 OPEN "R",#2,DISK$+"NBILLS.DAT",107
5930 FIELD #2,4 AS NEXPCDF$,103 AS NDUMMY1$
5940 I = 0 : J = 0
5950 I = I + 1
5960 IF I > BILLCNT THEN GOTO 6040
5970 GET #1,I
5980 IF CVS(EXPCDF$) = 0 THEN GOTO 5950
5990 LSET NEXPCDF$ = EXPCDF$
6000 LSET NDUMMY1$ = DUMMY1$
6010 J = J + 1
6020 PUT #2,J
6030 GOTO 5950
6040 PRINT "Old file had " I-1 " bills. New file has " J " bills."
6050 CLOSE :BILLCNT = J : GOSUB 2100
6060 KILL DISK$+"BILLS.DAT" :
NAME DISK$+"NBILLS.DAT" AS DISK$+"BILLS.DAT" : RETURN
7040 REM ****************************************************************
7050 REM THIS SECTION WILL HANDLE THE MONTH END REPORT REQUEST FROM THE  *
7060 REM MAIN MENU                                                       *
7070 REM ****************************************************************
7080 OPEN "R",#1,DISK$+"BILLS.DAT",107
7090 FIELD #1,4 AS EXPCDF$,25 AS PAYEEF$,
6 AS DDATEF$,6 AS PDATEF$,4 AS AMTF$,
4 AS PFLAGF$,4 AS TFLAGF$,4 AS CHKNBRF$,50 AS COMMF$
7100 LINE INPUT "Output to screen (1) or printer (2)"; CHGFIELD$
7110 OUTTYPE$ = CHGFIELD$
7120 IF CHGFIELD$ <> "1" AND CHGFIELD$ <> "2" THEN GOTO 7100
7140 OPEN "O",#2,DISK$+"REPORT.FIL"
7150 OPEN "O",#3,DISK$+"SORT.DAT"
7160 LINE INPUT "Enter month name :";MONTHNAME$
7170 IF MONTHNAME$ = "" THEN GOTO 7160
7180 LINE INPUT "Enter starting date :";STARTDTE$
7190 IF STARTDTE$ = "" THEN GOTO 7180
7200 LINE INPUT "Enter ending date :";ENDDTE$
7210 IF ENDDTE$ = "" THEN GOTO 7200
7220 RECCNT = 0
7230 TSTARTDTE$ = MID$(STARTDTE$,5,2)+MID$(STARTDTE$,1,4)    ' YYMMDD FORMAT
7240 TENDDTE$ = MID$(ENDDTE$,5,2)+MID$(ENDDTE$,1,4)          ' YYMMDD FORMAT
7250 FOR I = 1 TO BILLCNT
7260 GET #1,I
7270 TESTDATE$ = MID$(PDATEF$,5,2)+MID$(PDATEF$,1,4)          ' YYMMDD FORMAT
7280 IF CVS(EXPCDF$) = 6      THEN GOTO 7360 ' IGNORE TRAVEL EXPENSES
7290 IF PDATEF$ = "      "    THEN GOTO 7360 ' IGNORE UNPAID BILLS
7300 IF TESTDATE$ < TSTARTDTE$ THEN GOTO 7360 ' IGNORE BILLS NOT DUE YET
7310 IF TESTDATE$ > TENDDTE$   THEN GOTO 7360 ' IGNORE BILLS USED EARLIER
7320 IF TFLAGF$ = "T   "      THEN GOTO 7360 ' IGNORE BILLS ALREADY IN TOTALS
7330 RECCNT = RECCNT + 1
7340 PRINT #3,USING "##";CVS(EXPCDF$);:PRINT #3,USING "\     \";TESTDATE$;
```

```
7350 SORTREC(RECCNT) = I
7360 NEXT I
7370 CLOSE #3
7380 IF RECCNT = 0 THEN PRINT "No records selected ": CLOSE #2 : GOTO 7760
7390 OPEN "I",#3,DISK$+"SORT.DAT"
7400 FOR I = 1 TO RECCNT
7410 SORTKEY$(I) = INPUT$(8,#3)
7420 NEXT I
7430 CLOSE #3
7440 GOSUB 830        ' GO SORT RECORDS BY DUE DATE
7450 TOTEXP = 0  : TOTDUE = 0
7460 HOLDCODE$ = ""
7470 FOR I = 1 TO 36 : MNTHTOT(I) = 0 : NEXT I
7490 FOR I = 1 TO RECCNT
7500 GET #1,SORTREC(I)
7505 IF I = 1 OR I MOD 60 = 0 THEN PRINT #2,CHR$(12) ' PUT OUT A FORM FEED
7510 IF I = 1 OR I MOD 60 = 0 THEN PRINT #2,
"                        Month End Report For " MONTHNAME$
7520 IF I = 1 OR I MOD 60 = 0 THEN PRINT #2,
"        Bill                 Amount   Due Date  Date Paid     Comments     "
7530 IF I = 1 OR I MOD 60 = 0 THEN PRINT #2,
" ------------------------   --------- --------- --------- ----------------"
7540 IF HOLDCODE$ = "" THEN HOLDCODE$ = EXPCDF$
7550 IF HOLDCODE$ = EXPCDF$ THEN GOTO 7610
7560 PRINT #2," Total ";:PRINT #2,
USING"\              \"; EXPDESC$(CVS(HOLDCODE$)) ;
7570 PRINT #2,USING "$$##,###.##";TOTEXP
7580 MNTHTOT(CVS(HOLDCODE$)) = MNTHTOT(CVS(HOLDCODE$)) + TOTEXP
7590 HOLDCODE$ = EXPCDF$
7600 TOTDUE = TOTDUE + TOTEXP : TOTEXP = 0
7610 PRINT #2,PAYEEF$ " ";
7620 PRINT #2,USING "$$##,###.##";CVS(AMTF$);
7630 IF PFLAGF$ = "P    " THEN PRINT #2,"P"; ELSE PRINT #2," ";
7640 PRINT #2," " MID$(DDATEF$,1,2) "/"
MID$(DDATEF$,3,2) "/" MID$(DDATEF$,5,2);
7650 PRINT #2,"   " MID$(PDATEF$,1,2) "/"
MID$(PDATEF$,3,2) "/" MID$(PDATEF$,5,2);
7660 PRINT #2,"   ";:print #2,using "\              \";COMMF$
7670 TOTEXP = TOTEXP + CVS(AMTF$)
7710 NEXT I
7720 MNTHTOT(CVS(HOLDCODE$)) = MNTHTOT(CVS(HOLDCODE$)) + TOTEXP
7730 PRINT #2," Total ";:PRINT #2,
USING "\              \";
EXPDESC$(CVS(HOLDCODE$)) ;:PRINT #2,
USING "$$##,###.##";TOTEXP :TOTDUE = TOTDUE + TOTEXP : TOTEXP = 0
7740 PRINT #2,"          Total Expenses = ";:PRINT #2,USING "$$##,###.##";TOTDUE
7750 PRINT #2,"  ":PRINT #2,"  "
7755 CLOSE #1,#2 : GOSUB 2300        ' GO PRINT THE REPORT FILE
7760 IF OUTTYPE$ = "1" THEN LINE INPUT "Enter return to continue";CHGFIELD$
7770 LINE INPUT "Ok to update expense totals (Y/N) :"; CHGFIELD$
7780 IF CHGFIELD$ <> "Y" AND CHGFIELD$ <> "N" THEN GOTO 7770
7790 IF CHGFIELD$ <> "Y" THEN CLOSE :GOSUB 2100 : RETURN
7800 OPEN "R",#3,DISK$+"TOTALS.DAT",4
7810 FIELD #3,4 AS TEXPF$
7820 IF TOTLCNT > 0 THEN GOTO 7880
7825 TOTLCNT = 36
7830 FOR I = 1 TO 36
7840 LSET TEXPF$ = MKS$(MNTHTOT(I))
7850 PUT #3,I
7860 NEXT I
7870 GOTO 7940
7880 FOR I = 1 TO 36
7890 IF MNTHTOT(I) = 0 THEN GOTO 7930
7900 GET #3,I
```

```
7910 LSET TEXPF$ = MKS$(CVS(TEXPF$) + MNTHTOT(I))
7920 PUT #3,I
7930 NEXT I
7940 PRINT "Totals updated "
7950 FOR I = 1 TO RECCNT
7960 GET #1,SORTREC(I)
7970 LSET TFLAGF$ = "T    "
7980 PUT #1,SORTREC(I)
7990 NEXT I
8000 PRINT "Records flaged as used in totals"
8010 LINE INPUT "Do you want the monthly breakdown report (Y/N) :"; CHGFIELD$
8020 IF CHGFIELD$ <> "Y" AND CHGFIELD$ <> "N" THEN GOTO 8010
8030 IF CHGFIELD$ = "Y" THEN OPEN "O",#2,DISK$+"REPORT.FIL" : GOSUB 980
8040 LINE INPUT "Ok to clear expense transactions (Y/N) :";CHGFIELD$
8050 IF CHGFIELD$ <> "Y" AND CHGFIELD$ <> "N" THEN GOTO 8040
8060 IF CHGFIELD$ <> "Y" THEN CLOSE : RETURN
8070 CLOSE
8080 OPEN "R",#2,DISK$+"NEWBILLS.DAT",107
8090 FIELD #2,4 AS NEXPCDF$,25 AS NPAYEEF$,6 AS NDDATEF$,
6 AS NPDATEF$,4 AS NAMTF$,4 AS NPFLAGF$,4 AS NTFLAGF$,
4 AS NCHKNBRF$,50 AS NCCMMF$
8092 OPEN "R",#1,DISK$+"BILLS.DAT",107
8094 FIELD #1,4 AS EXPCDF$,25 AS PAYEEF$,6 AS DDATEF$,
6 AS PDATEF$,4 AS AMTF$,4 AS PFLAGF$,4 AS TFLAGF$,4 AS CHKNBRF$,50 AS COMMF$
8100 J = 0 : I = 0
8110 I = I + 1
8120 IF I > BILLCNT THEN GOTO 8260
8130 GET #1,I
8140 IF TFLAGF$ = "T    " THEN GOTO 8110
8150 LSET NEXPCDF$   = EXPCDF$
8160 LSET NPAYEEF$   = PAYEEF$
8170 LSET NDDATEF$   = DDATEF$
8180 LSET NPDATEF$   = PDATEF$
8190 LSET NAMTF$     = AMTF$
8200 LSET NPFLAGF$   = PFLAGF$
8210 LSET NTFLAGF$   = TFLAGF$
8220 LSET NCHKNBRF$  = CHKNBRF$
8230 LSET NCCMMF$    = CCMMF$
8240 J = J + 1 : PUT #2,J
8250 GOTO 8110
8260 CLOSE : KILL DISK$+"BILLS.DAT" :
NAME DISK$+"NEWBILLS.DAT" AS DISK$+"BILLS.DAT"
8270 PRINT "Old file had " I-1 " bills.  New file has " J " bills"
8275 BILLCNT = J : GOSUB 2100
8280 IF OUTTYPE$ = "1" THEN LINE INPUT "Enter return to continue :";CHGFIELD$
8290 RETURN
10000 REM THIS LINE IS HERE TO PROVIDE A COMMON
DELETE-THRU LINE-NBR FOR CHAIN
```

PAYMENT4.BAS

```
3000 ON CHGFIELD GOSUB 2530,2530,2530,2530,2530,8710,
9310,9090,8300,6540,6540,6070,2192
3010 GOTO 2530
8710 REM ******************************************************************
8720 REM THIS SECTION WILL PRODUCE THE TRAVEL LOG REPORT REQUEST FROM THE  *
8730 REM MAIN MENU                                                         *
8740 REM ******************************************************************
8750 OPEN "R",#1,DISK$+"BILLS.DAT",107
```

```
8760 FIELD #1,4 AS EXPCDF$,25 AS PAYEEF$,6 AS DDATEF$,
6 AS PDATEF$,4 AS AMTF$,4 AS PFLAGF$,4 AS TFLAGF$,4 AS CHKNBRF$,50 AS COMMF$
8770 LINE INPUT "Output to screen (1) or printer (2)"; CHGFIELD$
8780 OUTTYPE$ = CHGFIELD$
8790 IF CHGFIELD$ <> "1" AND CHGFIELD$ <> "2" THEN GOTO 8770
8810 OPEN "O",#2,DISK$+"REPORT.FIL"
8820 J = 0 : TOTAMT = 0 : TOTMILE = 0
8830 FOR I = 1 TO BILLCNT
8840 GET #1,I
8850 IF CVS(EXPCDF$) <> 6 THEN GOTO 8990
8860 J = J + 1
8865 IF J = 1 OR J MOD 60 = 0 THEN PRINT #2,CHR$(12)      ' PUT OUT A FORM FEED
8870 IF J = 1 OR J MOD 60 = 0 THEN PRINT #2,
"                              Travel Log Report "
8880 IF J = 1 OR J MOD 60 = 0 THEN PRINT #2,
"     Location               Date      Miles  Tolls
Amount     Comment "
8890 IF J = 1 OR J MOD 60 = 0 THEN PRINT #2,
"_____     _____  _____  _____
_____  _____"
8900 PRINT #2,PAYEEF$ " ";
8910 PRINT #2," " MID$(DDATEF$,1,2) "/"
MID$(DDATEF$,3,2) "/" MID$(DDATEF$,5,2);
8920 PRINT #2," ";:PRINT #2,USING "#####";CVS(CHKNBRF$);      ' MILES
8930 PRINT #2," ";:PRINT #2,USING "##.##";CVS(PFLAGF$);       ' TOLLS
8940 PRINT #2," ";:PRINT #2,USING "$$##,###.##";CVS(AMTF$) ;  ' EXPENSE
8945 PRINT #2," ";:PRINT #2,USING "\                \";COMMF$
8950 TOTAMT = TOTAMT + CVS(AMTF$)              ' TOT MILEAGE EXP
8960 TOTMILE = TOTMILE + CVS(CHKNBRF$)         ' TOT MILES
8990 NEXT I
9000 PRINT #2,"Total miles = ";: PRINT #2,USING "#####";TOTMILE
9010 PRINT #2," ":PRINT #2," "
9020 OPEN "R",#3,DISK$+"TOTALS.DAT",4
9030 FIELD #3,4 AS TEXPF$
9032 IF TOTLCNT = 36 THEN GOTO 9040
9034 LSET TEXPF$ = MKS$(0)
9036 FOR I = 1 TO 36 : PUT #3,I : NEXT I
9040 LSET TEXPF$ = MKS$(TOTAMT)
9050 PUT #3,6                ' SAVE TOTAL MILEAGE EXPENSE IN TOTALS FILE
9060 CLOSE : TOTLCNT = 36 : GOSUB 2100
GOSUB 2300  ' GO PRINT THE REPORT FILE
9070 IF OUTTYPE$ = "1" THEN LINE INPUT "Enter return to continue :";CHGFIELD$
9080 RETURN
9090 REM ****************************************************************
9100 REM THIS SECTION WILL HANDLE THE TOTALS COMMAND FROM THE MAIN MENU   *
9110 REM ****************************************************************
9120 OPEN "R",#1,DISK$+"TOTALS.DAT",4
9130 FIELD #1,4 AS TEXPF$
9140 IF TOTLCNT < 36 THEN CLOSE :
PRINT "No totals on file yet":
LINE INPUT "Enter return to continue :"; CHGFIELD$ : RETURN
9150 FOR I = 1 TO 36
9160 GET #1,I
9170 WORKTOT(I) = CVS(TEXPF$)
9180 NEXT I
9190 TOTAMT = 0   : J = 0
9200 LINE INPUT "Expense Selection  :";CHGFIELD$
9210 IF CHGFIELD$ <> "" THEN GOTO 9240
9220 IF J = 0 THEN CLOSE : RETURN
9230 GOTO 9290
9240 CHGFIELD = VAL(CHGFIELD$)
9250 IF CHGFIELD < 1 OR CHGFIELD > 36 THEN PRINT
"Invalid selection code": GOTO 9200
```

```
9260 TOTAMT = TOTAMT + WORKTOT(CHGFIELD)
9270 J = J + 1
9280 GOTO 9200
9290 PRINT "Total expense = " TOTAMT
9300 GOTO 9190
9310 REM ******************************************************************
9320 REM THIS SECTION WILL HANDLE THE TO DATE COMMAND FROM THE MAIN MENU   *
9330 REM ******************************************************************
9340 OPEN "R",#1,DISK$+"TOTALS.DAT",4
9350 FIELD #1,4 AS TEXPF$
9360 LINE INPUT "Output to screen (1) or printer (2)"; CHGFIELD$
9370 OUTTYPE$ = CHGFIELD$
9380 IF CHGFIELD$ <> "1" AND CHGFIELD$ <> "2" THEN GOTO 9360
9400 OPEN "O",#2,DISK$+"REPORT.FIL"
9410 PRINT #2," "
9420 FOR I = 1 TO 36
9430 GET #1,I
9440 PRINT #2,USING "##";I ;:PRINT #2,"-";
9450 PRINT #2,USING "\                    \";EXPDESC$(I) ;
9460 PRINT #2,USING "$$##,###.##";CVS(TEXPF$)
9490 NEXT I
9500 PRINT #2," " : PRINT #2," "
9505 CLOSE : GOSUB 2300    ' GO PRINT THE REPORT FILE
9510 IF OUTTYPE$ = "1" THEN LINE INPUT "Enter return to continue ";CHGFIELD$
9520 CLOSE
9530 LINE INPUT "Delete existing travel records (Y/N) :";CHGFIELD$
9540 IF CHGFIELD$ <> "Y" AND CHGFIELD$ <> "N" THEN GOTO 9530
9550 IF CHGFIELD$ = "N" THEN GOTO 9780
9560 OPEN "R",#3,DISK$+"NEWBILLS.DAT",107
9570 FIELD #3,4 AS NEXPCDF$,25 AS NPAYEEF$,
6 AS NDDATEF$,6 AS NPDATEF$,4 AS NAMTF$,
4 AS NPFLAGF$,4 AS NTFLAGF$,4 AS NCHKNBRF$,50 AS NCOMMF$
9580 OPEN "R",#1,DISK$+"BILLS.DAT",107
9590 FIELD #1,4 AS EXPCDF$,25 AS PAYEEF$,6 AS DDATEF$,
6 AS PDATEF$,4 AS AMTF$,4 AS PFLAGF$,
4 AS TFLAGF$,4 AS CHKNBRF$,50 AS COMMF$
9600 J = 0 : I = 0
9610 I = I + 1
9620 IF I > BILLCNT THEN GOTO 9760
9630 GET #1,I
9640 IF CVS(EXPCDF$) = 6 THEN GOTO 9610
9650 LSET NEXPCDF$   = EXPCDF$
9660 LSET NPAYEEF$   = PAYEEF$
9670 LSET NDDATEF$   = DDATEF$
9680 LSET NPDATEF$   = PDATEF$
9690 LSET NAMTF$     = AMTF$
9700 LSET NPFLAGF$   = PFLAGF$
9710 LSET NTFLAGF$   = TFLAGF$
9720 LSET NCHKNBRF$  = CHKNBRF$
9730 LSET NCCOMMF$   = CCOMMF$
9740 J = J + 1 : PUT #3,J
9750 GOTO 9610
9760 CLOSE : KILL DISK$+"BILLS.DAT" :
NAME DISK$+"NEWBILLS.DAT" AS DISK$+"BILLS.DAT"
9770 PRINT "Old file had " I-1 " bills.  New file has " J " bills"
9780 CLOSE : BILLCNT = J : GOSUB 2100
9790 LINE INPUT "Delete existing totals (Y/N) :"; CHGFIELD$
9800 IF CHGFIELD$ <> "Y" AND CHGFIELD$ <> "N" THEN GOTO 9790
9810 IF CHGFIELD$ = "Y" THEN
KILL DISK$+"TOTALS.DAT" : TOTLCNT = 0 : GOSUB 2100
9820 LINE INPUT "Change mileage rate (Y/N) :";CHGFIELD$
9830 IF CHGFIELD$ <> "Y" AND CHGFIELD$ <> "N" THEN GOTO 9820
9840 IF CHGFIELD$ = "Y" THEN KILL DISK$+"RATE.FIL" : GOSUB 1800
```

```
9850 CLOSE : RETURN
10000 REM THIS LINE IS HERE AS A COMMON
DELETE-THRU LINE NUMBER FOR CHAIN
```

PAYMENT5.BAS

```
3000 ON CHGFIELD GOSUB 2530,2530,2530,2530,2530,8710,
9310,9090,8300,6540,6540,6070,2192
3010 GOTO 2530
6070 REM ***********************************************************************
6080 REM THIS SECTION WILL TAKE CARE OF THE INQUIRY COMMAND FROM THE MAIN MENU*
6090 REM ***********************************************************************
6100 OPEN "R",#1,DISK$+"BILLS.DAT",107
6110 FIELD #1,4 AS EXPCDF$,25 AS PAYEEF$,6 AS DDATEF$,
6 AS PDATEF$,4 AS AMTF$,4 AS PFLAGF$,4 AS TFLAGF$,
4 AS CHKNBRF$,50 AS COMMF$
6120 LINE INPUT "Enter start date :";STARTDTE$
6130 IF STARTDTE$ = "" THEN CLOSE : RETURN
6140 LINE INPUT "Enter end date :";ENDDTE$
6150 LINE INPUT "Enter expense code :";TEXPCD$
6160 IF TEXPCD$ = "DONE" THEN GOTO 6120
6170 IF TEXPCD$ = "" THEN TEXPCD = 0 : GOTO 6190
6180 TEXPCD = VAL(TEXPCD$) : IF TEXPCD < 1 OR TEXPCD > 36 THEN GOTO 6150
6190 RECCNT = 0
6200 TSTARTDTE$ = MID$(STARTDTE$,5,2)+MID$(STARTDTE$,1,4)    ' YYMMDD FORMAT
6210 IF ENDDTE$ <> "" THEN TENDDTE$   = MID$(ENDDTE$,5,2)+MID$(ENDDTE$,1,4)
6220 FOR I = 1 TO BILLCNT
6230 GET #1,I
6240 TESTDATE$ = MID$(DDATEF$,5,2)+MID$(DDATEF$,1,4)
6250 IF TESTDATE$ < TSTARTDTE$ THEN GOTO 6310
6260 IF ENDDTE$ <> "" AND (TESTDATE$ > TENDDTE$) THEN GOTO 6310
6270 IF TEXPCD$ <> "" AND (CVS(EXPCDF$) <> TEXPCD) THEN GOTO 6310
6280 RECCNT = RECCNT + 1
6290 SORTKEY$(RECCNT) = TESTDATE$
6300 SORTREC(RECCNT) = I
6310 NEXT I
6320 IF RECCNT = 0 THEN PRINT "No records selected ": GOTO 6150
6330 GOSUB 830      ' GO SORT RECORDS BY DUE DATE
6340 K = 0
6350 FOR I = 1 TO RECCNT
6360 GET #1,SORTREC(I)
6370 FOR J = 1 TO 3 : PRINT : NEXT J
6380 PRINT "Expense Selection = " CVS(EXPCDF$) "- " EXPDESC$(CVS(EXPCDF$))
6385 EXPCD = CVS(EXPCDF$)
6390 IF EXPCD = 6 THEN PRINT "To where        = " PAYEEF$ : GOTO 6410
6400 PRINT "Payee           = " PAYEEF$
6410 PRINT "Due date        =
" MID$(DDATEF$,1,2) "/" MID$(DDATEF$,3,2) "/" MID$(DDATEF$,5,2)
6420 PRINT "Amount          = " CVS(AMTF$)
6430 IF EXPCD = 6 THEN PRINT
"Tolls           = " CVS(PFLAGF$) : GOTO 6490
6440 PRINT "Date paid       =
" MID$(PDATEF$,1,2) "/" MID$(PDATEF$,3,2) "/" MID$(PDATEF$,5,2)
6450 IF EXPCD = 6 THEN PRINT "Miles           = " CVS(CHKNBRF$) : GOTO 6490
6460 IF CHKNBRF$ = "CASH" THEN PRINT
"Check number    = " CHKNBRF$ : GOTO 6490
6470 IF CHKNBRF$ = "      " THEN PRINT "Check number    = " : GOTO 6490
6480 PRINT "Check number    = " CVS(CHKNBRF$)
6490 PRINT "Comment         = " COMMF$
6500 K = K + 12       ' TWELVE LINES PER PRINTED RECORD
```

```
6510 IF K MOD SCREENHEIGHT = 0 THEN
LINE INPUT "Enter return to continue :";CHGFIELD$
6520 NEXT I
6530 GOTO 6150
6540 REM ********************************************************************
6550 REM THIS SECTION WILL PRODUCE THE PAST DUE REPORT AND CASH REQUIREMENTS *
6560 REM REPORT REQUESTS FROM THE MAIN MENU                                  *
6570 REM ********************************************************************
6580 IF CHGFIELD$ = "6" THEN RPTTYPE$ = "1" : GOTO 6600
6590 RPTTYPE$ = "2"
6600 OPEN "R",#1,DISK$+"BILLS.DAT",107
6610 FIELD #1,4 AS EXPCDF$,25 AS PAYEEF$,6 AS DDATEF$,
6 AS PDATEF$,4 AS AMTF$,4 AS PFLAGF$,4 AS TFLAGF$,
4 AS CHKNBRF$,50 AS COMMF$
6620 LINE INPUT "Output to screen (1) or printer (2)"; CHGFIELD$
6630 OUTTYPE$ = CHGFIELD$
6640 IF CHGFIELD$ <> "1" AND CHGFIELD$ <> "2" THEN GOTO 6620
6660 OPEN "O",#2,DISK$+"REPORT.FIL"
6670 LINE INPUT "Enter due date :";STARTDTE$
6680 IF STARTDTE$ = "" THEN STARTDTE$ = CDATE$
6690 RECCNT = 0
6700 TSTARTDTE$ = MID$(STARTDTE$,5,2)+MID$(STARTDTE$,1,4)     ' YYMMDD FORMAT
6710 FOR I = 1 TO BILLCNT
6720 GET #1,I
6730 TESTDATE$ = MID$(DDATEF$,5,2)+MID$(DDATEF$,1,4)
6740 IF CVS(EXPCDF$) = 6 THEN GOTO 6810         ' IGNORE TRAVEL EXPENSES
6750 IF PDATEF$ <> "         " THEN GOTO 6810   ' IGNORE PAID BILLS
6760 IF RPTTYPE$ = "1" AND TESTDATE$ > TSTARTDTE$
THEN GOTO 6810 ' IGNORE BILLS NOT DUE YET
6770 IF RPTTYPE$ = "2" AND TSTARTDTE$ >= TESTDATE$
THEN GOTO 6810 ' IGNORE BILLS PAST DUE
6780 RECCNT = RECCNT + 1
6790 SORTKEY$(RECCNT) = TESTDATE$
6800 SORTREC(RECCNT) = I
6810 NEXT I
6820 IF RECCNT = 0 THEN PRINT "No records selected ": GOTO 7020
6830 GOSUB 830       ' GO SORT RECORDS BY DUE DATE
6840 TOTDUE = 0
6850 J = 0
6860 FOR I = 1 TO RECCNT
6870 GET #1,SORTREC(I)
6875 IF I = 1 OR I MOD 60 = 0 THEN PRINT #2,CHR$(12)     ' PUT OUT FORM FEED
6880 IF I = 1 OR I MOD 60 = 0 THEN PRINT #2,
"       Bill                Amount     Due Date          Comment       "
6890 IF I = 1 OR I MOD 60 = 0 THEN PRINT #2,
"----------------------- --------- -------- -----------------------------"
6900 PRINT #2,PAYEEF$ " ";
6910 PRINT #2,USING "$$##,###.##";CVS(AMTF$);
6920 PRINT #2," " MID$(DDATEF$,1,2) "/" MID$(DDATEF$,3,2)
"/" MID$(DDATEF$,5,2);
6930 PRINT #2," ";: PRINT #2,USING "\                      \";COMMF$
6940 TOTDUE = TOTDUE + CVS(AMTF$)
6950 J = J + 1
6980 NEXT I
6990 IF RPTTYPE$ = "1" THEN PRINT #2,"        Total past due = ";
:PRINT #2,USING "$$##,###.##";TOTDUE
7000 IF RPTTYPE$ = "2" THEN PRINT #2,
"    Total cash required = ";:PRINT #2,USING "$$##,###.##";TOTDUE
7010 PRINT #2," ":PRINT #2," " :CLOSE : GOSUB 2300
7020 IF CHGFIELD$ = "1" THEN LINE INPUT "Enter return to continue";CHGFIELD$
7030 CLOSE : RETURN
8300 REM ********************************************************************
8310 REM THIS SECTION WILL HANDLE THE BREAKDOWN REPORT REQUEST FROM THE      *
8320 REM MAIN MENU                                                           *
```

```
8330 REM ********************************************************************
8340 LINE INPUT "Report from Totals File (1) or
Transaction file (2) :";RPTFILE$
8350 IF RPTFILE$ <> "1" AND RPTFILE$ <> "2" THEN GOTO 8340
8360 IF RPTFILE$ = "2" THEN GOTO 8420
8370 OPEN "R",#1,DISK$+"TOTALS.DAT",4
8380 FIELD #1,4 AS TEXPF$
8390 IF TOTLCNT <> 36 THEN PRINT
"No totals file yet ":LINE INPUT "Enter return to continue :";CHGFIELD$ :
CLOSE : RETURN
8400 FOR I = 1 TO 36 : GET #1,I :MNTHTOT(I) = CVS(TEXPF$) : NEXT I
8410 GOTO 8440
8420 OPEN "R",#1,DISK$+"BILLS.DAT",107
8430 FIELD #1,4 AS EXPCDF$,25 AS PAYEEF$,6 AS DDATEF$,
6 AS PDATEF$,4 AS AMTF$,4 AS PFLAGF$,4 AS TFLAGF$,
4 AS CHKNBRF$,50 AS COMMF$
8440 LINE INPUT "Output to screen (1) or printer (2)"; CHGFIELD$
8450 OUTTYPE$ = CHGFIELD$
8460 IF CHGFIELD$ <> "1" AND CHGFIELD$ <> "2" THEN GOTO 8440
8480 OPEN "O",#2,DISK$+"REPORT.FIL"
8490 IF RPTFILE$ = "1" THEN GOTO 8690          ' WE HAVE DATA .. GO DO REPORT
8500 LINE INPUT "Enter starting date :";STARTDTE$
8510 IF STARTDTE$ = "" THEN GOTO 8500
8520 LINE INPUT "Enter ending date :";ENDDTE$
8530 IF ENDDTE$ = "" THEN GOTO 8520
8540 RECCNT = 0
8550 TSTARTDTE$ = MID$(STARTDTE$,5,2)+MID$(STARTDTE$,1,4)     ' YYMMDD FORMAT
8560 TENDDTE$ = MID$(ENDDTE$,5,2)+MID$(ENDDTE$,1,4)           ' YYMMDD FORMAT
8570 FOR I = 1 TO 36 : MNTHTOT(I) = 0 : NEXT I                ' ZERO MNTHLY TOTAL
8580 FOR I = 1 TO BILLCNT
8590 GET #1,I
8600 TESTDATE$ = MID$(DDATEF$,5,2)+MID$(DDATEF$,1,4)          ' YYMMDD FORMAT
8610 IF CVS(EXPCDF$) = 6        THEN GOTO 8670  ' IGNORE TRAVEL EXPENSES
8620 IF PDATEF$ = "      "      THEN GOTO 8670  ' IGNORE UNPAID BILLS
8630 IF TESTDATE$ < TSTARTDTE$  THEN GOTO 8670  ' IGNORE BILLS NOT DUE YET
8640 IF TESTDATE$ > TENDDTE$    THEN GOTO 8670  ' IGNORE BILLS USED EARLIER
8650 RECCNT = RECCNT + 1
8660 MNTHTOT(CVS(EXPCDF$)) = MNTHTOT(CVS(EXPCDF$)) + CVS(AMTF$)
8670 NEXT I
8680 IF RECCNT = 0 THEN PRINT "No records selected ": CLOSE :
LINE INPUT "Enter return to continue :";CHGFIELD$ : RETURN
8690 GOSUB 980                                  ' GO PRODUCE REPORT
8700 CLOSE : RETURN
10000 REM THIS LINE IS HERE AS A COMMON
DELETE-THRU LINE NUMBER FOR CHAIN
```

CHAPTER SEVEN

HOW MUCH DO I CHARGE?

One evening as she was correcting students' homework for her high school BASIC class, Megan received an unexpected telephone call. Would she be interested in teaching BASIC at a local computer store two evenings a week? Megan jumped at the opportunity. Later, as she was savoring this good news, she froze. What would she charge? She decided she would let the people at the computer store make an offer, and she would accept.

Ronald, the owner of the computer store, however, had held off calling at first because he had no idea how much Megan charged; so he didn't know whether he could afford to pay her. But he finally called, figuring she would charge a fair price.

See the problem?

What to charge is a fundamental question for any business. It means the difference between profit and loss as well as between just getting by and maximizing your profit. To complicate the question, personal computers are a new technology. Hardware, software, and service innovations keep prices fluctuating. There's no hard and fast schedule of costs, nor is there likely to be one.

If you're starting out in business, the last thing you probably know is how much to charge for doing work. You undoubtedly can pinpoint, very expertly, all the work involved in doing a job, and you can do the work very well. But pricing is something most people just haven't had to deal with before.

Charging shouldn't be a scary subject. It isn't difficult, but it can take some creativity. The purpose of charging is to offer an agreeable and equitable basis for compensating you for your work. The charge has to be fair to your customer *and you.*

Charging really consists of two different questions: how to charge and how much to charge. Once you've answered them, you will have fully defined your business.

In most cases you simply can follow the market's prices. *But you don't have to.* It is, after all, *your* business. A fresh approach to pricing your offer, different from the market's, can be all that's needed to make you successful.

BASIC WAYS TO CHARGE

Charges can be based on *anything.* There are, however, five basic ways to charge.

You can charge:

1. *Based on given costs.*   The given costs may be for goods you are reselling or for other people's services you are representing. You often can go into a meeting or advertise your offer with a price list for such items as PCs, *finished* programs, and supplies (e.g., disks, blank mailing labels, printer paper).
2. *By the hour.*   The time you work is the basis for your charge. You may encounter resistance to this method, especially when you meet a prospective customer for the first time. A client may be reluctant to pay by the hour, but not because he or she doesn't trust you to give an honest accounting of your time. Business people, by nature, are hesitant to agree to *any* open-ended obligation. If a customer agrees to pay you by the hour to develop a program, for example, how does he know how long it will take? He may think it will take only 40 hours, but with enhancements and problems, it may end up taking 3 weeks, and in that case he may have to pay more than he can afford for the project. If you do charge by the hour, it's a good idea in the early stages of a business relationship to set an upper limit on the amount you can be owed. As you approach this limit, you can tell your customer how much work remains and ask if he wishes to continue.

     On the other hand, do you really want to charge by the hour? At first, it may seem a very fair way to be paid. However, you should ask yourself a few questions. Do you work quickly? Does your speed at typing, or uptake of new material, or programming give you a competitive edge? If you're a genius at program design and can produce one in a quarter of the time it takes somebody else to do the same job, then you would be very foolish to charge by the hour since you would do yourself a serious injustice.

An hourly charge may be imposed with proposals. As you have seen, quite a bit of time and effort is necessary to prepare a proposal, and there's always the risk you will not get the work, so you will have toiled for nothing. To overcome this risk, a consultation charge may be imposed, in which case the prospective customer would agree to pay you an hourly fee from the time you begin talking at your first meeting. He or she would also agree to pay for any creative work done, such as developing program specifications. The fee is paid whether or not a prospect accepts the proposal. However, this is not a realistic approach in a standard business situation. This method usually isn't fair to the customer. Also, many potential customers are reluctant even to talk to anybody who charges such a fee. It may be done successfully, though, by someone who has a very high reputation in a field.

3. *Charge by the task.* A job may consist of many tasks. The amount of work necessary for each task will be about the same each time it is performed. A word processing service, for example, may charge by the page. The big job of preparing the entire manuscript consists of typing many pages. The time it takes to type a page generally will be the same, so the job's charge is figured by how many times the task must be repeated. A complex job, too, may consist of repeatable tasks. The direct mail service, for one, may be broken down into many tasks, such as printing envelopes, generating labels, attaching labels, and sealing envelopes.

4. *A fixed, scheduled fee.* A fixed, scheduled fee may be the basis of your charges when the time you will work cannot be anticipated, but you must be on call in the event you're needed. A software support service, for example, is likely to charge such a fee. If you offer such a service, you never know when a problem will occur, but you are always on duty and must be prepared to handle it. It's only fair to charge for the time when you're ready.

A fixed fee also may be charged when work cannot be defined in advance, but the customer wishes to schedule his or her costs. You may charge a fixed monthly fee, for example, to test programs. Some months you may test only one program and have a lot of free time, but other months you'll be testing into the early morning hours. In the end, it should balance out.

5. *A fixed price based on an estimate of work.* This approach is used for proposals. It puts a premium on your ability to estimate time and costs, but it's a method many business persons favor. A prospective customer can compare your estimate to others. In most cases, the lowest bid wins. (The exception would be when a considerable difference in quality exists between bidders.)

In many cases, the fairest way to charge is to combine ways. If you offer a company the service of locally supporting its PC software, for example, you might charge a monthly, fixed fee for being on call, add an additional hourly charge for the time needed to resolve a particular problem, and include the expense of traveling to the site of the problem.

Figuring out how to charge is so important that it alone can be the difference between going into a business or looking for another opportunity. When Maxine started her mail list business, for example, she faced a pricing problem that nearly did her in.

She planned to charge by combining ways. Some of her charges would be based on the cost of supplies (envelopes, paper, etc.) that she would resell. Her remaining charges would be hourly to reflect the work she actually did. But Maxine couldn't decide how to charge for running labels. It generally took only a few minutes to run them for a mailing; so if she charged by the time it took, she wouldn't make anything. Maxine was so puzzled she considered giving up because, more than anything else, she would be running labels.

Maxine hit on a creative solution. She would charge for her service of running off labels based on the cost of the labels. It struck her that her labor increased the value of *each* label. The charge realistically would correlate to the actual work being done, so it was fair to customers. Charging in this way meant she would make money on a mailing and justified going into the business.

You may have to do some serious thinking about *the business* of your business, too. In figuring out how to charge, don't worry about *how much* to charge. That's a separate question, which will be explored next.

PUTTING A PRICE TAG ON YOUR WORK

How you charge depends on how you define *units*. You may have decided to base your charges on *units* of *time*, or *materials*, or *tasks*. You now have to assign a price to each unit. Pricing, fortunately, isn't figured out in a vacuum. Your prices, to a large degree, are determined by three very real, down-to-earth facts. Your prices, specifically, are related to:

1. Your costs for goods or services
2. What other people already have been charging for the same or a similar offer
3. How much money your offer will save somebody

Your offer and how you have decided to charge will determine how the price will be computed. You will have to fill in the actual figure.

When you determine your price, you should play a few "what-if" games to see if your offer will be acceptable to a prospective customer at that price. On the other hand, can you increase your price and still have an appealing offer?

When you determine your final figure, avoid rounding off. Strangely enough, unrounded prices look more realistic and are more acceptable in most cases than rounded off ones. You might think a price tag of $4500.00 is more acceptable than one of $4501.99, but the latter, with change and all, looks "truer."

As you gain experience in your business, you will be able to refine the following pricing practices.

MARKING UP A COST

Marking up a cost is a practice that provides a profit by increasing the price above the cost. This pricing technique is familiar to most people. If you provide materials or the services of other people, you are entitled to an increase for your time and efforts in obtaining them, as well as for possibly tying up your own money in the interim. Since it's generally difficult to keep track of time and effort, a simple percentage of the original cost is computed to figure the profit.

As part of her programming service, for example, Susan supplies one of her customers with her code on three identical disks. Susan must pay $6.00 each for the disks. She is entitled to resell the disks at a higher price because she had to go to the store to buy them, decide on which ones to buy, and use her own money for the purchase. She marks the price up by 15 percent. Specifically, her profit on each disk is 15 percent (a standard for this type of resale) of the original cost. She adds the markup to the original cost and presents the total as the disk's cost to her customer.

Cost: $6.00

Profit: $6.00 × .15 = $ .90

Customer's charge: $6.00 + $ .90 = $6.90

Susan charges her customer $6.90 for each disk she supplies. She makes 90¢ on each one.

Related to this practice is the widely accepted assumption that the greater the value of goods or services you provide, the greater the value of your time and efforts. As a result, if you supply $10,000 worth of equipment to somebody, and it only takes you 5 minutes to do it, you're still entitled to (and should) charge your standard markup. If you usually mark up a cost 15 percent, your profit, in this case, is $1500, which you would add to the original cost in computing your charge. (Theoretically, your hourly rate then is $18,000, but don't put that on your resume if you ever have to apply for a job!)

This markup technique can be applied in nonlinear ways to pricing problems. Maxine, for example, used it to price the task of running labels. Here's how she did it.

She knew how much one standard roll of labels cost and how many labels were on it. Since she had to supply the labels from this roll, she marked up that cost by 15 percent. But that wasn't the end of it.

Maxine then asked herself how much would the labels increase in value if each one on the roll had a meaningful address printed on it. She decided— a bit arbitrarily—that it would be worth at least four times as much as the original cost. She computed how much she would charge if she had a job to print exactly one roll of labels. For her, that cost would be:

$$\left(\begin{array}{c}\text{Original}\\\text{cost of}\\\text{a roll}\end{array}\right) + \left(\begin{array}{c}\text{original}\\\text{cost of} \times 15\%\\\text{a roll}\end{array}\right) + \left(\begin{array}{c}\text{original}\\\text{cost of} \times 4\\\text{a roll}\end{array}\right) = \begin{array}{c}\text{charge}\\\text{per}\\\text{roll}\end{array}$$

Finally, she figured the price per label by dividing this charge by the number of labels in a roll:

$$\left(\begin{array}{c}\text{Charge}\\\text{per}\\\text{roll}\end{array}\right) \div \left(\begin{array}{c}\text{Number of}\\\text{labels per}\\\text{roll}\end{array}\right) = \begin{array}{c}\text{price}\\\text{per}\\\text{label}\end{array}$$

Knowing the price per label gave her the flexibility to charge for any size of mailing. She considered a few "what-if" cases by calculating charges for running off 100, 250, and 450 labels. Looking at the results, Maxine felt confident that a client would agree to her service at that price.

BECOMING AWARE OF WHAT OTHERS CHARGE

If your offer is based on your own skill, you have a different problem. You have to figure out what your skill is worth in dollars and cents. If you're presently using your skill in your job, a starting point for your price is your before-tax hourly wage or salary (which you can break down into an hourly wage for flexibility in computing charges). Your pay is, at minimum, what your services are worth.

You can raise your price because your pay excludes expenses you'll incur as a self-employed person. These expenses now are picked up by your company. Not reflected in your take-home pay are benefits (e.g., insurance coverage), equipment necessary for your work (e.g., a PC), planning (all the managers' salaries above you), time you're really not working on your job (or, looked at another way, your fee for being available for work), heat, lighting, water, and office space.

You, in fact, may not be paying for any of these expenses yourself. You may have a part-time business as a second job, in which case your benefits are paid by your company. You even may be staying after work at your company for your business. You still are entitled to increase your price because anyone who uses your service would have to pay these additional charges to someone else from outside the company. Your services could not be purchased at a cheaper price.

So much for theory. A specific price can be difficult to determine from a theoretical standpoint. To illustrate the difficulty, how much heat did you actually use for a specific job? It's impossible to tell.

You'll have to do some investigating to find out how much you can charge on the open market. You must determine what other people charge for the same type of offer.

If your manager hires outside temporary help to do a job like yours, you can tell the manager you're thinking about starting your own business and ask what the company pays for outside help. You should tell your manager about your intentions, otherwise it may be assumed you're looking for information to support a substantial raise at your next review. If your boss knows about your plans, he may be able to lead you to customers or even become one himself.

If your boss can't help, go to your personnel department, explain what you're thinking about doing, and ask if they can provide recent prices for outside help offering a similar service or product. If they can't provide the information, ask if they will direct you to someone in your company who can. There very likely will be somebody.

These suggestions for setting your prices won't help if you're not now working with the personal computer skill you want to use in your business. You may not even be working in a field remotely related to PCs. In fact, you may work in a tiny shop without a personnel department, where temporary help refers to anyone who hasn't been around for 10 years. How can you become aware of what other people charge?

You can call your competition and ask what they charge. It's amazing how much people will tell you. You, however, will have to be very truthful. You can say, "I'm interested in your offer. Can you tell me what you charge?" Or you can ask for a price list. It's dishonest to pretend to be a potential customer when you're not.

You may also call one or two people you think would be interested in your offer and simply ask what they would be willing to pay. They may give you valuable insight into your offer and might even invite you in to discuss becoming one of your customers.

If these direct approaches aren't suited to you, you can check the newspaper help wanted ads to see how much companies are willing to pay for your skills. Libraries usually save back issues, so you don't have to wait for an ad to appear. Check the papers in nearby areas, too. This will give you a starting price that you can mark up (add at least 25 percent to the company's advertised offer). If you can't find relevant ads, ask your librarian for help. Most libraries offer career materials and references that show what people earn.

Your local computer store will answer many questions, or can direct you to someone who can help. You also might call a placement officer at a local college.

To become aware of what price other people charge, you simply have to ask questions.

BASING A PRICE ON SAVINGS

If you start an innovative business, you will be unable to find comparative prices. Your business, however, will be directed at an already existing cost you can use to help you set your price. The innovative software testing business, for example, is directed at companies that presently use programmers to do testing. You will not find any comparative prices for similar services. The price you charge, however, can be based on what programmers charge. Your price will be a fraction of a programmer's salary and, as such, very attractive to most companies.

In this manner you can find salaries and costs on which to base your price.

FIGURING WHAT THE MARKET WILL BEAR

A special pricing problem occurs when your offer saves someone a lot more than it costs you for the offer. In this case, you can charge whatever you like and reap large profits—as long as somebody will buy.

Melanie, for example, developed a series of programs for a lawyer, who paid her for her work, but did not care about the rights to the software. She contacted another lawyer and realized that the same programs she already had developed needed only a bit of work to satisfy his needs. She wondered what price she should charge for the software. If she based her charge on the time she spent making the modifications, the second lawyer would get a lot of software for free. On the other hand, if she charged the second lawyer the same price as the first, she would be paid twice for the same work.

Melanie decided to charge the two lawyers the same price when she realized that the second one couldn't get software to do all he wanted at a cheaper price—he would have to pay somebody else to start from scratch. The price she offered was acceptable, and the lawyer was happy to get the software a lot sooner than he expected.

That wasn't the end of it. Melanie realized that with a few adjustments she could create a generalized series of programs suitable to any lawyer's needs. She made the set of programs available on five disks. Her costs to produce a package were inconsequential—the time she spent copying the programs from the master disks and the cost of the disks. She advertised the software at the same price she charged the original lawyer. Many lawyers bought packages, and she earned large profits from her previous work.

You may think that eventually competition will move into the field and that the price for the software naturally will go down, right? Wrong. The *last* thing the competition will tamper with is price—competitors will want to make the same large profits as Melanie. The competition, consequently, will try to distinguish itself by offering new features and enhancements. Only when these new capabilities become marginal will companies begin to lower prices to gain a share of the market.

PRICING FLEXIBILITY

A single price usually cannot be set for an offer. An offer often consists of doing many different kinds of work, each with a different value. Steve, for example, started a computerized bookkeeping service. One customer wanted him to create five programs and then run them each month. Steve faced a pricing problem until he became flexible on his pricing. Though he did all the work himself, he charged one price for the programming, and another, much lower one, for the monthly service. Though you may decide to charge by the hour, the price you charge for an hour of your time very well may vary, too.

This pricing flexibility can work in your favor. The value of your offer increases each time you provide an additional service or supply material, and you, correspondingly, increase your price. Ken, for instance, has decided to test software. He is figuring his price based on using somebody else's personal computer to run the programs. If he has to use his own computer, the value of his service will increase, and so will the price he intends to charge.

PRICING A PROPOSAL

When you prepare a proposal, you may have to use many of these practices to come up with a total price for the work you deliver. Three different parts of your proposed offer must be priced:

1. Your labor, i.e., the effort you must put in to complete the work
2. Materials, supplies, expenses, and outside labor, i.e., the effort others must put in for the project
3. Sales calls and proposal preparation

In approaching a project, you will break a job down into tasks and figure the time necessary to do each one. To figure pricing, begin by making a list of each task and the time you estimate it will take to do it.

Decide which tasks on the list other people will do and which ones you'll do. Call the people you want to do the work, verify your time estimates with them, and ask for their prices. Tabulate on your price computation list the costs for the tasks others will do (time × price), your markup by task, the markup *price* by task, and the total charge. Your list will look something like this:

Task	Time	Price	Task Cost	Markup	Markup Price	Charge (Cost + Markup)
Write assignment program	40 h	$40/h	$1600	15%	$240	$1840

You will do the remaining tasks yourself. Assign your prices to these tasks. The prices may vary depending on the level of skill required to do each one. Do not markup these prices. Put the cost for the work (your price × time) directly in the charge column:

Task	Time	Price	Task Cost	Markup	Markup Price	Charge (Cost + Markup)
Specification assignment program	10 h	$45/h				$450

At the bottom of your list add two more tasks: sales calls and proposal preparation. Both are part of your work and you should be paid for doing them. Figure out the time you already have spent on them and estimate how much more you will need. Assign each task a price (how much is your time worth?), and compute the charge.

On another sheet, list the supplies and materials you will need for the project. Determine the exact cost for each item and add your markup.

Finally, list your anticipated expenses, such as local travel to and from the job, parking fees, train fares, and meals. If long-distance travel or over-night stays are required for the job, you will have to find out in your meeting how the prospective customer intends to pay for these expenses. Some will reimburse you on presentation of receipts. Some will give you daily allot-ments to spend as you see fit. In both cases you will have to add a note to your proposal under Terms stating this relationship, e.g., "All overnight accommodations and long-distance travel expenses will be paid by (company name)." For the remaining companies, you will have to estimate your expenses.

Total the charges for supplies, materials, and, if necessary, expenses. Add the result to your charges.

By adding up all the charges, you will have the project's total price. Before you finalize it, play with the figure. Figure out what the client will be paying per hour for the work. Is it reasonable? Does it look too low? If so, increase your markup for outside help, your prices for sales calls and proposal preparation, and price for your own time to do the work. Figure out how much you actually will make on the job. Is it enough to make the effort worthwhile? Should you substantially increase your charges? Finally, ask yourself if you can defend the price. If you can, you're finished.

On your proposal, show only your total price for the project. Never show how you came up with that figure. Too many questions can be raised about why you set one markup for one person's services and a different one for another, as well as many similar ones. If your client has questions, consult your notes.

WHEN TO VARY WHAT YOU CHARGE

The practices presented so far will help you define your basic charges, but you may want to vary them at times.

You can increase your prices if a customer needs your work in a hurry. You estimate you can complete a job in 2 months, but your customer says he needs it in 1 month. To meet her requirements, you may need to put off other clients, miss calling on a prospect, or hire somebody to help do the work. You're entitled to charge a premium for these sacrifices.

You also can increase your prices if you have to work on a holiday, or during unusual hours or conditions. You may offer a service, for example, to support software from 9 to 6. If a prospect wants support for an evening shift (6 to midnight), you should charge a higher price. It's only fair. Your life must be restructured for your customer's convenience so you should be reimbursed.

You should consider *decreasing* your prices if you can pinpoint losing or missing business due to high prices. In a market prone to technological changes, it's easy to be caught off guard by lower prices. Dramatically less expensive technologies may have become available since you originally figured your prices, and you failed to adjust. Ability to adjust in this situation will give you a competitive edge over older, established businesses that have based their prices on paying for older, higher-priced computers.

A price reduction can be traded for a benefit. For example, Bob developed a BASIC program for a group of dentists. They liked the results and asked him to do a year's worth of work. In exchange, they expected a lowered hourly rate and Bob agreed. Why? The long-term commitment saved Bob from making other sales calls, some of which were bound to be a waste of time. Each time he did another program, Bob would know his subject better so the time necessary for him to begin working would be less though his charges would still reflect the research time. Bob also gained the benefit of a steady cash flow that enabled him to quit his job and go into business full time.

Your prices also may be lowered to gain an advantage over your competition. For instance, you may lower prices when you start out in business to develop referrals that can be very valuable to you in gaining new customers.

Because there are many advantages to you in long-term contracts, you can try to induce one by structuring your prices. A direct mail business, for example, can charge different prices to handle daily, weekly, monthly, and as-required mailings. The cheapest rate would be for a mailing every day. Work can be scheduled in advance and time can be used productively in this case. The most expensive rate would be for "as-required" mailing that could happen at any time, causing you to drop whatever you're doing.

You may give discounts on materials and supplies to induce large purchases. You won't make as much per unit, but you should sell more units with less sales calls.

You, finally, can raise or lower your prices whenever you want. It's your business. Jason proposed to develop a sophisticated stock analysis program for $9000. When he presented the proposal, his prospect told him he was impressed with the plan, but he had only $6000 for the project. They negotiated and settled on a price of $6700, but Jason would retain the software rights. Apparently, Jason was losing $1300, but was he really? First, he now would be paid for researching the proposal, which had taken a lot of time. Nearly all the project's price was based on Jason's labor, so he really was only lowering his price. He also now could try to resell the program, and, as well, he was free to work on other projects. Jason completed the job in 6 weeks and pocketed $6700 that he would have missed had he rigidly stuck to his price.

ARE YOU IN BUSINESS?

You now have the information you need to answer the most important question you can pose before you start your own business: Can you make a profit?

Every business, as you've seen, has expenses. To make a profit, you have to earn more than your expenses. Can you do it? Is the amount worth the effort?

In making your decision, distinguish between "real" expenses and tax writeoffs. Jim conducts a part-time programming business from his home. His real expenses include the cost of his supplies. His PC and peripherals really aren't expenses because he bought them before he had any idea he would go into business. However, he can take them as tax deductions. He also has writeoffs for the portion of his home bills he attributes to his business for heat, water, and electricity—all of which would be used whether or not he had a business.

Estimate your expenses for a year. The easiest way to do this is to estimate expenses for 1 month, which is easy to do, and multiply that result by 12 for a year's total. Estimate how much you realistically can expect to make in a year from your business. Compare your expenses and your business income. Do you have a profit or a loss?

You may show a loss. The difference between a profit and a loss in some cases can be considered an investment. Many businesses show losses for their first years, but show increasing profits after that. In the beginning, there are start-up costs for buying equipment, supplies, office furniture, and for announcing your offer, but these expenses certainly won't reoccur every month. Similarly, in the beginning there is no customer base, so a lot of "free" time must be spent making sales calls just to get going.

Many people start their businesses as second jobs to help them through these early stages. As their customer bases grow and their expenses decrease, they find they can turn a part-time business into a full-time career. Other people dive right into a full-time business and live off their savings. Still others ask investors to put up venture capital to back their businesses.

As you decide whether or not you can afford to start your business, don't let early losses scare you off. Look ahead, and try to see if you'll be able to stand on your own two feet in your business in the not too distant future.

SCHEDULING PAYMENTS

Once you and a customer agree on the scope of work to be done and the price to be paid, you still have to agree on how payments for that work are to be made. Scheduling of payments is an integral part of your agreement or proposal.

For a long-term, ongoing contract, payments usually are made on a calendar basis, such as monthly or bimonthly. This payment period normally isn't less than a month because businesses, as a rule, pay all their ongoing expenses only once a month.

For a one-time transaction (for developing a program or buying hardware, for instance), you have choices. You can ask for cash on delivery, in which case payment is made when you deliver materials or complete a service. While you may want cash on delivery, companies won't. Most companies have billing procedures that take 30, 60, or even 90 days. There really is no reason for a company delaying your payment this long, but, unfortunately, it is an accepted business practice.

You always run the risk that after you've done all your work, you won't be paid at all. You can reduce this risk significantly by scheduling payments for portions of the total price as work is completed. In this case, your customer okays or accepts your work to a predetermined point before authorizing the partial payment. Your customer may appraise your progress and, if necessary, redirect your work (in which case, you reestimate your prices). Your customer pays only for acceptable work that has been done. You gain a sizable reduction in the risk you have to assume. Instead of risking no payment for a total job, you stand to lose, at most, payment for only one stage. If the first payment is made, you proceed to the next step. If it's not, you stop doing the work.

Janet, who proposed to develop a payroll program (see Chap. 5), took this partial payments approach. In her proposal she specified her total price for the work and then scheduled payments by steps for: acceptance of detailed specification, prototype, and tested program. The actual cost for developing the prototype was much larger than for testing, but the payments were made equal. Figure 7-1, which you can use as a model for developing your own partial payments schedules, shows exactly what Janet inserted in her proposal for price.

INVOICING

Whenever you deliver work, either in final form or for a partial payment, you need to bring along an invoice that shows how much you expect to be paid. Your customers will use your invoices for their records. In many companies, duplicates or even triplicates are required. Your customer may sign your invoice on work acceptance and send it with any required paperwork to the Accounts Payable Department, where it will be processed and a check

PRICE

The cost of this project is $3,405.75.

Payments for this work are to be made according to the following schedule:

Acceptance of detailed specifications	$1,135.25
Acceptance of workable prototype	$1,135.25
Acceptance of tested program	$1,135.25

Payments are to be made within 30 days.

Fig. 7-1   Partial payments schedule (proposal insert).

sent to you. If you're dealing with a small company or individual, your customer may take your invoice and hand you a check.

An invoice shows:

1. Billing date, i.e., the date when you deliver the invoice
2. Who you are, or who the check is to be made out to
3. Who you are invoicing
4. A description of work done
5. How much that work costs
6. Optionally, a reference number you can use to readily find the invoice

Blank invoices, suitable for most businesses, are available in any office supply store, but you don't need a printed form. You can type an invoice yourself as long as you show all the required information. Figure 7-2 shows an invoice you can use to model your own. If you type your own, always be sure to make a copy for your own records.

If your customer has agreed to pay your expenses, you should submit receipts or other verification.

When you receive your first payment check, you will feel very proud. You will have gone the distance in your business. You will have begun to *really* make money with a personal computer.

```
INVOICE

                              December 1, 1984.

TO:    Dr. John Velspar
       240 Main St.
       Stratford, Ct. 06497

FROM:  Jack Johnson
       829 Feldcrest Ave.
       New York, N.Y. 10020


DESCRIPTION OF WORK                    COST
BOOKKEEPING PROGRAM                 $1,200.00
DATA ENTRY                             425.00
STAFF TRAINING                         300.00
                        TOTAL:      $1,925.00
```

Fig. 7-2 An invoice.

Pricing has befuddled many businesses. A person may have a brilliant idea for a business but have the wrong method of charging and fail, or avoid the business altogether because it appears unprofitable. With a thorough understanding of your own costs, an awareness of the market, and creativity, you will overcome these hurdles and prosper.

CHAPTER
EIGHT
PROFITS ON
THE BOOKS:
AN ACCOUNTS
RECEIVABLE
PROGRAM

When you send out your invoice, you Aren't Rich yet. You still have to collect your money. A/R really isn't the abbreviation for Aren't Rich yet, but it could be. An A/R or Accounts Receivable Program is designed to help you collect what you're owed.

WHY YOU NEED AN A/R PROGRAM

As more and more invoices are sent, it's easy to lose track of what you're owed. You'll be so busy doing new work and making sales calls, you won't have time to stay on top of payments coming in. There's the danger that you could do a lot of work and never make much money because you fail to collect what's due. If you pay for materials, you will lose money when you fail to collect. In fact, if you do enough business without collecting, you really could go into a hole.

Ken, who operated a job shop, ran into another problem. His timing on collecting bills and doing new business was off. He was owed over $40,000.00, but he had to declare bankruptcy because he couldn't collect on time to meet his own debts.

An A/R Program will make you aware of where you stand with your customers. Well-organized reports will show you who owes you money, how much is owed, and when the debt was incurred. An A/R Program makes it easy to keep track of your "receivables"—and that's why it's so important.

Your customers also are just as busy as you are. It's easy for them to forget who and how much they owe. An A/R Program solves this problem by automatically printing monthly statements that can be mailed to customers. As another aid, your A/R Program can print labels for the envelopes.

In your business you may not send out invoices. Even so, you will still need an A/R Program to help you keep track of the money you make. Payments may be made in cash, for example, in which case you'll need to record as easily as possible how much you made each day. You also need to know how much you made each month and for the year as a whole. An A/R Program can help you do that, as well. Such a program also can be used to stay on top of customer layaway plans and charges.

Your two bookkeeping programs (A/R and A/P) will tell you whether or not your business is making any money at all. Specifically, your total income, which you determine with your A/R Program, minus your total expenses (determined with your A/P Program) will show if you have a profit or a loss:

$$
\begin{array}{r}
\text{Total income as of date X} \\
- \ \underline{\text{Total expenses as of date X}} \\
\text{Profit (or loss) as of date X}
\end{array}
$$

Date X can be any day, but it's usually the last day of a month, quarter, or year. Any profit you may have made in a year is of interest to somebody else, too—the people at the Internal Revenue Service. You'll need income information to figure out federal, state, and local taxes. A good A/R Program can give you a comprehensive view of your accounts so the IRS won't haunt you if you're audited.

An A/R Program, ironically, also can help improve your customer relations. It can make you confident you will be on top of what you're owed. You won't be inclined to pester and alienate customers for payments only a few days after you send a bill, nor will you feel you can accept business only on a COD basis.

HOW YOUR A/R PROGRAM MAKES MONEY

If you're already in business, or if you're just starting your own business, your A/R and A/P Programs will let you handle your books yourself without spending a lot of time, so you'll be free for your main business.

You'll save money because you won't have to pay someone else for bookkeeping. You'll make money by getting all the tax deductions you're entitled to and collecting all the money you're owed. The reports, also, will give you a greater insight into your business than you could ever hope for from keeping records by hand.

You'll use your A/R and A/P Programs to complete your tax forms. With the information these programs provide, you'll be able to complete your tax forms quickly and accurately.

Your programs can be as valuable to others as they are to you, as well.

One person who needs help with bookkeeping is the small business person. He has to be a Jack-of-all-trades. He has to do his work, keep customers happy, call on prospects, maybe visit his family now and then, and—oh, yes, keep his own books, which is the last thing he wants to do. So, the books usually are done late at night, when he's tired and prone to mistakes. Just sending out invoices is a major chore. Typing up monthly statements is a nightmare. All those other things he should do—such as figuring out who is overdue in paying him—are just impossible. So, the small business loses.

Personal computer manufacturers have focused sales efforts on big companies, and have virtually ignored small businesses. If a small business wants to buy a personal computer, it has to seek the manufacturer out. The manufacturers are not going out of their way to sell to small businesses. Also, most owners of small businesses are inexperienced with computers and wary of committing their businesses to machines they don't feel comfortable operating. Very few have even taken the time to make themselves aware of benefits personal computers offer. How could they? They don't have the time.

You can help these people. Your *Programs For Profit* A/P Program and A/R Program enable you to offer a basic bookkeeping service for small businesses.

As you define your markets, you should not overemphasize *small*. True, your programs won't handle General Motors' bookkeeping, but your A/R Program is designed to store over 3500 invoices on a single disk. If you use one disk for each customer, that's about 10 invoices a day for a year. You, of course, can use more than one disk for each customer.

Markets include advertising agencies, air conditioning contractors, aluminum siding businesses, television repair services, architects, builders, artists, bakers, beauty salons, remodelers, cleaners, carpet installers and cleaners, small manufacturers, burglar alarm sales and installation services, painters, plumbers, diners, rubbish removal services, trailer renting and leasing services, upholsterers, and on and on.

You also can service retail stores because your A/R Program can keep records of daily income, layaways, and charges. These markets include doctors, dentists, boutiques, stores for men's and women's wear, and sporting goods shops.

Go through your telephone directory Yellow Pages and your library's business directories to find other markets in your area.

Focus your efforts on one or two markets. You will find that each business has its own jargon. By concentrating on a market, you'll pick up its language. You will sound experienced in the field and talking to prospective customers and closing deals will be easier. A person also will feel more comfortable signing up for your service if she knows you've already done work for other people in *her* line of work.

If you don't know where to begin, start by placing a general ad in the newspaper and see what business you pick up. An example of such an ad, which you can use as a model for your own, is shown in Fig. 8-1.

When you have singled out a market, you can direct a mail campaign at it to introduce your offer. An example of a letter you can send is shown in Fig. 8-2. The introductory offer referred to in the letter is a discount on the price of your service for 2 months. The reduced price will attract buyers and give you the chance to show how valuable your service can be in a real, workaday situation. You'll be giving up profits, but you'll be gaining on-the-job training, learning the market's language, and building a list of references. Once you've built a customer base, drop your introductory offer and instead mention in your letter that you specialize in the market.

To prepare for a meeting with a prospective customer, print realistic and extensive reports that show exactly what you offer. Use names in your reports that sound real. Explain to your prospects the benefits of your service. When they see what your A/R and A/P Programs can do for them, they will want your help.

```
          BOOKKEEPING SERVICE
      – Computerized To Save You Money –
         Accurate, Timely Information
  Call: Fred Grant, 555-5555 between 9 and 8:30
```

Fig. 8-1 An advertisement for a bookkeeping service.

You may encounter prospects who will want you to take over *more* of their bookkeeping tasks. They may want you to handle their payroll and general ledger, too. If anyone wants you to start by taking over everything—and no sensible person should—you should point out that it will be wiser to begin with a trial. If all goes well, and you fully expect it will, more of the bookkeeping can be computerized. You also will need the trial to see if this business is right for you. If you decide it is, you can ask to take over other bookkeeping chores. You then will collect data about your customers' payroll and look for a suitable application program.

You very likely will not be starting to keep records on the first day of a new year, so you'll have to become acquainted with the old bookkeeping system and figure out what already has occurred in the year. You may have to go back years to find all open invoices. To get started, consequently, you may have to type a lot of data and spend a lot of time. Don't charge an enormous initial fee for this service, since it may frighten off a prospect. Once you have a customer's data in the program, he or she will use your service for quite awhile. So, spread the initial data entry fee over several months.

KEEPING BUSINESS RECORDS

Whether you'll be keeping somebody else's books or your own, you will need to know how income records are kept. They may be kept in many dif-

February 18, 1984

566 Jackson Heights
Bayview, Alabama 36541
(205) 555-5555

Mr. Ernie Bomway
331 Arnststern Blvd.
Clarksville, Alabama 36543

Dear Mr. Bomway,

Bookkeeping is tricky. Spend too much time on your books and you'll lose customers. Spend too little and you'll lose your business.

An inexpensive bookkeeping service can make this problem disappear.

I offer a service that uses a personal computer, so my price is far less than what others charge who still work by hand. My service also can give you information others simply can't. Whenever you like, for example, I'll give you a report that shows how much money is owed you, starting with the customer who owes you the most. Right next to every customer's name and balance is his telephone number so you can get right on the phone and call him.

You'll gain all the benefits computers can offer you, but you won't have to use one yourself.

If you would like to discuss this bookkeeping service and a special introductory offer, please call me at 555-5555.

Very truly,

Your Name

Fig. 8-2 A direct mail letter for a bookkeeping service.

ferent ways. Your A/R Program is designed for basic methods suitable to most businesses.

Keeping records for income is simplest with cash transactions, in which case service is rendered or goods delivered and cash is handed over immediately. Restaurants, diners, delis, drugstores, grocery stores, gas stations, office supply stores, and many others conduct business in this way. Throughout the day, sales are rung up on a cash register. At day's end, the register tape is totaled. To keep books for this type of business, you only need to record the daily totals, which constitute the business income.

Other types of income may be recorded in a similar way. Royalties, for example, are sent out by companies to patent holders, authors, designers, programmers, etc. These royalties, which are income, are recorded as they arrive.

Record keeping becomes more involved when payments are not made immediately and bills are used. A dentist, for example, may be asked to bill a family at the end of a month during which children come in at various times for work. The family could pay the dentist after each visit, but it's easier to make one or more payments each month. A woman may buy four dresses from a store, but instead of paying cash, she opens a charge account. A man may buy an air conditioner on a layaway plan and pay a proportion of the total price each month. A consultant, finally, may deliver a computer program and documentation to a company, which requires time to process the invoice and issue a check for payment.

In these cases, records for income as well as for who owes money and how much is owed often are kept with a ledger book and two boxes. One box contains all invoices, some of which are marked "paid." The other box, called the Customer File, contains index cards with information about customers. Specifically, on a card is a customer's name, address, telephone number, and balance. Transactions (either a new bill for goods and/or services, or a payment) are listed in the ledger book (see Fig. 8-3).

The Customer File also shows how much you're owed, which is your Accounts Receivable. The ledger book contains figures for determining income. Specifically, the payments are totaled. The invoice box provides detailed documentation about the transactions should any questions about a specific invoice arise.

The amount of unpaid bills in the ledger book, when added, *should* equal the Accounts Receivable amount as shown in the Customer File. They often don't. The difference may be due to a copying or mathematical error, or any number of other clerical problems, which are understandable when you consider what has to be done to maintain these books.

Before a payment check is cashed, the business person should record the

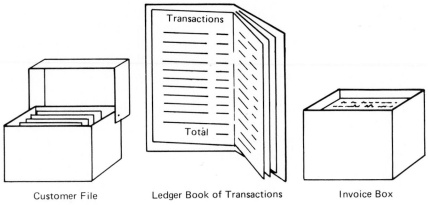

Customer File   Ledger Book of Transactions   Invoice Box

Fig. 8-3 Transactions.

amount in the ledger book. He or she should go into the invoice box, find the invoice that's being paid, and mark it "paid." Finally, he or she should open the Customer File, pull the customer's card, cross off the old balance and write in the new one. Sounds like a great way to spend an evening after a full day's work, doesn't it? No wonder the businessman or woman can only shrug when asked what a present Accounts Receivable total is. Who wants to take the time to add it all up?

Businesses often send out monthly statements, or reminders, in the hope of collecting money. Someone must sit down with the Customer File in this case and type (or write by hand) on a preprinted statement form the customer's name, address, and present balance. (The bookkeeping term for this type of statement is *Balance Forward.*) If the person doing the billing wants to spend even more time, he can open his ledger book and write on the statements all the customer's transactions that have occurred in the billing period. (This type of statement is called *Open Item.*) All the envelopes then have to be addressed.

Your A/R Program *dramatically* simplifies this work by removing the tedious chores of copying entries, performing calculations, and preparing statements. Your A/R Program also significantly increases the value of your income information with meaningful reports.

With your A/R Program, you'll record transactions in a Transaction File stored on disk, instead of in a ledger book. Your Customer File will be on the same disk. You'll still need to keep the invoice box for detailed documentation about transactions.

You'll first set up a Customer File that contains a "card" for each customer by responding to prompts for the customer's name, telephone number, and address (see Fig. 8-4). Though the customer's balance will be on the card, you don't have to worry about it because your A/R Program will handle it automatically. When a bill is made out or a payment received, you'll record it in the Transaction File.

That's really all you have to do, and that's even simpler than you think because so much has been computerized to save you work and prevent errors. When you enter an invoice, the amount that customer owes is automatically increased. When a payment is applied to an invoice, the customer's balance is reduced automatically. If you receive payment for an invoice's full amount, you can press the carriage return and the figure will be entered for you, saving you retyping. If you send out an invoice on the same day you record it, you can press the carriage return and that date will be recorded. To help you send out your invoices, the program prints labels, as well. You'll find many more helpful features as you begin to use this program yourself.

A single command is used to prepare all your monthly statements *and* mailing labels. The statements are set up to allow you to impose finance charges for late payments.

Another command generates a report that shows for the month and so far into the year total cash and total payments. Outstanding receivables also are shown. This report alone will save hours of computational time.

A Detailed Month End Report also can be printed. This report very

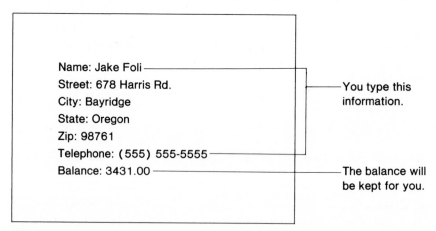

Fig. 8-4 A customer's card.

neatly shows each invoice for which payment was received during the month and how much of the bill was paid. All of a customer's transactions are shown together, so the business in many ways becomes more visible than ever before. It would be far too time-consuming to attempt to prepare this report by hand.

Another report can be generated that lists customers by the amount they owe you. The customer who owes you the most is at the top of the list. Next to each customer's name is his or her telephone number so you can call to collect overdue money.

An Old Debt capability helps you to determine overdue invoices. This capability also can be used to quickly remove invoices for which you have no hope of ever being paid so your A/R balance can reflect your receivables realistically.

All the companies and customers with which business is done also can be listed. *All* unpaid invoices can be listed, a capability which lets you easily convert to another program if you should ever wish to do so.

Your A/R Program provides an online historical file of *all* transactions so you can track down information in a hurry. This capability enables the program to show you:

- Exactly how much any customer owes you and how much he or she already has paid you
- Information about any invoice, open *or* closed
- All invoices paid by a single company check

Safety checks, finally, have been built into the program to prevent errors from being introduced. Your A/R Program, for example, will not allow an invoice with an unpaid balance to be deleted unless the balance is zero or the invoice declared a bad debt.

OPERATING YOUR A/R PROGRAM

Your A/R Program allows you to keep accurate and up-to-date A/R records with minimum time and effort. Meaningful reports can be generated that allow captured information to be fully used.

Though your A/R Program allows you to keep track of invoices and cash simultaneously, you do not need to record both. You may record only invoices, or only cash, depending on what's appropriate to the business.

Each client's records must be stored on a separate disk. The disk cover should be labeled with: the client's name and telephone number; the earliest date recorded and, when the disk is full, the last date; the client's customers' names and their IDs; the reports the client wants; and what type of cash is recorded in item 1 and item 2, if you use either one.

Each disk will store about 3500 records. More than one disk can be used for a single year.

When you access your A/R Program, you may:

- Set up on a disk "cards" that name and, optionally, record other information about customers you'll be invoicing
- Record invoices and print mailing labels
- Record cash or invoice payments
- Change information
- Delete information
- List invoices to pick out overdue ones and bad debts
- Print Monthly Statements
- Prepare Month End and Descending Balances Reports
- Perform a year end procedure so records for a new year can be kept
- List companies
- List all open invoices
- Make inquiries

If you'll be using your A/R Program for your own business, try to record an invoice when you're preparing to send it out—you'll save time because the program will print a mailing label. *Be sure to keep a copy of your invoice for reference about details.* Try to record a payment when it's received so your information will be up to date. If you'll be using your A/R Program in a bookkeeping service, all information for a client can be recorded once or twice a month.

Each month you'll print Month End Reports for the previous month and, if you wish, Monthly Statements. At any time you may print a Descending Balances Report and make inquiries into your records.

At the beginning of a new year, you'll print bad debts. You'll also perform a year end procedure that moves your open invoices into the new year and closes the book on the old year.

At income tax time, you'll use the A/R Program December Month End Report Summary and your A/P Program records to prepare your taxes.

The procedures for these tasks are presented in detail with the appropriate commands. At this chapter's end, a schedule for applying the commands is provided.

ACCESSING THE A/R PROGRAM

To access your A/R Program, type **RUN INCOME** in response to your system prompt:

A: **RUN INCOME**

The A/R Program will be loaded and you will be prompted:

ENTER THE CURRENT DATE AS MMDDYY:

Type the date. Your response sets the date for the session. If you type it wrong, exit the program, access it again, and set it correctly.

You will be shown the menu of A/R Program commands:

```
* * * * * * * * * * * * * * * * * * * * * * * * * * * * * * * * * * * * * * * * * *
                      Accounts Receivable Program

                      Available commands are:

            1 – Cards          2 – Billing
            3 – Payments       4 – Change
            5 – Delete         6 – Old Debt
            7 – Month End      8 – Descending balances
            9 – Inquiry       10 – Companies
           11 – Open          12 – Year end
           13 – Statements    14 – EXIT
* * * * * * * * * * * * * * * * * * * * * * * * * * * * * * * * * * * * * * * * * *
```

The following descriptions provide all you will need to know to use these commands effectively.

NOTE:

Your A/R Program is too large to be loaded as a single unit. Consequently, the program has been split into eight programs (see the program list under "Accounts Receivable Program Source Code" at the end of this chapter). When you first request (access) a command, the appropriate program will be loaded. If, for example, you first use command 6, the INCOME4.BAS program is loaded. If you should then use command 1, the INCOME1.BAS program will be loaded automatically as a replacement. You should not experience *any* delay.

This separation of programs is organized around functions for programming clarity. Each of the INCOME programs includes all of the functions needed to perform all aspects of its corresponding command(s).

SETTING UP COMPANY CARDS

If bills, charges, or invoices are used by a business, you'll have to set up company cards on your disk. If these devices are not used, cards will not be set up and you can proceed directly to the PAYMENTS command.

NOTE:

In all remaining descriptions of A/R Program procedures, bills, charges, and invoices are referred to simply as invoices.

The A/R Program will prompt you for this card information. You only need to enter a company's name. If you wish to use the Descending Balances Report, you also will have to enter the company's telephone number. If you set up two or more accounts for the same company, you also should define a customer's name for each account. The remaining information will be used for mailing labels. If you do not intend to print these labels for statements or invoices, you do not have to type this information.

The program will assign each new company an identification number or ID. This ID will save you from having laboriously to type the company name in command procedures. The ID allows you to set up different accounts for the same company, too. You'll want to set up different accounts, for example, if you do business with two different product managers at the same company and need to bill them separately. Your A/R Program allows you to keep track of each product manager's invoices separately, *and* can show you the total amount owed by the company.

IDs are required input for the other A/R Program commands so you'll need a list of the assignments for later use. (This list can be printed with the COMPANIES command.)

The CARDS command (1) sets cards up and assigns IDs. *A card must be set up for a company before any invoice can be recorded for it.*

The procedure for setting up a card is:

1. COMMAND SELECTION: Type 1 for the CARDS command.
2. ENTER COMPANY NAME: Type the company name, using 20 or less characters. In response, the program will display the ID assigned. A company name must be specified. Duplicate company names can be entered; they will be differentiated by unique IDs and customer names. If you'll be dealing on a customer basis (e.g., you run a men's clothing store), type the customer's name here, *not in response to prompt 3.* If you do not wish to set up a card once you have started this procedure, press the carriage return before typing anything and you will be returned to the Menu Level.
3. ENTER CUSTOMER NAME: Type your customer's name, using 20 or less characters. (Optional)
4. ENTER DEPARTMENT NAME: Type the department you're doing business with, using 15 or less characters. (Optional)
5. ENTER STREET ADDRESS: Type the street address, using 15 or less characters. (Optional)
6. ENTER POST OFFICE BOX NUMBER: Type the customer's post office box number, using 10 or less characters. (Optional)
7. ENTER CITY NAME: Type the name of the city or town in which the company is located, using 15 or less characters. (Optional)
8. ENTER STATE ABBREVIATION: Type the two-character state abbreviation. These abbreviations are listed in Appendix B. (Optional)
9. ENTER ZIP CODE: Type the zip code. (Optional)
10. ENTER PHONE NUMBER: Type the customer's telephone number. (Optional)

At this time the card will be set up and you will be prompted to set up another by ENTER NAME:. If you do not want to set anymore up, press the carriage return and you'll be returned to the Menu Level.

The procedure for setting up a card is illustrated in Fig. 8-5.

RECORDING AN INVOICE

The BILLING command (2) records invoices. If you'll be mailing the invoice, you also can print a label.

```
                 Accounts Receivable Program
                    Available commands are:
           1 – Cards              2 – Billing
           3 – Payments           4 – Change
           5 – Delete             6 – Old Debt
           7 – Month End          8 – Descending balances
           9 – Inquiry           10 – Companies
          11 – Open              12 – Year end
          13 – Statements        14 – EXIT
```

Command selection [1–14 or ?1–?14] :**1**   The CARDS command is
selected.

Enter Company Name :**JASON CO.**   The company name is typed.
New customer: ID = 2   The program assigns the account
an identification number.

Enter Customer Name :**ROBERT GREEN**
Enter Department Name :**ACCOUNTING DEPT.**
Enter Street Address :**45 PINEGROVE ST**
Enter Post Office Box Number :⟨**CR**⟩   —Data for a mailing label is entered.
Enter City Name :**RIVERDALE**
Enter State Abbreviation :**MA**
Enter Zip Code :**04563**
Enter Phone Number :**4155555555**   The customer's telephone number
is typed.

Enter Company Name :⟨**CR**⟩   No other cards are to be set up so
the carriage return is pressed.
At this time, you will be
returned to the Menu Level.

Fig. 8-5 The CARDS command.

Each invoice must have a unique number, which later will be used to identify the invoice. You can send out invoices you bought at an office supply store or ones you have made yourself, but each one must have a number. Invoices that you buy come with preprinted numbers.

If you offer a bookkeeping service, you often will have to convert books well into the year. In these instances, you will need to record invoices which *already* have been paid as well as unpaid ones for use of the historical inquiry capability. If you do not wish to use this capability, simply record all unpaid invoices, and create a single invoice for the entire amount collected that year up to the time of the conversion. You later will use the PAYMENTS command to record a full payment for this newly created invoice. These techniques will assure you of accurate, up-to-date records.

For this procedure, you will need the ID of the company to which the invoice is sent.

The procedure for recording an invoice is:

1. COMMAND SELECTION: Type 2 for the BILLING command.
2. ENTER COMPANY ID: Type the ID of the company to which the invoice is sent. In response, the name of the company will be displayed so you can verify you typed the right number. If you entered the wrong one, press the carriage return in response to all remaining prompts.
3. ENTER INVOICE NUMBER: Type the invoice number, using 5 or less alphanumeric characters (i.e., numbers and/or letters).
4. ENTER AMOUNT: Type the amount of the invoice using as many numbers as you need. *Do not type a $ or any commas. Do not type a negative number.*
5. ENTER DATE: Press the carriage return to record the current date as the date when the invoice is sent. If the invoice was sent on a different date, type it instead.
6. ENTER COMMENT: Type any comment you wish to record, using 30 or less characters. This comment will appear on monthly statements and the open invoices report (which is generated with the OPEN command). If you do not wish to record a comment, press the carriage return.
7. PRINT LABEL? (Y/N):   Type **Y** *(it must be a capital)* if you want a label printed. Type **N** if you don't. Labels will be printed for all invoices at once when you finish this procedure.

At this time, the program will record the invoice and update the company's record in the Customer File.

You will be prompted to record another invoice by ENTER COMPANY ID: If you don't wish to record another, press the carriage return. If you did not wish any labels printed, you will be returned to the Menu Level. If you wanted labels, the program will prompt SET UP PRINTER AND HIT CARRIAGE RETURN WHEN READY. Load a roll of labels in the printer and press the carriage return to start printing. When your requested labels are printed, you will be returned to the Menu Level.

Record invoices when you send them out. For a bookkeeping service, record all invoices for a client at least once a month and enter the exact date the invoice was sent out.

The procedure for recording an invoice is illustrated in Fig. 8-6.

Command selection [1–14 or ?1–?14] :**2**	The BILLING command is selected.
Enter Company ID :**2**	The ID for the Jason Co. is entered and the program verifies the company.
Company name = JASON CO.	
Enter Invoice Number :**32** ⎤	The invoice number, amount, and
Enter Amount :**728.56** ⎬	the date the invoice was sent
Enter Date :**021984** ⎦	are entered.
Enter Comment :**PROGRAM ENHANCEMENTS**	A comment is typed as a reminder of what the invoice was for.
Print label ? (Y / N) :**Y**	A label is to be printed.
Master record updated	
Enter Company ID :⟨**CR**⟩	Since no other invoices are to be recorded, the carriage return is pressed.
Set up printer and hit carriage return when ready :⟨**CR**⟩	A roll of labels is loaded on the printer and the carriage return pressed. The requested label is printed on the printer and echoed on the screen. At this time, you will be returned to the Menu Level.

JASON CO.
ROBERT GREEN   ACCOUNTING DEPT ⎤
45 PINEGROVE ST   ⎬— The label.
RIVERDALE   ,MA 04563   ⎦

Fig. 8-6 The BILLING command.

RECORDING INCOME

The PAYMENTS command (3) is used to record cash and invoice payments. The procedures for recording these two types of income are different and presented below separately.

When you end the procedure, the program will display the total amount of invoice payments and the total amount of cash you have recorded. When you are finished looking at these totals, press the carriage return, the screen will be cleared, and you'll be returned to the Menu Level.

The PAYMENTS command is used to record cash. Cash is money paid on the spot. It can be dollar bills or checks. (Yes, checks are considered cash in bookkeeping.)

Your A/R Program enables you to keep track of where the cash came from, or its source. Cash may be recorded as coming from one of eight sources:

```
* * * * * * * * * * * * * * * * * * * * * * * * * * * * * * * * * * * * * * * * * *
        1 – Daily Income        2 – Interest Payment
        2 – Insurance Payment   4 – Royalties
        5 – Rebate              6 – Miscellaneous
        7 – Item 1              8 – Item 2
* * * * * * * * * * * * * * * * * * * * * * * * * * * * * * * * * * * * * * * * * *
```

Many businesses' primary source of income is *daily cash*. You'll record each day's amount. *Interest payment* is cash received from *business* savings. An *insurance payment* is money from an insurance company to cover damages (the cost of the damage is entered with the A/P Program as an expense). *Royalties* are payments received for software, published works, etc. A *rebate* is a repayment of the purchase price by a company. *Miscellaneous* is anything not accounted for in these other categories. *Item 1* and *item 2* can be used to record sources particular to a market that are not included elsewhere. You very likely will not use all these sources, but they're there should you need them.

The procedure for recording cash is:

1. COMMAND SELECTION: Type **3** for the PAYMENTS command.
2. ENTERING INVOICE PAYMENT (1) OR CASH (2): Type **2** to record cash. The program will display the menu of cash sources.
3. ENTER SOURCE (1–8): Type the number that describes the source of cash.
4. ENTER AMOUNT: Type the amount of cash you have from that source for a specific date. *Do not type a $ or commas.*
5. ENTER DATE: If you are recording cash on the day it is received, press the carriage return and the current date will be recorded. If you're recording it on a different day, type the date.
6. ENTER COMMENT: Type any comment you wish to record. The comment will be displayed for changes and deletions. At this time, the cash will be recorded.
7. ENTER SOURCE (1–8): If you wish to record another cash transaction, type the number that describes the cash source. You may enter the same source code as before to record a transaction for a different day, or a different source code. Repeat steps 4 through 7. If you have recorded all the cash, press the carriage return.

8. ENTER INVOICE PAYMENT (1) OR CASH (2): Type 1 to record invoice payments, or press the carriage return to end the procedure and return to the Menu Level.

The procedure for recording cash is illustrated in Fig. 8-7.

The PAYMENTS command also is used to record invoice payments. To record a payment, you'll identify the company that sent the check and the program will display *all* unpaid invoices for that company. You'll decide how to apply the payment.

When you record the payment, a lot happens inside the computer. The Transaction File is updated with the payment information and the invoice balance is automatically reduced by the payment amount. The balance on the customer's card is updated. In addition, the payment automatically is recorded in a third file, the Payments File. This Payments File is designed specifically to allow details about partial payments to be saved for later reference. It's importance can be seen best by an example. When a partial payment is recorded, the Transaction File is updated, which is fine. When the *next* partial payment for the invoice is posted, however, the payment amount and date in the Transaction File are again updated, so the two records now look like one payment. The Payments File saves the details (see Fig. 8-8).

Prepare to record payments by collecting all checks. Add up the amount of the checks and write the total on a pad. At the end of this procedure, the program will display the total payment amount you have recorded, which must *exactly* match the total on your pad. If it doesn't, reconcile the difference by carefully checking your work and using the CHANGE command to correct mistakes. For this procedure, you will need the ID or name of the company making the payment.

For your own business, try to record payments as they're received. If you offer a bookkeeping service, record payments after you record invoices.

The procedure for recording an invoice payment is:

1. COMMAND SELECTION: Type 3 for the PAYMENTS command.
2. ENTERING INVOICE PAYMENT (1) OR CASH (2): Type 1 to record payment of an invoice.
3. ENTER COMPANY NAME OR ID NUMBER: Type either the ID or the name of the company that made the payment. The program will display *all* open invoices for that company. If the list of the company's invoices will not fit on the screen, you will be shown as many as will fit and asked to press the carriage return to see more. When you have seen all of them, the dialogue will continue.

Command Selection [1–14 or ?1–?14] :**3**   The PAYMENTS command is
                                                        selected.

Entering Invoice payment(1) or   Cash is to be recorded.
   Cash(2) :**2**

Source Selection

1 –Daily Income	2 –Interest Payment
3 –Insurance Payment	4 –Royalties
5 –Rebate	6 –Miscellaneous
7 –Item 1	8 –Item 2

Enter source (1–8) :**2**   The cash has been received from
                                                        interest on a money market
                                                        checking account, so interest
                                                        payment is entered.

Enter amount :**423.65**
Enter date :**072484**   ⎤———————Data about the cash is typed.
Enter comment :**MM ACCOUNT**⎦

                                                        The cash is recorded, and the
                                                        sources again are displayed.

Source Selection

1 –Daily Income	2 –Interest Payment
3 –Insurance Payment	4 –Royalties
5 –Rebate	6 –Miscellaneous
7 –Item 1	8 –Item 2

Enter source (1–8) :⟨**CR**⟩   The carriage return is pressed
                                                        since no more cash needs to be
                                                        recorded.

Entering Invoice payment(1) or   The carriage return is pressed to
   Cash(2) :⟨**CR**⟩   end the posting procedures.
All payments and cash entered and
   transactions posted
Total payments =
   Total cash = 423.65
Enter return to continue⟨**CR**⟩   The carriage return is pressed to
                                                        clear the screen and return to
                                                        the Menu Level.

Fig. 8-7 Recording cash.

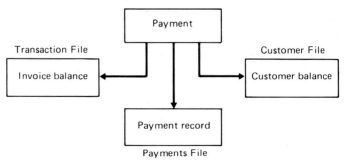

Fig. 8-8 Payments file.

4. ENTER INVOICE NUMBER: Type the number of the invoice for which you have a payment. The program will display the number so you can verify you have correctly entered it.
5. IS THIS CORRECT (Y/N)?:   Check the invoice number and make sure it's the one you want. If it is, type **Y**. If not, type **N** and you will be able to correct it.
6. ENTER PAYMENT DATE: Type the date the payment was received. If you are recording the payment on the same day it is received, only press the carriage return and the current date will be recorded automatically.
7. ENTER CHECK NUMBER: Type the payment check number. If you are uninterested in using the historical inquiry capabilities, you do not have to enter this number.
8. ENTER AMOUNT OF PAYMENT: If the payment is for the full invoice amount, press the carriage return and that amount will be recorded. If the payment is for a *different* amount, type it. *Do not type a $ or a comma*. The amount you type must be equal or less than the invoice balance. An amount greater than the balance will be rejected. If the check amount is greater, you must apply the remainder to one or more of the company's open invoices.
9. ENTER COMMENTS: Type any comment you wish for the payment. This comment will be displayed when inquiries about payments are made.

The program will display the payment information it has recorded for your verification. Check to make sure you have entered everything correctly. If you have made a mistake, use the CHANGE command when you have completed this procedure to correct it. The program also will display the updated invoice balance and customer balance.

So you can apply a payment to another invoice for this customer, the program again will list all open invoices and prompt ENTER INVOICE #:. Repeat steps 4 through 9 to record another payment. If you have recorded all payments made by this customer, press the carriage return. This procedure is designed to simplify applying a single check to many invoices, recording payments once a month for your clients, and distributing a check among different invoices.

If the customer has no more open invoices, the program will prompt for a new company name or ID.

10.   ENTER COMPANY NAME OR ID NUMBER: Type either the ID or the name of another company that has made a payment and repeat steps 4 through 9. If you have recorded all payments, press the carriage return.

11.   ENTERING INVOICE PAYMENT (1) OR CASH (2):   Type 2 to record cash received and you will use the procedure previously presented. If you do not have any cash to record, press the carriage return and you will be returned to the Menu Level.

Figure 8-9 shows two examples that illustrate how invoice payments are recorded. In the first, a customer has two open invoices and a payment is recorded for one of them. In the second, a partial payment is recorded.

CHANGING INFORMATION

The CHANGE command (4) is used to change information you already have stored for invoices, cards, cash payments, and invoice payments. You *very rarely* should have to change any of this information, but you have the capability to do so if you need it.

NOTE:

Changing certain information for invoices, cash payments, or invoice payments may require you to reprint Month End Reports to accurately show the revised figures. Specific changes that require reprints are listed in Table 8-1.

The general procedure for making a change is given below. In subsequent examples, steps 1 and 2 will remain the same. Following steps (from 3

Command selection [1–14 or ?1–?14] :**3**   The PAYMENTS command is
                                                 selected.

Entering Invoice payment(1) or   Invoice payments are to be
   Cash(2) :**1**   recorded.
Enter Company name or ID number :**2**   A customer's ID is entered and all
                                                 invoices for the customer are
                                                 shown.

Invoice # = 38
Company name = JASON CO.
Balance = 453.98
Invoice # = 42
Company name = JASON CO.
Balance = 2314.98
Enter Invoice # :**38**   A payment is to be made on
                                                 invoice 38.

Is this correct (Y / N) :**Y**
Enter Payment Date :**071284**   ┐
Enter Check number :**542**   ├── Data for the invoice is entered.
Enter amount of payment :⟨**CR**⟩   │   The carriage return is pressed
Enter comments :⟨**CR**⟩   ┘   because the check is for the
Invoice = 38   invoice amount.
Date = 07 / 12 / 84
Check Nbr = 542
AMOUNT = 453.98
COMMENT =
Invoice record updated balance =   0   ┐──── The program shows the
Customer balance updated to   2314.98 │   information that is recorded as
Payment has been recorded   ┘   well as the up-to-date status of
                                             the customer's account.
Invoice # = 42   The remaining invoice is
Company name = JASON CO.   displayed.
Balance = 2314.98
Enter Invoice # :⟨**CR**⟩

                                        Since no other payments have
                                        been received from the
                                        customer, the carriage return is
                                        pressed, ending payments for
                                        this customer.
Enter Company name or ID number :**5** Another customer's ID is entered.
Invoice # = 37
Company name = ZEPCO INC.
Balance = 3426.34
Enter Invoice # :**37**
Is this correct (Y / N) :**Y**

Fig. 8-9   Recording invoice payments. (*Cont. on following page.*)

Enter Payment Date :**07 1684**
Enter Check number :**9871**
Enter amount of payment :**1500**

Enter comments :**PARTIAL PAYMENT**
Invoice = 37
Date = 07 / 16 / 84
Check Nbr = 9871
AMOUNT = 1500
COMMENT = PARTIAL PAYMENT
Invoice record updated
    balance =   1926.34
Customer balance updated to   1926.34
Payment has been recorded

Invoice # = 37
Company name = ZEPCO INC
Balance = 1926.34

Enter Invoice # :⟨**CR**⟩

Enter Company name or ID number :⟨**CR**⟩

Fig. 8-9 *Cont.*

Data for the invoice is entered.

The payment amount is less than
the invoice balance so the
amount is typed.

Note the outstanding balance
remaining for the invoice.

Since the invoice still is open, it
again is displayed. No other
payments have been received,
though.

The carriage return is pressed,
ending posting payments for
this customer.

All payments are recorded, so the
carriage return is pressed,
ending the payments procedure.

on) differ according to specific information categories being discussed. In
these examples, procedures begin with the number 3.

1. COMMAND SELECTION: Type **4** for the CHANGE command.
2. CHANGE INVOICES (1), CARDS (2), CASH PAYMENTS (3),
   INVOICE PAYMENTS (4):   Type the number that describes the
   information you want to change and the program will prompt you for the
   changes. The procedure for each type of information varies from this
   point on, as described below.

CHANGING INVOICES.   Only *open* invoices without partial payments can be changed. To change an invoice with a partial payment, or a

TABLE 8-1 CHANGES THAT REQUIRE REPORT REPRINTS

Type of Change	Reports to Reprint
For invoice:	
1. Amount	Detailed and Summary Month End Reports from the original invoice date.
2. Date sent	If the new date is within the same month as the old one, only the Detailed Month End Report for the month that's changed.
	If the new date is in a different month, all Detailed and Summary Month End Reports from the earliest date in the change.
3. Company ID	Detailed Month End Report for the month with the change.
For cash payment:	
1. Amount	Detailed and Summary Month End Reports from the original cash payment date.
2. Date	If the new date is in a different month, all Detailed and Summary Month End Reports from the earliest date in the change.
For invoice payment:	
1. Invoice number	Detailed and Month End Report for the month with the change.
2. Date	If the new date is within the same month, only the Detailed Month End Report for that month.
	If the new date is in a different month, all Detailed and Summary Month End Reports from the earliest date in the change.
3. Amount	Detailed and Summary Month End Reports from the original transaction date.

completely paid invoice, you first must change the invoice payment amount to zero (use the CHANGE command, Changing Invoice Payments procedure). After you have made your invoice changes, you may need to change the payment amounts back to the original entries.

To change an invoice, type 1 in response to the CHANGE INVOICE (1), etc. prompt in step 2.

3. ENTER INVOICE #: Type the number of the invoice you want to change. The program will display the name of the company to which you sent the invoice and the other invoice information:

> INVOICE #: 42   :JASON CO.
> 1.   AMOUNT: 2314.98
> 2.   DATE SENT: 04 / 03 / 84
> 3.   COMMENT: ORDER ENTRY PR.
> 4. COMPANY ID: 2

4. CHANGE WHAT (1–4)?: Type the number of the line on the invoice you want to change. The program then will prompt you for the new line, which you type. You will be prompted for another change to this invoice. When you have changed this invoice, press the carriage return in response to the prompt and the changes will be recorded. If you changed an amount, your customer's A/R balance is updated automatically.
5. ENTER INVOICE #: Type the number of another invoice that you want to change, or, if you have no more changes, press the carriage return and you will be returned to step 2.

The procedure for changing an invoice is illustrated in Fig. 8-10.

Command selection [1–14 or ?1–?14] :**4**	The CHANGE command is selected.
Change Invoices(1), Cards(2), Cash Payments(3) Invoice Payments(4) :**1**	An invoice is to be changed.
Enter Invoice # :**42**	The invoice is identified.
Invoice # : 42 : JASON CO.	
(1) Amount : 2314.98	The program displays the
(2) Date sent : 04 / 03 / 84	presently stored data.
(3) Comment : ORDER ENTRY PROGRAM	
(4) Company ID : 2	
Change what ? (1–4) :**2**	The date is to be changed.
Enter date sent :**041384**	The new date is entered.
Change what ? (1–4) :⟨**CR**⟩	No other changes to this invoice are to be made.
Invoice Record Updated	
Enter Invoice # :⟨**CR**⟩	No other invoice changes are to be made. At this time, you will be prompted CHANGE INVOICES (1) etc.

Fig. 8-10 Changing an invoice.

CHANGING CARDS. To change a card, type 2 in response to the CHANGE INVOICE, etc., prompt in step 2.

3. ENTER COMPANY ID: Type the ID number for the customer's card you want to change. The program will display the card with its present information, ask you for the line you want to change, and prompt for the change. The same character limits are in effect for making changes to a line as for setting up a card. (Note that you cannot change a card's ID assignment.) When you are finished changing lines on this card, press the carriage return in response to CHANGE WHAT? You will be able to specify an ID for another customer's card. When you're done making changes to cards, press the carriage return in response to ENTER COMPANY ID and you will be returned to step 2.

The procedure for changing information on a card is illustrated in Fig. 8-11.

Change Invoices(1), Cards(2), _A card is to be changed._
   Cash Payments(3) Invoice Payments(4) :**2**
Enter Company ID :**1** _The customer ID is entered and the card displayed._

(1) Company name = WERN INC.
(2) Customer name = FRED JERKINS
(3) Department   = CUSTOMER SUPPOR
(4) Street   = 234 YATES ROAD
(5) City   = CULVER CITY
(6) State   = NE
(7) Zip   = 78654
(8) Telephone   = 5435555555
(9) P.O. Number =

Change what ? (1–9) :**2** _The name of the customer is to be changed._

Enter Customer name :**FRED R. JENKINS** _The new name is entered._
Change what ? (1–9) :⟨**CR**⟩ _No other changes are to be made._
Record updated
Enter Company ID :⟨**CR**⟩ _No other cards are to be changed. At this time, you will be prompted CHANGE INVOICES (1) etc., again._

Fig. 8-11 Changing a card.

CHANGING CASH PAYMENTS.   To change a cash payment, type **3** in response to the CHANGE INVOICE, etc., prompt in step 2. The program will display the Source Selection Menu.

3.   ENTER SOURCE CODE (1–8):   Type the number of the source for which you want to change an entry.

For all sources except Daily Income (1), the program will display all entries for the source. Daily Income is a special case since it is very likely that a business may have one entry per day, resulting in a cumbersome display of 365 records. For Daily Income, consequently, you will be prompted ENTER DATE OF PAYMENT and you will type the date for which a change is to be made.

If more entries are stored than can fit on the screen, the program will display as many as it can and ask you to press the carriage return to see more. Each cash payment in this list will be numbered. As the list is displayed, note the number of the line you want to change.

4.   CHANGE WHICH LINE?:   Type the number of the line in the list that you want to change.

The program will display all information you have recorded for this payment:

```
1     SOURCE = Interest Payment
2     AMOUNT = 423.65
3     DATE = 07/24/84
4     COMMENT = MM ACCOUNT
```

5.   CHANGE WHICH (1–4)?:   Type the number for the line of information you want to change. The program will prompt for the change and you will type it. If the source is to be changed (i.e., you type 1), the Source Selection Menu will be displayed again and you merely type the number of the new source. When the change is specified, the program then will prompt for another change to this payment record. When you have made all your changes, press the carriage return in response to the prompt. The change will be stored and the Year-To-Date Cash Balance will be updated automatically.

The program again will display all entries for this source so you can change another one. When you are finished with this source, press the carriage return in response to CHANGE WHICH LINE and you will be able to change entries for another source.

The program again will display the Source Selection Menu. When you are done changing payments, press the carriage return in response to ENTER SOURCE CODE and you will be returned to step 2.

The procedure for changing a cash record is illustrated in Fig. 8-12.

CHANGING INVOICE PAYMENTS.   To change an invoice payment, type **4** in response to the CHANGE INVOICES, etc., prompt in step 2.

3. ENTER INVOICE NUMBER: Type the number of the invoice for which the payment was received. The program will display a numbered list of all payments made for this invoice.
4. CHANGE WHICH LINE?:   Type the number of the payment in the list that you want to change. The program will display the payment record as a numbered list.
5. CHANGE WHICH (1–5)?:   Type the number of the payment line you wish to change. You will be prompted to enter the new line, which you type. If you change the amount, the balance due on the invoice and the amount the customer owes will be adjusted automatically. If you change the invoice number, all affected balances are adjusted automatically. For example, if you apply the payment to a different customer's account, both account and all invoices balances are adjusted automatically. The program will prompt you for another change. When you have made all your changes, press the carriage return in response to CHANGE WHICH and you will be able to change another payment.

When all payments are changed, press the carriage return in response to ENTER INVOICE NUMBER and you will be returned to step 2.

When you are finished making all your changes, press the carriage return in response to CHANGE INVOICES, etc., and you will be returned to the Menu Level.

The procedure for changing an invoice payment is illustrated in Fig. 8-13.

DELETING INFORMATION

The DELETE command (5) *permanently* removes from your records open invoices, cards, cash payments, and invoice payments. You *very rarely* will have to use this command.

Command selection [1–14 or ?1–?14] :**4**   The CHANGE command is
                                                        selected.

Change Invoices(1), Cards(2),   A cash record is to be changed.
   Cash Payments(3) Invoice Payments(4) :**3**

Source Selection

1 –Daily Income   2 –Interest Payment
3 –Insurance Payment   4 –Royalties
5 –Rebate   6 –Miscellaneous
7 –Item 1   8 –Item 2

Enter source code (1–8) :**1** ⎤────────── A DAILY INCOME record for
Enter date of payment :**040883** ⎦   April 8, 1983 will be changed.
(1) Source = Daily Income ⎤
      Amount = 500
      Date = 04/08/83
      Comment =
(2) Source = Daily Income
      Amount = 500   More than one record was
      Date = 04/08/83   recorded for that day. All
      Comment =   records are displayed.
(3) Source = Daily Income
      Amount = 500
      Date = 04/08/83
      Comment = ⎦
Change which line :**2**   The second record will be
                                          changed.

(1) SOURCE   = Daily Income ⎤
(2) AMOUNT   = 500
(3) DATE   = 04/08/83   The record is displayed.
(4) COMMENT = ⎦
Change which (1–4) ? :**1**   The source will be changed.

Source Selection

1 –Daily Income   2 –Interest Payment
3 –Insurance Payment   4 –Royalties
5 –Rebate   6 –Miscellaneous
7 –Item 1   8 –Item 2

Enter source (1–8) :**4**   This cash will be recorded with
                                          royalties.

Change which (1–4) ? :⟨**CR**⟩   No more changes to this record
                                          will be made.

Fig. 8-12 Changing a cash record. (*Cont. on following page.*)

Record updated
Change which line :⟨**CR**⟩   No more changes for this date will
                                                                          be made.

Source Selection

1 –Daily Income	2 –Interest Payment
3 –Insurance Payment	4 –Royalties
5 –Rebate	6 –Miscellaneous
7 –Item 1	8 –Item 2

Enter source code (1–8) :⟨**CR**⟩   No more changes to cash will be
                                                                          made.

Change Invoices(1), Cards(2),
  Cash Payments(3) Invoice
  Payments(4) :⟨**CR**⟩

Fig. 8-12   (*Cont.*)

The command lets you first flag the records you want to delete. When you have made all your selections, the flagged records are removed.

NOTE:

Month End Reports must be reprinted if you delete an open invoice or a cash record. When the reports are reprinted, balances will show updated figures.

The general procedure for deleting a transaction is given below. In subsequent examples, steps 1 and 2 will remain the same. Following steps (from 3 on) differ according to specific information categories being discussed. In these examples, procedures begin with the number 3.

1. COMMAND SELECTION: Type 5 for the DELETE command.
2. DELETE: OPEN INVOICES (1), CARDS (2), CASH PAYMENT (3), INVOICE PAYMENT (4):   Type the number that describes the type of record you want to delete and the program will prompt you through the remainder of the appropriate procedure, as described below.

DELETING OPEN INVOICES.   Type 1 in response to the DELETE prompt (step 2) to delete an open invoice.

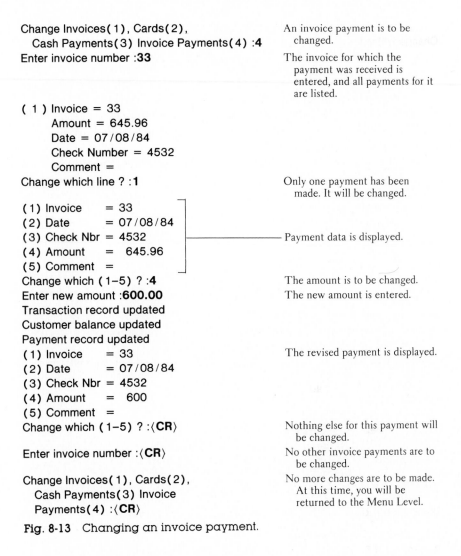

Change Invoices(1), Cards(2),
   Cash Payments(3) Invoice Payments(4) :**4**
Enter invoice number :**33**

An invoice payment is to be changed.

The invoice for which the payment was received is entered, and all payments for it are listed.

(1) Invoice = 33
    Amount = 645.96
    Date = 07 / 08 / 84
    Check Number = 4532
    Comment =
Change which line ? :**1**

Only one payment has been made. It will be changed.

(1) Invoice   = 33
(2) Date   = 07 / 08 / 84
(3) Check Nbr = 4532
(4) Amount   = 645.96
(5) Comment =
Change which (1–5) ? :**4**
Enter new amount :**600.00**
Transaction record updated
Customer balance updated
Payment record updated

Payment data is displayed.

The amount is to be changed.
The new amount is entered.

(1) Invoice   = 33
(2) Date   = 07 / 08 / 84
(3) Check Nbr = 4532
(4) Amount   = 600
(5) Comment =
Change which (1–5) ? :⟨**CR**⟩

The revised payment is displayed.

Nothing else for this payment will be changed.

Enter invoice number :⟨**CR**⟩

No other invoice payments are to be changed.

Change Invoices(1), Cards(2),
   Cash Payments(3) Invoice
   Payments(4) :⟨**CR**⟩

No more changes are to be made. At this time, you will be returned to the Menu Level.

Fig. 8-13 Changing an invoice payment.

Only open invoices for which *no* payment (including partial payment) has been received can be deleted. The program prohibits you from deleting any invoice which has been paid—as it should. If you received payment, but delete the invoice, then what was the payment for?

To remove an invoice that has been paid, you first must use the CHANGE command to change the invoice payment(s) to zero.

Before deleting an invoice, see if the invoice can be listed as a bad debt, in which case you will use the BAD DEBT command to remove it. *If you delete an invoice, you will receive no bad debt credit.*

3. ENTER INVOICE #:   Type the number of the open invoice you want to delete. The program will display the invoice.
4. OK TO DELETE? (Y/N):   Type **Y** if you have verified that the invoice displayed is the one you want and it will be flagged. Type **N** if it isn't and no flag will be set.
5. ENTER INVOICE #:   Type the number of another open invoice you want to delete or press the carriage return to remove all the invoices you have flagged and return to step 2. When an invoice is removed, the amount the customer owes you will be adjusted automatically.

The procedure for deleting an invoice is illustrated in Fig. 8-14.

Command selection [1–14 or ?1–?14] :**5**	The DELETE command is selected.
Delete: Open Invoices(1),Cards(2), Cash Payment(3),Invoice Payments(4) :**1**	Open invoices are to be deleted.
Enter Invoice # :**42**	Invoice 42 is called up for deletion and displayed.
Invoice = 42 Company # = 2 Name = JASON CO. Invoice Amount = 2314.98 Date sent = 04/13/84 Ok to delete? (Y/N) :**Y**	Permission is given to flag the invoice.
Enter Invoice # :**1**	An attempt is made to delete an invoice (1) for which a payment has been recorded, but the program prohibits the deletion.
Paid Invoice cannot be deleted Enter Invoice # :⟨**CR**⟩	No more invoices are to be deleted now.
Old file had 8 invoices. New file has 7 invoices.	Cleaning is started and the flagged invoice removed. Note that only one invoice has been removed from the Transaction File.

Fig. 8-14 Deleting an invoice.

DELETING A CARD. To delete a card, type **2** in response to the DELETE prompt in step 2.

Only a customer with a zero amount due can have his or her card deleted. If a customer owes any money, you either can claim the amount as a bad debt and then delete the card, or delete all open invoices for the customer before deleting the card. *The program strictly prohibits you from deleting a card for a customer who owes money.*

3. ENTER COMPANY #: Type the ID number of the customer whose card you want to delete. The program will display the company name so you can verify it's the one you want.
4. OK TO DELETE: (Y/N): Type **Y** if the company displayed is the one you want to flag for deletion. Type **N** if it isn't and no flag will be set.
5. ENTER COMPANY #: Type the ID number of another customer or press the carriage return to remove all the cards you have flagged and return to step 2.

The procedure for deleting a card is illustrated in Figure 8-15.

DELETING CASH. To delete a record of cash you received, type **3** in response to the DELETE prompt in step 2. The program will display the Source Selection Menu.

3. ENTER SOURCE CODE: Type the number of the source for which the cash was recorded. For all sources except Daily Income (1), the program will display all entries for the source. Daily Income is a special case

Delete: Open Invoices(1),Cards(2), Cash Payment(3),Invoice Payments(4) :2	Cards are to be deleted.
Enter Company # :**6**	A company is identified and its card shown.
Company # = 6 Name = PALLOCK FISH Ok to delete? (Y / N) :**Y**	Permission is given to flag the card.
Enter Company # :⟨**CR**⟩	No more cards are to be deleted.
Old file had 6 customers. New file has 5 customers.	Cleaning is started and the flagged card removed. Note that the card had a 0 balance.

Fig. 8-15 Deleting a card.

since it is very likely that a business may have a cumbersome display of 365 records. For Daily Income, consequently, you will be prompted ENTER DATE OF PAYMENT and you will type the date for which a change is to be made. If more entries are stored than can fit on the screen, the program will display as many as it can and ask you to press the carriage return to see more. Each cash payment in this list will be numbered. As the list is displayed, note the number of the line you want to change.

4. DELETE WHICH?: Type the line number of the transaction you want to flag for deletion. This transaction amount does *not* have to be zero. The program will display the record you picked so you can verify it for deletion.

5. OK TO DELETE? (Y/N): Type **Y** if the cash record displayed is the one you want to flag. Type **N** if it isn't and no flag will be set.

6. DELETE WHICH?: Type the line number of another transaction you want to flag or press the carriage return to remove all the flagged cash records and return to step 2.

The procedure for deleting a record of cash received is illustrated in Fig. 8-16.

DELETING AN INVOICE PAYMENT. To delete an invoice payment, type **4** in response to the DELETE prompt in step 2.

The circumstances for deleting an invoice payment are very rare. *Only invoice payments with a zero payment amount can be deleted.* Before you can delete a payment, you will have to use the CHANGE command to reduce the payment amount for the transaction to zero.

All invoice payments with a zero balance will be listed.

3. OKAY TO DELETE? (Y/N): Type **Y** to delete *all* invoices displayed. Type **N** to end the procedure without deleting anything. If you type **N** and want to remove an invoice payment from the delete list, use the CHANGE command to assign the payment an amount, which you will remove after the deletion procedure.

When you have deleted everything you want, press the carriage return and you will be returned to the Menu Level.

The procedure for deleting an invoice payment is illustrated in Fig. 8-17.

Delete: Open Invoices(1),Cards(2),
   Cash Payment(3),Invoice Payments(4) :**3**

A record of a cash payment is to be deleted. The Source Selection Menu is displayed.

Source Selection

1 –Daily Income   2 –Interest Payment
3 –Insurance Payment   4 –Royalties
5 –Rebate   6 –Miscellaneous
7 –Item 1   8 –Item 2

Enter source code :**2**

A record of an interest payment is to be deleted. These records are displayed.

(1) Source = Interest Payment
Date = 07 / 24 / 84
Amount = 423.65
Comment = MONEY MARKET ACCOUNT
Delete which ? :**1**

The only interest payment record is selected for deletion and displayed.

  Source = Interest Payment
Date = 07 / 24 / 84
Amount = 423.65
Comment = MONEY MARKET ACCOUNT
Ok to delete? (Y / N) :**Y**

Permission is given to flag the record.

Record flagged for deletion
Delete which ? :⟨**CR**⟩

No more interest payment records are to be flagged.

Enter source code :⟨**CR**⟩

No more cash records are to be deleted.

Old file had 1 payments. New file
  has 0 payments.

Cleaning is started and the interest payment record deleted.

Fig. 8-16 Deleting a cash record.

REMOVING BAD DEBTS

The OLD DEBT command (6) is used to remove from your active accounts invoices that have not been fully paid and, in your judgment, never will be paid. A list of these debts can be printed for your permanent records. Removal adjusts the A/R balance automatically so you will know what you realistically can hope to collect. You should declare bad debts *before* you print your final Month End Reports for December.

Delete: Open Invoices(1),Cards(2),
  Cash Payment(3),Invoice Payments(4) :**4**
The following invoice payments with zero
  amounts will be deleted:

Invoice = 33
Date paid = 07/08/84
Amount =   0
Ok to delete? (Y/N) :**Y**

Old file had 5 payments. New file
  has 4 payments.

Delete: Open Invoices(1),Cards(2),
Cash Payment(3),Invoice
  Payments(4) :⟨**CR**⟩

Invoice payments are to be
deleted.

All payments with zero amount
are displayed. Only one
payment meets this condition.

Permission is given to delete
everything on the list and
cleaning is started.

No more deletions are to be made.
At this time, you will be
returned to the Menu Level.

Fig. 8-17 Deleting an invoice payment.

When you specify a period of time in this procedure, the program will search for and display all open invoices that had been sent out during that period. Successive sweeps can be used to approach the most recently sent invoices. You then can select the invoices for which you do not expect to receive payment and mark them as bad debts.

NOTE:

If you subsequently should be paid for a bad debt, you record it as cash received in the year it was paid.

The procedure for declaring a bad debt is:

1. COMMAND SELECTION: Type 6 for the OLD DEBT command.
2. ENTER STARTING DATE: Type the date on which to start looking for open invoices. If you press the carriage return, you will be prompted DO YOU WANT THE BAD DEBT DETAIL REPORT? Type **Y** if you want the report. You also will need to specify whether you want to see it displayed or printed. Once your choice is made, the report will be generated and you will be returned to the Menu Level. Type **N** if you don't want the report and you'll be returned to the Menu Level.

3. ENTER ENDING DATE: Type the ending date for the search. The program will list all unpaid invoices that were sent out in the period. For reference, the date each invoice was sent out also is printed. The invoices will be listed in the order in which you entered them. Every invoice will be numbered for easy identification.

4. ENTER RECORD NUMBER FOR BAD DEBT: If you do not wish to declare any of the displayed invoices as bad debts, press the carriage return and you again will be prompted for a new starting date. If you want to declare an invoice a bad debt, type its line number and you will be prompted for another line number. When you have declared all bad debts for this period, press the carriage return and the program will list all the invoices you have declared as bad debts.

5. OK TO CLEAR AMOUNTS AS BAD DEBTS? (Y/N):   Type **Y** if the invoices are the ones you want declared bad debts. The invoices will be closed and your receivables balance updated. Type **N** if you have declared an invoice you do not want included, and the list will be cleared so you can start over. If you have left out an invoice, type **Y** to save yourself the trouble of respecifying this list. Specify a period that will select the missing invoice, and declare it a bad debt in a list of its own.

6. ENTER STARTING DATE: Type the starting date for another search, or press the carriage return to end the procedure and you will be returned to the Menu Level.

The procedure for declaring a bad debt is illustrated in Fig. 8-18.

PRINTING THE MONTH END REPORTS

The MONTH END command (7) is used to generate the Month End Reports. The Month End Reports show income transactions that occurred during the month and how they affected your income and A/R positions. The Detailed Report shows all invoices paid during the month and each cash transaction that occurred. The Summary Report shows only totals for both the month and year to date.

The program generates the Month Summary from the Transaction File. You specify the beginning and end dates for a month. The program will search through your Transaction File for all records with date sent or date paid within that period. It will use these figures to compute month end and year-to-date totals (see Fig. 8-19).

The records are stored online all the time so you don't have to worry

Command selection [1–14 or ?1–?14] :**6**   The BAD DEBT command is
                                                 selected.

Enter starting date :**010182** ⎤──────────── The period to be scanned for
Enter ending date :**010184** ⎦   unpaid invoices is specified.
(1) Company id = 6   All invoices found are listed.
      Name = PALLOCK FISH
      Invoice # 1
      Invoice Amount =   1320.42
      Amount paid 0
      Balance due 1320.42
Enter record number for bad debt :**1**   The only open invoice for the
                                              period is flagged as a bad debt.

Enter record number for bad debt :⟨**CR**⟩   No other invoices are to be
                                              flagged.

(1) Company id = 6   The flagged invoice is displayed.
      Name = PALLOCK FISH
      Invoice # = 1
      Invoice Amount =   1320.42
      Amount paid 0
      Balance due 1320.42
OK to clear amounts as bad   Permission is given to record it as
  debts? (Y / N) :**Y**   a bad debt.
Enter starting date :⟨**CR**⟩   A Bad Debt Report is to be
                                              printed.

Do you want the Bad Debt Detail   The report is requested.
  report :**Y**
Output to screen (1) or printer (2) :**1** The report is displayed.

Invoice #	Company Name	Date Sent	Inv. Amount	Bad Debt Amount
1	PALLOCK FISH	02 / 25 / 82	$1,320.42	$1,320.42

Enter return to continue ⟨**CR**⟩   The carriage return is pressed to
                                             clear the screen. At this time,
                                             you will be returned to the
                                             Menu Level.

Fig. 8-18 Declaring a bad debt.

about deletions. The entire Transaction File is used to print Month End
Reports.

The Detailed Month End Report uses information from the Transaction
and the Payments File (when necessary for partial payments information).

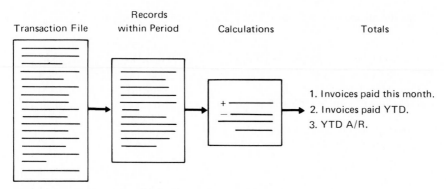

Fig. 8-19 Generation of Month End A/R Reports.

The procedure for generating these reports is:

1. COMMAND SELECTION: Type **7** for the MONTH END command.
2. OUTPUT TO SCREEN (1) OR PRINTER (2):   Type 1 to display the report, or **2** to print it.
3. ENTER REPORT YEAR AS YY: Type two digits for the year that is to be shown in the report.
4. ENTER REPORT MONTH AS MM: Type two digits for the month that is to be shown in the report.
5. REPORT PREPARED FOR: If you are using the program for a bookkeeping service, type your client's name and it will appear in the report title. If you're not, press the carriage return.
6. DO YOU WANT THE DETAILED REPORT? (Y/N):   Type **Y** and the detailed report will be generated. Type **N** if you do not want to see this report.
7. DO YOU WANT THE SUMMARY REPORT?:   Type **Y**, the report will be generated and you will be returned to the Menu Level. Type **N** if you don't want to see it and you will be returned to the Menu Level.

Either or both reports can be generated. The reports do not have to be prepared only at month's end. You can print these reports anytime, but you will only save the ones for the whole month.

The procedure for generating the Month End Reports is illustrated in Fig. 8-20. A detailed Month End Report is shown in Fig. 8-21 and a Summary Report in Fig. 8-22.

Command selection [1–14 or ?1–?14] :**7**   The MONTH END command is
                                               selected.

Output to screen (1) or printer (2) :**2**   Printed reports are requested.
Enter report year as yy :**84**   ⌐—— The report year and month are
Enter report month as mm :**07** ⌐   entered.
Report prepared for :**HARWARD CO.**   A client's name is entered for the
                                        title.

Do you want the Detailed Report (Y / N) :**Y** —— Both Month End Reports are
Do you want the Summary Report :**Y**   ordered.

When the reports are printed, you
will be returned to the Menu
Level.

Fig. 8-20   Generating the Month End Reports.

July
Detailed Month End Report
For HARWARD CO.

Invoices Paid:

Company Name	Invoice #	Amount	Date Sent	Date Paid	Payment Amt.
JASON CO.	32	$728.56	02/19/84	07/12/84	$728.56
JASON CO.	38	$453.98	03/14/84	07/12/84	$453.98
PHIL'S SERVICE	33	$645.96	02/14/84	07/08/84	$600.00
ZEPCO INC.	37	$3,426.34	03/30/84	07/16/84	$1,500.00

Cash Received:

Date Paid	Source	Amount
072484	2	$423.65

Total Payments : $3,282.54

Total Cash   : $ 423.65

Fig. 8-21   A Detailed Month End Report.

July
Summary Month End Report
For HARWARD CO.

This month
  Invoices paid   : $3,282.54
  Cash received   : $423.65
This year
  Invoices paid   : $29,332.54
  Cash received   : $2,947.65
Total outstanding receivables : $5,954.45
Total bad debts   :

Fig. 8-22 A Month End Summary Report.

PRINTING THE DESCENDING BALANCES REPORT

The Descending Balances Report lists customers in order of their balances, starting with the largest. Customers with high balances will be called to your attention. Next to the customer's name and balance will be his or her telephone number so you can call to collect your money. You can keep your A/R Program going while you talk on the telephone and, if questions arise about payments, you can use your historical inquiry capability to answer them. The report is generated from the Customer File.

A Descending Balances Report is shown in Fig. 8-23. The DESCENDING BALANCES command (8) is used to print this report. To generate the report, select the DESCENDING BALANCES command and specify

Company Name	Customer Name	Balance	Phone Nbr.
JASON CO.	ROBERT GREEN	$2,314.98	(415) 555-5555
ZEPCO INC.	LAWRENCE FINNEY	$1,926.34	(212) 555-5555
PALLOCK FISH	JEFF DAVIES	$1,320.42	(514) 555-5555
J & R SUPPLIES	THOMAS R. THORTON	$346.75	(203) 555-5555
WERN INC.	FRED R. JENKINS	$50.00	(543) 555-5555
PHIL'S SERVICE	JOHN GRUNNERY	$45.96	(203) 555-5555

Fig. 8-23 A Descending Balances Report.

whether you want it displayed on the screen or printed. The report will be generated and you will be returned to the Menu Level.

MAKING INQUIRIES

At times, you may want to find specific information from your records in a hurry. Your A/R Program inquiry capability will:

- List all invoices, both paid and unpaid, for a customer. This will show your complete business history with the customers.
- Show the up-to-date amount a company owes you. You'll see the amount for the whole company, even if you've set up many accounts for that company.
- List all invoices to which a specific check was applied.

The INQUIRY command (9) is used to make all these inquiries. The procedure for making an inquiry is:

1. COMMAND SELECTION: Type 9 for the INQUIRY command.
2. OUTPUT TO SCREEN (1) OR PRINTER (2):   Type the number for the manner in which you want to see the inquiry answered. The printer will provide a permanent record. The screen can be used to answer questions quickly.
3. INQUIRY BY COMPANY ID (1), COMPANY BALANCE BY NAME (2), OR CHECK NUMBER (3):   Type the number for the inquiry you want. The COMPANY ID inquiry lists all invoices for a customer. The COMPANY BALANCE BY NAME inquiry lists the total amount a company owes. The CHECK NUMBER inquiry shows all invoices that a check was used to pay.

   Depending on the type of inquiry, you will specify an ID, a company name, or a check number, and the information you're interested in will be shown. When you're done making a type of inquiry, press the carriage return and you can make another. When you're done making all inquiries, press the carriage return in response to the INQUIRY prompt and you'll be returned to the Menu Level.

The procedure for making inquiries, and an example of each type, are illustrated in Fig. 8-24.

Command selection [1–14 or ?1–?14] :**9**

The INQUIRY command is selected.

Output to screen (1) or printer (2) :**1**

The answers are to be displayed.

Inquiry by Company Id (1),
  Company Balance by Name (2),
  or Check Number (3) :**1**

An Inquiry by Company ID is first selected.

Enter Company Id :**1**

All invoices for company 1 are requested and displayed.

Company id = 1   Name = WERN INC.
Invoice # = 21   Amount 345.56
Amount paid =   345.56
Date sent = 03/04/84 Comment =

Company id = 1   Name = WERN INC.
Invoice # = 34   Amount 500
Amount paid =   500
Date sent = 01/01/83 Comment =

Enter Company Id :⟨**CR**⟩

No more company ID inquiries are needed now.

Inquiry by Company Id (1),
  Company Balance by Name (2),
  or Check Number(3) :**2**

An inquiry is made into a company's balance.

Enter Company Name :**ZEPCO INC.**

The name of the company is entered and its balance displayed.

Company id =   5 Name = ZEPCO INC.
Balance =   1926.34

Enter Company Name :⟨**CR**⟩

No more company balances are needed now.

Inquiry by Company Id (1),
  Company Balance by Name (2),
  or Check Number(3) :**3**

An inquiry into a check is made.

Enter Check number :**542**

Invoices that check number 542 was used to pay are requested.

Company id =   2 Name = JASON CO.
Invoice # = 32   Amount 728.56
Amount paid =   728.56 Date sent =
02/19/84

The invoices are listed. The report shows a single check of $1182.54 was used to pay 2 invoices on 7/12/84.

Fig. 8-24 Making inquiries. (*Cont. on following page.*)

Check number = 542 Payment date =
   07 / 12 / 84
Check amount =   728.56 Comment =
   TESTING

Company id =   2 Name = JASON CO.
Invoice # = 38   Amount   453.98
Amount paid =   453.98 Date sent =
   03 / 14 / 84
Check number = 542   Payment date =
   07 / 12 / 84
Check amount =   453.98 Comment =

Enter Check number :⟨**CR**⟩   No more check inquiries are
                                          needed.

Inquiry by Company Id (1),   No more inquiries are needed. At
   Company Balance by Name (2),   this time, you will be returned
   or Check Number(3) :⟨**CR**⟩   to the Menu Level.

Fig. 8-24   *Cont.*

LISTING COMPANIES

A Summary Report of companies shows each company's ID. An up-to-date copy of this summary should be attached to the cover of your disk with A/R records. A Detailed Report also can be listed that shows each company's card. The COMPANIES command (10) generates these reports.

To prepare a report, you have to specify whether you want to see it on the screen or printer, and which report you want. When the reports are prepared, you will be returned to the Menu Level. These reports are illustrated in Fig. 8-25.

LISTING OPEN INVOICES

The OPEN command (11) is used to list all open invoices for a period.

NOTE:

By setting a long enough period, *all* open invoices can be printed. The resulting report can be used to convert to another A/R Program should you ever wish to do so.

```
Id =  1 Company Name  = WERN INC.
Id =  2 Company Name  = JASON CO.
Id =  3 Company Name  = PHIL'S SERVICE
Id =  4 Company Name  = J & R SUPPLIES
Id =  5 Company Name  = ZEPCO INC.
Id =  6 Company Name  = PALLOCK FISH
```

Fig. 8-25a Company Summary Report.

```
Id =  1
Company Name   = WERN INC.
Customer Name  = FRED R. JENKINS
Department     = CUSTOMER SUPPOR
Street Address = 234 YATES ROAD
Post Office Box =
City           = CULVER CITY
State          = NE
Zip code       = 78654
Phone Number   = (543) 555-5555


Id =  2
Company Name   = JASON CO.
Customer Name  = ROBERT GREEN
Department     = ACCOUNTING DEPT
Street Address = 45 PINEGROVE ST
Post Office Box =
City           = RIVERDALE
State          = MA
Zip code       = 04563
Phone Number   = (415) 555-5555
```

.
.
.

Fig. 8-25b Detailed Company Report.

The procedure for preparing this report is:

1. COMMAND SELECTION: Type 11 for the OPEN command.
2. OUTPUT TO SCREEN (1) OR PRINTER (2): Type the number for where you want to see the report.
3. ENTER STARTING DATE: The program will search for invoices within a period. Type the starting date for that period.
4. ENTER ENDING DATE: Type the period's ending date. The program will prepare your report.

5.   ENTER STARTING DATE: Type the starting date for a report that lists invoices in another period. If you do not wish another report, press the carriage return and you will be returned to the Menu Level.

An Open Invoices Report for January 1, 1982 to April 15, 1984 is shown in Fig. 8-26.

PERFORMING THE YEAR END PROCEDURE

The YEAR END command (12) is used to perform the year end procedure. The command clears from a disk all records of cash and paid invoices for a year, freeing space for a new year's work. Specifically, the command:

1.   Clears the Transaction File of all cash records for the year so the year-to-date cash total is zero, as appropriate for a new year.
2.   Clears the Payments File and the Transaction File of all paid invoices for the year so the Invoice Payment total is zero, as appropriate for the new year.
3.   Leaves the Customer File unaffected so the A/R balance is unchanged. Consequently, you do not have to reenter all your Customer File information on a new disk.
4.   Leaves unpaid invoices on your Transaction File so they don't need to be reentered.

You should initiate this procedure *after* you print December Month End Reports. Any cash or invoice payments that have been entered for the new year will not be affected by this procedure.

Company id =	2	Name = JASON CO.	Invoice # 42	Date sent = 04 / 13 / 84
Invoice Amount =	2314.98	Amount paid 0	Comment = INPUT ERROR PROBLEMS COR	
Company id =	4	Name = J & R SUPPLIES	Invoice # 35	Date sent = 02 / 23 / 84
Invoice Amount =	346.75	Amount paid 0	Comment =	
Company id =	3	Name = PHIL'S SERVICE	Invoice # 33	Date sent = 02 / 14 / 84
Invoice Amount =	645.96	Amount paid 600	Comment =	
Company id =	6	Name = PALLOCK FISH	Invoice # 1	Date sent = 02 / 25 / 82
Invoice Amount =	1320.42	Amount paid 0	Comment =	
Company id =	5	Name = ZEPCO INC.	Invoice # 37	Date sent = 03 / 30 / 84
Invoice Amount =	3426.34	Amount paid 1500	Comment =	

Fig. 8-26   An Open Invoices Report.

NOTE:

Make a copy of your data disk and use the copy for this procedure. You then will have a permanent, online record of the previous year's work that may be used for inquiries.

If you run out of space on your disk during the year, you can use the YEAR END command to start a continuation disk. In this case, you will copy the data disk and use the copy in this procedure. At the end of the year, you will need to add the Cash and Invoice Payments amounts from the two disks for yearly figures.

The year end procedure is:

1. COMMAND SELECTION: Type 12 for the YEAR END command.
2. ENTER YEAR TO CLOSE OUT AS YY: Type the last two digits of the year for which records are to be cleared. At the beginning of 1985, for example, you would type 84 to clear the 1984 records.

    Clearing will be started. The program will print messages that show clearing results from each file. When you are done looking at the report, press the carriage return, the screen will be cleared and you will be returned to the Menu Level.

The Year End Procedure is illustrated in Fig. 8-27.

Command selection [1–14 or ?1–?14] :**12**   The YEAR END command is selected.

Enter year to close out as yy :**84**   Records for 1984 are to be cleared.

Old cash file had 328 payments.   Note that 11 open invoices are
New file has 0 payments   left.
Old Transaction file had 912 records.
New file has 11 records.
Old Payment file had 115 records.
New file has 0 records.
Enter return to continue 〈**CR**〉   At this time, you will be returned to the Menu Level.

Fig. 8-27   The Year End Procedure.

PRINTING MONTHLY STATEMENTS

The STATEMENTS command (13) is used to print monthly statements. A monthly statement is a reminder notice. It lacks the legal significance of a contract or agreement.

In your agreement or contract, you state when payment is due. Payments can be due on invoice presentation. Or, you can allow your customers to pay in 30, 60, or 90 days after you present the invoice. If payment is not sent within the agreed time, you are entitled to impose a finance charge on the unpaid amount as long as you have stated this contingency in your agreement. The finance charge is usually 15 percent. Statements may be mailed anytime in a month.

For each customer with an open balance, the program will list all open invoices and show the total amount owed. Mailing labels for these customers also can be printed. The invoices are designed to fit on standard 8½″ × 11″ paper, one statement per sheet. You may wish to preprint a statement border that shows your address and who to make a check payable to. An example of such a border is shown in Fig. 8-30.

Before printing monthly statements, complete the following steps:

1. Post all payments so your records are up to date. If you will not be imposing finance charges, you can skip the remaining steps and begin printing statements.
2. Print an open invoices report with the OPEN command (11) to determine overdue invoices. Set the ending date for the report to the scheduled payment date and the starting date at least 1 year earlier to pick up old invoices. If you expect payments in 30 days, for example, set the ending date to 30 days before the current date, i.e., if the current date is 05/25/85, set the ending date to 04/25/85. Check the report and decide which customers, if any, should be penalized with a finance charge.
3. Compute the finance charges for the customers' invoices and mark them next to the customer's name on the report.
4. Create invoices for the finance charges. Record FINANCE CHARGE as the comment.

You now are ready to run monthly statements and print labels. To do so, you'll use the following procedure.

1. COMMAND SELECTION: Type 13 for the STATEMENTS command.
2. OUTPUT TO SCREEN (1) OR PRINTER (2): Type 1 if you wish to preview all statements. Type 2 to print them.

3. ENTER FINANCE CHARGE PERCENTAGE: Type a two-digit number that will appear in the statement line about finance charges. If you will be imposing a finance charge of 15 percent, type 15. If you are not imposing finance charges, press the carriage return. (Note that this number is used only as text for the statements; it is *not* used in any calculations.)
4. ENTER NUMBER OF DAYS BEFORE FINANCE CHARGE IMPOSED: Type the number of days that you allow customers to pay. If you are not using finance charges, press the carriage return. This information is used only for text on the statements; it is not used in any calculations.

At this time, the statements will be printed. When the last statement is printed, you will be prompted PRINT LABELS (Y/N). If you wish to print mailing labels, remove the statements paper from your printer and insert a roll of labels; type **Y**, which starts the printing of the labels. If you do not wish labels printed, type **N**, and you will be returned to the Menu Level.

The procedure for printing statements is illustrated in Fig. 8-28. A statement is shown in Fig. 8-29, and a statement on a preprinted border is shown in Fig. 8-30.

ENDING A/R PROGRAM OPERATION

When you are done with the A/R Program, respond to COMMAND SELECTION by typing **14** to EXIT. You will be returned to the operating system level.

Remove your data disk from its drive and return it to its cover.

Command selection [1–14 or ?1–?14] :**13**	The STATEMENTS command is selected.
Output to screen (1) or printer (2) :**2**	Statements are to be printed.
Enter finance charge Percentage :**12.5**	
Enter number of days before finance charge imposed :**30**	Data which will be printed on all statements is entered. When the carriage return is pressed, statement printing begins.

Fig. 8-28   Printing monthly statements.

J & R SUPPLIES
THOMAS R. THORTON   ,ACCOUNTING
612 FERUHL ROAD
COFFINGTON   ,CT

Date	Invoice #	Comment	Amount	Balance
02/23/84	35	STATIONARY, STAPLES, PENS, ETC..	$346.75	$346.75

···· Total Amount Due as of 08/31/84 : $346.75
Please pay this amount. Invoices not
paid in   30   days are subject to a
12.5 % finance charge.

Fig. 8-29   A monthly statement.

SCHEDULE OF ACTIVITIES

Time	Action
Program start-up	1. Use CARDS command (1) to create cards for companies if appropriate.
	2. Use BILLING command (2) to record open invoices. If a company has any opening balances unrelated to unpaid invoices, create a special invoice.
	3. Check work by generating reports with MONTH END (7), COMPANIES (10), and OPEN (11) commands.
	4. Use CHANGE command (4) and DELETE command (5) to correct mistakes, if necessary.
	5. Use COMPANIES command (10) to print reference list of company IDs. Attach list to disk cover.
Day of transaction (your business)	1. If sending an invoice to a new customer, set up a card for the customer with the CARDS command.
	2. Use BILLING command (2) to record each invoice sent out.
	3. Use PAYMENTS command (3) to record all payments and cash received.

```
J & R SUPPLIES
THOMAS R. THORTON, ACCOUNTING
612 FERUHL ROAD
COFFINGTON    CT
```

WALDEN OFFICE CENTER
24 Chesnut Drive
Kent, Vermont 01002
(802) 555-5555

Make Check Payable To:
    WALDEN OFFICE CENTER

Date	Invoice #	Comment	Amount	Balance
02/23/84	35	STATIONARY, STAPLES, PENS, ETC	$346.75	$346.75

**** Total Amount Due as of 08/31/84: $346.75
     Please pay this amount. Invoices not
     paid in 30 days are subject to a
     12.5% finance charge.

Questions about charges and payments should be directed to Ext. 651.

Fig. 8-30   A monthly statement in preprinted border.

Time	Action
Beginning of month (your service)	1. If sending an invoice to a new customer, set up a card with the CARDS command (1).
	2. Use BILLING command (2) to record all invoices sent last month.
	3. Use PAYMENTS command (3) to record all payments and cash received last month.
Beginning of month (all businesses)	1. Use MONTH END command (7) to print reports. Keep reports in folder.
	2. Use DESCENDING BALANCES command (8) to print report, if desired.
Late in month (all businesses)	1. Use PAYMENTS command (3) to record checks.
	2. Use OPEN command (11) to determine invoices on which to impose finance charges.
	3. Use BILLING command (2) to create finance charge invoices.
	4. Use STATEMENTS command (13) to print monthly statements and mailing labels.
Beginning of year (all businesses)	1. When program is accessed, set current date to December 31 of the previous year.
	2. Use BAD DEBT command (6) to declare bad debts and print bad debt report.
	3. Initiate beginning of month procedure.
	4. Determine storage capacity left on disk and decide if it will be enough for all records in the coming year. If it isn't, start a new disk.
Tax preparation	1. Use December Month End Reports to complete taxes.

ACCOUNTS RECEIVABLE PROGRAM
COMMAND SUMMARY

Command Number and Name	Function
1–CARDS	Sets up customer information card.
2–BILLING	Records invoices sent out.
3–PAYMENTS	Records invoice payments and cash received.
4–CHANGE	Changes information on cards, invoices, cash records, and invoice payments.
5–DELETE	Deletes open invoices, cards for customers with zero balances, cash records, and invoice payments with zero amounts.
6–BAD DEBT	Used to declare unpaid invoices as bad debts.
7–MONTH END	Generates Month End Reports.
8–DESCENDING BALANCES	Generates Descending Balances Report.
9–INQUIRY	Shows all invoices for a customer, the total amount a company owes, and invoices that a check was used to pay.
10–COMPANIES	Lists company IDs and cards.
11–OPEN	Lists all open invoices for a specified period.
12–YEAR END	Clears paid invoices from Transaction File.
13–STATEMENTS	Prints monthly statements and mailing labels.
14–EXIT	Ends program operation.

ACCOUNTS RECEIVABLE PROGRAM SOURCE CODE

The A/R Program consists of eight programs:

1. INCOME.BAS acts as a monitor and comprises the functions common to the entire A/R Program set, including the EXIT request (no. 14) from the main menu.
2. INCOME1.BAS handles the CARDS request (no. 1) from the main menu.
3. INCOME2.BAS handles the BILLING (no. 2) and PAYMENTS (no. 3) requests from the main menu.
4. INCOME3.BAS handles the CHANGE request (no. 4) from the main menu.
5. INCOME4.BAS handles the DELETE (no. 5) and OLD DEBT (no. 6) requests from the main menu.
6. INCOME5.BAS handles the MONTH END request (no. 7) from the main menu.
7. INCOME6.BAS handles the DESCENDING BALANCES (no. 8) and INQUIRY (no. 9) requests from the main menu.
8. INCOME7.BAS handles the COMPANIES (no. 10), OPEN (no. 11), YEAR END (no. 12), and STATEMENTS (no. 13) requests from the main menu.

You should type in all eight programs in the order of their corresponding names, assigning each program its respective name. All eight programs must be stored on the same disk.

INCOME.BAS

```
10 REM ***************************************************************
20 REM This program will provide most of the common functions of an    *
30 REM Accounts Receivable system.                                     *
40 REM The following functions are provided:                           *
50 REM   1. Cards               To update the Customer file            *
60 REM   2. Billing             To record invoices sent                *
70 REM   3. Payments            To record payments received            *
80 REM   4. Change              To update existing information         *
90 REM   5. Delete              To clean an open invoice               *
100 REM  6. Old Debt            To total and remove bad debts          *
110 REM  7. Month End           Detailed and summary month-end report  *
120 REM  8. Descending Balances Report of master file balances         *
130 REM  9. Inquiry             Report of invoices for a customer      *
140 REM 10. Companies           Report from customer master           *
150 REM 11. Open                Report of open invoices                *
152 REM 12. Year end            Year end file maint.                   *
```

```
154 REM  13.  Statements          Print statements for customers    *
156 REM  14.  Exit                Leave the program                 *
160 REM ***************************************************************
170 DIM RECNO(99)
180 DIM RECNOS(99)
190 MERGEDFILE$ = " "
200 GOSUB 6200
300 GOTO 5000
800 REM ***************************************************************
810 REM THIS SECTION WILL DISPLAY THE CASH SOURCE SELECTION TABLE     *
820 REM ***************************************************************
830 PRINT TAB(LEFTMARG); "          Source Selection               ";
840 I = 1
850 PRINT TAB(LEFTMARG); I "-" SOURCETBL$(I) "     " I+1 "-" SOURCETBL$(I+1)
860 I = I + 2 : IF I < 9 THEN GOTO 850
870 PRINT : RETURN
900 REM ***************************************************************
910 REM CONVERT A DATE IN MMDDYY FORMAT TO YYMMDD                     *
920 REM ***************************************************************
930 HOLDDATE$ = SPACE$(6)
940 MID$(HOLDDATE$,1,2) = MID$(MAKEDATE$,5,2)    ' MOVE YEAR VALUE TO FRONT
950 MID$(HOLDDATE$,3,2) = MID$(MAKEDATE$,1,2)    ' MOVE DAY VALUE TO MIDDLE
960 MID$(HOLDDATE$,5,2) = MID$(MAKEDATE$,3,2)    ' MOVE MONTH VALUE TO END
970 RETURN
1000 REM **************************************************************
1010 REM THIS SECTION IS FOR THE HELP FACILITY FROM THE MAIN MENU     *
1020 REM ON ENTRY THE VARIABLE A$ WILL HAVE A ? IN THE LEFTMOST POSITION *
1030 REM THE VALUE OF THE REST OF A$ VARIABLE WILL DETERMINE WHICH IF ANY *
1040 REM HELP MESSAGE WILL BE PRINTED                                 *
1050 REM **************************************************************
1060 AA$ = MID$(A$,2)                     ' GET THE REST OF THE HELP REQUEST
1070 AA = VAL(AA$)                        ' MAKE IT NUMERIC
1080 IF AA < 1 OR AA > 14 THEN PRINT "Valid help requests are ?1 through ?14" : RETURN
1090 ON AA GOSUB  1110,1120,1130,1150,1170,1190,
1200,1210,1230,1250,1270,1272,1274,1280
1100 RETURN
1110 PRINT
"Cards : This command will allow the addition of customer records." : RETURN
1120 PRINT
"Billing : This command will record invoices that have been sent." : RETURN
1130 PRINT
"Payment : This command will record the payment of open invoices and the "
1140 PRINT
"          receipt of cash income." : RETURN
1150 PRINT
"Change : This command will allow the changing of information for : "
1160 PRINT
"          customer records, invoices sent, payments made,
and cash received." : RETURN
1170 PRINT
"Delete : This command will allow the removal of customer, invoice, payment "
1180 PRINT
"          and cash records from the system." : RETURN
1190 PRINT
"Bad Debt : This command will record specified open invoices as
bad debts " : RETURN
1200 PRINT
"Month End : This command will produce a monthly
detail and/or summary report" : RETURN
1210 PRINT
"Descending Balances : This command will produce
a report of all customers "
1220 PRINT
"                      by descending balances." : RETURN
```

```
1230 PRINT
"Inquiry : This command will allow the examination of
the invoice and payment "
1240 PRINT
"          files based on customer id, customer name
or check number" : RETURN
1250 PRINT
"Companies : This command will produce a
detailed listing of all customers "
1260 PRINT
"          and/or a summary listing of all customers " : RETURN
1270 PRINT
"Open : This command will produce a listing of all open invoices " : RETURN
1272 PRINT
"Year end : This command will clear all closed invoices and payments for a"
1273 PRINT
"          given year" :RETURN
1274 PRINT
"Statements : This command will print statements for all customers "
1275 PRINT
"          with unpaid invoices ":RETURN
1280 PRINT
"Exit : This command will terminate the program" : RETURN
2000 REM ***********************************************************
2010 REM OPEN THE CUSTOMER FILE RANDOMLY                           *
2020 REM ***********************************************************
2030 OPEN "R",#2,DISK$+"CUSTOMER.DAT",124
2040 FIELD #2, 4 AS IDF$,20 AS COF$,20 AS NAF$,15 AS DEPF$,
15 AS STREETF$,15 AS CITYF$,2 AS STATEF$,9 AS ZIPF$,10 AS PHONEF$,
4 AS BALF$,10 AS PONUMF$
2050 RETURN
2060 REM ***********************************************************
2070 REM OPEN THE TRANSACTION FILE RANDOMLY                        *
2080 REM ***********************************************************
2090 OPEN "R",#3,DISK$+"TRANSACT.DAT",87
2100 FIELD #3, 4 AS TIDF$,20 AS TCOF$,5 AS INVF$,4 AS AMTF$,
4 AS PPAMTF$,6 AS DATESF$,6 AS DATEPF$,4 AS CHKNBRF$,
4 AS BADDEBTF$,30 AS COMF$
2110 RETURN
3010 REM ***********************************************************
3020 REM THIS SUBROUTINE WILL FIND THE REQUESTED INVOICE IN THE TRANSACTION*
3030 REM FILE AND RETURN THE RECORD NUMBER IN THE VARIABLE "TRANSID".  IF  *
3040 REM THE INVOICE NUMBER IN THE VARIABLE "TINV$" IS NOT FOUND THEN      *
3050 REM "TRANSID" WILL BE SET TO ZERO                                     *
3060 REM ***********************************************************
3070 TRANSID = 0 : II = 0
3080 II = II + 1          ' INCREMENT THE RECORD NBR
3090 IF II > TRANCNT THEN RETURN        ' EOF .. RECORD NOT FOUND
3100 GET #3,II                          ' GET THE RECORD
3110 IF CVI(TIDF$) = 0 THEN GOTO 3080   ' DELETED RECORD
3120 IF INVF$ = TINV$ THEN TRANSID = II : RETURN    ' RECORD FOUND .. GET OUT
3130 GOTO 3080                                      ' TRY AGAIN
3140 REM ***********************************************************
3150 REM THIS SUBROUTINE WILL FIND THE REQUESTED COMPANY IN THE CUSTOMER   *
3160 REM FILE AND RETURN THE RECORD NUMBER IN THE VARIABLE "COID". IF THE  *
3170 REM COMPANY NUMBER IN THE VARIABLE "TCOID" IS NOT FOUND THEN "COID"   *
3180 REM WILL BE SET TO ZERO                                               *
3190 REM ***********************************************************
3200 COID = 0 : II = 0
3210 II = II + 1               ' INCREMENT THE RECORD NBR
3220 IF II > CUSTCNT THEN RETURN' EOF .. RECORD NOT FOUND
3230 GET #2,II                 ' GET THE RECORD
3240 IF CVI(IDF$) = 0 THEN GOTO 3210     ' DELETED RECORD
3250 IF TCOID = CVI(IDF$) THEN COID = II : RETURN  ' RECORD FOUND .. GET OUT
```

```
3260 GOTO 3210                              ' TRY AGAIN
5000 REM ******************************************************************
5010 REM THIS IS THE MAIN PROCESSING LOOP OF THE PROGRAM               *
5020 REM ******************************************************************
5030 FOR I = 1 TO SCREENHEIGHT:PRINT:NEXT I     'CLEAR THE SCREEN
5040 PRINT TAB(LEFTMARG);
"        Accounts Receivable Program               ";
5050 PRINT TAB(LEFTMARG);
"          Available commands are:              ";
5060 PRINT TAB(LEFTMARG);
" 1 - Cards              2 - Billing            ";
5070 PRINT TAB(LEFTMARG);
" 3 - Payments           4 - Change            ";
5080 PRINT TAB(LEFTMARG);
" 5 - Delete             6 - Old Debt          ";
5090 PRINT TAB(LEFTMARG);
" 7 - Month End          8 - Descending balances";
5100 PRINT TAB(LEFTMARG);
" 9 - Inquiry           10 - Companies         ";
5110 PRINT TAB(LEFTMARG);
"11 - Open              12 - Year end          ";
5115 PRINT TAB(LEFTMARG);
"13 - Statements        14 - EXIT              ";
5120 PRINT TAB(LEFTMARG);
" " ;: LINE INPUT "Command selection [1-14 or ?1-?14] :";A$
5130 IF A$ = "" THEN GOTO 5120
5140 IF A$ = "?" THEN GOTO 5040
5150 IF MID$(A$,1,1) = "?" THEN GOSUB 1000 : GOTO 5120
5160 A = VAL(A$)
5170 IF A < 1 OR A > 14 THEN PRINT "Invalid selection" : GOTO 5120
5171 FOR I = 1 TO SCREENHEIGHT : PRINT : NEXT I
5172 IF A = 14 THEN CLOSE : END           ' CLOSE FILES AND GET OUT
5173 IF A > 1 THEN GOTO 5182
5174 IF MERGEDFILE$ <> "1" THEN MERGEDFILE$ = "1" :
CHAIN MERGE "INCOME1.BAS",6000,ALL,DELETE 6000-13000 :GOTO 5120
5175 GOTO 6000
5182 IF A > 3 THEN GOTO 5186
5184 IF MERGEDFILE$ <> "2" THEN MERGEDFILE$ = "2" :
CHAIN MERGE "INCOME2.BAS",6000,ALL,DELETE 6000-13000 :GOTO 5120
5185 GOTO 6000
5186 IF A > 4 THEN GOTO 5189
5187 IF MERGEDFILE$ <> "3" THEN MERGEDFILE$ = "3" :
CHAIN MERGE "INCOME3.BAS",6000,ALL,DELETE 6000-13000 : GOTO 5120
5188 GOTO 6000
5189 IF A > 5 THEN GOTO 5192
5190 IF MERGEDFILE$ <> "4" THEN MERGEDFILE$ = "4" :
CHAIN MERGE "INCOME4.BAS",6000,ALL,DELETE 6000-13000 : GOTO 5120
5191 GOTO 6000
5192 IF A > 7 THEN GOTO 5195
5193 IF MERGEDFILE$ <> "5" THEN MERGEDFILE$ = "5" :
CHAIN MERGE "INCOME5.BAS",6000,ALL,DELETE 6000-13000 : GOTO 5120
5194 GOTO 6000
5195 IF A > 9 THEN GOTO 5198
5196 IF MERGEDFILE$ <> "6" THEN MERGEDFILE$ = "6" :
CHAIN MERGE "INCOME6.BAS",6000,ALL,DELETE 6000-13000 : GOTO 5120
5197 GOTO 6000
5198 IF MERGEDFILE$ <> "7" THEN MERGEDFILE$ = "7" :
CHAIN MERGE "INCOME7.BAS",6000,ALL,DELETE 6000-13000 : GOTO 5120
5199 GOTO 6000
5200 REM ******************************************************************
5201 REM THIS SUBROUTINE WILL SAVE THE RECORD COUNTS IN THE ARFILES.CNT FILE*
5203 REM ******************************************************************
5205 OPEN "R",#1,DISK$+"ARFILES.CNT",16
5210 FIELD #1,4 AS CUSTCNT$,4 AS TRANCNT$,4 AS PAYMCNT$,4 AS CASHCNT$
```

```
5220 LSET CUSTCNT$ = MKS$(CUSTCNT)
5230 LSET TRANCNT$ = MKS$(TRANCNT)
5240 LSET PAYMCNT$ = MKS$(PAYMCNT)
5250 LSET CASHCNT$ = MKS$(CASHCNT)
5260 PUT #1,1
5270 CLOSE #1:RETURN
5300 REM ******************************************************************
5301 REM THIS SUBROUTINE WILL EITHER PRINT OR LPRINT THE CONTENTS OF THE  *
5302 REM FILE REPORT.FIL DEPENDING ON THE VALUE OF THE VARIABLE OUTTYPE$  *
5303 REM ******************************************************************
5305 OPEN "I",#1,DISK$+"REPORT.FIL"
5310 J = 0
5320 IF EOF(1) THEN GOTO 5370
5325 J = J + 1
5330 LINE INPUT #1,A$
5340 IF OUTTYPE$ = "2" THEN LPRINT A$ : GOTO 5320
5350 IF J MOD (SCREENHEIGHT -1) = 0 THEN
LINE INPUT "Enter return to continue :";CHGFIELD$
5360 PRINT A$ : GOTO 5320
5370 CLOSE #1 : FOR J = 1 TO 4 : PRINT : NEXT J
5380 RETURN
6000 REM THIS IS WHERE THE CHAINED PROGRAMS WILL BE LOADED
6200 REM ******************************************************************
6210 REM PROMPT FOR THE DISK DRIVE DESIGNATOR TO BE USED FOR ALL DISK FILES*
6220 REM IN THIS PROGRAM                                                  *
6230 REM ******************************************************************
6240 LINE INPUT "Drive the datafile will be on :" ; TDISK$
6250 IF TDISK$ = "" THEN PRINT "The default drive will be used":RETURN
6260 IF MID$(TDISK$,1,1) < "A" OR MID$(TDISK$,1,1) > "P" THEN GOTO 6240
6270 DISK$ = SPACE$(2) : LSET DISK$ = MID$(TDISK$,1,1)+":"
6300 REM ******************************************************************
6310 REM PROMPT THE USER FOR THE CURRENT DATE AND SAVE THIS VALUE FOR USE  *
6320 REM WHENEVER A CARRIAGE-RETURN IS ENTERED AT A PROMPT FOR A DATE      *
6330 REM ******************************************************************
6340 LINE INPUT "Enter the current date as mmddyy :";CDATE$
6350 IF CDATE$ = "" OR LEN(CDATE$) <> 6 THEN PRINT "Invalid date" : GOTO 6340
6360 PRINT "Current system date = "
MID$(CDATE$,1,2) "/" MID$(CDATE$,3,2) "/" MID$(CDATE$,5,2)
6370 DIM MONTH$(12)
6380 MONTH$(1) = "January " :  MONTH$(7) = "  July   "
6390 MONTH$(2) = "February" :  MONTH$(8) = " August "
6400 MONTH$(3) = "  March " :  MONTH$(9) = "September"
6410 MONTH$(4) = " April " :   MONTH$(10) = " October "
6420 MONTH$(5) = "  May  " :   MONTH$(11) = "November "
6430 MONTH$(6) = " June  " :   MONTH$(12) = "December "
6440 REM ************ DEFINE THE CASH PAYMENT SOURCE TABLE VALUES
6450 SOURCETBL$(1) = "Daily Income       "
6460 SOURCETBL$(2) = "Interest Payment "
6470 SOURCETBL$(3) = "Insurance Payment"
6480 SOURCETBL$(4) = "Royalties        "
6490 SOURCETBL$(5) = "Rebate           "
6500 SOURCETBL$(6) = "Miscellaneous    "
6510 SOURCETBL$(7) = "Item 1           "
6520 SOURCETBL$(8) = "Item 2           "
6550 REM ******************************************************************
6560 REM THIS SECTION WILL READ THE SCREEN HEIGHT AND WIDTH SIZES FROM    *
6570 REM THE PARAMETER FILE .. IF NO PARAMETER FILE EXISTS PROMPT FOR THE *
6580 REM VALUES AND CREATE ONE FOR NEXT TIME .. IN ANY CASE SET THE       *
6590 REM VARIABLES SCREENHEIGHT AND SCREENWIDTH AND GO TO THE NEXT STEP   *
6600 REM ******************************************************************
6610 OPEN "R",#1,DISK$+"PARAMTER.FIL",8
6620 FIELD #1,4 AS SCREENHEIGHT$,4 AS SCREENWIDTH$
6640 I = 1 : GET #1,I
6650 SCREENHEIGHT = CVI(SCREENHEIGHT$)
```

```
6660 SCREENWIDTH  = CVI(SCREENWIDTH$)
6670 IF SCREENHEIGHT > 0 AND SCREENWIDTH > 0 THEN GOTO 6770
6680 LINE INPUT "Enter screen height value (1-24) :" ; SCREENPARM$
6690 SCREENHEIGHT = VAL(SCREENPARM$)
6700 IF SCREENHEIGHT < 1 OR SCREENHEIGHT > 24 THEN GOTO 6680
6710 LINE INPUT "Enter screen width value (30-80) :" ; SCREENPARM$
6720 SCREENWIDTH = VAL(SCREENPARM$)
6730 IF SCREENWIDTH < 30 OR SCREENWIDTH > 80 THEN GOTO 6710
6740 LSET SCREENHEIGHT$ = MKI$(SCREENHEIGHT)
6750 LSET SCREENWIDTH$  = MKI$(SCREENWIDTH)
6760 I = 1 : PUT #1,I
6770 CLOSE #1 : SCRNCTR = 40 :LEFTMARG = SCREENWIDTH/2 - 20
7000 OPEN "R",#1,DISK$+"ARFILES.CNT",16
7010 FIELD #1,4 AS CUSTCNT$,4 AS TRANCNT$,4 AS PAYMCNT$,4 AS CASHCNT$
7020 GET #1,1
7030 CUSTCNT = CVS(CUSTCNT$)
7040 TRANCNT = CVS(TRANCNT$)
7050 PAYMCNT = CVS(PAYMCNT$)
7060 CASHCNT = CVS(CASHCNT$)
7070 CLOSE #1 : RETURN
13000 REM THIS IS THE LAST LINE THAT THE CHAINED PROGRAMS WILL OVERLAY
```

INCOME1.BAS

```
6000 ON A GOSUB 6020,6490,7210,6010,6010,6010,6010,6010,6010,6010,6010,6010
6010 GOTO 5000
6020 REM ****************************************************************
6030 REM This section will handle the Cards request from the main menu   *
6040 REM ****************************************************************
6050 OPEN "R",#1,DISK$+"CUSTOMER.KEY",4
6060 FIELD #1,4 AS LASTREC$
6070 LASTREC = 0
6090 GET #1,1
6100 LASTREC = CVI(LASTREC$)
6110 CLOSE #1
6120 GOTO 6140
6130 PRINT"No previous customers entered"
6140 GOSUB 2000                              ' GO OPEN CUSTOMER FILE
6150 LINE INPUT "Enter Company Name :";TNAME$
6160 IF TNAME$="" THEN GOTO 6420
6170 LASTREC = LASTREC + 1  : ID = LASTREC
6180 PRINT "New customer: ID = " ID
6190 LINE INPUT "Enter Customer Name :";NA$
6200 LINE INPUT "Enter Department Name :";DEP$
6210 LINE INPUT "Enter Street Address :";STREET$
6220 LINE INPUT "Enter Post Office Box Number :";PONUM$
6230 LINE INPUT "Enter City Name :";CITY$
6240 LINE INPUT "Enter State Abbreviation :";STATE$
6250 LINE INPUT "Enter Zip Code :";ZIP$
6260 LINE INPUT "Enter Phone Number :";PHONE$
6270 REM *************** NOW MOVE VALUES TO BUFFER FIELDS ***********
6280 LSET IDF$=MKI$(ID)
6290 LSET COF$=TNAME$
6300 LSET NAF$=NA$
6310 LSET DEPF$=DEP$
6320 LSET STREETF$=STREET$
6330 LSET CITYF$ = CITY$
6340 LSET STATEF$=STATE$
6350 LSET ZIPF$=ZIP$
6360 LSET PHONEF$=PHONE$
```

```
6370 LSET BALF$=MKS$(0)
6380 LSET PONUMF$=PONUM$
6390 REM *************** NOW PUT THE RECORD INTO THE FILE
6400 CUSTCNT = CUSTCNT + 1 : PUT #2,CUSTCNT
6410 GOTO 6150
6420 CLOSE #2
6430 OPEN "R",#1,DISK$+"CUSTOMER.KEY",4
6440 FIELD #1,4 AS LASTREC$
6450 LSET LASTREC$ = MKI$(LASTREC)
6460 PUT #1,1
6470 CLOSE
6475 GOSUB 5200           ' GO SAVE RECORD COUNTS
6480 RETURN
13000 REM *** THIS LINE IS HERE TO HAVE A COMMON
DELETE THRU LINE NUMBER FOR CHAINING FILES
```

INCOME2.BAS

```
6000 ON A GOSUB 6020,6490,7210,6010,6010,6010,6010,6010,6010,6010,6010,6010
6010 GOTO 5000
6490 REM *****************************************************************
6500 REM This section will handle the Billing request from the main menu *
6510 REM *****************************************************************
6520 OPEN "R",#1,DISK$+"LABEL.DAT",4
6530 FIELD #1,4 AS LIDF$
6540 LCNT = 0
6550 GOSUB 2060            ' GO OPEN TRANSACTION FILE
6560 GOSUB 2000            ' GO OPEN CUSTOMER FILE
6570 IF CUSTCNT > 0 THEN GOTO 6610
6580 PRINT "No customers in customer file" : CLOSE :
6590 LINE INPUT "Enter return to continue :";CHGFIELD$ : RETURN
6610 PRINT : PRINT : PRINT
6620 LINE INPUT "Enter Company ID :";TID$
6630 IF TID$ <> "" THEN GOTO 6660
6640 IF LCNT = 0 THEN CLOSE :KILL DISK$+"LABEL.DAT" :GOSUB 5200 :RETURN
6650 GOTO 7070
6660 TCOID = CVI(MKI$(VAL(TID$)))
6670 GOSUB 3140                          ' GO FIND CUSTOMER
6680 IF COID = 0 THEN PRINT "Company ID is invalid" : GOTO 6620
6690 LASTTRAN = LASTTRAN + 1
6700 PRINT "Company name = " COF$
6710 LINE INPUT "Enter Invoice Number :";INV$
6720 IF INV$ = "" THEN PRINT "Invoice number cannot be blank": GOTO 6710
6730 TINV$ = SPACE$(5)
6740 LSET TINV$ = INV$                   ' SET TRANSACTION FILE KEY
6750 GOSUB 3010                          ' GO GET A RECORD
6760 IF TRANSID <> 0 THEN PRINT "Invoice # already exists ": GOTO 6710
6770 LINE INPUT "Enter Amount :";AMT$
6780 IF AMT$ = "" OR VAL(AMT$) < .01 THEN
PRINT "Amount must be positive":GOTO 6770
6790 LINE INPUT "Enter Date :";DATES$
6800 LINE INPUT "Enter Comment :" ; TCOM$
6810 IF DATES$ = "" THEN DATES$ = CDATE$
6820 LINE INPUT "Print label ? (Y/N) :";LABEL$
6830 IF LABEL$ <> "Y" AND LABEL$ <> "N" THEN GOTO 6820
6840 IF LABEL$ = "N" THEN GOTO 6880
6850 LCNT = LCNT + 1
6860 LSET LIDF$ = MKI$(COID)
6870 PUT #1,LCNT
```

```
6880 REM *** NOW MOVE FIELDS TO RECORD BUFFER
6890 LSET TIDF$= MKI$(TCOID)
6900 LSET TCOF$= COF$
6910 LSET INVF$= INV$
6920 LSET AMTF$= MKS$(VAL(AMT$))
6930 LSET PPFLGF$= "N"
6940 LSET PPAMTF$= MKS$(0)
6950 LSET DATESF$= DATES$
6960 LSET DATEPF$= "        "
6970 LSET CHKNBRF$= "      "
6980 LSET BADDEBTF$ = MKS$(0)
6990 LSET COMF$    = TCOM$
7000 REM *** NOW PUT THE RECORD INTO THE TRANSACTION FILE
7010 TRANCNT = TRANCNT + 1
7020 PUT #3,TRANCNT
7030 REM *** NOW UPDATE THE MASTER FILE
7040 LSET BALF$ = MKS$(CVS(BALF$) + VAL(AMT$))
7050 PUT #2,COID : PRINT "Master record updated"
7060 GOTO 6620
7070 REM ************************ NOW PUT OUT THE LABELS
7080 LINE INPUT "Set up printer and hit carriage return when ready :";
CHGFIELD$
7090 FOR I = 1 TO LCNT
7100 GET #1,I
7110 J = CVI(LIDF$)
7120 GET #2,J
7130 LPRINT COF$
7140 LPRINT NAF$ DEPF$
7150 LPRINT STREETF$
7160 IF PONUMF$ <> "" THEN LPRINT PONUMF$
7170 LPRINT CITYF$ "," STATEF$ " " ZIPF$
7180 LPRINT
7190 NEXT I
7200 CLOSE : KILL DISK$+"LABEL.DAT" :GOSUB 5200 : RETURN
7210 REM *****************************************************************
7220 REM * THIS SECTION WILL HANDLE THE PAYMENT REQUEST FROM THE MAIN MENU  *
7230 REM *****************************************************************
7240 TOTPYMT = 0 : TOTCASH = 0
7250 GOSUB 2000              ' GO OPEN CUSTOMER FILE
7260 IF CUSTCNT < 1 THEN PRINT "There are no customers records":CLOSE:RETURN
7270 GOSUB 2060              ' GO OPEN TRANSACTION FILE
7280 IF TRANCNT < 1 THEN PRINT "There are no transaction records":CLOSE:RETURN
7300 PRINT : PRINT : PRINT : PRINT :
LINE INPUT "Entering Invoice payment(1) or Cash(2) :";CHG$
7310 IF CHG$ = "" THEN CLOSE : GOTO 8310
7320 IF CHG$ = "1" THEN GOTO 7350
7330 IF CHG$ = "2" THEN GOTO 8070
7340 GOTO 7300
7350 REM *****************************************************************
7360 REM THIS SECTION WILL HANDLE THE A/R PAYMENT REQUEST                *
7370 REM *****************************************************************
7380 OPEN "R",#1,DISK$+"PAYMENT.DAT",44
7390 FIELD #1,1 AS PDELF$,5 AS PINVF$,10 AS PDATEPF$,4 AS PCHKNBRF$,
4 AS PAMTF$,20 AS PCOMMF$
7400 TOTPYMT = 0
7420 PRINT : PRINT : PRINT : PRINT :
LINE INPUT "Enter Company name or ID number :" ; ABC$
7430 IF ABC$ = "" THEN CLOSE #1:GOTO 7300
7440 CO$ = SPACE$(20) : LSET CO$ = ABC$
7450 FOR I = 1 TO LEN(ABC$)
7460 IF MID$(ABC$,I,1) < "0" OR MID$(ABC$,I,1) > "9" THEN GOTO 7490
7470 NEXT I
7480 TID = VAL(CO$) : GOTO 7500
7490 TID = 0
```

```
7500 TRANSNBR = 0 : J = 0
7510 TRANSNBR = TRANSNBR + 1
7520 IF TRANSNBR > TRANCNT THEN GOTO 7610
7530 GET #3,TRANSNBR
7540 IF TID > 0 AND TID = CVI(TIDF$) THEN GOTO 7570
7550 IF TID = 0 AND CO$ = TCOF$ THEN GOTO 7570
7560 GOTO 7510
7570 IF CVS(AMTF$) - CVS(PPAMTF$) < .01 THEN
GOTO 7510        ' DON'T SHOW 0 BALANCES
7580 PRINT "Invoice # = " INVF$ " Company name = " TCOF$
" Balance = " CVS(AMTF$) - CVS(PPAMTF$)
7590 J = J + 1
7600 GOTO 7510
7610 IF J < 1 THEN PRINT "No Invoices found for this company":GOTO 7420
7620 LINE INPUT "Enter Invoice # :" ; INV$
7630 IF INV$ = "" THEN GOTO 7420
7640 TINV$ = SPACE$(5) : LSET TINV$ = INV$
7650 TRANSNBR = 0
7660 TRANSNBR = TRANSNBR + 1
7670 IF TRANSNBR > TRANCNT THEN PRINT "Invoice not found " : GOTO 7620
7680 GET #3,TRANSNBR
7690 IF TINV$ <> INVF$ THEN GOTO 7660
7700 IF CVS(AMTF$) - CVS(PPAMTF$) < .01 THEN
PRINT "Invoice has been paid " :GOTO 7620
7710 LINE INPUT "Is this correct (Y/N) :" ; CHGFIELD$
7720 IF CHGFIELD$ <> "Y" AND CHGFIELD$ <> "N" THEN GOTO 7710
7730 IF CHGFIELD$ <> "Y" THEN GOTO 7620
7740 LINE INPUT "Enter Payment Date :" ; PDATEP$
7750 IF PDATEP$ = "" THEN PDATEP$ = CDATE$
7760 LINE INPUT "Enter Check number :" ; PCHKNBR$
7770 LINE INPUT "Enter amount of payment :" ;
PAMT$          'NULL ENTRY=BALANCE
7780 IF PAMT$ = "" THEN PAMT = CVS(AMTF$) - CVS(PPAMTF$):GOTO 7800
7790 PAMT = VAL(PAMT$)
7800 IF PAMT > CVS(AMTF$)-CVS(PPAMTF$) THEN PRINT "Amt. too large ":GOTO 7770
7810 LINE INPUT "Enter comments :" ; PCOMM$
7820 PAYMCNT = PAYMCNT + 1
7830 LSET PDELF$    = "N"
7840 LSET PINVF$    = INV$
7850 LSET PDATEPF$  = PDATEP$
7860 LSET PCHKNBRF$ = PCHKNBR$
7870 LSET PCOMMF$   = PCOMM$
7880 LSET PAMTF$    = MKS$(PAMT)
7890 PUT #1,PAYMCNT
7900 TOTPYMT = TOTPYMT + PAMT
7910 PRINT "Invoice = " PINVF$ " Date = "
MID$(PDATEPF$,1,2) "/" MID$(PDATEPF$,3,2) "/" MID$(PDATEPF$,5,2)
" Check Nbr = " PCHKNBRF$ " AMOUNT  = " CVS(PAMTF$)
7920 PRINT "COMMENT = " PCOMMF$
7930 REM **** NOW UPDATE THE INVOICE RECORD (TRANSACTION FILE)
7940 LSET PPAMTF$   = MKS$(CVS(PPAMTF$) + CVS(PAMTF$))
7950 LSET DATEPF$   = PDATEP$
7960 LSET CHKNBRF$  = PCHKNBRF$
7970 PUT #3,TRANSNBR
7980 REM **** NOW UPDATE THE CUSTOMER RECORD (CARDS FILE)
7990 PRINT "Invoice record updated  balance = " CVS(AMTF$) - CVS(PPAMTF$)
8000 TCOID = CVI(TIDF$)             ' GET CUSTOMER FILE KEY
8010 GOSUB 3140                    ' GO GET CUSTOMER RECORD
8020 IF COID = 0 THEN
PRINT "FATAL ERROR .. CUSTOMER RECORD NOT FOUND":GOTO 7300
8030 LSET BALF$ = MKS$(CVS(BALF$) - CVS(PAMTF$))
8040 PUT #2,COID
8050 PRINT "Customer balance updated to " CVS(BALF$)
8060 PRINT "Payment has been recorded" :PRINT:PRINT:PRINT:PRINT:GOTO 7500
```

```
8070 REM ********************************************************************
8080 REM THIS SECTION WILL HANDLE THE CASH PAYMENT REQUEST            *
8090 REM ********************************************************************
8100 OPEN "R",#1,DISK$+"CASH.DAT",38
8110 FIELD #1,4 AS SOURCEF$,4 AS CAMTF$,10 AS CDATEPF$,20 AS CCOMMF$
8130 GOSUB 800                                ' GO PRINT SOURCE TABLE
8140 PRINT : PRINT
8150 LINE INPUT "Enter source (1-8) : " ; SOURCE$
8160 IF SOURCE$ = "" THEN CLOSE #1 : GOTO 7300
8170 SOURCE = VAL(SOURCE$)
8180 IF SOURCE < 1 OR SOURCE > 8 THEN GOTO 8150
8190 LINE INPUT "Enter amount :" ; CAMT$
8200 IF CAMT$ = "" THEN GOTO 8130
8210 CAMT = VAL(CAMT$)
8220 LINE INPUT "Enter date :" ; CDATEP$
8230 IF CDATEP$ = "" THEN CDATEP$ = CDATE$
8240 LINE INPUT "Enter comment :" ; CCOMM$
8250 LSET SOURCEF$ = MKS$(SOURCE)
8260 LSET CAMTF$   = MKS$(CAMT)
8270 LSET CDATEPF$ = CDATEP$
8280 LSET CCOMMF$  = CCOMM$
8290 CASHCNT = CASHCNT + 1 : PUT #1,CASHCNT
8300 TOTCASH = TOTCASH + CAMT:GOTO 8130
8310 PRINT "All payments and cash entered and transactions posted"
8320 PRINT "Total payments = " TOTPYMT " Total cash = " TOTCASH
8330 CLOSE : LINE INPUT "Enter return to continue" ;
CHGFIELD$ :GOSUB 5200: RETURN
13000 REM *** THIS LINE IS HERE TO HAVE A COMMON
DELETE THRU LINE NUMBER FOR CHAINING FILES
```

INCOME3.BAS

```
6000 ON A GOSUB 6010,6010,6010,6020,8560,6010,6010,6010,6010,6010,6010,6010
6010 GOTO 5000
6020 REM ********************************************************************
6030 REM * THIS SECTION WILL HANDLE THE CHANGE REQUEST FROM THE MAIN MENU  *
6040 REM ********************************************************************
6050 LASTREC = 0
6060 GOSUB 2000                              ' GO OPEN CUSTOMER FILE
6070 IF CUSTCNT > 0 THEN GOTO 6100
6080 PRINT "There are no customers to update"
6090 LINE INPUT "Enter return to continue :";CHGFIELD$ : CLOSE : RETURN
6100 GOSUB 2060                              ' GO OPEN TRANSACTION FILE
6110 LINE INPUT "Change Invoices(1), Cards(2), Cash
Payments(3) Invoice Payments(4) :";CHG$
6120 IF CHG$ = "" THEN CLOSE : RETURN
6130 CHG = VAL(CHG$) : IF CHG < 1 THEN GOTO 6110
6140 PRINT : PRINT : PRINT : PRINT
6150 ON CHG GOSUB 6200,6810,7180,7700
6160 GOTO 6110
6170 REM ********************************************************************
6180 REM THIS SECTION WILL HANDLE THE INVOICE CHANGE REQUEST             *
6190 REM ********************************************************************
6200 LINE INPUT "Enter Invoice # :"; INV$
6210 IF INV$ = "" THEN RETURN
6220 TINV$ = SPACE$(5) : LSET TINV$ = INV$
6230 GOSUB 3010                              ' FIND INVOICE
6240 IF TRANSID = 0 THEN PRINT"Invoice not found":GOTO 6200
6250 IF CVS(PPAMTF$) > 0 THEN
PRINT "Paid Invoice cannot be changed": GOTO 6200
```

```
6260 TCOID = CVI(TIDF$)
6270 GOSUB 3140                        ' FIND COMPANY RECORD
6280 IF COID = 0 THEN PRINT "Error .. customer record not found" : GOTO 6200
6290 PRINT : PRINT : PRINT : PRINT
6300 PRINT "    Invoice #  :  " INVF$ "  :  " TCOF$
6310 PRINT "(1) Amount      :  " CVS(AMTF$)
6320 PRINT "(2) Date sent   :  "
MID$(DATESF$,1,2) "/" MID$(DATESF$,3,2) "/" MID$(DATESF$,5,2)
6330 PRINT "(3) Comment     :  " COMF$
6340 PRINT "(4) Company ID  :  " CVI(TIDF$)
6350 LINE INPUT "Change what ? (1-4) :" ; CHGFIELD$
6360 IF CHGFIELD$ = "" THEN PUT #3,TRANSID : PRINT "Record Updated":GOTO 6200
6370 CHGFIELD = VAL(CHGFIELD$)
6380 IF CHGFIELD < 1 OR CHGFIELD > 4 THEN GOTO 6350
6390 ON CHGFIELD GOSUB 6410,6470,6510,6540
6400 GOTO 6350
6410 LINE INPUT "Enter amount     :" ;AMT$
6420 LSET BALF$=MKS$(CVS(BALF$) - CVS(AMTF$) + VAL(AMT$))
6430 PUT #2,COID
6440 LSET AMTF$=MKS$(VAL(AMT$))
6450 PRINT "New Customer Balance = " CVS(BALF$)
6460 RETURN
6470 LINE INPUT "Enter date sent  :" ;DATES$
6480 IF DATES$ = "" THEN DATES$ = CDATE$     ' IF DATE IS BLANK MAKE IT TODAY
6490 LSET DATESF$ = DATES$
6500 RETURN
6510 LINE INPUT "Enter Comment     :" ; COMM$
6520 LSET COMF$ = COMM$
6530 RETURN
6540 HID = COID                            ' SAVE CURRENT CO. RECORD #
6550 LINE INPUT "Enter Company ID :" ; TID$
6560 TCOID = CVI(MKI$(VAL(TID$)))          ' GET NEW CO RECORD
6570 GOSUB 3140                  ' FIND CO RECORD
6580 IF COID = <> 0 THEN GOTO 6630
6590 PRINT "Error .. customer record not found"
6600 COID = HID                            ' RESTORE OLD CO RECORD #
6610 GET #2,COID                           ' RETRIEVE OLD CO RECORD
6620 RETURN                                ' GET OUT
6630 PRINT "New Company name = " COF$
6640 LINE INPUT "Ok to update (Y/N) :" ;CHGFIELD$
6650 IF CHGFIELD$ <> "Y" AND CHGFIELD$ <> "N" THEN GOTO 6640
6660 IF CHGFIELD$ <> "Y" THEN RETURN
6670 LSET BALF$ = MKS$(CVS(BALF$) + CVS(AMTF$)) ' INCREASE BALANCE DUE
6680 PUT #2,COID                           ' UPDATE NEW COMPANY BALANCE
6690 PRINT "New Company = " COF$ " Balance = " CVS(BALF$)
6700 LSET TIDF$ = MKI$(TCOID)              ' UPDATE CO. NBR IN TRANS REC
6710 LSET TCOF$ = COF$                     ' UPDATE CO. NAME IN TRANS REC
6720 COID = HID                            ' RESTORE OLD CO. RECORD #
6730 GET #2,COID                           ' GET OLD COMPANY RECORD
6740 IF COID = 0 THEN PRINT "Error .. customer record not found" : RETURN
6750 LSET BALF$ = MKS$(CVS(BALF$) - CVS(AMTF$)) ' REDUCE BALANCE DUE
6760 PRINT "Old Company = " COF$ " Balance = " CVS(BALF$)
6770 PUT #2,COID                           ' UPDATE OLD COMPANY BALANCE
6780 PRINT "Both Company records updated"
6790 PUT #3,TRANSID : PRINT "Invoice record updated"
6800 RETURN
6810 REM ************************************************************************
6820 REM THIS SECTION WILL PROCESS THE CARDS CHANGE REQUEST           *
6830 REM ************************************************************************
6840 LINE INPUT "Enter Company ID :";TID$
6850 IF TID$ = "" THEN RETURN
6860 TCOID = CVI(MKI$(VAL(TID$)))
6870 GOSUB 3140
6880 IF COID = 0 THEN PRINT "Invalid Customer ID" : GOTO 6840
```

```
6890 PRINT "(1) Company name  = " COF$
6900 PRINT "(2) Customer name = " NAF$
6910 PRINT "(3) Department     = " DEPF$
6920 PRINT "(4) Street         = " STREETF$
6930 PRINT "(5) City           = " CITYF$
6940 PRINT "(6) State          = " STATEF$
6950 PRINT "(7) Zip            = " ZIPF$
6960 PRINT "(8) Telephone      = (
" MID$(PHONEF$,1,3) ") " MID$(PHONEF$,4,3) "-" MID$(PHONEF$,7,4)
6970 PRINT "(9) P.O. Number    = " PONUMF$
6980 PRINT : PRINT : PRINT
6990 LINE INPUT "Change what ? (1-9) :";CHGFIELD$
7000 IF CHGFIELD$ = "" THEN PUT #2,COID : PRINT "Record updated" : GOTO 6840
7010 CHGFIELD = VAL(CHGFIELD$)
7020 IF CHGFIELD < 1 OR CHGFIELD > 9 THEN GOTO 6990
7030 ON CHGFIELD GOSUB 7050,7100,7110,7120,7130,7140,7150,7160,7170
7040 GOTO 6990
7050 LINE INPUT "Enter Company Name :"; CO$
7060 LSET COF$=CO$
7070 PRINT "You must change company name for all open invoices. "
7080 PRINT "For a list of invoices, use INQUIRY command and old company name"
7090 RETURN
7100 LINE INPUT "Enter Customer name :" ; NA$    :LSET NAF$=NA$        :RETURN
7110 LINE INPUT "Enter Department name :" ; DEP$ :LSET DEPF$=DEP$      :RETURN
7120 LINE INPUT "Enter Street address :";STREET$ :LSET STREETF$=STREET$:RETURN
7130 LINE INPUT "Enter City name :";CITY$        :LSET CITYF$=CITY$    :RETURN
7140 LINE INPUT "Enter State abbrev. :";STATE$   :LSET STATEF$=STATE$  :RETURN
7150 LINE INPUT "Enter Zip Code :";ZIP$          :LSET ZIPF$=ZIP$      :RETURN
7160 LINE INPUT "Enter Phone number :";PHONE$    :LSET PHONEF$=PHONE$  :RETURN
7170 LINE INPUT "Enter P.O. number :";PONUM$     :LSET PONUMF$=PONUM$  :RETURN
7180 REM ****************************************************************
7190 REM THIS SECTION WILL ALLOW THE CHANGE OF CASH PAYMENTS          *
7200 REM ****************************************************************
7210 OPEN "R",#1,DISK$+"CASH.DAT",38
7220 FIELD #1,4 AS SOURCEF$,4 AS CAMTF$,10 AS CDATEPF$,20 AS CCOMMF$
7240 GOSUB 800                              ' GO PRINT SOURCE CODE TABLE
7250 PRINT : PRINT
7260 LINE INPUT "Enter source code (1-8) :" ; TSOURCE$
7270 IF TSOURCE$ = "" THEN CLOSE #1:RETURN
7280 TSOURCE = VAL(TSOURCE$)
7290 IF TSOURCE < 1 OR TSOURCE > 8 THEN
PRINT "Invalid source code " : GOTO 7240
7300 IF TSOURCE = 1 THEN LINE INPUT "Enter date of payment :";TDATE$
7310 J = 0 : I = 0
7320 I = I + 1 : IF I > CASHCNT THEN GOTO 7410
7330 GET #1,I
7340 IF CVS(SOURCEF$) <> TSOURCE  THEN GOTO 7320
7350 IF TSOURCE = 1 AND TDATE$ <> MID$(CDATEPF$,1,6) THEN GOTO 7320
7360 J = J + 1 : RECNOS(J) = I           ' REMEMBER THE RECORD NUMBER
7370 IF J MOD (SCREENHEIGHT/2) = 0 THEN
LINE INPUT "Enter return to continue :"; CHGFIELD$
7380 PRINT "(" J ") Source = " SOURCETBL$(CVS(SOURCEF$))
" Amount = " CVS(CAMTF$)
7390 PRINT "        Date =
" MID$(CDATEPF$,1,2) "/" MID$(CDATEPF$,3,2) "/" MID$(CDATEPF$,5,2)
" Comment = " CCOMMF$
7400 GOTO 7320
7410 IF J < 1 THEN PRINT "No records found for this source " : GOTO 7240
7420 LINE INPUT "Change which line :" ; RID$
7430 IF RID$ = "" THEN GOTO 7240
7440 IF RID$ = "?" THEN GOTO 7310         ' GO SHOW CHOICES AGAIN
7450 RID = VAL(RID$)
7460 IF RID > J OR RID < 1 THEN PRINT "Invalid record number " : GOTO 7420
7470 GET #1,RECNOS(RID)
```

```
7480 PRINT : PRINT : PRINT : PRINT
7490 PRINT "(1) SOURCE   = " SOURCETBL$(CVS(SOURCEF$))
7500 PRINT "(2) AMOUNT   = " CVS(CAMTF$)
7510 PRINT "(3) DATE     = " MID$(CDATEPF$,1,2) "/"
MID$(CDATEPF$,3,2) "/" MID$(CDATEPF$,5,2)
7520 PRINT "(4) COMMENT  = " CCOMMF$
7530 LINE INPUT "Change which (1-4) ? :" ; CHGFLD$
7540 IF CHGFLD$ = "" THEN PUT #1,RECNOS(RID) :
PRINT "Record updated": GOTO 7420
7550 CHG = VAL(CHGFLD$)
7560 IF CHG < 1 THEN GOTO 7530
7570 ON CHG GOSUB 7590,7650,7660,7690
7580 GOTO 7530
7590 GOSUB 800  ' GO PRINT SOURCE TABLE
7600 LINE INPUT "Enter source (1-8) :" ; SOURCE$
7610 IF SOURCE$ = "" THEN RETURN
7620 SOURCE = VAL(SOURCE$)
7630 IF SOURCE < 1 OR SOURCE > 8 THEN GOTO 7600
7640 LSET SOURCEF$ = MKS$(SOURCE) : RETURN
7650 LINE INPUT
"Enter amount :" ; CAMT$ : LSET CAMTF$ = MKS$(VAL(CAMT$)):RETURN
7660 LINE INPUT "Enter date :" ; CDATEP$ :
7670 IF CDATEP$ = "" THEN CDATEP$ = CDATE$
7680 LSET CDATEPF$ = CDATEP$ : RETURN
7690 LINE INPUT "Enter comment :" ; CCOMM$ : LSET CCOMMF$ = CCOMM$ : RETURN
7700 REM ****************************************************************
7710 REM THIS SECTION WILL HANDLE THE A/R PAYMENT CHANGE REQUEST        *
7720 REM ****************************************************************
7730 OPEN "R",#1,DISK$+"PAYMENT.DAT",44
7740 FIELD #1,1 AS PDELF$,5 AS PINVF$,10 AS PDATEPF$,
4 AS PCHKNBRF$,4 AS PAMTF$,20 AS PCOMMF$
7760 PRINT : PRINT : PRINT : PRINT :LINE INPUT "Enter invoice number :" ; INV$
7770 TINV$ = SPACE$(5) : LSET TINV$ = INV$
7780 IF INV$ = "" THEN CLOSE #1 : RETURN
7790 IF INV$ = "0" THEN GOTO 7760            ' DO NOT ALLOW INVOICE # = 0
7800 J = 0 : I = 0
7810 I = I + 1 : IF I > PAYMCNT THEN GOTO 7890
7820 GET #1,I
7830 IF TINV$ <> PINVF$  THEN GOTO 7810
7840 J = J + 1 : RECNOS(J) = I             ' REMEMBER THE RECORD NUMBER
7850 IF J MOD (SCREENHEIGHT/2) = 0 THEN
LINE INPUT"Enter return to continue";CHGFIELD$
7860 PRINT "(" J ") Invoice = " PINVF$ " Amount =
" CVS(PAMTF$) " Date = " MID$(PDATEPF$,1,2) "/" MID$(PDATEPF$,3,2)
"/" MID$(PDATEPF$,5,2)
7870 PRINT "        Check Number = " PCHKNBRF$ " Comment = " PCOMMF$
7880 GOTO 7810
7890 IF J < 1 THEN PRINT "No records found for this invoice " : GOTO 7760
7900 LINE INPUT "Change which line ? :" ; RID$
7910 IF RID$ = "" THEN GOTO 7760
7920 IF RID$ = "?" THEN GOTO 7800           ' GO SHOW CHOICES AGAIN
7930 RID = VAL(RID$)
7940 IF RID > J OR RID < 1 THEN PRINT "Invalid record number " : GOTO 7900
7950 GET #1,RECNOS(RID)
7960 PRINT : PRINT : PRINT : PRINT
7970 PRINT "(1) Invoice   = " PINVF$
7980 PRINT "(2) Date      =
" MID$(PDATEPF$,1,2) "/" MID$(PDATEPF$,3,2) "/" MID$(PDATEPF$,5,2)
7990 PRINT "(3) Check Nbr = " PCHKNBRF$
8000 PRINT "(4) Amount    = " CVS(PAMTF$)
8010 PRINT "(5) Comment   = " PCOMMF$
8020 LINE INPUT "Change which (1-5) ? :" ; CHGFIELD$
8030 IF CHGFIELD$ = "" THEN GOTO 7760
8040 CHGFIELD = VAL(CHGFIELD$)
```

```
8050 IF CHGFIELD < 1 THEN GOTO 8020
8060 ON CHGFIELD GOSUB 8080,8340,8370,8390,8540
8070 GOTO 7960
8080 LINE INPUT "Enter new invoice # :" ; NINV$
8090 IF NINV$ = "" THEN RETURN
8100 TINV$ = SPACE$(5) : LSET TINV$ = NINV$     ' SET KEY FOR SEARCH
8110 GOSUB 3010                       ' GO FIND TRANSACTION RECORD
8120 IF TRANSID = 0 THEN
PRINT "Error ... invoice record not found ": GOTO 8080
8130 HTRANSID = TRANSID ' SAVE RECORD NUMBER OF NEW INV.
8140 TINV$ = SPACE$(5) : LSET TINV$ = PINVF$     ' SET KEY FOR SEARCH
8150 GOSUB 2010
8160 IF TRANSID = 0 THEN PRINT "Error ... invoice record not found ": RETURN
8170 LSET PPAMTF$ = MKS$(CVS(PPAMTF$) - CVS(PAMTF$)) 'REDUCE AMT PAID
8180 PUT #3,TRANSID : PRINT "Old Invoice record updated "
8190 TCOID = CVI(TIDF$)                       ' SET CO KEY FOR SEARCH
8200 GOSUB 3140                        ' GO FIND COMPANY RECORD
8210 IF COID = 0 THEN PRINT "Error ..old customer record not found " : RETURN
8220 LSET BALF$ = MKS$(CVS(BALF$) + CVS(PAMTF$))     'INCREASE BALANCE DUE
8230 PUT #2,COID : PRINT "Old Customer balance updated "
8240 GET #3,HTRANSID    ' GET NEW INV .. SAVED KEY
8250 LSET PPAMTF$ = MKS$(CVS(PPAMTF$) + CVS(PAMTF$))    ' INCREASE AMT PAID
8260 PUT #3,HTRANSID : PRINT "New Invoice record updated "
8270 TCOID = CVI(TIDF$)                        ' SET CO KEY FOR SEARCH
8280 GOSUB 3140                        ' GO FIND COMPANY RECORD
8290 IF COID = 0 THEN PRINT "Error .. new customer record not found " : RETURN
8300 LSET BALF$ = MKS$(CVS(BALF$) - CVS(PAMTF$))     ' REDUCE BALANCE DUE
8310 PUT #2,COID : PRINT "New Customer balance updated "
8320 LSET PINVF$ = NINV$                    'REPLACE INVOICE NBR
8330 PUT #1,RECNOS(RID) : PRINT "Payment record updated" : RETURN
8340 LINE INPUT "Enter Date paid :" ; PDATEP$
8350 IF PDATEP$ = "" THEN PDATEP$ = CDATE$
8360 LSET PDATEPF$ = PDATEP$ : PUT #1,RECNOS(RID):RETURN
8370 LINE INPUT "Enter Check number :" ; PCHKNBR$ : LSET PCHKNBRF$ = PCHKNBR$
8380 PUT #1,RECNOS(RID):RETURN
8390 LINE INPUT "Enter new amount :" ; PAMT$
8400 PAMT = VAL(PAMT$)
8410 IF PAMT < 0 THEN PRINT "Amount cannot be negative" : GOTO 8390
8420 TINV$ = SPACE$(5) : LSET TINV$ = PINVF$
8430 GOSUB 3010                ' GO FIND TRANSACTION RECORD
8440 IF TRANSID = 0 THEN PRINT "Error ... invoice record not found " : RETURN
8450 LSET PPAMTF$ = MKS$(CVS(PPAMTF$) - CVS(PAMTF$) + VAL(PAMT$))
8460 PUT #3,TRANSID : PRINT "Transaction record updated "
8470 TCOID = CVI(TIDF$)
8480 GOSUB 3140
8490 IF COID = 0 THEN PRINT "Error .. customer record not found " : RETURN
8500 LSET BALF$ = MKS$(CVS(BALF$) + CVS(PAMTF$) - VAL(PAMT$))
8510 PUT #2,COID : PRINT "Customer balance updated "
8520 LSET PAMTF$ = MKS$(VAL(PAMT$))
8530 PUT #1,RECNOS(RID) : PRINT "Payment record updated" : RETURN
8540 LINE INPUT "Enter Comment :" ; PCOMM$ : LSET PCOMMF$ = PCOMM$
8550 PUT #1,RECNOS(RID):RETURN
13000 REM *** THIS LINE IS HERE TO HAVE A COMMON
DELETE THRU LINE NUMBER FOR CHAINING FILES
```

INCOME4.BAS

```
6000 ON A GOSUB 6010,6010,6010,6020,8560,6010,6010,6010,6010,6010,6010,6010
6010 GOTO 5000
8560 REM *********************************************************************
```

```
8570 REM THIS SECTION WILL HANDLE THE CLEAR REQUEST FROM THE MAIN MENU    *
8580 REM ******************************************************************
8590 LINE INPUT "Delete: Open Invoices(1),Cards(2),
Cash Payment(3),Invoice Payments(4) :" ; CHGFIELD$
8600 IF CHGFIELD$ = "" THEN CLOSE : RETURN
8610 CHGFIELD = VAL(CHGFIELD$)
8620 IF CHGFIELD < 1 THEN GOTO 8590
8630 PRINT : PRINT : PRINT : PRINT
8640 ON CHGFIELD GOSUB 8660,9130,9510,10100
8650 GOTO 8590
8660 REM ******************************************************************
8670 REM THIS WILL CLEAR AND DELETE SELECTED TRANSACTION (INVOICE) RECORDS *
8680 REM PROMPT FOR ALL INVOICES TO DELETE .. SET COMPANY ID TO ZERO      *
8690 REM ******************************************************************
8700 GOSUB 2000                          ' GO OPEN CUSTOMER FILE
8710 GOSUB 2060                          ' GO OPEN TRANSACTION FILE
8720 IF TRANCNT > 0 THEN GOTO 8750
8730 PRINT "There are no transaction records":CLOSE
8740 LINE INPUT 'Enter return to continue :";CHGFIELD$ : RETURN
8750 LINE INPUT "Enter Invoice # :" ;INV$
8760 IF INV$ = "" THEN GOTO 8950
8770 TINV$ = SPACE$(5) : LSET TINV$ = INV$
8780 GOSUB 3010                          ' GO FIND ENTERED INVOICE
8790 IF TRANSID = 0 THEN PRINT "Invoice not found" : GOTO 8750
8800 IF CVS(PPAMTF$) > 0 THEN PRINT "Paid Invoice cannot be deleted":GOTO 8750
8810 PRINT "Invoice = " INVF$ " Company # = " CVI(TIDF$) " Name = " TCOF$
8820 PRINT " Invoice amount = " CVS(AMTF$)
" Date sent = " MID$(DATESF$,1,2) "/" MID$(DATESF$,3,2)
"/" MID$(DATESF$,5,2)
8830 LINE INPUT "Ok to delete? (Y/N) :" ; CHGFIELD$
8840 IF CHGFIELD$ <> "Y" AND CHGFIELD$ <> "N" THEN GOTO 8830
8850 IF CHGFIELD$ <> "Y" THEN GOTO 8750
8860 IF CVS(AMTF$) = 0 THEN GOTO 8920     ' ZERO AMOUNT SKIP NEXT STEP
8870 TCOID = CVI(TIDF$)                   ' SET CUSTOMER FILE KEY
8880 GOSUB 3140                           ' GO FIND RECORD
8890 IF COID = 0 THEN PRINT "Error .. customer record not found " : RETURN
8900 LSET BALF$ = MKS$(CVS(BALF$) - CVS(AMTF$))   ' ADJUST BALANCE DUE
8910 PUT #2,COID                          ' REWRITE CUSTOMER RECORD
8920 LSET TIDF$ = MKI$(0)                 ' SET COMPANY ID TO 0
8930 PUT #3,TRANSID
8940 GOTO 8750
8950 REM ******************************************************************
8960 REM THIS SECTION WILL RE-ORGANIZE THE INVOICE FILE AND ELIMINATE ALL  *
8970 REM RECORDS WITH A COMPANY ID VALUE OF 0                             *
8980 REM ******************************************************************
8990 CLOSE                                ' CLOSE ALL OPEN FILES
9000 OPEN "R",#1,DISK$+"TRANSACT.DAT",87
9010 FIELD #1,4 AS TIDF$,77 AS FILLER$    ' ONLY DEFINE NEEDED FIELDS
9020 OPEN "R",#2,DISK$+"NEWTRANS.DAT",87
9030 FIELD #2,4 AS NTIDF$,77 AS NFILLER$           ' OUTPUT RECORD = INPUT RECORD
9040 I = 0 : J = 0
9050 I = I + 1
9060 IF I > TRANCNT THEN GOTO 9110
9070 GET #1,I                             ' GET INPUT RECORD
9080 IF CVI(TIDF$) = 0 THEN GOTO 9050
9090 LSET NTIDF$ = TIDF$ : LSET NFILLER$ = FILLER$  ' COPY THE RECORD
9100 J = J + 1 : PUT #2,J : GOTO 9050     ' PUT OUTPUT RECORD
9110 PRINT "Old file had " I - 1 " invoices.  New file has " J " invoices."
9120 CLOSE : KILL DISK$+"TRANSACT.DAT" :
NAME DISK$+"NEWTRANS.DAT" AS DISK$+"TRANSACT.DAT":
TRANCNT = J : GOSUB 5200 :RETURN
9130 REM ******************************************************************
9140 REM PROMPT FOR ALL COMPANIES (CARDS) TO DELETE .. SET CO # TO ZERO    *
9150 REM ******************************************************************
```

```
9160 GOSUB 2000                           ' GO OPEN CUSTOMER FILE
9170 IF CUSTCNT > 0 THEN GOTO 9200
9180 PRINT "There are no customer records":CLOSE
9190 LINE INPUT "Enter return to continue :";CHGFIELD$ :RETURN
9200 LINE INPUT "Enter Company # :" ;ID$
9210 IF ID$ = "" THEN GOTO 9330
9220 TCOID = CVI(MKI$(VAL(ID$)))
9230 GOSUB 3140                           ' FIND CUSTOMER RECORD
9240 IF COID = 0 THEN PRINT "Company not found" : GOTO 9200
9250 IF CVS(BALF$) > 0 THEN PRINT
"Company with outstanding balance cannot be deleted":GOTO 9200
9260 PRINT "Company # = " CVI(IDF$) " Name = " COF$
9270 LINE INPUT "Ok to delete? (Y/N) :" ; CHGFIELD$
9280 IF CHGFIELD$ <> "Y" AND CHGFIELD$ <> "N" THEN GOTO 9270
9290 IF CHGFIELD$ <> "Y" THEN GOTO 9200
9300 LSET IDF$ = MKI$(0)                          ' SET COMPANY ID TO 0
9310 PUT #2,COID
9320 GOTO 9200
9330 REM ***********************************************************************
9340 REM THIS SECTION WILL RE-ORGANIZE THE CARDS FILE AND ELIMINATE ALL     *
9350 REM RECORDS WITH A COMPANY ID VALUE OF 0                               *
9360 REM ***********************************************************************
9370 CLOSE                                ' CLOSE ALL OPEN FILES
9380 OPEN "R",#1,DISK$+"CUSTOMER.DAT",124
9390 FIELD #1,4 AS IDF$,120 AS FILLER$    ' ONLY DEFINE NEEDED FIELDS
9400 OPEN "R",#2,DISK$+"NEWCUST.DAT",124
9410 FIELD #2,4 AS NIDF$,120 AS NFILLER$          ' OUTPUT RECORD = INPUT RECORD
9420 I = 0 : J = 0
9430 I = I + 1
9440 IF I > CUSTCNT THEN GOTO 9490
9450 GET #1,I                             ' GET INPUT RECORD
9460 IF CVI(IDF$) = 0 THEN GOTO 9430
9470 LSET NIDF$ = IDF$ : LSET NFILLER$ = FILLER$  ' COPY THE RECORD
9480 J = J + 1 : PUT #2,J : GOTO 9430     ' PUT OUTPUT RECORD
9490 PRINT "Old file had " I - 1 " customers.  New file has " J " customers."
9500 CLOSE : KILL DISK$+"CUSTOMER.DAT" :
NAME DISK$+"NEWCUST.DAT" AS DISK$+"CUSTOMER.DAT":
CUSTCNT = J : GOSUB 5200 :RETURN
9510 REM ***********************************************************************
9520 REM THIS WILL CLEAR AND DELETE SELECTED CASH PAYMENT RECORDS          *
9530 REM PROMPT FOR ALL PAYMENT RECORDS TO DELETE .. SET SOURCE TO ZERO    *
9540 REM ***********************************************************************
9550 OPEN "R",#1,DISK$+"CASH.DAT",38
9560 FIELD #1, 4 AS SOURCEF$,4 AS CAMTF$,10 AS CDATEPF$,20 AS CCOMMF$
9570 IF CASHCNT > 0 THEN GOTO 9600
9580 PRINT "There are no Cash payment records":CLOSE
9590 LINE INPUT "Enter return to continue :";CHGFIELD$ : RETURN
9600 GOSUB 800                            ' DISPLAY CASH SOURCE MENU
9610 PRINT : PRINT :
9620 LINE INPUT "Enter source code :" ; SOURCE$
9630 IF SOURCE$ = "" THEN GOTO 9890
9640 I = 0 : J = 0
9650 I = I + 1
9660 IF I > CASHCNT THEN GOTO 9750
9670 GET #1,I
9680 IF CVS(SOURCEF$) <> VAL(SOURCE$) THEN GOTO 9650
9690 J = J + 1
9700 IF J MOD (SCREENHEIGHT/2) = 0 THEN
LINE INPUT"Enter return to continue";CHGFIELD$
9710 PRINT "(" J ") Source = " SOURCETBL$(CVS(SOURCEF$))
" Date = " MID$(CDATEPF$,1,2) "/" MID$(CDATEPF$,3,2) "/" MID$(CDATEPF$,5,2)
9720 PRINT "        Amount = " CVS(CAMTF$) " Comment = " CCOMMF$
9730 RECNO(J) = I   ' SAVE RECORD NUMBER
9740 GOTO 9650
```

```
9750 IF J < 1 THEN PRINT "No Cash records with this source" : GOTO 9600
9760 LINE INPUT "Delete which ? :" ; TRECNO$
9770 IF TRECNO$ = "" THEN GOTO 9620
9780 IF TRECNO$ = "?" THEN GOTO 9640
9790 TRECNO = VAL(TRECNO$)
9800 IF TRECNO < 1 OR TRECNO > J THEN PRINT " Invalid line number" : GOTO 9760
9810 GET #1,RECNO(TRECNO)
9820 IF CVS(SOURCEF$) = 0 THEN PRINT "Record already deleted" : GOTO 9760
9830 PRINT "Source = " SOURCETBL$(CVS(SOURCEF$))
" Date = " MID$(CDATEPF$,1,2) "/" MID$(CDATEPF$,3,2)
"/" MID$(CDATEPF$,5,2) " Amount = " CVS(CAMTF$) " Comment = " CCOMMF$
9840 LINE INPUT "Ok to delete? (Y/N) :" ; CHGFIELD$
9850 IF CHGFIELD$ <> "Y" AND CHGFIELD$ <> "N" THEN GOTO 9840
9860 IF CHGFIELD$ <> "Y" THEN GOTO 9760
9870 LSET SOURCEF$ = MKS$(0)
9880 PUT #1,RECNO(TRECNO) : PRINT "Record flagged for deletion" :GOTO 9760
9890 REM *******************************************************************
9900 REM THIS SECTION WILL RE-ORGANIZE THE CASH FILE AND ELIMIANTE ALL     *
9910 REM RECORDS WITH A SOURCE CODE OF ZERO                                *
9920 REM *******************************************************************
9930 CLOSE                                      ' CLOSE ALL OPEN FILES
9940 OPEN "R",#1,DISK$+"CASH.DAT",38
9950 FIELD #1, 4 AS SOURCEF$,4 AS CAMTF$,10 AS CDATEPF$,20 AS CCOMMF$
9960 OPEN "R",#2,DISK$+"NEWCASH.DAT",38
9970 FIELD #2, 4 AS NSOURCEF$,4 AS NCAMTF$,10 AS NCDATEPF$,20 AS NCCOMMF$
9980 I = 0 : J = 0
9990 I = I + 1
10000 IF I > CASHCNT THEN GOTO 10080
10010 GET #1,I                                  ' GET INPUT RECORD
10020 IF CVS(SOURCEF$) = 0 THEN GOTO 9990
10030 LSET NSOURCEF$ = SOURCEF$                  ' COPY THE RECORD
10040 LSET NCAMTF$   = CAMTF$                    ' ...
10050 LSET NCDATEPF$ = CDATEPF$                  ' ...
10060 LSET NCCOMMF$  = CCOMMF$                   ' ...
10070 J = J + 1 : PUT #2,J : GOTO 9990    ' PUT OUTPUT RECORD
10080 PRINT "Old file had " I - 1 " payments.  New file has " J " payments."
10090 CLOSE : KILL DISK$+"CASH.DAT" :
NAME DISK$+"NEWCASH.DAT" AS DISK$+"CASH.DAT":
CASHCNT = J : GOSUB 5200 : RETURN
10100 REM *******************************************************************
10110 REM THIS SECTION WILL CLEAR AND DELETE ALL A/R PAYMENT RECORDS WHICH  *
10120 REM HAVE A ZERO PAYMENT AMOUNT                                        *
10130 REM *******************************************************************
10140 OPEN "R",#1,DISK$+"PAYMENT.DAT",44
10150 FIELD #1,1 AS PDELF$,5 AS PINVF$,10 AS PDATEPF$,
4 AS PCHKNBRF$,4 AS PAMTF$,20 AS PCOMMF$
10160 IF PAYMCNT > 0 THEN GOTO 10190
10170 PRINT "There are no A/R payment records":CLOSE
10180 LINE INPUT "Enter return to continue :";CHGFIELD$ : RETURN
10190 I = 0 : J = 0
10200 PRINT "The following invoice payments with zero amounts will be deleted:"
10210 I = I + 1
10220 IF I > PAYMCNT THEN GOTO 10290
10230 GET #1,I
10240 IF CVS(PAMTF$) <> 0 THEN GOTO 10210
10250 IF J MOD SCREENHEIGHT = 0 THEN
LINE INPUT"Enter return to continue";CHGFIELD$
10260 PRINT "Invoice = " PINVF$ " Date paid = "
MID$(PDATEPF$,1,2) "/" MID$(PDATEPF$,3,2)
"/" MID$(PDATEPF$,5,2) " Amount = " CVS(PAMTF$)
10270 J = J + 1
10280 GOTO 10210
10290 IF J > 0 THEN GOTO 10320
10300 PRINT "No A/R payment records with zero amount" : CLOSE
```

```
10310 LINE INPUT "Enter return to continue :";CHGFIELD$ : RETURN
10320 LINE INPUT "Ok to delete? (Y/N) :" ; CHGFIELD$
10330 IF CHGFIELD$ <> "Y" AND CHGFIELD$ <> "N" THEN GOTO 10320
10340 IF CHGFIELD$ <> "Y" THEN CLOSE #1:RETURN
10350 REM ***************************************************************
10360 REM THIS SECTION WILL RE-ORGANIZE THE A/R PAYMENT FILE AND ELIMINATE ALL*
10370 REM RECORDS WITH AN AMOUNT OF ZERO                                 *
10380 REM ***************************************************************
10390 CLOSE                                    ' CLOSE ALL OPEN FILES
10400 OPEN "R",#1,DISK$+"PAYMENT.DAT",44
10410 FIELD #1,1 AS PDELF$,5 AS PINVF$,10 AS PDATEPF$,
4 AS PCHKNBRF$,4 AS PAMTF$,20 AS PCOMMF$
10420 OPEN "R",#2,DISK$+"NEWPYMT.DAT",44
10430 FIELD #2,1 AS NPDELF$,5 AS NPINVF$,10 AS NPDATEPF$,
4 AS NPCHKNBRF$,4 AS NPAMTF$,20 AS NPCOMMF$
10440 I = 0 : J = 0
10450 I = I + 1
10460 IF I > PAYMCNT THEN GOTO 10550
10470 GET #1,I                                 ' GET INPUT RECORD
10480 IF CVS(PAMTF$)    = 0 THEN GOTO 10450
10490 LSET NPDELF$      = PDELF$               ' COPY THE RECORD
10500 LSET NPINVF$      = PINVF$               ' ...
10510 LSET NPDATEPF$    = PDATEPF$             ' ...
10520 LSET NPCHKNBRF$   = PCHKNBRF$            ' ...
10530 LSET NPCOMMF$     = PCOMMF$              ' ...
10540 J = J + 1 : PUT #2,J : GOTO 10450        ' OUTPUT RECORD
10550 PRINT "Old file had " I - 1 " payments.  New file has " J " payments."
10560 CLOSE : KILL DISK$+"PAYMENT.DAT" :
NAME DISK$+"NEWPYMT.DAT" AS DISK$+"PAYMENT.DAT":
PAYMCNT = J : GOSUB 5200 : RETURN              '
13000 REM *** THIS LINE IS HERE TO HAVE A COMMON
DELETE THRU LINE NUMBER FOR CHAINING FILES
```

INCOME5.BAS

```
6000 ON A GOSUB 6010,6010,6010,6010,6010,
9090,6400,6020,8280,6010,6010,6010,6010,6010
6010 GOTO 5000
6400 REM ***************************************************************
6410 REM * THIS SECTION WILL HANDLE THE MONTH END REQUEST FROM THE MAIN MENU*
6420 REM ***************************************************************
6430 LINE INPUT "Output to screen (1) or printer (2) :" ; CHGFIELD$
6440 IF CHGFIELD$ <> "1" AND CHGFIELD$ <> "2" THEN GOTO 6430
6450 IF CHGFIELD$ = "1" THEN PRINTER$ = "N" : GOTO 6470
6460 PRINTER$ = "Y"
6470 LINE INPUT "Enter report year as yy :" ; RPTYR$
6480 IF RPTYR$ = "" THEN CLOSE : RETURN
6490 IF RPTYR$ < "01" OR RPTYR$ > "99" THEN GOTO 6470
6500 LINE INPUT "Enter report month as mm :"; RPTMN$
6510 IF RPTMN$ < "01" OR RPTMN$ > "12" THEN GOTO 6500
6520 LINE INPUT "Report prepared for :" ; RPTNAME$
6530 RNAMELEN = LEN(RPTNAME$) : IF RNAMELEN > 30 THEN RNAMELEN = 30
6540 LINE INPUT "Do you want the Detailed Report (Y/N) :"; CHGFIELD$
6550 IF CHGFIELD$ <> "Y" AND CHGFIELD$ <> "N" THEN GOTO 6540
6560 IF CHGFIELD$ <> "Y" THEN GOTO 7650
6570 GOSUB 2060                                ' GO OPEN TRANSACTION FILE
6580 IF TRANCNT > 0 THEN GOTO 6610
6590 PRINT "There are no transaction records":CLOSE
6600 LINE INPUT "Enter return to continue :";CHGFIELD$ : RETURN
6610 OPEN "R",#1,DISK$+"PAYMENT.DAT",44
```

```
6620 FIELD #1,1 AS PDELF$,5 AS PINVF$,10 AS PDATEPF$,
4 AS PCHKNBRF$,4 AS PAMTF$,20 AS PCOMMF$
6630 IF PAYMCNT > 0 THEN GOTO 6660
6640 PRINT "There are no payment records" : CLOSE
6650 LINE INPUT "Enter return to continue :";CHGFIELD$ : RETURN
6660 OPEN "O",#2,DISK$+"SORTKEY.DAT"
6670 J = 0
6680 FOR I = 1 TO PAYMCNT
6690 GET #1,I
6700 IF CVS(PAMTF$) = 0 THEN GOTO 6790
6710 IF MID$(PDATEPF$,5,2) <> RPTYR$ OR
MID$(PDATEPF$,1,2) <> RPTMN$ THEN GOTO 6790
6720 TINV$ = PINVF$                         'SET TRANS FILE KEY FOR RANDOM READ
6730 GOSUB 3010                             'GO READ TRANSACTION FILE
6740 IF TRANSID <> 0 THEN GOTO 6770
6750 PRINT "Error .. transaction record not found" : CLOSE
6760 LINE INPUT "Enter return to continue :";CHGFIELD$ : RETURN
6770 PRINT #2,USING "\              \";TCOF$;:PRINT #2,
USING "#####";CVI(TIDF$);: PRINT #2,
USING "\    \";INVF$;:PRINT #2,
USING "\      \";PDATEPF$;:PRINT #2,USING "########.##";CVS(PAMTF$);
6780 J = J + 1
6790 NEXT I
6800 CLOSE #1,#2
6810 IF J < 1 THEN PRINT "No records selected for this period":CLOSE:GOTO 6470
6820 OPEN "I",#2,DISK$+"SORTKEY.DAT"
6830 FOR I = 1 TO J
6840 SORTKEYS$(I) = INPUT$(49,#2)
6850 NEXT I
6860 CLOSE #2
6870 SWITCHED = 0
6880 FOR I = 1 TO J-1
6890 IF SORTKEYS$(I) < SORTKEYS$(I+1) OR
SORTKEYS$(I) = SORTKEYS$(I+1) THEN GOTO 6920
6900 HOLDKEYS$ = SORTKEYS$(I) :
SORTKEYS$(I) = SORTKEYS$(I+1) : SORTKEYS$(I+1) = HOLDKEYS$
6910 SWITCHED = 1
6920 NEXT I
6930 IF SWITCHED = 1 THEN GOTO 6870
6940 GOSUB 2000                             ' GO OPEN CUSTOMER FILE
6950 TOTPYMT = 0 : TOTCASH = 0
6960 FOR I = 1 TO J
6970 TINV$ = MID$(SORTKEYS$(I),26,5)        ' GET INVOICE RECORD KEY
6980 DATEPAID$ = MID$(SORTKEYS$(I),31,8)    ' GET DATE PAID FROM SORT REC
6990 AMTPAID  = VAL(MID$(SORTKEYS$(I),39,11)) ' GET AMOUNT PAID
7000 TOTPYMT  = TOTPYMT + AMTPAID
7010 GOSUB 3010                             ' GO GET THE INVOICE RECORD
7020 IF TRANSID = 0 THEN PRINT "Error .. invoice not found" : RETURN
7030 TCOID = CVI(TIDF$)                      ' GET CUSTOMER RECORD KEY
7040 GOSUB 3140                             ' GO GET GET CUSTOMER RECORD
7050 IF COID = 0 THEN
PRINT "Error .. Customer record not found " TCOID : RETURN
7060 IF I <> 1 AND I MOD SCREENHEIGHT <> 0 THEN GOTO 7080
7070 IF PRINTER$ = "Y" THEN GOTO 7210 ELSE GOTO 7090
7080 IF PRINTER$ = "Y" THEN GOTO 7270 ELSE GOTO 7150
7090 PRINT:PRINT:PRINT: PRINT TAB(32); MONTH$(VAL(RPTMN$))
7100 PRINT TAB(25) ; "Detailed Month End Report"
7110 PRINT TAB((SCREENWIDTH - (RNAMLEN+10))/2) ; "For " RPTNAME$
7120 PRINT : PRINT "Invoices Paid: " : PRINT
7130 PRINT
"Company Name        Invoice #   Amount    Date Sent
Date Paid   Payment Amt."
7140 PRINT
"_____  _____ _____  _____
_____  _____"
```

```
7150 PRINT USING "\                    \";COF$;:PRINT " ";
7160 PRINT USING "\    \";INVF$;:PRINT "    ";
7170 PRINT USING "$$##,###.##";CVS(AMTF$);:PRINT "    ";
7180 PRINT MID$(DATESF$,1,2) "/"
MID$(DATESF$,3,2) "/" MID$(DATESF$,5,2) "    ";
7190 PRINT MID$(DATEPAID$,1,2) "/"
MID$(DATEPAID$,3,2) "/" MID$(DATEPAID$,5,2) "    ";
7200 PRINT USING "$$##,###.##";AMTPAID  : GOTO 7330
7210 LPRINT:LPRINT:LPRINT: LPRINT TAB(32); MONTH$(VAL(RPTMN$))
7220 LPRINT TAB(25) ; "Detailed Month End Report"
7230 LPRINT TAB((SCREENWIDTH - (RNAMLEN+10))/2) ; "For " RPTNAME$
7240 LPRINT : LPRINT "Invoices Paid: " : LPRINT
7250 LPRINT
"Company Name          Invoice #   Amount    Date Sent
Date Paid   Payment Amt."
7260 LPRINT
"_____  _____  _____   _____
_____  _____"
7270 LPRINT USING "\                    \";COF$;:LPRINT " ";
7280 LPRINT USING "\    \";INVF$;:LPRINT "    ";
7290 LPRINT USING "$$##,###.##";CVS(AMTF$);:LPRINT "    ";
7300 LPRINT MID$(DATESF$,1,2) "/"
MID$(DATESF$,3,2) "/" MID$(DATESF$,5,2) "    ";
7310 LPRINT MID$(DATEPAID$,1,2) "/"
MID$(DATEPAID$,3,2) "/" MID$(DATEPAID$,5,2) "    ";
7320 LPRINT USING "$$##,###.##";AMTPAID
7330 NEXT I
7340 IF PRINTER$ = "Y" THEN GOTO 7360
7350 J = 0 : PRINT : PRINT "Cash Received: " : PRINT :GOTO 7370
7360 J = 0 : LPRINT " " : LPRINT "Cash Received: " : LPRINT " " : GOTO 7370
7370 OPEN "R",#1,DISK$+"CASH.DAT",38
7380 FIELD #1,4 AS SOURCEF$,4 AS CAMTF$,10 AS CDATEPF$,20 AS COOMMF$
7390 IF PRINTER$ = "Y" THEN GOTO 7410
7400 IF CASHCNT < 1 THEN PRINT "No cash records on file" : GOTO 7580
7410 IF CASHCNT < 1 THEN LPRINT "No cash records on file" : GOTO 7580
7420 FOR I = 1 TO CASHCNT
7430 GET #1,I
7440 IF CVS(CAMTF$) = 0 THEN GOTO 7520
7450 IF MID$(CDATEPF$,5,2) <> RPTYR$ THEN GOTO 7570
7460 IF MID$(CDATEPF$,1,2) <> RPTMN$ THEN GOTO 7570
7470 TOTCASH = TOTCASH + CVS(CAMTF$)
7480 J = J + 1
7490 IF PRINTER$ = "Y" THEN GOTO 7540
7500 IF J = 1 OR J/60 = 0 THEN PRINT "Date Paid    Source     Amount"
7510 IF J = 1 OR J/60 = 0 THEN PRINT "_____    _____    _____"
7520 PRINT MID$(CDATEPF$,1,2) "/"
MID$(CDATEPF$,3,2) "/" MID$(CDATEPF$,5,2) "    ";:
PRINT USING "##";CVS(SOURCEF$);:PRINT "      ";: PRINT
USING "$$##,###.##";CVS(CAMTF$)
7530 GOTO 7570
7540 IF J = 1 OR J/60 = 0 THEN LPRINT "Date Paid    Source     Amount"
7550 IF J = 1 OR J/60 = 0 THEN LPRINT "_____    _____    _____"
7560 LPRINT MID$(CDATEPF$,1,2) "/" MID$(CDATEPF$,3,2) "/"
MID$(CDATEPF$,5,2) "      ";: LPRINT
USING "##";CVS(SOURCEF$);:LPRINT "      ";:
LPRINT USING "$$##,###.##";CVS(CAMTF$)
7570 NEXT I
7580 IF PRINTER$ = "Y" THEN GOTO 7620
7590 PRINT : PRINT "   Total Payments : ";:PRINT USING "$###,###.##";TOTPYMT
7600 PRINT : PRINT "   Total Cash     : ";:PRINT USING "$###,###.##";TOTCASH
7610 GOTO 7640
7620 LPRINT : LPRINT "   Total Payments : ";:LPRINT USING "$###,###.##";TOTPYMT
7630 LPRINT : LPRINT "   Total Cash     : ";:LPRINT USING "$###,###.##";TOTCASH
7640 CLOSE
7650 LINE INPUT "Do you want the Summary Report :" ;CHGFIELD$
```

```
7660 IF CHGFIELD$ <> "Y" AND CHGFIELD$ <> "N" THEN GOTO 7650
7670 IF CHGFIELD$ <> "Y" THEN FOR I = 1 TO 500 : NEXT I : RETURN
7680 GOSUB 2060                          ' GO OPEN TRANSACTION FILE
7690 OPEN "R",#1,DISK$+"CASH.DAT",38
7700 FIELD #1,4 AS SOURCEF$,4 AS CAMTF$,10 AS CDATEPF$,20 AS CCOMMF$
7710 IF CASHCNT < 1 THEN PRINT "No cash records on file" : GOTO 7810
7720 YRLYCASH = 0 : MONTHCASH = 0
7730 FOR I = 1 TO CASHCNT
7740 GET #1,I
7750 IF CVS(CAMTF$) = 0 THEN GOTO 7800
7760 IF MID$(CDATEPF$,5,2) <> RPTYR$ THEN GOTO 7800
7770 YRLYCASH = YRLYCASH + CVS(CAMTF$)
7780 IF MID$(CDATEPF$,1,2) <> RPTMN$ THEN GOTO 7800
7790 MONTHCASH = MONTHCASH + CVS(CAMTF$)
7800 NEXT I
7810 CLOSE #1
7820 YRLYPYMT = 0 : MONTHPYMT = 0
7830 OPEN "R",#1,DISK$+"PAYMENT.DAT",44
7840 FIELD #1,1 AS PDELF$,5 AS PINVF$,10 AS PDATEPF$,
4 AS PCHKNBRF$,4 AS PAMTF$,20 AS PCOMMF$
7850 IF PAYMCNT < 1 THEN PRINT "There are no payment records" : GOTO 8010
7860 J = 0
7870 FOR I = 1 TO PAYMCNT
7880 GET #1,I
7890 IF CVS(PAMTF$) = 0 THEN GOTO 7940
7900 IF MID$(PDATEPF$,5,2) <> RPTYR$ THEN GOTO 7940
7910 YRLYPYMT = YRLYPYMT + CVS(PAMTF$)
7920 IF MID$(PDATEPF$,1,2) <> RPTMN$ THEN GOTO 7940
7930 MONTHPYMT = MONTHPYMT + CVS(PAMTF$)
7940 NEXT I
7950 TOTBAD = 0 : TOTAR = 0
7960 FOR I = 1 TO LOF(3)/87
7970 GET #3,I
7980 IF CVI(TIDF$) = 0 THEN GOTO 8020
7990 TOTAR = TOTAR + (CVS(AMTF$) - CVS(PPAMTF$))
8000 TOTBAD = TOTBAD + CVS(BADDEBTF$)
8010 NEXT I
8020 CLOSE
8030 IF PRINTER$ = "Y" THEN GOTO 8160
8040 PRINT:PRINT:PRINT: PRINT TAB(32); MONTH$(VAL(RPTMN$))
8050 PRINT TAB(25) ; "Summary Month End Report"
8060 PRINT TAB((SCREENWIDTH - (RNAMLEN+10))/2) ; "For " RPTNAME$
8070 PRINT "This month "
8080 PRINT "        Invoices paid : ";:PRINT USING "$$##,###.##"; MONTHPYMT
8090 PRINT "        Cash received : ";:PRINT USING "$$##,###.##"; MONTHCASH
8100 PRINT "This year  "
8110 PRINT "        Invoices paid : ";:PRINT USING "$$##,###.##"; YRLYPYMT
8120 PRINT "        Cash received : ";:PRINT USING "$$##,###.##"; YRLYCASH
8130 PRINT "Total outstanding receivables : " ;:
PRINT USING "$$##,###.##"; TOTAR
8140 PRINT "Total bad debts            : " ;:
PRINT USING "$$##,###.##"; TOTBAD
8150 PRINT : LINE INPUT "Enter return to continue :" ;CHGFIELD$ : RETURN
8160 LPRINT:LPRINT:LPRINT: LPRINT TAB(32); MONTH$(VAL(RPTMN$))
8170 LPRINT TAB(25) ; "Summary Month End Report"
8180 LPRINT TAB((SCREENWIDTH - (RNAMLEN+10))/2) ; "For " RPTNAME$
8190 LPRINT "This month "
8200 LPRINT "        Invoices paid : ";:LPRINT USING "$$##,###.##"; MONTHPYMT
8210 LPRINT "        Cash received : ";:LPRINT USING "$$##,###.##"; MONTHCASH
8220 LPRINT "This year  "
8230 LPRINT "        Invoices paid :`";:LPRINT USING "$$##,###.##"; YRLYPYMT
8240 LPRINT "        Cash received : ";:LPRINT USING "$$##,###.##"; YRLYCASH
8250 LPRINT "Total outstanding receivables : " ;:
LPRINT USING "$$##,###.##"; TOTAR
```

```
8260 LPRINT "Total bad debts                    : " ;;
LPRINT USING "$$##,###.##"; TOTBAD
8270 RETURN
9090 REM **************************************************************
9100 REM THIS SECTION WILL HANDLE THE BAD DEBT REQUEST FROM THE MAIN MENU   *
9110 REM **************************************************************
9120 GOSUB 2000                            ' GO OPEN CUSTOMER FILE
9130 GOSUB 2060                            ' GO OPEN TRANSACTION FILE
9140 LINE INPUT "Enter starting date :" ; STARTDATE$
9150 IF STARTDATE$ <> "" THEN GOTO 9200
9160 LINE INPUT "Do you want the Bad Debt Detail report :";CHGFIELD$
9170 IF CHGFIELD$ <> "Y" AND CHGFIELD$ <> "N" THEN GOTO 9160
9180 IF CHGFIELD$ <> "Y" THEN CLOSE : RETURN
9190 GOTO 9750
9200 IF LEN(STARTDATE$) <> 6 THEN PRINT "INVALID DATE FORMAT" :GOTO 9140
9210 LINE INPUT "Enter ending date :" ; ENDDATE$
9220 IF ENDDATE$ = "" THEN ENDDATE$ = CDATE$
9230 IF LEN(ENDDATE$) <> 6 THEN GOTO 9210
9240 MAKEDATE$ = STARTDATE$
9250 GOSUB 910
9260 STARTDATE$ = HOLDDATE$
9270 MAKEDATE$ = ENDDATE$
9280 GOSUB 910                        ' PUT ENDDATE IN YYMMDD FORMAT
9290 ENDDATE$ = HOLDDATE$
9300 J = 0
9310 FOR I = 1 TO TRANCNT
9320 GET #3,I
9330 IF CVI(TIDF$) = 0 THEN GOTO 9430   ' DELETED TRANSACTION
9340 MAKEDATE$ = DATESF$
9350 GOSUB 910                        ' RE ARRANGE FILE DATE TO YYMMDD
9360 IF HOLDDATE$ < STARTDATE$ OR HOLDDATE$ > ENDDATE$ THEN GOTO 9430
9370 IF CVS(AMTF$) - CVS(PPAMTF$) < .01 THEN GOTO 9430 ' IT HAS BEEN PAID
9380 J = J + 1
9390 PRINT "(" J ") Company id = " CVI(TIDF$)
" Name = " TCOF$ " Invoice # " INVF$
9400 PRINT "       Invoice Amount = " CVS(AMTF$)
" Amount paid " CVS(PPAMTF$) " Balance due " CVS(AMTF$) - CVS(PPAMTF$)
9410 PRINT "       Date Sent = " MID$(DATESF$,1,2)
"/" MID$(DATESF$,3,2) "/" MID$(DATESF$,5,2)
9420 RECNO(J) = I                        ' SAVE TRANS FILE RECORD NBR
9430 NEXT I
9440 IF J < 1 THEN PRINT "No open invoices in this period" : GOTO 9140
9450 K = 0
9460 LINE INPUT "Enter record number for bad debt :" ; TRECNO$
9470 IF TRECNO$ = "" THEN GOTO 9530
9480 TRECNO = VAL(TRECNO$)
9490 IF TRECNO < 1 OR TRECNO > J THEN PRINT "Invalid record number" :GOTO 9460
9500 K = K + 1
9510 HRECNO(K) = RECNO(TRECNO)
9520 GOTO 9460
9530 IF K < 1 THEN GOTO 9140
9540 FOR I = 1 TO K
9550 J = HRECNO(I) : GET #3,J
9560 PRINT "(" J ") Company id = " CVI(TIDF$)
" Name = " TCOF$ " Invoice # = " INVF$
9570 PRINT "       Invoice Amount = " CVS(AMTF$)
" Amount paid " CVS(PPAMTF$) " Balance due " CVS(AMTF$) - CVS(PPAMTF$)
9580 NEXT I
9590 LINE INPUT "OK to clear amounts as bad debts? (Y/N) :" ; CHGFIELD$
9600 IF CHGFIELD$ <> "Y" AND CHGFIELD$ <> "N" THEN GOTO 9590
9610 IF CHGFIELD$ <> "Y" THEN GOTO 9140
9620 FOR I = 1 TO K
9630 GET #3,HRECNO(I)
9640 BADDEBT = CVS(AMTF$) - CVS(PPAMTF$)
```

```
9650 LSET BADDEBTF$ = MKS$(CVS(BADDEBTF$) + BADDEBT)
9660 LSET PPAMTF$   = MKS$(CVS(PPAMTF$) + BADDEBT)
9670 TCOID = CVI(TIDF$)                          'SET CUST KEY FOR READ
9680 GOSUB 3140                                  'GO READ CUST. FILE
9690 IF COID = 0 THEN PRINT "Error .. customer record not found" : RETURN
9700 LSET BALF$ = MKS$(CVS(BALF$) - BADDEBT)
9710 PUT #2,COID                                 ' REPLACE CUSTOMER RECORD
9720 PUT #3,HRECNO(I)                            ' REPLACE TRANSACTION RECORD
9730 NEXT I
9740 GOTO 9140
9750 LINE INPUT "Output to screen (1) or printer (2) :" ; CHGFIELD$
9760 IF CHGFIELD$ <> "1" AND CHGFIELD$ <> "2" THEN GOTO 9750
9765 OUTTYPE$ = CHGFIELD$
9770 OPEN "O",#1,DISK$+"REPORT.FIL"
9790 J = 0
9800 FOR I = 1 TO TRANCNT
9810 GET #3,I
9820 IF CVI(TIDF$) = 0 OR CVS(BADDEBTF$) < 0 THEN GOTO 9890
9830 J = J + 1
9835 IF J = 1 OR J MOD 60 = 0 THEN PRINT #1,CHR$(12)    ' PUT OUT A FORM FEED
9840 IF J = 1 OR J MOD 60 = 0 THEN
PRINT #1,
"Invoice #            Company Name      Date Sent   Inv. Amount  Bad Debt Amount"
9850 IF J = 1 OR J MOD 60 = 0 THEN
PRINT #1,
"_____            _____     _____  _____  _____"
9860 PRINT #1,
INVF$ "          " TCOF$ "     "
MID$(DATESF$,1,2) "/" MID$(DATESF$,3,2) "/" MID$(DATESF$,5,2) "     ";
9870 PRINT #1,USING "$$##,###.##"; CVS(AMTF$);:PRINT #1,"        ";
9880 PRINT #1,USING "$$##,###.##"; CVS(BADDEBTF$)
9890 NEXT I :PRINT #1,"   "
9895 CLOSE : GOSUB 5300        ' GO PRINT REPORT ON REQUESTED DEVICE
9900 IF CHGFIELD$ = "1" THEN LINE INPUT "Enter return to continue " ;CHGFIELD$
9910 CLOSE : RETURN
13000 REM ***** THIS LINE IS HERE TO PROVIDE A COMMON
DELETE THRU LINE NUMBER FOR CHAINING
```

INCOME6.BAS

```
6000 ON A GOSUB 6010,6010,6010,6010,6010,9090,6400,6020,8280,
6010,6010,6010,6010,6010
6010 GOTO 5000
6020 REM *************************************************************
6030 REM * THIS SECTION WILL HANDLE THE DESCENDING BALANCE REPORT REQUEST  *
6040 REM *************************************************************
6050 LINE INPUT "Output to screen (1) or printer (2) :" ; CHGFIELD$
6060 IF CHGFIELD$ <> "1" AND CHGFIELD$ <> "2" THEN GOTO 6050
6070 OUTTYPE$ = CHGFIELD$
6080 OPEN "O",#1,DISK$+"REPORT.FIL"
6090 I = 0 : J = 0
6100 GOSUB 2000                              ' GO OPEN CUSTOMER FILE
6110 IF CUSTCNT > 0 THEN GOTO 6140
6120 PRINT "No existing customers" : CLOSE
6130 LINE INPUT "Enter return to continue :";CHGFIELD$ : RETURN
6140 I = I + 1
6150 IF I > CUSTCNT THEN GOTO 6190
6160 GET #2,I
6170 IF CVI(IDF$) = 0 THEN GOTO 6160
6180 J = J + 1 : BAL(J) = CVS(BALF$) : RECNO(J) = I : GOTO 6140
```

```
6190 IF J > 0 THEN GOTO 6220
6200 PRINT "No existing customers" : CLOSE
6210 LINE INPUT "Enter return to continue :";CHGFIELD$ : RETURN
6220 SWITCHED = 0
6230 FOR I = 1 TO J-1
6240 IF BAL(I) > BAL(I+1) OR BAL(I) = BAL(I+1) THEN GOTO 6280
6250 HOLDBAL = BAL(I) : BAL(I) = BAL(I+1) : BAL(I+1) = HOLDBAL
6260 HOLDREC = RECNO(I) : RECNO(I) = RECNO(I+1) : RECNO(I+1) = HOLDREC
6270 SWITCHED = 1
6280 NEXT I
6290 IF SWITCHED = 1 THEN GOTO 6220
6295 IF I MOD 60 = 0 OR I = 1 THEN PRINT #1,CHR$(12)       ' PUT OUT A FORM FEED
6300 IF I MOD 60 = 0 OR I = 1 THEN PRINT #1,
"     Company Name          Customer Name          Balance      Phone Nbr."
6310 IF I MOD 60 = 0 OR I = 1 THEN PRINT #1,
"_____  _____  _____  _____"
6320 FOR I = 1 TO J
6330 GET #2,RECNO(I)
6340 PRINT #1,COF$ "   " NAF$ "   " ;: PRINT #1,USING "$$##,###.##";CVS(BALF$);
6350 PRINT #1," (" MID$(PHONEF$,1,3) ") "
MID$(PHONEF$,4,3) "-" MID$(PHONEF$,7,4)
6370 NEXT I
6372 CLOSE : GOSUB 5300        ' GO PRINT REPORT ON REQUESTED DEVICE
6380 IF OUTTYPE$ = "1" THEN LINE INPUT "Enter c/r to continue";CHGFIELD$
6390 RETURN
8280 REM ************************************************************************
8290 REM THIS ROUTINE WILL HANDLE THE INQUIRY REQUEST FROM THE MAIN MENU      *
8300 REM ************************************************************************
8310 LINE INPUT "Output to screen (1) or printer (2) :" ; CHGFIELD$
8320 OUTTYPE$ = CHGFIELD$
8330 IF CHGFIELD$ <> "1" AND CHGFIELD$ <> "2" THEN GOTO 8310
8360 GOSUB 2060                          ' GO OPEN TRANSACTION FILE
8370 LINE INPUT "Inquiry by Company Id (1),
Company Balance by Name (2), or Check Number(3) :" ; CHGFIELD$
8380 IF CHGFIELD$ = "" THEN CLOSE : RETURN
8390 CHGFIELD = VAL(CHGFIELD$)
8400 IF CHGFIELD < 1 THEN GOTO 8370
8410 ON CHGFIELD GOSUB 8430,8660,8840
8420 GOTO 8370
8430 REM ************************************************************************
8440 REM THIS SECTION WILL HANDLE INQUIRY BY COMPANY ID NUMBER                *
8450 REM ************************************************************************
8460 OPEN "R",#2,DISK$+"PAYMENT.DAT",44
8470 FIELD #2,1 AS PDELF$,5 AS PINVF$,10 AS PDATEPF$,
4 AS PCHKNBRF$,4 AS PAMTF$,20 AS PCOMMF$
8480 PRINT " " : LINE INPUT "Enter Company Id :" ; TID$
8490 IF TID$ = "" THEN CLOSE #2:RETURN
8500 TID = CVI(MKI$(VAL(TID$)))
8510 IF TID < 1 THEN PRINT " Invalid Company id ": GOTO 8480
8515 OPEN "O",#1,DISK$+"REPORT.FIL"
8520 J = 0
8530 FOR I = 1 TO TRANCNT
8540 GET #3,I
8550 IF TID <> CVI(TIDF$) THEN GOTO 8640
8560 PRINT #1,"   "
8570 PRINT #1," Company id = " CVI(TIDF$) " Name = " TCOF$ "
8580 PRINT #1," Invoice # = " INVF$ " Amount " CVS(AMTF$)
8590 PRINT #1," Amount paid = " CVS(PPAMTF$)
" Date sent = " MID$(DATESF$,1,2) "/"
MID$(DATESF$,3,2) "/" MID$(DATESF$,5,2) " Comment = " COMF$
8600 PRINT #1,"   "
8610 J = J + 5           ' FIVE LINES PER PRINTED RECORD
8640 NEXT I
8645 CLOSE #1:GOSUB 5300        ' GO PRINT REPORT ON REQUESTED DEVICE
```

```
8650 GOTO 8480
8660 REM ********************************************************************
8670 REM THIS SECTION WILL HANDLE INQUIRY COMPANY BALANCE BY COMPANY NAME   *
8680 REM ********************************************************************
8690 GOSUB 2000                              ' GO OPEN CUSTOMER FILE
8700 LINE INPUT "Enter Company Name :" ; TCO$
8710 IF TCO$ = "" THEN CLOSE #2:RETURN
8720 CO$ = SPACE$(20) : LSET CO$ = TCO$
8725 OPEN "O",#1,DISK$+"REPORT.FIL"
8730 J = 0
8740 FOR I = 1 TO CUSTCNT
8750 GET #2,I
8760 IF CVI(IDF$) = 0 OR CO$ <> COF$ THEN GOTO 8820      'CO ID OF 0 = DELETED
8770 PRINT #1," Company id = " CVI(IDF$)
" Name = " COF$ " Balance = " CVS(BALF$)
8780 PRINT #1," "
8790 J = J + 2      ' TWO LINES PER PRINTED RECORD
8820 NEXT I
8825 CLOSE #1 : GOSUB 5300      ' GO PRINT REPORT ON REQUESTED DEVICE
8830 GOTO 8700
8840 REM ********************************************************************
8850 REM THIS SECTION WILL HANDLE INQUIRY BY CHECK NUMBER                   *
8860 REM ********************************************************************
8870 OPEN "R",#2,DISK$+"PAYMENT.DAT",44
8880 FIELD #2,1 AS PDELF$,5 AS PINVF$,10 AS PDATEPF$,
4 AS PCHKNBRF$,4 AS PAMTF$,20 AS PCOMMF$
8890 LINE INPUT "Enter Check number :" ; TCHKNBR$
8900 IF TCHKNBR$ = "" THEN CLOSE #2:RETURN
8910 CHKNBR$ = SPACE$(4) : LSET CHKNBR$ = TCHKNBR$
8915 OPEN "O",#1,DISK$+"REPORT.FIL"
8930 FOR I = 1 TO PAYMCNT
8940 GET #2,I
8950 IF CVS(PAMTF$) = 0 OR PCHKNBRF$ <> CHKNBR$ THEN GOTO 9070 '0 AMT = DELETE
8960 TINV$ = PINVF$                           ' SET TRANS FILE KEY
8970 GOSUB 3010                               ' READ TRANS FILE
8980 IF TRANSID = 0 THEN PRINT "ERROR .. transaction record not found" : RETURN
8990 PRINT #1," Company id = " CVI(TIDF$)
" Name = " TCOF$ " Invoice # = " INVF$ " Amount " CVS(AMTF$)
9000 PRINT #1," Amount paid = " CVS(PPAMTF$)
" Date sent = " MID$(DATESF$,1,2) "/" MID$(DATESF$,3,2) "/" MID$(DATESF$,5,2)
9010 PRINT #1," Check number = " PCHKNBRF$
" Payment date = " MID$(PDATEPF$,1,2) "/"
MID$(PDATEPF$,3,2) "/" MID$(PDATEPF$,5,2) " Check amount = " CVS(PAMTF$)
9020 PRINT #1," Comment = " PCOMMF$
9030 PRINT #1," "
9070 NEXT I
9075 CLOSE #1:GOSUB 5300      ' GO PRINT REPORT ON REQUESTED DEVICE
9080 GOTO 8890
9090 REM ********************************************************************
9100 REM THIS SECTION WILL HANDLE THE BAD DEBT REQUEST FROM THE MAIN MENU   *
9110 REM ********************************************************************
9120 GOSUB 2000                              ' GO OPEN CUSTOMER FILE
9130 GOSUB 2060                              ' GO OPEN TRANSACTION FILE
9140 LINE INPUT "Enter starting date :" ; STARTDATE$
9150 IF STARTDATE$ <> "" THEN GOTO 9200
9160 LINE INPUT "Do you want the Bad Debt Detail report :";CHGFIELD$
9170 IF CHGFIELD$ <> "Y" AND CHGFIELD$ <> "N" THEN GOTO 9160
9180 IF CHGFIELD$ <> "Y" THEN CLOSE : RETURN
9190 GOTO 9750
9200 IF LEN(STARTDATE$) <> 6 THEN PRINT "INVALID DATE FORMAT" :GOTO 9140
9210 LINE INPUT "Enter ending date :" ; ENDDATE$
9220 IF ENDDATE$ = "" THEN ENDDATE$ = CDATE$
9230 IF LEN(ENDDATE$) <> 6 THEN GOTO 9210
9240 MAKEDATE$ = STARTDATE$
```

```
9250 GOSUB 910
9260 STARTDATE$ = HOLDDATE$
9270 MAKEDATE$ = ENDDATE$
9280 GOSUB 910                    ' PUT ENDDATE IN YYMMDD FORMAT
9290 ENDDATE$ = HOLDDATE$
9300 J = 0
9310 FOR I = 1 TO TRANCNT
9320 GET #3,I
9330 IF CVI(TIDF$) = 0 THEN GOTO 9430   ' DELETED TRANSACTION
9340 MAKEDATE$ = DATESF$
9350 GOSUB 910                    ' RE ARRANGE FILE DATE TO YYMMDD
9360 IF HOLDDATE$ < STARTDATE$ OR HOLDDATE$ > ENDDATE$ THEN GOTO 9430
9370 IF CVS(AMTF$) - CVS(PPAMTF$) < .01 THEN GOTO 9430 ' IT HAS BEEN PAID
9380 J = J + 1
9390 PRINT "(" J ") Company id = " CVI(TIDF$)
" Name = " TCOF$ " Invoice # " INVF$
9400 PRINT "       Invoice Amount = " CVS(AMTF$)
" Amount paid " CVS(PPAMTF$) " Balance due " CVS(AMTF$) - CVS(PPAMTF$)
9410 PRINT "      Date Sent = " MID$(DATESF$,1,2)
"/" MID$(DATESF$,3,2) "/" MID$(DATESF$,5,2)
9420 RECNO(J) = I                              ' SAVE TRANS FILE RECORD NBR
9430 NEXT I
9440 IF J < 1 THEN PRINT "No open invoices in this period" : GOTO 9140
9450 K = 0
9460 LINE INPUT "Enter record number for bad debt :" ; TRECNO$
9470 IF TRECNO$ = "" THEN GOTO 9530
9480 TRECNO = VAL(TRECNO$)
9490 IF TRECNO < 1 OR TRECNO > J THEN PRINT "Invalid record number" :GOTO 9460
9500 K = K + 1
9510 HRECNO(K) = RECNO(TRECNO)
9520 GOTO 9460
9530 IF K < 1 THEN GOTO 9140
9540 FOR I = 1 TO K
9550 J = HRECNO(I) : GET #3,J
9560 PRINT "(" J ") Company id = " CVI(TIDF$)
" Name = " TCOF$ " Invoice # = " INVF$
9570 PRINT "      Invoice Amount =
" CVS(AMTF$) " Amount paid "
CVS(PPAMTF$) " Balance due " CVS(AMTF$) - CVS(PPAMTF$)
9580 NEXT I
9590 LINE INPUT "OK to clear amounts as bad debts? (Y/N) :" ; CHGFIELD$
9600 IF CHGFIELD$ <> "Y" AND CHGFIELD$ <> "N" THEN GOTO 9590
9610 IF CHGFIELD$ <> "Y" THEN GOTO 9140
9620 FOR I = 1 TO K
9630 GET #3,HRECNO(I)
9640 BADDEBT = CVS(AMTF$) - CVS(PPAMTF$)
9650 LSET BADDEBTF$ = MKS$(CVS(BADDEBTF$) + BADDEBT)
9660 LSET PPAMTF$   = MKS$(CVS(PPAMTF$) + BADDEBT)
9670 TCOID = CVI(TIDF$)                         'SET CUST KEY FOR READ
9680 GOSUB 3140                                 'GO READ CUST. FILE
9690 IF COID = 0 THEN PRINT "Error .. customer record not found" : RETURN
9700 LSET BALF$ = MKS$(CVS(BALF$) - BADDEBT)
9710 PUT #2,COID                               ' REPLACE CUSTOMER RECORD
9720 PUT #3,HRECNO(I)                          ' REPLACE TRANSACTION RECORD
9730 NEXT I
9740 GOTO 9140
9750 LINE INPUT "Output to screen (1) or printer (2) :" ; CHGFIELD$
9760 IF CHGFIELD$ <> "1" AND CHGFIELD$ <> "2" THEN GOTO 9750
9770 OUTTYPE$ = CHGFIELD$
9780 OPEN "O",#1,DISK$+"REPORT.FIL"
9790 J = 0
9800 FOR I = 1 TO TRANCNT
9810 GET #3,I
9820 IF CVI(TIDF$) = 0 OR CVS(BADDEBTF$) < 0 THEN GOTO 9890
```

```
9830 J = J + 1
9835 IF J = 1 OR J MOD 60 = 0 THEN PRINT #1,CHR$(12)     ' PUT OUT A FORM FEED
9840 IF J = 1 OR J MOD 60 = 0 THEN PRINT #1,
"Invoice #          Company Name      Date Sent    Inv. Amount  Bad Debt Amount"
9850 IF J = 1 OR J MOD 60 = 0 THEN PRINT #1,
"_____   _____   _____   _____  _____"
9860 PRINT #1,
INVF$ "         " TCOF$ "    " MID$(DATESF$,1,2) "/"
MID$(DATESF$,3,2) "/" MID$(DATESF$,5,2) "      ";
9870 PRINT #1,USING "$$##,###.##"; CVS(AMTF$);:PRINT #1,"         ";
9880 PRINT #1,USING "$$##,###.##"; CVS(BADDEBTF$)
9890 NEXT I :PRINT #1,"   " : CLOSE : GOSUB 5300 ' GO PRINT REPORT
9900 IF CHGFIELD$ = "1" THEN LINE INPUT "Enter return to continue " ;CHGFIELD$
9910 CLOSE : RETURN
13000 REM ***** THIS LINE IS HERE TO PROVIDE A COMMON
DELETE THRU LINE NUMBER FOR CHAINING
```

INCOME7.BAS

```
6000 ON A GOSUB 6010,6010,6010,6010,6010,6010,6010,
6010,6010,6020,6450,6960,7760,6010
6010 GOTO 5000
6020 REM ****************************************************************
6030 REM * THIS SECTION WILL HANDLE THE COMPANIES REQUEST FROM THE MAIN MENU*
6040 REM ****************************************************************
6050 LINE INPUT "Output to screen (1) or printer (2) :" ; CHGFIELD$
6060 OUTTYPE$ = CHGFIELD$
6070 IF CHGFIELD$ <> "1" AND CHGFIELD$ <> "2" THEN GOTO 6050
6100 GOSUB 2000                              ' GO OPEN CUSTOMER FILE
6110 IF CUSTCNT < 1 THEN PRINT
"No existing customers" : FOR I = 1 TO 1000 : NEXT I : CLOSE : RETURN
6120 LINE INPUT "Do you want detail report :" ; CHGFIELD$
6130 IF CHGFIELD$ <> "Y" AND CHGFIELD$ <> "N" THEN GOTO 6120
6140 IF CHGFIELD$ <> "Y" THEN GOTO 6320
6145 OPEN "O",#1,DISK$+"REPORT.FIL"
6150 FOR I = 1 TO CUSTCNT
6160 GET #2,I
6170 IF CVI(IDF$) = 0 THEN GOTO 6310
6180 PRINT #1," "
6190 PRINT #1,"Id = " CVI(IDF$)
6200 PRINT #1,"Company Name     = " COF$
6210 PRINT #1,"Customer Name    = " NAF$
6220 PRINT #1,"Department       = " DEPF$
6230 PRINT #1,"Street Address   = " STREETF$
6240 PRINT #1,"Post Office Box  = " PONUMF$
6250 PRINT #1,"City             = " CITYF$
6260 PRINT #1,"State            = " STATEF$
6270 PRINT #1,"Zip code         = " ZIPF$
6280 PRINT #1,"Phone Number     =
" "(" MID$(PHONEF$,1,3) ") " MID$(PHONEF$,4,3) "-" MID$(PHONEF$,7,4)
6310 NEXT I
6315 CLOSE #1 : GOSUB 5300    ' GO PRINT REPORT ON REQUESTED DEVICE
6320 LINE INPUT "Do you want summary report :";CHGFIELD$
6330 IF CHGFIELD$ <> "Y" AND CHGFIELD$ <> "N" THEN GOTO 6320
6340 IF CHGFIELD$ <> "Y" THEN GOTO 6420
6345 OPEN "O",#1,DISK$+"REPORT.FIL"
6350 FOR I = 1 TO CUSTCNT
6360 GET #2,I
6370 IF CVI(IDF$) = 0 THEN GOTO 6310
```

```
6380 PRINT #1," Id = " CVI(IDF$) " Company Name   = " COF$
6410 NEXT I
6415 CLOSE #1:GOSUB 5300       ' GO PRINT REPORT ON REQUESTED DEVICE
6420 IF OUTTYPE$ = "1" THEN LINE INPUT "Enter return to continue :";CHGFIELD$
6430 CLOSE
6440 RETURN
6450 REM *****************************************************************
6460 REM THIS SECTION WILL HANDLE THE OPEN REPORT REQUEST FROM THE MAIN MENU *
6470 REM *****************************************************************
6480 LINE INPUT "Output to screen (1) or printer (2) :" ; CHGFIELD$
6490 OUTTYPE$ = CHGFIELD$
6500 IF CHGFIELD$ <> "1" AND CHGFIELD$ <> "2" THEN GOTO 6480
6530 GOSUB 2060                        ' GO OPEN TRANSACTION FILE
6540 LINE INPUT "Enter starting date :" ; STARTDATE$
6550 IF STARTDATE$ <> "" THEN GOTO 6580
6560 IF OUTTYPE$ = "1" THEN LINE INPUT "Enter return to continue :"; CHGFIELD$
6570 CLOSE : RETURN
6580 IF LEN(STARTDATE$) <> 6 THEN GOTO 6540
6590 LINE INPUT "Enter ending date :" ; ENDDATE$
6600 IF ENDDATE$ = "" THEN ENDDATE$ = CDATE$
6610 IF LEN(ENDDATE$) <> 6 THEN GOTO 6590
6620 MAKEDATE$ = STARTDATE$            ' PUT STARTDATE$ IN YYMMDD FORMAT
6630 GOSUB 910                         ' RESULTS IN HOLDDATE$
6640 STARTDATE$ = HOLDDATE$
6650 MAKEDATE$ = ENDDATE$              ' PUT ENDDATE$ IN YYMMDD FORMAT
6660 GOSUB 910                         ' PUT RESULT IN HOLDDATE$
6670 ENDDATE$ = HOLDDATE$
6680 J = 0
6690 FOR I = 1 TO TRANCNT
6700 GET #3,I
6710 IF CVI(TIDF$) = 0 THEN GOTO 6790  ' DELETED TRANSACTION
6720 MAKEDATE$ = DATESF$               ' PUT FILEDATE INTO YYMMDD FORMAT
6730 GOSUB 910                         ' PUT RESULT IN HOLDDATE$
6740 IF HOLDDATE$ < STARTDATE$ OR HOLDDATE$ > ENDDATE$ THEN GOTO 6790
6750 IF CVS(AMTF$) - CVS(PPAMTF$) < .01 THEN GOTO 6790 ' IT HAS BEEN PAID
6760 J = J + 1
6770 SORTKEYS$(J) = TCOF$
6780 RECNO(J) = I
6790 NEXT I
6800 IF J < 1 THEN PRINT "No open invoices in this period" : GOTO 6540
6810 SWITCHED = 0
6820 FOR I = 1 TO J - 1
6830 IF SORTKEYS$(I+1) > SORTKEYS$(I) THEN GOTO 6880
6840 IF SORTKEYS$(I+1) = SORTKEYS$(I) THEN GOTO 6880
6850 HOLDSORT$ = SORTKEYS$(I) : SORTKEYS$(I) =
SORTKEYS$(I+1) : SORTKEYS$(I+1) = HOLDSORT$
6860 HOLDRECNO = RECNO(I) : RECNO(I) = RECNO(I+1) : RECNO(I+1) = HOLDRECNO
6870 SWITCHED = 1
6880 NEXT I
6885 OPEN "O",#1,DISK$+"REPORT.FIL"
6890 FOR I = 1 TO J
6900 GET #3,RECNO(I)
6910 PRINT #1,"Company id = " CVI(TIDF$)
" Name = " TCOF$ " Invoice # " INVF$
" Date sent   " MID$(DATESF$,1,2) "/"
MID$(DATESF$,3,2) "/" MID$(DATESF$,5,2)
6920 PRINT #1,"Invoice Amount = " CVS(AMTF$)
" Amount paid " CVS(PPAMTF$) " Comment = " COMF$
6930 PRINT #1," "
6940 NEXT I
6945 CLOSE #1 : GOSUB 5300      ' GO PRINT REPORT ON REQUESTED DEVICE
6950 GOTO 6540
6960 REM *****************************************************************
6970 REM THIS SECTION WILL HANDLE THE YEAR END PROCESSING REQUEST        *
```

```
6980 REM *********************************************************************
6990 LINE INPUT "Enter year to close out as yy :";XYEAR$
7000 IF XYEAR$ = "" THEN CLOSE : RETURN
7010 OPEN "R",#1,DISK$+"CASH.DAT",38
7020 FIELD #1,4 AS SOURCEF$,4 AS CAMTF$,10 AS CDATEPF$,20 AS CCOMMF$
7030 OPEN "R",#2,DISK$+"NCASH.DAT",38
7040 FIELD #2,4 AS NSOURCEF$,4 AS NCAMTF$,10 AS NCDATEPF$,20 AS NCCOMMF$
7050 IF CASHCNT < 1 THEN CLOSE :
PRINT "There are no cash records to delete":GOTO 7160
7060 J = 0
7070 FOR I = 1 TO CASHCNT
7080 GET #1,I
7090 IF MID$(CDATEPF$,5,2) = XYEAR$ THEN GOTO 7130
7100 LSET NSOURCEF$ = SOURCEF$ : LSET NCAMTF$ = CAMTF$ :
LSET NCDATEPF$ = CDATEPF$ : LSET NCCOMMF$ = CCOMMF$
7110 J = J + 1
7120 PUT #2,J
7130 NEXT I
7140 CLOSE : PRINT "Old cash file had " I-1 " payments.
New file has " J " payments"
7150 KILL DISK$+"CASH.DAT" : NAME DISK$+"NCASH.DAT" AS DISK$+"CASH.DAT"
7155 CASHCNT = J : GOSUB 5200 ' GO SAVE FILE COUNTS
7160 REM ******** NOW REORG THE TRANSACTION FILE
7170 REM ******** KEEPING ANY RECORDS PAID AFTER YEAR= XYEAR
7180 GOSUB 2060              ' GO OPEN TRANS FILE AS #3
7190 OPEN "R",#1,"HTRANS.DAT",5
7200 FIELD #1,5 AS HINVF$
7210 OPEN "R",#2,DISK$+"PAYMENT.DAT",44
7220 FIELD #2,1 AS PDELF$,5 AS PINVF$,10 AS PDATEPF$,
4 AS PCHKNBRF$,4 AS PAMTF$,20 AS PCOMMF$
7230 HCNT = 0
7240 IF TRANCNT < 1 THEN GOTO 7750
7250 FOR I = 1 TO TRANCNT
7260 GET #3,I
7270 IF MID$(DATESF$,5,2) <> XYEAR$   THEN
GOTO 7370         'KEEP INV FOR OTHER YEAR
7280 IF CVS(AMTF$) - CVS(PPAMTF$) > 0   THEN GOTO 7370   'KEEP OPEN INVOICES
7290 KEEPCNT = 0
7300 FOR J = 1 TO PAYMCNT        ' FIND ALL PAYMENTS FOR THIS INVOICE
7310 GET #2,J
7320 IF PINVF$ <> INVF$ THEN GOTO 7350           ' INV. # MUST MATCH
7330 IF MID$(PDATEPF$,5,2)  <= XYEAR$ THEN GOTO 7350    ' KEEP AFTER THIS YEAR
7340 KEEPCNT = KEEPCNT + 1        ' FOUND PAYMENT THIS YEAR
7350 NEXT J
7360 IF KEEPCNT = 0 THEN GOTO 7380
7370 HCNT = HCNT + 1:LSET HINVF$ = INVF$:PUT #1,HCNT    ' SAVE INV #
7380 NEXT I                                            ' NEXT INV. RECORD
7390 IF HCNT = 0 THEN
PRINT "No invoice or payment records are being deleted":GOTO 7750
7400 CLOSE #2                                          ' CLOSE PAYMENT FILE
7410 NTRANS = 0
7420 OPEN "R",#2,DISK$+"NTRANS.DAT",87
7430 FIELD #2,87 AS NREC$
7440 FIELD #3,87 AS OREC$
7450 FOR I = 1 TO TRANCNT                              ' GET AN INVOICE
7460 GET #3,I
7470 KEEPCNT = 0
7480 FOR J = 1 TO HCNT
7490 GET #1,J
7500 IF HINVF$ = INVF$ THEN KEEPCNT = KEEPCNT + 1
7510 NEXT J
7520 IF KEEPCNT = 0 THEN GOTO 7540
7530 LSET NREC$ = OREC$: NTRANS = NTRANS + 1 : PUT #2,NTRANS ' KEEP THIS RECORD
```

```
7540 NEXT I                                           ' NEXT INVOICE REC
7550 CLOSE #2:CLOSE #3:
PRINT "Old Transaction file had " I-1 " records.
New file has " NTRANS " records."
7560 KILL DISK$+"TRANSACT.DAT" :
NAME DISK$+"NTRANS.DAT" AS DISK$+"TRANSACT.DAT"
7565 TRANCNT = NTRANS
7570 OPEN "R",#2,DISK$+"PAYMENT.DAT",44
7580 FIELD #2,1 AS PDELF$,5 AS PINVF$,10 AS PDATEPF$,
4 AS PCHKNBRF$,4 AS PAMTF$,20 AS PCOMMF$
7590 FIELD #2,44 AS OPREC$
7600 OPEN "R",#3,DISK$+"NPAYMENT.DAT",44
7610 FIELD #3,44 AS NPREC$
7620 NPAYREC = 0
7630 FOR I = 1 TO PAYMCNT                             ' GET A PAYMENT REC
7640 GET #2,I
7650 KEEPCNT = 0
7660 FOR J = 1 TO HCNT
7670 GET #1,J
7680 IF HINVF$ = PINVF$ THEN KEEPCNT = KEEPCNT + 1
7690 NEXT J
7700 IF KEEPCNT = 0 THEN GOTO 7720
7710 LSET NPREC$ = OPREC$: NPAYREC = NPAYREC + 1 :
PUT #3,NPAYREC ' KEEP THIS RECORD
7720 NEXT I                                           ' NEXT INVOICE REC
7730 CLOSE:PRINT "Old Payment file had " I-1 " records.
New file has " NPAYREC " records."
7740 KILL DISK$+"PAYMENT.DAT" :
NAME DISK$+"NPAYMENT.DAT" AS DISK$+"PAYMENT.DAT"
7745 PAYMCNT = NPAYREC :CLOSE : GOSUB 5200 ' GO SAVE RECORD COUNTS
7750 LINE INPUT "Enter return to continue ";CHGFIELD$ :CLOSE : RETURN
7760 REM *****************************************************************
7770 REM THIS SECTION WILL HANDLE THE STATEMENT REQUEST FROM THE MAIN MENU  *
7780 REM *****************************************************************
7790 LINE INPUT "Output to screen (1) or printer (2) :" ; CHGFIELD$
7800 OUTTYPE$ = CHGFIELD$
7810 IF CHGFIELD$ <> "1" AND CHGFIELD$ <> "2" THEN GOTO 7790
7830 OPEN "O",#1,DISK$+"REPORT.FIL"
7840 GOSUB 2060                             ' GO OPEN TRANSACTION FILE
7850 GOSUB 2000                             ' GO OPEN CUSTOMER FILE
7860 LINE INPUT "Enter finance charge Percentage :";FINCHG$
7870 FINCHG = VAL(FINCHG$)
7880 LINE INPUT "Enter number of days before finance charge imposed :";FINDAY$
7890 FINDAY = VAL(FINDAY$)
7900 FOR I = 1 TO CUSTCNT
7910 GET #2,I
7920 ICNT = 0 : TOTDUE = 0
7930 IF CVI(IDF$) = 0 THEN GOTO 8230
7940 FOR J = 1 TO TRANCNT
7950 GET #3,J
7960 IF IDF$ <> TIDF$    THEN GOTO 8140
7970 IF CVS(AMTF$) - CVS(PPAMTF$) < .01 THEN GOTO 8140
7980 ICNT = ICNT + 1
7990 IF ICNT > 1 THEN GOTO 8080
8000 IF OUTTYPE$ = "2" THEN PRINT #1,CHR$(12) ELSE PRINT #1," ":PRINT #1," "
8010 PRINT #1,COF$
8020 PRINT #1,NAF$;:PRINT #1," ";:PRINT #1,DEPF$
8030 PRINT #1,STREETF$
8040 PRINT #1,CITYF$;:PRINT #1,",";:PRINT #1,
STATEF$;:PRINT #1," ";:PRINT #1,ZIPF$
8050 PRINT #1," " :PRINT #1," ":PRINT #1," "
8060 PRINT #1,
" Date    Invoice #             Comment              Amount      Balance"
```

```
8070 PRINT #1,
"_____  _____  _____  _____  _____
8080 PRINT #1,MID$(DATESF$,1,2);:
PRINT #1,"/";:PRINT #1,MID$(DATESF$,3,2);:
PRINT #1,"/";:PRINT #1,MID$(DATESF$,5,2);
8090 PRINT #1," ";:PRINT #1,USING "\       \";INVF$;
8100 PRINT #1," ";:PRINT #1,USING "\                    \";COMF$;
8110 PRINT #1," ";:PRINT #1,USING "$$#,###.##";CVS(AMTF$);
8120 TOTDUE = TOTDUE + CVS(AMTF$) - CVS(PPAMTF$)
8130 PRINT #1," ";:PRINT #1,USING "$$#,###.##";(CVS(AMTF$) - CVS(PPAMTF$))
8140 NEXT J
8150 IF TOTDUE = 0 THEN GOTO 8230
8160 PRINT #1," " : PRINT #1,"**** Total Amount Due as of ";
8170 PRINT #1,MID$(CDATE$,1,2);:PRINT #1,"/";:
PRINT #1,MID$(CDATE$,3,2);:PRINT #1,"/";:
PRINT #1,MID$(CDATE$,5,2);:PRINT #1," :";
8180 PRINT #1,USING "$$#,###.##";TOTDUE
8190 PRINT #1,"         Please pay this amount.  Invoices not "
8200 PRINT #1,"         paid in ";:
PRINT #1,FINDAY;:PRINT #1," days are subject to a"
8210 PRINT #1,"         ";:PRINT #1,FINCHG;:PRINT #1,"% finance charge."
8230 NEXT I
8235 CLOSE #1 : GOSUB 5300 ' GO PRINT REPORT ON REQUESTED DEVICE
8240 IF OUTTYPE$ = "1" THEN LINE INPUT "Enter return to continue :";CHGFIELD$
8260 LINE INPUT "Print labels (Y/N) : " ; CHGFIELD$
8270 IF CHGFIELD$ = "N" THEN CLOSE : RETURN
8280 IF CHGFIELD$ <> "Y" THEN GOTO 8260
8290 FOR I = 1 TO CUSTCNT
8300 GET #2,I
8310 IF CVS(BALF$) = 0 THEN GOTO 8380
8320 LPRINT COF$
8330 LPRINT NAF$ "," DEPF$
8340 LPRINT STREETF$
8350 LPRINT CITYF$ "," STATEF$ " " ZIPF$
8360 LPRINT " "
8370 LPRINT " "
8380 NEXT I
8390 LINE INPUT "Enter return to continue :";CHGFIELD$
8400 CLOSE : RETURN
13000 REM ***** THIS LINE IS HERE TO PROVIDE A COMMON
DELETE THRU LINE NUMBER FOR CHAINING
```

CHAPTER NINE
SELLING SOFTWARE

Selling personal computer software still is in its infancy. Conglomerates, small companies, and individuals are feeling their way into this potentially enormous market, and are selling it using the same approach suggested in the beginning of Chap. 3 for you to start a business—they're looking at what has proven successful before.

It's not surprising to find a diversity of ways to sell software. Unquestionably, there will be new ways as the market evolves and matures. Not every method will be successful. Which ones will? At this point, nobody knows for sure, but everyone agrees that the winners will make enormous profits.

SELLING YOUR OWN SOFTWARE

You can sell your own software directly to buyers using the techniques already presented for ads and direct mail. You will get the *entire* price for your program, but your distribution will be limited. You also can install and then sell your own programs to increase your profits per program, but again, your distribution will be reduced even more.

On the other hand, you can sell your own software nationally by placing classified ads in one or more of the many personal computer magazines. People interested in your program will write to you, enclosing a check for the software. You usually provide user documentation and a disk on which is stored your program.

To enhance your credibility on a national level, you can send your software to many of the PC magazines for review. Send the magazine (one at a time) an introductory letter describing your software, a disk that operates on *their* PC (by studying the magazine, you should be able to tell which machines it has available), documentation, and anything else you think is suitable. If your program is reviewed, you then can include in your classified ads the line: "This program was reviewed in. . . . " and name the magazine. It's prestigious, but difficult to have a program reviewed because there are so many programs competing for space.

You also could try writing an article *about* your programs or the areas they serve. The article can be indirectly about your offering if that's what it will take to gain exposure. Regardless of the article's focus, be sure to include instructions for obtaining the program, i.e., your address and/or telephone number. You'll also be paid for the article. Of course writing an article is difficult. Many people have spent years developing the skills necessary to write one. Unless you feel you already have these skills, you may want to advertise for a co-author who'll put the article together. You may have to pay the writer before the article is sold.

Selling programs yourself presents the problem of support. How do you support a program nationally? In most cases you don't, which is why buyers are hesitant to buy. Your user documentation has to be of a very high quality. It should make your program easy to use and anticipate *all* foreseeable problems. Your reputation, consequently, will be built based on the quality of your software *and* its supporting documentation.

Distribution is the main problem with selling your own software, but if you start small, you can create a company and overcome this problem with regional outlets.

SELLING DIRECTLY TO A COMPUTER STORE

For a percentage of the program's price, a computer store may agree to sell your program, but few stores, quite frankly, will be interested. Too many people already have preceded you with poor software and given "walk-ins" a bad name. So you should be prepared for a cold reception. Franchised stores also may not have the right to offer software independently without first obtaining approval from the home office.

To increase your chances of getting a fair hearing, you should act professionally. That means sending a letter introducing your software and requesting a meeting. If the store manager invites you in, you should arrive prepared with a *high-quality* program, documentation, a plan for support, your predetermined price for the program, and an agreement. Act professionally and you'll be treated professionally.

You, again, face the problem of support. The store manager will want you to support your own software. He or she will have neither the time nor help to do it.

One technique that has been used to interest stores was to give the store a master disk and allow it to make as many copies as it wanted for sale. Only one restriction was imposed on the store. It would have to buy a user manual for each program it sold. This technique has not proven very successful for end users, who have found they need support, or for the stores, which have found it a pain to copy the disks and do paperwork.

You, however, do find software in computer stores. How did it get there? Computer stores, like the many other stores that today sell software, obtain it from three sources:

1. A marketing representative, who represents one or more companies, sells software directly to the store or franchise.
2. The store contacts a hardware or software company for software. The store may need to buy a minimum number of programs and commit itself to buying a specified number in future months. This minimum purchase requirement prevents individuals from buying the software at an outlet's discount. The software is listed in catalogs distributed by the companies.
3. The store contacts a mail order house that offers software.

A store uses all these sources for its software supplies. At first, this may sound discouraging. After all, what chance do you have against such competition? A very good chance, if you team up with them, as explained below.

SELLING THROUGH A MAIL ORDER HOUSE

You can sell your software through mail order houses, such as Discount Software Group and Software Distributors, Inc. Mail order houses accept programs and sell them to individuals and stores. The houses advertise long lists of programs in the computer magazines and provide contact telephone numbers (often a 24-hour, 800 number) and a response address for requesting programs. Many houses are set up to accept credit card purchases over the telephone. These houses also print catalogs listing their programs with brief descriptions. Anyone who buys a program, including computer stores, goes on the house's mail list and receives a new catalog.

The house takes a percentage of the program's selling price. Though you don't make as much per program as you would if you sold your program yourself, you should sell more programs.

Some houses also will support the programs they offer, which solves your problem of supporting software on a national level. Some houses specialize in software for specific personal computers.

The details for submitting a program vary from house to house, so you should contact the one you're interested in before you send anything. Generally, the procedures will be the same.

To submit your work to Discount Software Group, for instance, you would send your program on a disk along with your program's user manual to:

DISCOUNT SOFTWARE GROUP
10150 West Jefferson Blvd.
Culver City, California 90230

Do not send a source code listing.

You can find the names and addresses of other houses in PC magazines. You also can ask local outlets for the names of the mail order houses that they buy from.

In evaluating your program, a house will look at:

1. *The marketability of the program.* The house will ask itself if people will buy your program. It will look at similar programs presently available and decide if yours has defined a different position in its line.
2. *The quality of the documentation.* A house may read the documentation before examining the program. The user manual presents capabilities, features, and often provides background, all of which help the evaluation process. The manual also shows how much support the program will require.
3. *The quality of the program.* Does the program do what the documentation says it will do?

Based on its evaluation, the house either will send you an agreement or return your materials. If your program is rejected, *don't be discouraged.* Immediately send it to another house. Your program may have been rejected at one house for many reasons that have little to do with the quality and value of your program. The house, for instance, may have too many other programs in your line. Or, the evaluator may not have understood your market. Or, the evaluator simply may have failed to write a convincing "buy" recommendation. So, keep sending your program out until a house accepts it.

The mail order houses need a constant flow of software to stay competitive and keep their offerings abreast of the changing PC field.

SELLING THROUGH A PC MANUFACTURER

Personal computer manufacturers, such as the Tandy Corporation, IBM, and the Digital Equipment Corporation, accept programs for their machines from individuals. The programs accepted appear in the company's catalogs as part of its software lines, so your program gains high visibility, the prestige of a nationally known manufacturer, and the efforts of major marketing forces. A manufacturer, also, will generally support the program.

The manufacturer may buy your program outright or offer you a royalty (a percentage of each program sold).

Manufacturers *need* software from people outside their companies. The software increases the value of the PC. The most common question asked before a PC is bought is, "What can I do with it?" Software answers that question.

Of all the software sold at Radio Shack outlets, 50 percent is bought by the Tandy Corporation from outsiders. Of that percent, roughly one-half is supplied, *not by software companies,* but by small PC operators. With over 6000 Radio Shack outlets, Tandy offers you a very profitable opportunity for selling software.

It shouldn't surprise you, then, to discover that manufacturers actively search for programs to buy. They go through mail order catalogs and PC magazines for program reviews and classified ads. They are looking for programs to start new marketing lines, or programs that will fill a gap in a present offering. If your program appears in one of these places and it's wanted, the manufacturer will contact you.

You, however, do not need to wait to be contacted. You can contact a manufacturer directly. The procedure for submitting your program varies among manufacturers, but usually you write or call the manufacturer and request that submission information be sent to you.

To submit a program to IBM, for example, you will write a brief letter that simply states your interest in submitting a program—do not submit the program at this time. Send the letter to:

IBM Software Submission
Department 765 PC
Old Orchard Road
Armonk, N.Y. 10504

IBM will send you:

1. An information packet that will tell you what IBM looks for in a program, standards it requires, and details of the submission procedure
2. A software submission agreement, which protects your rights and assures you that IBM will not steal your program

After reading the packet, you will send a description of your program for evaluation. If it likes the description, IBM will request the program code and user documentation for final evaluation. At this time, your program will be rigorously tested, its marketability will be judged, and forecasts of sales will be run. IBM also will decide how well your program fits with its present offering. To help you decide how well your program will fit, you can buy the IBM *Guide To P.C. Offerings*, which lists the IBM personal computer software.

If your program is accepted, you will sign a nonexclusive agreement with IBM, which states that you will be able to sell your own software any way you wish, while IBM also sells it. This clause is very advantageous to you. Based on its sales forecasts, IBM will match the appropriate marketing and advertising resources to your program. At minimum, your program will be included in the IBM catalog. You will gain an extensive dealer network offering more than 770 stores; and you will have the prestige of the IBM name behind you.

Not all manufacturers accept programs. KAYPRO, for example, buys a very few programs and bundles the software with the hardware. KAYPRO, however, will review your software for inclusion in a list of approved software that is available to dealers and individuals. In this case, you're not actively represented, but your offer does gain exposure. Some manufacturers don't even have these lists, so check your market.

You will be pleasantly surprised by how helpful the people representing manufacturers are.

As you can imagine, it takes time to have your program evaluated, but the potential for profit makes the wait worthwhile.

SELLING THROUGH A PC SOFTWARE COMPANY

Personal computer software companies, such as Visicorp, Inc., and Micropro, Inc., are in the business of selling software. You will gain the considerable prestige and outlets that these companies have if your program is sold by them.

Companies constantly are on the lookout (again in PC magazines and mail order house catalogs) for programs to add to their offerings. Once again, if a company is interested in your program, you will be contacted.

These companies do need new programs, but some simply lack the staff for evaluating "outsiders'" programs. Other companies, such as Visicorp, are interested in outsider's programs.

Visicorp looks for programs that fit in its product lines and product strategy. The procedure for selling your program through Visicorp begins with a letter. In the letter, you will describe your program using *nonproprietary* information. The letter will be used to evaluate the program. If Visicorp is interested, you will be contacted for the program. Send your letter to:

Director of Product Marketing
Visicorp, Inc.
2895 Zanker Road
San Jose, California 95134

Many companies, also will at least look at a *brief* description of a program. Do not include any proprietary information in the description. Conclude the letter by asking the company if it wishes to see your program and documentation.

SELLING THROUGH A PUBLISHING COMPANY

Books, such as this one, that contain software are published each year. Some of these books have little if any text to support their source code. The books span a wide range of applications and user sophistication. A number of publishing houses also now are planning to offer software on disks, either alone or with a source code book.

The publishing house will give you a percentage or royalty of the price of each book sold. For software sold on disk, the house may buy the program or offer you a royalty.

You contact a publishing house with a "proposal" that:

1. Examines what other books (or programs) are available like yours.
2. Shows what differentiates your work from the others.
3. States what you intend to do.
4. Includes, for a book, a table of contents and at least one sample chapter.

You can find the names and addresses of houses that publish software books by going to a bookstore and looking in the computer section. At the bookstore, you'll also be able to see what has already been published.

Once again, if your proposal is rejected by one house, immediately send it out to another until your work is accepted. Publishing houses are investing heavily in software and further exploration can be very profitable.

Other traditional "communications" companies also are getting into the PC software sales field. CBS, for example, has entered the field. Procedures for outside submissions at most of these companies are not yet finalized.

SELLING THROUGH A DATA BASE SERVICE

Programs also can be sold through data base services, such as The Source. In this case, your program is considered data and you are responsible for maintaining it.

A data base service allows data to be accessed from locations geographically remote from the main computer. Your buyer down-loads your program to his or her own disk via a communications line by accessing the central data base. You are paid a percentage of the access time or a fee for your program. The only people who can buy your program are those who have modems and who subscribe to the service, which, as of now, restricts the market.

User documentation presents a problem. It's handled by being stored with the program in the data base so each user prints a manual on demand, but this technique does not allow diagrams or photographs to be included.

Support is another problem area. The introduction of changes can cause havoc with any support effort since it may be difficult to determine which user has what code unless you're careful.

A local computer store should be able to tell you the names of services in your area.

RETAILING SOFTWARE

Computer stores that sell primarily PC hardware are common today. Recently, a few stores have begun to appear that specialize in software. These stores don't sell PCs, but they may sell supplies, such as printer paper. In fact, franchises in software stores are now offered. These stores may become as common in a few years as record stores are today.

A software store also can rent programs in the same way today's video stores rent video movies.

You don't need a franchise to start a software store. If you're successful, though, you may be able to offer franchises to others. You will need start-up money for your store, as well as furnishings, programs, help, and enough money to keep yourself going until your store catches on. You can get your software from the mail order house catalogs, software companies, PC manufacturers, and book publishers.

Now that the computer store has put PCs in people's hands, software stores should become more popular.

RELATED OPPORTUNITIES

The way software is sold is creating many new opportunities, including the following four.

REPRESENTING PROGRAMS

You can profit from PCs, even if you don't know how to program, by selling other people's programs.

You can check the classified ads in magazines and look through catalogs, just like the hardware manufacturers and software companies do, pick out the programs you think could sell well, and write directly to the programmers, asking for the right to represent their software in your general area. You then can call on computer and software stores, offering an extensive list of programs. You also can put ads in the paper and PC magazines. If you know how to program, you can increase your profits by offering to locally support the software, as well.

Many software companies are still small and unable to pay a full-time marketing representative to sell their programs in all geographic areas. You can contact these small companies, too.

EVALUATING SOFTWARE FOR PROFIT

As you have read, some PC software companies can't afford a full-time staff to evaluate "outside" submissions. You can offer a service to evaluate software for them. You will work at home, accept program submissions, and try to match programs to your client's needs. You will need to investigate your client's businesses and know the program lines they presently offer and the ones they want to offer.

To start your service, you can run ads in the PC magazines. The ads will describe your service, state that there is no charge to the programmer to submit a program (you will be paid by software companies), and request submissions (disk with code and user manual).

BECOMING A SOFTWARE AGENT

Instead of representing software houses, you can represent programmers and gain a commission on programs that you place in catalogs, or with software companies or PC manufacturers.

You will place your ads in the PC magazines, describing your service and inviting submissions, but stating that a commission will be charged on profits. There will be no charge to evaluate the software.

As pointed out, some people's skill is in selling, and some, with skills in other areas, will be happy to focus on what they're good at and leave the selling to you.

STARTING YOUR OWN SOFTWARE CATALOG

Software catalogs are important to selling software. You can start your own. Run an ad in the PC magazines, inviting program submissions. If your catalog will be a special-purpose one, you should spell out the specific types of programs for which you'll be looking.

Once you have the software, you will run ads in PC magazines listing and briefly describing your programs. When somebody orders a program, you will send it out and add the person's name and address to your mail list, using your *Programs For Profit* Mail List Program. As you periodically print updated catalogs, you'll send one to everyone on your mail list. By doing a bit of research, you also can add names and addresses of computer and software stores.

FOR MORE INFORMATION ON MARKETS . . .

A book such as *Programs For Profit* simply cannot cover the changeable software marketplace comprehensively. However, *Programmer's Market* (Writer's Digest Books) does. The book is a detailed directory of over 500 software markets. You'll learn who to contact at a company, how many programs the company offers, how many were written by outsiders, submission procedures, contract and payment terms, and current titles. New editions will be published each year. If you can't find it in a bookstore, you can order *Programmer's Market* by calling 1-800-543-4644 (except Ohio, Alaska, and Hawaii).

CONCLUSION

Personal computers have created many profitable opportunities in selling software. The technology also allows profits to be made by selling something else—information. The following chapter discusses this in detail.

CHAPTER TEN

SELLING INFORMATION: A FOOTBALL INFORMATION PROGRAM

Data bases of commercial information are common in most fields. An extensive one holds the U.S. census data, and a highly specialized one stores reliability statistics for parts used in military hardware—I didn't know such statistics were kept or why until I came across that data base. There are data bases of parts that simulate electronic components (i.e., you think you've got a real, physical part, but it's really just information) and data bases of economic statistics. All these diverse data bases have one thing in common. They were developed to sell information.

The Football Information Program presented in this chapter will let you enter this field with your own data bases of commercial information. Before looking at the program, you may want to take a brief look at how money can be made in this field.

DATA BASE OPPORTUNITIES

Large companies have invested millions of dollars to create vast data bases, which give people access to information that would be too impractical to collect and maintain alone. An increasing number of these data bases are accessible by PCs with modems—and that opens new marketing opportunities.

The abilities to access a specific data base and use its information for reports can be integrated in your offers. You can write software, for example, for the following applications with data base tie-ins:

- For a doctor, bookkeeping software, a program for recording patients' medical histories, and a tie-in to the seven data bases of up-to-date medical literature provided by Dialog Information Services (a Lockheed division). With the tie-in a doctor could locate and immediately access articles of interest.
- For an investor, portfolio management software with a VisiLink software tie-in to the economic, financial, business, and industry data bases provided by Data Resources, Inc.

You also can use data bases yourself to access information for your own newsletter. In your newsletter, you can increase the information's value by interpreting it for subscribers. You also can extract information for reports prepared for specific clients.

Though there are many data bases today, there will be more. Companies will be offering more data bases. You also can start you own data bases. You don't need to invest millions of dollars, just time and perseverance. As you'll see, you have the software to get going.

SELLING FOOTBALL INFORMATION

Computer reports have appeared on American television screens, most of which are not attached to home computers. In the fall, online computer reports are displayed for—of all things—football games!

The dizzying feats of computation and record searches vie for attention with the play on the field. All sorts of incredible statistics pop up. The data is analyzed on the spot and constantly updated. For a lot of viewers, though, these statistics aren't very timely. These viewers already have put down their bets.

What bettor hasn't cringed when watching a game played in a downpour to learn the team he bet on wins less than 20 percent of its games on a wet field? A person with $10 on a team can't fully appreciate learning 2 minutes into the game that her team hasn't beaten its opponent in the last 4 years.

For the bettor, there's another serious problem with all these television statistics—they don't take into account point spreads. Knowing that a team won its last six games is interesting, but knowing how often it beat the spread is what really counts.

The Football Information Program is designed to let you make money in your spare time by sending out a weekly newsletter of interest to bettors during the football season.

This newsletter helps a bettor win primarily by highlighting the handicappers' biases. Most bettors make the mistake of betting "on a game." Actually, a person wagers *against another person*. In fact, what's *really* at stake is the handicapper's ability to appraise teams. The spread standings show the teams that are underrated and overrated by the handicapper. Teams at the top are badly underrated, the ones at the bottom overrated. The handicapper's judgment will change very slowly over the season. The other report information shows unusual events that may affect the outcome of a game.

Your Football Information Program makes capturing data for professional and college teams quick and simple. A single command will generate the report that constitutes your newsletter.

The market for this newsletter is very specific: bettors on football games. It's quite a big market. More Americans bet on football than any other sport. To introduce your newsletter to this audience, you'll put ads in the sports section of weekly and Sunday newspapers in your area. (In this application, the first person in your area who has a program and runs an ad wins the market.) Placing ads in more than one paper will cost more, but it'll increase your subscribers.

An ad that you can use as a model for your own is shown in Fig. 10-1. Start your ads late in July, after training camps open, so people will have time to subscribe for the opening games. Before the season starts, replace the ad line "Base Your Picks On" with "Coming This Season," and add a line so the bottom copy reads: "Football Stats Goes Into The Mail Each Tuesday During The Season. First Mailing is August (*day*). Get on . . . " During the season, you can add a teaser line to attract interest: "Last week's Football Stats showed the Browns win in the cold—and they did! This week you can learn a lot more!"

Base Your Picks On
FOOTBALL STATS
A Weekly Newsletter of Key Football Statistics

- Pro and college teams in their point spread standings. Teams that consistently beat the spread are at the top in this league—no matter where they stand in other leagues! When a team at the top of point spread standings plays one at the bottom, the winner is you!
- Revealing stats about wins and losses based on each team's past performance!

FOOTBALL STATS GOES INTO THE MAIL EACH TUESDAY DURING THE SEASON. GET ON THE LIST WITH PROFESSIONALS TODAY!

- -

Send me FOOTBALL STATS for:

3 week trial subscription—only $_______
Season Subscription (16 Full Weeks)—only $_______

Enclose check payable to _______________ and mail to:
(your name)

YOUR NAME, YOUR STREET ADDRESS OR P.O. BOX NUMBER, CITY, STATE, ZIP

Complete following information:

Name	Street	
City	State	Zip

Fig. 10-1 Advertisement for Football Stats Report.

When people respond to your ad, you'll:

1. Use your Mail List Program to record the names and addresses of people who have sent checks.
2. Use your Tickler Program (which is presented in Chap. 12) to record the names and addresses of people who want only a trial subscription. For these people, set the trigger date (you'll learn what that is in Chap. 12) to 2 weeks before the end of the trial period. On that date, people with subscriptions running out will be called to your attention so you can send notices for payments prorated for the remainder of the season. Remove from your mail list the names of people who do not send checks for the remainder of the season.

During August, you'll have to go to the library. You'll need a newspaper that shows point spreads (use the Friday edition with the latest line when you find a newspaper). You'll have to look at issues for the last 3 years. You'll need Monday and Tuesday's editions for game results. Weather information, which you'll need, can be taken from game reports or national weather maps, which are printed also. In August, you'll also record preseason games as they are played.

A week before the season opens, you should have all your historical and preseason football information in your data base. You'll run your first Football Stats Report and take it to a printing or copying service to make copies for your subscribers. Also type (or have typeset) the explanation of the report (shown in Fig. 10-8) and have copies made. Run labels with your Mail List Program and put them on your envelopes. When the reports and explanations are printed, pick them up and send them out. Put them in the mail Monday before the first weekend of the season.

During the season, here's what you'll do:

1. Before the games, run labels and put them on your envelopes.
2. Sunday evening, record the weekend's results.
3. Monday night or Tuesday morning, record the results of the Monday night game. Tuesday, record match-ups and point spreads for the coming weekend. (Alternatively, you can record the match-ups on any prior day, and before Sunday, add the point spreads.) Print the Football Stats Report. Early Tuesday, drop the report off at a printer's or a copying service.
4. Late Tuesday, pick up the reports. Spend Tuesday evening stuffing envelopes and affixing postage. Put them in the mail Tuesday night or, *at the latest*, Wednesday morning. You have to give the post office enough time

to deliver your reports by Thursday. (Many people bet where betting slips are collected Friday afternoon, *before* people get home and have a chance to look at their mail.)

You'll send out your newsletter through the regular season. Subsequent seasons will be much simpler than the first because all your research already is in your data base. In late July, you'll start running your ads. You'll use your mail list to print labels for subscription renewals. That's it!

NOTE:

It won't take much programming to adapt your Football Information Program to baseball, basketball, or hockey.

OPERATING YOUR FOOTBALL INFORMATION PROGRAM

Your Football Information Program enables you to set up and maintain a data base of football information and generate Football Stats Reports from it. Information can be stored for both college and professional teams (either league).

Maintenance of your data base is virtually eliminated because the program *automatically* deletes 3-year-old records, which generally no longer reflect a team's present character. Specifically, records for the same week in the season 3 years ago are deleted after the report is generated. This data base, consequently, requires only one disk.

After you access the program, you may:

- Add game records
- Specify match-ups
- Change a game record
- Delete a game record
- Print the Football Stats Report
- Make inquiries to check your data

The procedures for these activities are presented below.

ACCESSING THE FOOTBALL INFORMATION PROGRAM

To access the Football Information Program, type **RUN FOOTBALL** in response to your system prompt:

A: **RUN FOOTBALL**

The program will be loaded and the Football Program Command Menu will be displayed:

```
* * * * * * * * * * * * * * * * * * * * * * * * * * * * * * * * * * * * * * * * * * * * *
                        Football Program

                  Available commands are:
                  1 – Data     2 – Results
                  3 – Change   4 – Delete
                  5 – Report   6 – Inquiry
                  7 – Exit
* * * * * * * * * * * * * * * * * * * * * * * * * * * * * * * * * * * * * * * * * * * * * *
```

Command selection [1–7 or ?1–?7] :

The following descriptions present all you will need to use these commands effectively.

STORING FOOTBALL INFORMATION

The DATA command (1) is used:

1. When you first set up your data base to record 3 years of data for games that already have been played. In this case, you will respond to each prompt for data about each game.
2. During each preseason to record preseason results. In this case, you will not record data about weather conditions.
3. During the regular season to record match-ups and point spreads for the coming week(s). Scores and playing conditions for these games will be recorded with the RESULTS commands.

During the regular season, you need to record only match-ups for the coming week to print your report. If you do not have point spreads early in the week, you should not delay entering the match-ups and generating your report. The point spreads can be added at any later time (before you generate your next report) with the CHANGE command.

Records are stored for games, *not* teams. That is, the data base contains no records about the COWBOYS, but it does have records about the COW-BOY-GIANT games, COWBOY-EAGLES games, etc.

On a single data disk, records for 70 teams (28 pro and 42 college teams, for example) can be stored for each weekend. If you wish, you can set up one disk for pros and the other for up to 70 college teams.

The procedure for storing information in your football data base is:

1. COMMAND SELECTION: Type 1 for the DATA command.
2. ENTER TEAM TYPE: PRO (1) OR COLLEGE (2):   In the report, pro and college teams are listed separately. Type 1 to add data for pro games and 2 for college games.
3. ENTER SEASON YEAR: Type two digits for the year in which these are played.
4. ENTER WEEK NUMBER: Type the number of the week for which you want to record games. Regular season opening games are played on week 1, the last games on week 16. Preseason games are played on weeks P1 (first preseason game) through P5 (last preseason game). Note that the letter P must precede the preseason game number.
5. ENTER TEAM NAME: Type the name of a team using 15 or less characters, e.g., 49ERS. The program does not distinguish between home and away teams so either one can be entered first.
6. ENTER OPPONENT NAME: Type the name of the team playing the first team, using 15 or less characters.
7. WHICH TEAM IS FAVORED TO WIN (1/2):   Type 1 if the first team you entered (step 5) is favored, or 2 for the second (step 6). If the point spread for the upcoming weekend is not yet available, type the number for the team you think will be favored; if you're wrong, change the designation later with the CHANGE command. (Note that point spread data for an upcoming weekend is not used in the report.)
8. WHAT POINT SPREAD: Type the point spread. Do not type a + or − before the number. The favored team automatically is assigned + points, and the other team the − points. If the point spread for an upcoming weekend is not yet available, type 0 and later use the CHANGE command to enter it.

9. WEATHER CONDITIONS: NOT PLAYED YET (0), CLEAR (1), RAIN (2), SNOW (3), HOT (4):   Type the number that best describes the weather conditions under which the game was played. Use CLEAR (1) for games played under a dome. NOT PLAYED YET (0) will be used during the regular season to allow match-ups to be recorded so the report can be run. If 0 is entered, the procedure ends, the record is stored, and you can start to enter another game record; the game record will be completed with the RESULTS command.

10. ENTER TEAM SCORE: Type the number of points scored by the first team you entered (step 5).

11. ENTER OPPONENT SCORE: Type the number of points scored by the opponent.

The record for this game will be stored. You'll need to type similar records for all the other weekend's games.

The program will prompt for another team name, and you'll type one for an unrecorded game or press the carriage return, which allows you to specify another week. If you are not entering records for another week, press the carriage return to "step up" so you can specify another season. Press the carriage return and you'll be able to select PRO or COLLEGE games again, restarting this procedure. When you're done, respond to the PRO OR COLLEGE prompt by pressing the carriage return and you'll be returned to the Menu Level.

NOTE:

For a season, all college teams in a report must have participated in the same number of games. If college teams play in different numbers of games, the college spread standings will be invalid. If you begin tracking Baylor, for example, at the beginning of a season, you must continue throughout the season or delete its past records. On the other hand, if Florida State University begins to appear on betting slips during the third week of the season but you haven't been tracking its games, you must go back to the beginning of the season and record each game it has played already.

The procedure for storing a game record is illustrated in Fig. 10-2.

Football Program

Available commands are:
1–Data   2–Results
3–Change   4–Delete
5–Report   6–Inquiry
7–Exit

Command selection [1–7 or ?1–?7] :**1**   The DATA command is selected.

Enter team type PRO(1) or COLLEGE(2) :**1**   A PRO game is to be recorded.
Enter season year :**83**   Specifically, a record of the 1983
Enter week number :**1**   season's opening game between
Enter team name :**PATRIOTS**   the Patriots and Jets is to be
Enter opponent name :**JETS**   added to the data base.
Which team is favored to win(1 / 2) :**2**   The Jets were favored to win by
What point spread :**10**   10.
Weather conditions: Not Played Yet (0),
   Clear (1), Rain (2), Snow (3), Hot (4)
Enter weather conditions (0–4) :**1**   The game was played under clear
          conditions.

Enter team score :**24**
Enter opponent score :**21**   The game score is entered.
Data has been recorded
Enter team name :⟨**CR**⟩
Enter week number :⟨**CR**⟩
Enter season year :⟨**CR**⟩   No more records for any teams,
Enter team type PRO(1) or   PRO or COLLEGE, are to be
   COLLEGE(2) :⟨**CR**⟩   added at this time.

          You now will be returned to the
          Menu Level.

Fig. 10-2   Recording a game.

RECORDING RESULTS

The RESULTS command (2) is used to record game scores and weather conditions during the season. The program will prompt you to define the weekend for which scores are to be entered. The weekend's match-ups will be displayed one at a time. For each game, you type the score and weather. If you do not have scores for a game, press the carriage return in response to ENTER TEAM SCORE, the game will be passed over, and the next game displayed. At a later time, the score can be entered with the RESULTS command or CHANGE command.

The program will prompt for all games played on your specified weekend, even if scores for a game already have been recorded. The games will be displayed in the order in which they were stored (with the DATA command).

The procedure for recording results is illustrated in Fig. 10-3.

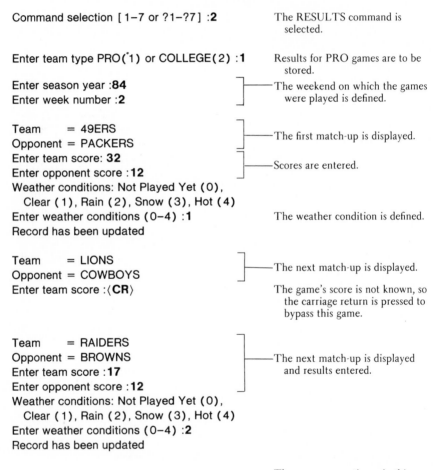

Command selection [1–7 or ?1–?7] :**2**   The RESULTS command is
                                              selected.

Enter team type PRO(˙1) or COLLEGE(2) :**1**   Results for PRO games are to be
                                                 stored.

Enter season year :**84**   The weekend on which the games
Enter week number :**2**   were played is defined.

Team   = 49ERS
Opponent = PACKERS   The first match-up is displayed.
Enter team score: **32**
Enter opponent score :**12**   Scores are entered.
Weather conditions: Not Played Yet (0),
   Clear (1), Rain (2), Snow (3), Hot (4)
Enter weather conditions (0–4) :**1**   The weather condition is defined.
Record has been updated

Team   = LIONS
Opponent = COWBOYS   The next match-up is displayed.
Enter team score :⟨**CR**⟩   The game's score is not known, so
                                              the carriage return is pressed to
                                              bypass this game.

Team   = RAIDERS
Opponent = BROWNS   The next match-up is displayed
Enter team score :**17**   and results entered.
Enter opponent score :**12**
Weather conditions: Not Played Yet (0),
   Clear (1), Rain (2), Snow (3), Hot (4)
Enter weather conditions (0–4) :**2**
Record has been updated

                                              The program continues in this
                                              way until all games have been
                                              displayed. At that time, you will
                                              be returned to the Menu Level.

Fig. 10-3   Recording results.

CHANGING A GAME RECORD

The CHANGE command (3) is used to change a game record. The command may be used to complete records as well as to change lines in completed ones. You first have to identify the record you want and then the line you want to change. As many lines as you wish can be changed.

The procedure for changing a record is:

1. COMMAND SELECTION: Type **3** for the CHANGE command.
2. ENTER TEAM TYPE PRO (1) OR COLLEGE (2):   Type **1** to change the record of a pro game or type **2** for a college game.
3. ENTER SEASON YEAR: Type two digits for the year in which the game you want to change occurred.
4. ENTER WEEK NUMBER: Type the number of the week into the season that the game was played.
5. ENTER TEAM NAME: Type the name of the first team you recorded for this game. If you stored a record for a Jets-Bills game by specifying the Jets first, you must specify the Jets in response to this prompt. If you specify the Bills, the record you want will not be found. The program will display the record you requested. Each line in the record will be numbered.
6. CHANGE WHAT?:   Type the number of the line you want to change. The program will prompt for the replacement line and you will type it. The program again will prompt CHANGE WHAT? and you can specify the number of a line you want to change, or press the carriage return to store the changed record.

At this time you will be prompted to begin this procedure again. When all your changes are made, press the carriage return and you will be returned to the Menu Level.

The procedure for changing a game record is illustrated in Fig. 10-4.

DELETING A GAME RECORD

The DELETE command (4) is used to remove a game record from your data base. You first have to identify the record you want deleted. The program will show you the record and if it's the one you want, flag it for deletion. When you've flagged all the ones you want to delete, cleaning will be started and the records will be removed.

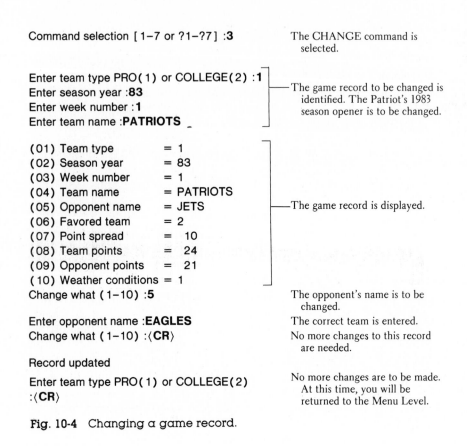

Command selection [1–7 or ?1–?7] :**3**   The CHANGE command is
selected.

Enter team type PRO(1) or COLLEGE(2) :**1**
Enter season year :**83**   The game record to be changed is
Enter week number :**1**   identified. The Patriot's 1983
Enter team name :**PATRIOTS** _   season opener is to be changed.

(01) Team type   = 1
(02) Season year   = 83
(03) Week number   = 1
(04) Team name   = PATRIOTS
(05) Opponent name = JETS   The game record is displayed.
(06) Favored team   = 2
(07) Point spread   = 10
(08) Team points   = 24
(09) Opponent points = 21
(10) Weather conditions = 1
Change what (1–10) :**5**   The opponent's name is to be
changed.

Enter opponent name :**EAGLES**   The correct team is entered.
Change what (1–10) :⟨**CR**⟩   No more changes to this record
are needed.

Record updated

Enter team type PRO(1) or COLLEGE(2)   No more changes are to be made.
:⟨**CR**⟩   At this time, you will be
returned to the Menu Level.

Fig. 10-4 Changing a game record.

The procedure for deleting a game record is:

1. COMMAND SELECTION: Type 4 for the DELETE command.
2. ENTER TEAM TYPE PRO (1) OR COLLEGE (2): Type 1 to delete
   a record of a pro game or type 2 for a college game.
3. ENTER SEASON YEAR: Type two digits for the year in which the
   game you want to delete occurred.
4. ENTER WEEK NUMBER: Type the number of the week into the
   season that the game was played.
5. ENTER TEAM NAME: Type the name of the first team you
   recorded for the game. The program will display the record you
   requested.

6. OK TO DELETE? (Y/N):   Type **Y** to flag the record for deletion or **N** to save it.

   At this time, you will be prompted to begin the procedure again. When all your records are flagged for deletion, press the carriage return and cleaning will be started. The program will display a report of how many records were in the data base before cleaning and how many remain. Press the carriage return to clear the screen and you'll be returned to the Menu Level.

The procedure for deleting a game record is illustrated in Fig. 10-5.

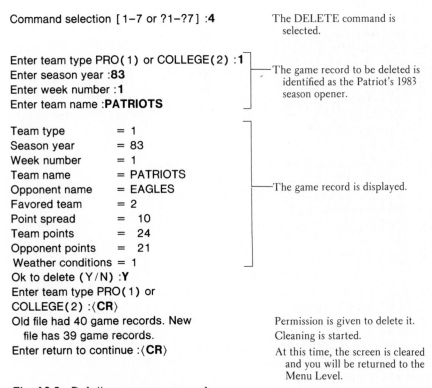

Command selection [1–7 or ?1–?7] :**4**   The DELETE command is selected.

Enter team type PRO(1) or COLLEGE(2) :**1**
Enter season year :**83**   The game record to be deleted is identified as the Patriot's 1983 season opener.
Enter week number :**1**
Enter team name :**PATRIOTS**

Team type   = 1
Season year   = 83
Week number   = 1
Team name   = PATRIOTS
Opponent name = EAGLES   The game record is displayed.
Favored team   = 2
Point spread   = 10
Team points   = 24
Opponent points = 21
Weather conditions = 1
Ok to delete (Y / N) :**Y**
Enter team type PRO(1) or
COLLEGE(2) :⟨**CR**⟩
Old file had 40 game records. New   Permission is given to delete it.
   file has 39 game records.   Cleaning is started.
Enter return to continue :⟨**CR**⟩   At this time, the screen is cleared and you will be returned to the Menu Level.

Fig. 10-5 Deleting a game record.

PRINTING THE FOOTBALL STATS REPORT

The REPORT command (5) generates the Football Stats Report from information in your data base.

NOTE:

Before a valid report can be generated, you must have 3 years of data, scores from the previous weekend (or preseason), and match-ups for the coming weekend.

The procedure for generating the report is:

1. COMMAND SELECTION: Type 5 for the REPORT command.
2. OUTPUT TO SCREEN (1) OR PRINTER (2):   Type 1 to preview a display of the report; type 2 to print it.
3. ENTER DATA FOR REPORT HEADING: Type the date using as many characters as you wish, exactly as you want to see it on your report.
4. ENTER NAME FOR REPORT HEADING: Type your name, if you wish. The name will be displayed in the report heading.
5. ENTER TEAM TYPE PRO (1) OR COLLEGE (2):   Separate reports are prepared for pro and college "spread standings." Type the number for the report you want. *Both* reports should be sent to clients unless you structure your business otherwise (e.g., charge one price for either the pro or college report, and a discounted price for both).
6. ENTER SEASON YEAR: Type two digits for the year the games in the report are played.
7. ENTER WEEK NUMBER: Type the number of the *upcoming* season's week. At this time, the report will be generated.
8. OK TO DELETE 3-YEAR-OLD RECORDS FOR THIS WEEK? (Y/ N):   If you have prepared a report for only PRO (or only COLLEGE) games, and you wish a report for the other games, type N. If you have printed both reports (or you wish to print only one), type Y. After the appropriate action is taken, you will be returned to the Menu Level.

The procedure for generating a report is illustrated in Fig. 10-6. An example of a Pro Football Stats Report is shown in Fig. 10-7. *Data for this report is fictitious.* An explanation of the report, which you can include with your mailings, is shown in Fig. 10-8.

Command selection [1–7 or ?1–?7] : **5**

The REPORT command is selected.

Output to screen (1) or printer (2) : **2**

The report is to be printed.

Enter date for report
  heading :**SEPTEMBER 14, 1984**

Heading information is typed.

Enter name for report heading :**THE PRO**

A name is entered in the heading.

Enter team type PRO(1) or COLLEGE(2) :**1**
Enter season year :**84**
Enter week number :**2**

The games to be used are defined.

At this time, the Football Stats Report is printed for PRO teams.

Ok to delete 3-year old records for
  this week (Y / N) :**Y**

The report for college teams already has been printed, so the old records are deleted.

Old file had 1344 game records. New
  file has 1316 game records.
Enter return to continue :⟨**CR**⟩

When the carriage return is pressed, you will be returned to the Menu Level.

Fig. 10-6 Generating the Football Stats Report.

NOTE:

For the season's first weekend, standings for PRO teams are based on preseason play. Standings for college teams are based on the final weekend of play for the previous season. For all subsequent weekends, only games for this season are used to determine the standings.

MAKING INQUIRIES

The INQUIRY command (6) enables you to look at all your data. This capability will be used to make sure you entered data correctly. It also can be used when you make changes or for deletion to see which team you typed first for a game record. The game records are listed in order of entry.

Football Stats
By THE PRO on SEPTEMBER 14 1984

Team	Wins	Losses	Last Meeting Against Opponent	Results For This Week In Previous Season	Clear	Rain	Snow	Hot
						Weather Performance		
JETS	5	0	7	1	27%	18%	50%	8%
DOLPHINS	5	0	3	2	22%	42%	20%	25%
RAIDERS	5	0	7	0	95%	20%	0%	15%
CHARGERS	4	1	−7	3	60%	30%	0%	100%
FALCONS	4	1	−7	0	14%	50%	30%	0%
PACKERS	3	2	−21	2	35%	10%	0%	100%
COWBOYS	3	2	6	0	8%	17%	0%	8%
REDSKINS	3	2	13	1	12%	0%	0%	100%
VIKINGS	3	2	7	0	33%	33%	0%	45%
BUCS	3	2	−24	3	80%	5%	40%	35%
SEAHAWKS	2	2	10	0	25%	16%	0%	100%
49ERS	2	2	1	1	25%	22%	0%	8%
STEELERS	2	3	−13	0	14%	35%	0%	17%
BENGALS	2	3	8	2	37%	0%	15%	50%
BROWNS	2	3	−3	2	75%	10%	0%	60%
OILERS	2	3	−10	1	40%	50%	0%	20%
RAMS	1	4	−4	0	32%	20%	60%	18%
COLTS	1	4	4	1	35%	45%	0%	32%
EAGLES	1	4	−8	0	46%	60%	0%	0%
BEARS	1	4	−6	2	27%	18%	80%	18%
GIANTS	1	4	−3	1	27%	10%	0%	18%
CARDINALS	1	4	24	3	22%	20%	0%	54%
LIONS	0	5	−7	1	19%	35%	90%	37%
SAINTS	0	5	7	0	50%	10%	0%	63%
CHIEFS	0	5	3	2	65%	24%	20%	84%
BRONCOS	0	5	21	1	72%	60%	0%	16%
PATRIOTS	0	5	−7	3	50%	10%	50%	26%
BILLS	0	5	0	0	28%	0%	0%	29%

Note: The "Spread Standing" spans Wins and Losses. The "ACTUAL SCORE" box spans Last Meeting Against Opponent and Results For This Week In Previous Season. Weather Performance spans Clear, Rain, Snow, Hot.

Fig. 10-7 A Football Stats Report.

The procedure for making an inquiry is:

1. COMMAND SELECTION: Type 6 for the INQUIRY command.
2. OUTPUT TO SCREEN (1) OR PRINTER (2):   Type 2 to print the report, in which case you'll be returned to the Menu Level once all records are printed. Type 1 to see a display of records. As many records as

Here's How To Read Your Report:

● Assume that the Chargers are favored by 4 to beat the Seahawks. The actual game score is Chargers 27, Seahawks 24. It's a league win for the Chargers. But if you're betting on the game, who cares about the league and its standings! If you bet on the Chargers, you lose with the points: Chargers 27, Seahawks 28!

  What really counts when you bet are the spread standings—how the teams did after the point spread is added in. That's exactly what Football Stats shows you!

  The teams at the top of the spread standings consistently beat the spread. The teams at the bottom lose with the spread. It's a good bet that a team at the top of the spread standings will beat one at the bottom—no matter what the league standings are.

● The spread standing's Wins and Losses columns shows exactly how many times a team did and didn't beat the spread this year. When teams have the same number of wins and losses, the standings are computed by looking at the margin of the handicapper's errors for the previous week's games. The more underrated the team is, the higher its standing. Assume the Jets and Bengals, for example, are both 4–1 this season. The Jets were favored to beat the Cowboys by 2, but actually beat them by 21 (a spread margin of 19). The Bengals, on the other hand, were favored to beat the Browns by 7, but won by only 4 (a spread margin of 3). Though the two teams have identical records, the Jets (with 19) would be higher in the spread standings than the Bengals (with 3).

● Last Meeting Against Opponent shows the point difference the last regular season time the two teams matched this week met. A plus number shows the team won by that many points, a minus that it lost by those points. Assume the Cowboys and Vikings are playing this week, and the score the last time they met in the regular season was Cowboys 35, Vikes 28. The entry in this column for the Cowboys will be 7 and the entry for the Vikes −7. Compare these figures to this week's spread for the game and ask yourself how much the teams have changed since that last meeting.

Fig. 10-8 What the Football Stats Report means. (*Cont. on following page.*)

- Results For This Week In Previous Season shows how many wins a team has recorded in games played this far into the season. If the Patriots, for example, always win their seventh game, the Patriot entry for the seventh week of this season will be 3 (only three seasons are examined for a very good reason, which is explained below). A team that wins or loses on a given week ought to be looked at. If you save your reports, you'll see trends about each team's character develop. You'll see teams that fade or finish out the season strong.

- Weather Performance shows how often a team wins under four different weather conditions. If the Dolphins, for example, win 80 percent of their games played in the rain, and rain is forecast for their game, the Dolphins should be looked at as a good winning shot.

    Only 3 years of historical records are kept for the Actual Score columns because it takes about 3 years for a team's nature to change. It's not often an owner brings in a new coaching staff and a whole new team for a season. Players are gradually replaced and the team slowly evolves. Records older than 3 years often are too reflective of an old coach or team to be helpful.
    That's your report. Good luck in your picks!

Fig. 10-8   *Cont.*

will fit your screen will be displayed at once, and you'll be prompted ENTER RETURN TO CONTINUE: Keep pressing the carriage return in response. When the carriage return is pressed after the last record is printed, you'll be returned to the Menu Level.

An example of an Inquiry Report is shown in Fig. 10-9. *The data in this report is fictitious.*

ENDING PROGRAM OPERATION

The EXIT command (7) ends operation of the Football Information Program and returns you to the operating system level. Remove your data base disk and return it to its cover.

```
Team type            = 1
Season year          = 81
Week number          = 1
Team name            = BEARS
Opponent name        = COWBOYS
Favored team         = 1
Point spread         =   6
Team points          =  12
Opponent points      =   7
Weather conditions   = 4

Team type            = 1
Season year          = 81
Week number          = 1
Team name            = JETS
Opponent name        = GIANTS
Favored team         = 2
Point spread         =   2
Team points          =   6
Opponent points      =   7
Weather conditions   = 4

Team type            = 1
Season year          = 81
Week number          = 1
Team name            = DOLPHINS
Opponent name        = 49ERS
Favored team         = 1
Point spread         =   3
Team points          =   7
Opponent points      =   4
Weather conditions   = 4

Team type            = 1
Season year          = 81
Week number          = 2
Team name            = BEARS
Opponent name        = GIANTS
Favored team         = 1
Point spread         =   3
Team points          =  14
Opponent points      =  12
Weather conditions   = 2
```

.
.
.

Fig. 10-9 A Football Inquiry Report.

FOOTBALL INFORMATION PROGRAM
COMMAND SUMMARY

Command Number and Name	Function
1–DATA	Adds game records to the data base.
2–RESULTS	Records scores and weather conditions.
3–CHANGE	Changes a game record.
4–DELETE	Deletes a game record.
5–REPORT	Generates the Football Stats Report.
6–INQUIRY	Lists all records stored in the data base.
7–EXIT	Ends program operation.

FOOTBALL INFORMATION
PROGRAM SOURCE CODE

```
10 ' ***********************************************************************
20 ' THIS PROGRAM WILL RECORD AND REPORT ON THE PERFORMANCE OF FOOTBALL   *
30 ' TEAMS.  AVAILABLE COMMANDS ARE:                                      *
40 '      DATA    : TO RECORD FOOTBALL DATA.                              *
50 '      CHANGE  : TO UPDATE ANY INFORMATION IN THE DATA RECORDS         *
60 '      DELETE  : TO REMOVE ANY DATA RECORD                             *
70 '      REPORT  : TO REPORT ON THE PERFORMANCE OF THE TEAMS             *
80 '      EXIT    : TO LEAVE THE PROGRAM                                  *
90 ' ***********************************************************************
100 GOSUB 5070' GO GET DISK DESIGNATOR
110 GOSUB 5150' GO SET SCREEN HEIGHT AND WIDTH
120 DIM SORTKEY(140),SORTREC(140),PCTWINS(4)
130 SCREENCNTR   = SCREENWIDTH/2
140 LEFTMARG     = SCREENCNTR - 20
150 FOR I = 1 TO SCREENHEIGHT : PRINT : NEXT I   ' SCROLL THE SCREEN CLEAR
160 PRINT TAB(LEFTMARG) ; "          Football Program              "
170 PRINT
180 PRINT TAB(LEFTMARG) ; "          Available commands are:"
190 PRINT TAB(LEFTMARG) ; " 1-Data                   2-Results     "
200 PRINT TAB(LEFTMARG) ; " 3-Change                 4-Delete      "
210 PRINT TAB(LEFTMARG) ; " 5-Report                 6-Inquiry     "
220 PRINT TAB(LEFTMARG) ; " 7-Exit                                 "
230 PRINT TAB(LEFTMARG) ;
"  " ; : LINE INPUT "Command selection [1-7 or ?1-?7] :" ;
CHGFIELD$
240 IF CHGFIELD$ = "" THEN GOTO 230
250 IF MID$(CHGFIELD$,1,1) = "?" THEN GOSUB 5380 : GOTO 230
260 CHGFIELD = VAL(CHGFIELD$)
270 IF CHGFIELD < 1 OR  CHGFIELD > 7 THEN GOTO 230
280 FOR I = 1 TO SCREENHEIGHT : PRINT : NEXT I
290 ON CHGFIELD GOSUB 320,4260,940,1610,1870,3990,310
300 GOTO 150
310 CLOSE : END
320 ' ***********************************************************************
330 ' THIS SECTION WILL ALLOW THE ENTRY OF NEW GAME INFORMATION INTO THE *
340 ' FILES                                                              *
350 ' ***********************************************************************
360 GOSUB 5780              ' GO OPEN GAME FILE
370 LINE INPUT "Enter team type PRO(1) or COLLEGE(2) :";TTYPE$
380 IF TTYPE$ = "" THEN CLOSE :GOSUB 5890 : RETURN
390 IF TTYPE$ <> "1" AND TTYPE$ <> "2" THEN GOTO 370
400 LINE INPUT "Enter season year :";SEASON$
410 IF SEASON$ = "" THEN GOTO 370
420 SEASON$ = MID$(SEASON$,1,2)
430 SEASON = VAL(SEASON$)
440 IF SEASON < 0 OR SEASON > 99 THEN GOTO 400
450 LINE INPUT "Enter week number :";WEEK$
460 IF WEEK$ = "" THEN GOTO 370
470 WEEK$ = MID$(WEEK$,1,2)
480 IF WEEK$ = "P1" OR WEEK$ = "P2" OR WEEK$ = "P3" OR
WEEK$ = "P4" OR WEEK$ = "P5" THEN GOTO 510
490 WEEK = VAL(WEEK$)
500 IF WEEK < 1 OR WEEK > 52 THEN GOTO 450
510 LINE INPUT "Enter team name `:"; TEAMA$
520 IF TEAMA$ = "" THEN GOTO 370
530 LINE INPUT "Enter opponent name :";TEAMB$
540 IF TEAMB$ = "" THEN GOTO 510
550 LINE INPUT "Which team is favored to win(1/2) :";FAVORED$
560 IF FAVORED$ <> "1" AND FAVORED$ <> "2" THEN GOTO 550
```

```
570 LINE INPUT "What point spread :";SPREAD$
580 IF SPREAD$ = "" THEN GOTO 570
590 SPREAD = VAL(SPREAD$)
600 IF SPREAD < 0 THEN GOTO 570
610 PRINT "Weather conditions: Not Played Yet (0),
Clear (1), Rain (2), Snow (3), Hot (4)"
620 LINE INPUT "Enter weather conditions (0-4) :";WEATHER$
630 WEATHER$ = MID$(WEATHER$,1,1)
640 IF WEATHER$ < "0" OR WEATHER$ > "4" THEN GOTO 610
650 IF WEATHER$ <> "0" THEN GOTO 690
660 POINTSA$ = "0"
670 POINTSB$ = "0"
680 GOTO 770
690 LINE INPUT "Enter team score :";POINTSA$
700 IF POINTSA$ = "" THEN GOTO 690
710 POINTSA = VAL(POINTSA$)
720 IF POINTSA < 0 THEN GOTO 690
730 LINE INPUT "Enter opponent score :";POINTSB$
740 IF POINTSB$ = "" THEN GOTO 730
750 POINTSB = VAL(POINTSB$)
760 IF POINTSB < 0 THEN GOTO 730
770 ' ********************************************************************
780 ' OK NOW PUT THE INFORMATION INTO THE RECORD AND WRITE IT OUT      *
790 ' ********************************************************************
800 LSET TTYPEF$ = TTYPE$
810 LSET SEASONF$ = SEASON$
820 LSET WEEKF$ = WEEK$
830 LSET TEAMAF$ = TEAMA$
840 LSET TEAMBF$ = TEAMB$
850 LSET FAVOREDF$ = FAVORED$
860 LSET SPREADF$ = MKS$(SPREAD)
870 LSET PTSAF$ = MKS$(POINTSA)
880 LSET PTSBF$ = MKS$(POINTSB)
890 LSET WEATHERF$ = WEATHER$
900 GAMECNT = GAMECNT + 1
910 PUT #1,GAMECNT
920 PRINT "Data has been recorded"
930 GOTO 510
940 ' ********************************************************************
950 ' THIS SECTION WILL PROCESS THE CHANGE REQUEST FROM THE MAIN MENU   *
960 GOSUB 5780        ' GO OPEN GAME FILE
970 GOSUB 4740     ' GO FIND THE DESIRED RECORD
980 IF FOUND$ = "Q" THEN CLOSE : RETURN
990 FOR I = 1 TO 4 : PRINT : NEXT I
1000 PRINT "(01) Team type        = " TTYPEF$
1010 PRINT "(02) Season year       = " SEASONF$
1020 PRINT "(03) Week number       = " WEEKF$
1030 PRINT "(04) Team name         = " TEAMAF$
1040 PRINT "(05) Opponent name     = " TEAMBF$
1050 PRINT "(06) Favored team      = " FAVOREDF$
1060 PRINT "(07) Point spread      = " CVS(SPREADF$)
1070 PRINT "(08) Team points       = " CVS(PTSAF$)
1080 PRINT "(09) Opponent points   = " CVS(PTSBF$)
1090 PRINT "(10) Weather conditions = " WEATHERF$
1100 LINE INPUT "Change what (1-10) :";CHGFIELD$
1110 IF CHGFIELD$ = "" THEN PUT #1,RECNO : PRINT "Record updated": GOTO 970
1120 CHGFIELD = VAL(CHGFIELD$)
1130 IF CHGFIELD < 1 OR CHGFIELD > 10 THEN GOTO 1100
1140 ON CHGFIELD GOSUB 1160,1190,1250,1320,1350,1380,1410,1460,1510,1560
1150 GOTO 1100
1160 LINE INPUT "Enter team type PRO(1) or COLLEGE(2) :";TTYPE$
1170 IF TTYPE$ <> "1" AND TTYPE$ <> "2" THEN GOTO 1160
1180 LSET TTYPEF$ = TTYPE$ : RETURN
1190 LINE INPUT "Enter season year :";SEASON$
```

```
1200 IF SEASON$ = "" THEN GOTO 1190
1210 SEASON$ = MID$(SEASON$,1,2)
1220 SEASON = VAL(SEASON$)
1230 IF SEASON < 0 OR SEASON > 99 THEN GOTO 1190
1240 LSET SEASONF$ = SEASON$ : RETURN
1250 LINE INPUT "Enter week number :";WEEK$
1260 IF WEEK$ = "" THEN GOTO 1250
1270 WEEK$ = MID$(WEEK$,1,2)
1280 IF WEEK$ = "P1" OR WEEK$ = "P2" OR WEEK$ = "P3" OR
WEEK$ = "P4" OR WEEK$ = "P5" THEN GOTO 1310
1290 WEEK = VAL(WEEK$)
1300 IF WEEK < 1 OR WEEK > 52 THEN GOTO 1250
1310 LSET WEEKF$ = WEEK$ : RETURN
1320 LINE INPUT "Enter team name :"; TEAMA$
1330 IF TEAMA$ = "" THEN GOTO 1320
1340 LSET TEAMAF$ = TEAMA$ : RETURN
1350 LINE INPUT "Enter opponent name :";TEAMB$
1360 IF TEAMB$ = "" THEN GOTO 1350
1370 LSET TEAMBF$ = TEAMB$ : RETURN
1380 LINE INPUT "Which team is favored to win(1/2) :";FAVORED$
1390 IF FAVORED$ <> "1" AND FAVORED$ <> "2" THEN GOTO 1380
1400 LSET FAVOREDF$ = FAVORED$ : RETURN
1410 LINE INPUT "What point spread :";SPREAD$
1420 IF SPREAD$ = "" THEN GOTO 1410
1430 SPREAD = VAL(SPREAD$)
1440 IF SPREAD < 0 THEN GOTO 1410
1450 LSET SPREADF$ = MKS$(SPREAD) : RETURN
1460 LINE INPUT "Enter team score :";POINTSA$
1470 IF POINTSA$ = "" THEN GOTO 1460
1480 POINTSA = VAL(POINTSA$)
1490 IF POINTSA < 0 THEN GOTO 1460
1500 LSET PTSAF$ = MKS$(POINTSA) : RETURN
1510 LINE INPUT "Enter opponent score :";POINTSB$
1520 IF POINTSB$ = "" THEN GOTO 1510
1530 POINTSB = VAL(POINTSB$)
1540 IF POINTSB < 0 THEN GOTO 1510
1550 LSET PTSBF$ = MKS$(POINTSB) : RETURN
1560 PRINT "Weather conditions: Not Played Yet (0),
Clear (1), Rain (2), Snow (3), Hot (4)"
1570 LINE INPUT "Enter weather conditions (0-4) :";WEATHER$
1580 WEATHER$ = MID$(WEATHER$,1,1)
1590 IF WEATHER$ < "0" OR WEATHER$ > "4" THEN GOTO 1560
1600 LSET WEATHERF$ = WEATHER$ : RETURN
1610 ' ****************************************************************
1620 ' THIS SECTION WILL PROCESS THE DELETE REQUEST FROM THE MAIN MENU   *
1630 ' ****************************************************************
1640 GOSUB 5780              ' GO OPEN GAME FILE
1650 GOSUB 4740              ' GO FIND THE DESIRED RECORD
1660 IF FOUND$ = "Q" THEN GOTO 1840
1670 FOR I = 1 TO 4 : PRINT : NEXT I
1680 PRINT "Team type        = " TTYPEF$
1690 PRINT "Season year      = " SEASONF$
1700 PRINT "Week number      = " WEEKF$
1710 PRINT "Team name        = " TEAMAF$
1720 PRINT "Opponent name    = " TEAMBF$
1730 PRINT "Favored team     = " FAVOREDF$
1740 PRINT "Point spread     = " CVS(SPREADF$)
1750 PRINT "Team points      = " CVS(PTSAF$)
1760 PRINT "Opponent points  = " CVS(PTSBF$)
1770 PRINT "Weather conditions = " WEATHERF$
1780 LINE INPUT "Ok to delete (Y/N) :";CHGFIELD$
1790 IF CHGFIELD$ <> "Y" AND CHGFIELD$ <> "N" THEN GOTO 1780
1800 IF CHGFIELD$ <> "Y" THEN GOTO 1650
1810 LSET TTYPEF$ = "0" ' FLAG THE RECORD FOR DELETION
```

```
1820 PUT #1,RECNO
1830 GOTO 1650
1840 CLOSE
1850 GOSUB 5530
1860 RETURN
1870 ' ****************************************************************
1880 ' THIS SECTION WILL HANDLE THE PERFORMANCE REPORT REQUEST FROM THE   *
1890 ' MAIN MENU                                                          *
1900 ' ****************************************************************
1910 GOSUB 5780              ' GO OPEN GAME FILE
1920 OPEN "R",#2,DISK$+"HOLD.DAT",80
1930 FIELD #2,30 AS HTEAMAF$,30 AS HTEAMBF$,4 AS PREVMEETF$,
4 AS PREVPTSAF$,4 AS PREVPTSBF$,4 AS HINDEX1F$,4 AS HINDEX2F$
1940 OPEN "R",#3,DISK$+"TEMPGAME.DAT",78
1950 FIELD #3,30 AS TEAMNAME$,4 AS TOTGAMES$,4 AS SPRDWINS$,
4 AS SPRDLOSS$,4 AS REALWIN1$,4 AS REALWIN2$,4 AS REALWIN3$,
4 AS REALWIN4$,4 AS WEEKGAMES$,4 AS WEEKWINS$,4 AS SPRDDTE$,
4 AS SPRDPTS$,4 AS PREVPTS$
1960 LINE INPUT "Output to screen (1) or printer (2) : ";CHGFIELD$
1970 OUTTYPE$ = CHGFIELD$
1980 IF CHGFIELD$ <> "1" AND CHGFIELD$ <> "2" THEN GOTO 1960
1990 LINE INPUT "Enter date for report heading :";RPTDATE$
2000 LINE INPUT "Enter name for report heading :";RPTNAME$
2010 LINE INPUT "Enter team type PRO(1) or COLLEGE(2) :";TTYPE$
2020 IF TTYPE$ = "" THEN CLOSE : RETURN
2030 IF TTYPE$ <> "1" AND TTYPE$ <> "2" THEN GOTO 2010
2040 LINE INPUT "Enter season year :";SEASON$
2050 IF SEASON$ = "" THEN GOTO 2010
2060 SEASON$ = MID$(SEASON$,1,2)
2070 SEASON = VAL(SEASON$)
2080 IF SEASON < 0 OR SEASON > 99 THEN GOTO 2040
2090 LINE INPUT "Enter week number :";TWEEK$
2100 IF TWEEK$ = "" THEN GOTO 2040
2110 WEEK$ = SPACE$(2) : LSET WEEK$ = TWEEK$
2120 WEEK$ = MID$(WEEK$,1,2)
2130 IF WEEK$ = "P1" OR WEEK$ = "P2" OR WEEK$ = "P3" OR
WEEK$ = "P4" OR WEEK$ = "P5" THEN PRINT
"Standings not available for Pre-season games":GOTO 2090
2140 WEEK = VAL(WEEK$)
2150 IF WEEK < 1 OR WEEK > 52 THEN GOTO 2090
2160 IF WEEK = 1 AND TTYPE$ = "2" THEN PRINT
"Spread Standings are based on last years final results"
2170 IF WEEK = 1 AND TTYPE$ = "1" THEN PRINT
"Spread Standings are based on Pre-season results"
2180 RECNO = 0
2190 MAXTEAM = 0
2192 HCNT = 0
2200 FOR I = 1 TO GAMECNT
2210 GET #1,I
2220 IF TTYPEF$ <> TTYPE$ THEN GOTO 2590'IGNORE RECORDS WITH WRONG TYPE
2230 IF SEASONF$ > SEASON$ THEN GOTO 2590'IGNORE FUTURE SEASON RECORDS
2240 IF (SEASONF$ = SEASON$) AND (WEEKF$ > WEEK$) THEN
GOTO 2590 'IGNORE FUTURE GAMES THIS SEASON
2260 IF WEEK <> 1 AND MID$(WEEKF$,1,1) = "P" THEN GOTO 2590
' IGNORE PRE-SEASON GAMES EXCEPT IN WEEK1
2270 TEAM$ = TEAMAF$
2280 GOSUB 3900'FIND TEAM IN TEMP FILE OR ADD IT
2290 INDEX1 = TEAMNBR
2300 TEAM$ = TEAMBF$
2310 GOSUB 3900'FIND OPPONENT TEMP FILE OR ADD IT
2320 INDEX2 = TEAMNBR
2330 IF (SEASONF$ = SEASON$) AND (WEEKF$ = WEEK$) THEN
GOSUB 3660 : GOTO 2590 'SAVE MATCHUP INFO FOR THIS WEEK AND GET OUT_
2340 IF WEEK <> 1 THEN GOTO 2380
```

```
2350 IF (TTYPE$ = "1") AND ((MID$(WEEKF$,1,1) <> "P")
OR (SEASONF$ <> SEASON$)) THEN
SCORE1 = 0 : SCORE2 = 0 : GOTO 2420
2360 IF (TTYPE$ = "2") AND (VAL(SEASONF$) = VAL(SEASON$) -1)
THEN GOTO 2390
2370 IF (TTYPE$ = "2") AND (VAL(SEASONF$) <> VAL(SEASON$) -1)
THEN SCORE1 = 0 : SCORE2 = 0 : GOTO 2420
2380 IF SEASONF$ <> SEASON$ THEN SCORE1 = 0 : SCORE2 = 0 : GOTO 2420
2390 SCORE1 = CVS(PTSAF$) : SCORE2 = CVS(PTSBF$)
2400 IF VAL(FAVOREDF$) = 1 THEN SCORE1 = SCORE1 + CVS(SPREADF$)
2410 IF VAL(FAVOREDF$) = 2 THEN SCORE2 = SCORE2 + CVS(SPREADF$)
2420 ' **********************************************************
2430 ' NOW PROCESS EACH TEAM FROM THE RECORD SEPERATELY        *
2440 ' **********************************************************
2445 IF VAL(WEATHERF$) = 0 THEN GOTO 2590      ' IGNORE GAMES NOT PLAYED
2450 SPREADSCORE = SCORE1 - SCORE2
2460 IF SCORE1 > SCORE2 THEN SPREADWIN = 1 ELSE SPREADWIN = 0
2470 IF SCORE1 < SCORE2 THEN SPREADLOSS = 1 ELSE SPREADLOSS = 0
2480 IF CVS(PTSAF$) > CVS(PTSBF$) THEN REALWIN = 1 ELSE REALWIN = 0
2490 TEAMNBR = INDEX1
2500 GOSUB 3480                              ' GO UPDATE TEAM STATS
2510 ' **********************************************************
2520 SPREADSCORE = SCORE2 - SCORE1
2530 IF SCORE2 > SCORE1 THEN SPREADWIN = 1 ELSE SPREADWIN = 0
2540 IF SCORE2 < SCORE1 THEN SPREADLOSS = 1 ELSE SPREADLOSS = 0
2550 IF CVS(PTSBF$) > CVS(PTSAF$) THEN REALWIN = 1 ELSE REALWIN = 0
2560 TEAMNBR = INDEX2
2570 GOSUB 3480                              ' GO UPDATE TEAM STATS
2580 ' **********************************************************
2590 NEXT I                                  ' GO FIND ANOTHER RECORD
2600 ' **********************************************************
2610 ' NOW FIND AND UPDATE PREVIOUS MATCHUP RESULTS IN TEMP FILE RECORDS
2615 ' AND BUILD SORT KEYS AS WE GO THROUGH
2620 ' **********************************************************
2625 K = 0
2630 FOR I = 1 TO HCNT
2640 GET #2,I
2650 GOSUB 3740                              ' GO FIND LAST MEETING
2660 GET #3,CVS(HINDEX1F$)
2670 LSET PREVPTS$ = MKS$(CVS(PREVPTSAF$) - CVS(PREVPTSBF$))
2680 K = K + 1
2682 SORTKEY(K) = (CVS(SPRDWIN$) * 100) + CVS(SPRDPTS$)
2684 SORTREC(K) = CVS(HINDEX1F$)
2686 PUT #3,CVS(HINDEX1F$)
2690 GET #3,CVS(HINDEX2F$)
2700 LSET PREVPTS$ = MKS$(CVS(PREVPTSBF$) - CVS(PREVPTSAF$))
2710 K = K + 1
2712 SORTKEY(K) = (CVS(SPRDWIN$) * 100) + CVS(SPRDPTS$)
2714 SORTREC(K) = CVS(HINDEX2F$)
2716 PUT #3,CVS(HINDEX2F$)
2720 NEXT I
2810 ' **********************************************************
2820 ' NOW SORT THE RECORDS IN THE ARRAYS WE JUST BUILT
2830 ' **********************************************************
2840 SWITCHED = 0
2850 FOR I = 1 TO (K-1)
2860 IF SORTKEY(I) >= SORTKEY(I+1) THEN GOTO 2900
2870 HOLDKEY = SORTKEY(I):SORTKEY(I) = SORTKEY(I+1):SORTKEY(I+1)=HOLDKEY
2880 HOLDREC = SORTREC(I):SORTREC(I) = SORTREC(I+1):SORTREC(I+1)=HOLDREC
2890 SWITCHED = 1
2900 NEXT I
2910 IF SWITCHED = 1 THEN GOTO 2840
2920 ' **********************************************************
2930 ' NOW PRODUCE THE REPORT USING THE RECORDS IN THE TEMP FILE
```

```
2940 ' IN THE SORTED SEQUENCE
2950 ' **********************************************************
2960 IF OUTTYPE$ = "1" THEN PAGELEN = SCREENHEIGHT ELSE PAGELEN = 66
2970 CLOSE #2
2980 OPEN "O",#2,DISK$+"REPORT.FIL"
2990 FOR I = 1 TO K
3000 GET #3,SORTREC(I)
3010 REALWINS(1) = CVS(REALWIN1$)
3020 REALWINS(2) = CVS(REALWIN2$)
3030 REALWINS(3) = CVS(REALWIN3$)
3040 REALWINS(4) = CVS(REALWIN4$)
3050 PCTWINS(1) = 0 : PCTWINS(2) = 0 : PCTWINS(3) = 0 : PCTWINS(4) = 0
3060 IF CVS(TOTGAME$) = 0 THEN GOTO 3110
3070 PCTWINS(1) = REALWINS(1)/CVS(TOTGAME$) * 100
3080 PCTWINS(2) = REALWINS(2)/CVS(TOTGAME$) * 100
3090 PCTWINS(3) = REALWINS(3)/CVS(TOTGAME$) * 100
3100 PCTWINS(4) = REALWINS(4)/CVS(TOTGAME$) * 100
3110 IF (I <> 1) AND (I MOD (66-14) <> 0) THEN GOTO 3250
3120 IF OUTTYPE$ = "2" THEN PRINT #2,CHR$(12)
3130 PRINT #2,
"                                  Football Stats                            "
3140 PRINT #2,
"                            By " RPTNAME$ " on " RPTDATE$: PRINT #2,"  "
3150 PRINT #2," "
3160 IF WEEK = 1 AND TTYPE$ = "1" THEN PRINT #2,
"Spread Standings based on Pre-season results"
3170 IF WEEK = 1 AND TTYPE$ = "2" THEN PRINT #2,
"Spread Standings based on Final results of last season"
3180 PRINT #2,
"                      ********** A C T U A L    S C O R E **********"
3190 PRINT #2,
"                           *              Results                        *"
3200 PRINT #2,
"                           * Last      For This                          *"
3210 PRINT #2,
"                Spread     *Meeting    Week In                           *"
3220 PRINT #2,
"                Standing   *Against    Previous    Weather Performance   *"
3230 PRINT #2,
"   Team     Wins   Losses *Opponent   Season    Clear  Rain  Snow   Hot*"
3240 PRINT #2,
"_____  ____  _____ *_____  _____  _____  ____  ____  ___*"
3250 PRINT #2,
USING "\                  \";TEAMNAME$;:PRINT #2,"  ";
3260 PRINT #2,
USING "####";CVS(SPRDWIN$); :PRINT #2,"    ";
3270 PRINT #2,
USING "####";CVS(SPRDLOSS$);:PRINT #2,"     ";
3280 PRINT #2,
USING "####";CVS(PREVPTS$); :PRINT #2,"      ";
3290 PRINT #2,
USING "####";CVS(WEEKWIN$); :PRINT #2,"   ";
3300 PRINT #2,
USING "####";PCTWINS(1);    :PRINT #2,"% ";
3310 PRINT #2,
USING "####";PCTWINS(2);    :PRINT #2,"% ";
3320 PRINT #2,
USING "####";PCTWINS(3);    :PRINT #2,"% ";
3330 PRINT #2,
USING "####";PCTWINS(4);    :PRINT #2,"%"
3340 NEXT I
3350 CLOSE #2
3360 CLOSE #3
3370 GOSUB 5980        ' GO PRINT REPORT.FIL ON REQUESTED DEVICE
```

```
3380 LINE INPUT
"Ok to delete 3-year old records for this week (Y/N) :";CHGFIELD$
3390 IF CHGFIELD$ <> "Y" AND CHGFIELD$ <> "N" THEN GOTO 3380
3400 IF CHGFIELD$ = "N" THEN CLOSE : RETURN
3410 FOR I = 1 TO GAMECNT
3420 GET #1,I
3430 IF (VAL(SEASONF$) = (VAL(SEASON$) -3)) AND
WEEKF$ = WEEK$ THEN LSET TTYPE$ = "O" :PUT #1,I
3440 NEXT I
3450 CLOSE
3460 GOSUB 5530          ' GO REORGANIZE THE FILE
3470 CLOSE : RETURN
3480 ' ***********************************************************
3490 ' THIS SUBROUTINE WILL UPDATE THE TEMP FILE RECORD VARIABLES FOR THE *
3500 ' THE RECORD NUMBER REFRENCED BY THE VARIABLE TEAMNBR              *
3510 ' ***********************************************************
3520 GET #3,TEAMNBR                                    ' GET THE RECORD
3530 LSET TOTGAME$  = MKS$(CVS(TOTGAME$) + 1)          ' UPDATE TOTAL GAMES
3540 LSET SPRDWIN$  = MKS$(CVS(SPRDWIN$) + SPREADWIN)   ' UPDATE SPREAD WINS
3550 LSET SPRDLOSS$ = MKS$(CVS(SPRDLOSS$) + SPREADLOSS) ' UPDATE SPREAD LOSSES
3560 IF REALWIN <> 1 THEN GOTO 3610
3570 IF VAL(WEATHERF$) = 1 THEN LSET REALWIN1$ = MKS$(CVS(REALWIN1$) + 1)
3580 IF VAL(WEATHERF$) = 2 THEN LSET REALWIN2$ = MKS$(CVS(REALWIN2$) + 1)
3590 IF VAL(WEATHERF$) = 3 THEN LSET REALWIN3$ = MKS$(CVS(REALWIN3$) + 1)
3600 IF VAL(WEATHERF$) = 4 THEN LSET REALWIN4$ = MKS$(CVS(REALWIN4$) + 1)
3610 IF WEEK$ = WEEKF$ THEN
LSET WEEKGAME$ = MKS$(CVS(WEEKGAME$) + 1):
LSET WEEKWIN$ = MKS$(CVS(WEEKWIN$) + REALWIN)
3620 IF SCORE1 = 0 AND SCORE2 = 0 THEN
GOTO 3642    ' FOR WEEK1 SPECIAL PROCESSING
3630 SPREADDATE$ = SEASONF$+WEEKF$                ' GET LAST SPREAD DATE/AMT
3640 IF SPREADDATE$ > SPRDDTE$ THEN
LSET SPRDDTE$ = SPREADDATE$ : LSET SPRDPTS$ = MKS$(SPREADSCORE)
3642 PUT #3,TEAMNBR
3650 RETURN
3660 ' ***********************************************************
3670 ' THIS SUBROUTINE WILL SAVE THE CURRENT WEEK MATCHUPS IN A HOLD FILE *
3680 ' ***********************************************************
3690 LSET HTEAMAF$ = TEAMAF$ : LSET HTEAMBF$ = TEAMBF$
3700 LSET PREVMEETF$ = "    ":LSET PREVPTSAF$ = MKS$(0):
LSET PREVPTSBF$ = MKS$(0)
3710 LSET HINDEX1F$ = MKS$(INDEX1) : LSET HINDEX2F$ = MKS$(INDEX2)
3720 HCNT = HCNT + 1 : PUT #2,HCNT
3730 RETURN
3740 ' ***********************************************************
3750 ' GET LATEST MATCHUP RESULTS FOR THIS PAIR OF TEAMS              *
3760 ' ***********************************************************
3770 FOR J = 1 TO GAMECNT
3780 GET #1,J
3790 IF HTEAMAF$ = TEAMAF$ AND HTEAMBF$ = TEAMBF$ THEN GOTO 3820
3800 IF HTEAMAF$ = TEAMBF$ AND HTEAMBF$ = TEAMAF$ THEN GOTO 3820
3810 GOTO 3880
3820 IF SEASONF$ > SEASON$ THEN GOTO 3880
3830 IF (SEASONF$ = SEASON$) AND (WEEKF$ >= WEEK$) THEN GOTO 3880
3840 MEETF$ = SPACE$(4) : LSET MEETF$ = SEASONF$+WEEKF$
3850 IF PREVMEETF$ = "    " THEN LSET PREVMEETF$ = MEETF$
3860 IF MEETF$ < PREVMEETF$ THEN GOTO 3880
3870 LSET PREVPTSAF$ = PTSAF$ :
LSET PREVPTSBF$ = PTSBF$ : LSET PREVMEETF$ = MEETF$
3880 NEXT J
3890 RETURN
3900 ' ***********************************************************
3910 ' THIS SUBROUTINE WILL FIND THE TEAM IN THE TEMP FILE AND RETURN THE *
3920 ' RECORD NUMBER IN THE VARIABLE TEAMNBR                            *
```

```
3930 ' ****************************************************************
3940 IF MAXTEAM = 0 THEN GOTO 3972
3950 FOR J = 1 TO MAXTEAM
3951 GET #3,J
3960 IF TEAM$ = TEAMNAME$ THEN TEAMNBR = J : RETURN
3970 NEXT J
3972 MAXTEAM = MAXTEAM + 1
3973 TEAMNBR = MAXTEAM
3974 LSET TEAMNAME$ = TEAM$
3975 LSET TOTGAME$ = MKS$(0):LSET SPRDWIN$ = MKS$(0):LSET SPRDLOSS$ = MKS$(0)
3976 LSET REALWIN1$ = MKS$(0):LSET REALWIN2$ = MKS$(0):LSET REALWIN3$ = MKS$(0)
3977 LSET REALWIN4$ = MKS$(0):LSET WEEKGAME$ = MKS$(0):LSET WEEKWIN$ = MKS$(0)
3978 LSET SPRDDTE$ = MKS$(0):LSET SPRDPTS$ = MKS$(0):LSET PREVPTS$ = MKS$(0)
3980 PUT #3,MAXTEAM : RETURN
3990 ' ****************************************************************
4000 ' THIS SECTION WILL PRINTOUT THE CONTENTS OF THE GAME FILE      *
4010 ' ****************************************************************
4020 GOSUB 5780          ' GO OPEN GAME FILE
4030 FIELD #1,1 AS TTYPEF$,2 AS SEASONF$,2 AS WEEKF$,
30 AS TEAMAF$,30 AS TEAMBF$,1 AS WEATHERF$,4 AS PTSAF$,
4 AS PTSBF$,1 AS FAVOREDF$,4 AS SPREADF$
4040 LINE INPUT "Output to screen (1) or printer (2) : ";CHGFIELD$
4050 OUTTYPE$ = CHGFIELD$
4060 IF CHGFIELD$ <> "1" AND CHGFIELD$ <> "2" THEN GOTO 4040
4070 OPEN "O",#2,DISK$+"REPORT.FIL"
4080 FOR I = 1 TO GAMECNT
4090 GET #1,I
4100 PRINT #2,"Team type          = " TTYPEF$
4110 PRINT #2,"Season year        = " SEASONF$
4120 PRINT #2,"Week number        = " WEEKF$
4130 PRINT #2,"Team name          = " TEAMAF$
4140 PRINT #2,"Opponent name      = " TEAMBF$
4150 PRINT #2,"Favored team       = " FAVOREDF$
4160 PRINT #2,"Point spread       = " CVS(SPREADF$)
4170 PRINT #2,"Team points        = " CVS(PTSAF$)
4180 PRINT #2,"Opponent points    = " CVS(PTSBF$)
4190 PRINT #2,"Weather conditions = " WEATHERF$
4200 PRINT #2,"  " : PRINT #2,"  "
4210 NEXT I
4220 CLOSE
4230 GOSUB 5980     ' GO PRINT REPORT.FIL ON REQUESTED DEVICE
4240 IF OUTTYPE$ = "1" THEN LINE INPUT "Enter return to continue";CHGFIELD$
4250 RETURN
4260 ' ****************************************************************
4270 ' THIS SECTION WILL PROCESS THE RESULTS REQUEST FROM THE MAIN MENU  *
4280 ' ****************************************************************
4290 GOSUB 5780          ' GO OPEN GAME FILE
4300 LINE INPUT "Enter team type PRO(1) or COLLEGE(2) :";TTYPE$
4320 IF TTYPE$ <> "1" AND TTYPE$ <> "2" THEN GOTO 4300
4330 LINE INPUT "Enter season year :";SEASON$
4340 IF SEASON$ = "" THEN GOTO 4300
4350 SEASON$ = MID$(SEASON$,1,2)
4360 SEASON = VAL(SEASON$)
4370 IF SEASON < 0 OR SEASON > 99 THEN GOTO 4330
4380 LINE INPUT "Enter week number :";TWEEK$
4390 IF TWEEK$ = "" THEN GOTO 4300
4400 WEEK$ = SPACE$(2):LSET WEEK$ = TWEEK$
4410 WEEK$ = MID$(WEEK$,1,2)
4420 IF WEEK$ = "P1" OR WEEK$ = "P2" OR WEEK$ = "P3" OR
WEEK$ = "P4" OR WEEK$ = "P5" THEN GOTO 4450
4430 WEEK = VAL(WEEK$)
4440 IF WEEK < 1 OR WEEK > 52 THEN GOTO 4380
4450 ' ****************************************************************
```

```
4460 ' NOW FIND EACH MATCH UP RECORD WITH THE PROMPTED VALUES AND UPDATE  *
4470 ' ********************************************************************
4480 FOR I = 1 TO GAMECNT
4490 GET #1,I
4500 IF TTYPE$ <> TTYPEF$ THEN GOTO 4720
4510 IF SEASON$ <> SEASONF$ THEN GOTO 4720
4520 IF WEEK$ <> WEEKF$ THEN GOTO 4720
4530 PRINT : PRINT : PRINT :
4540 PRINT "Team     = " TEAMAF$
4550 PRINT "Opponent = " TEAMBF$
4560 LINE INPUT "Enter team score : ";POINTSA$
4570 IF POINTSA$ = "" THEN GOTO 4720
4580 POINTSA = VAL(POINTSA$)
4590 IF POINTSA < 0 THEN GOTO 4560
4600 LSET PTSAF$ = MKS$(POINTSA)
4610 LINE INPUT "Enter opponent score :";POINTSB$
4620 IF POINTSB$ = "" THEN GOTO 4610
4630 POINTSB = VAL(POINTSB$)
4640 IF POINTSB < 0 THEN GOTO 4610
4650 LSET PTSBF$ = MKS$(POINTSB)
4660 PRINT "Weather conditions: Not Played Yet (0),
Clear (1), Rain (2), Snow (3), Hot (4)"
4670 LINE INPUT "Enter weather conditions (0-4) :";WEATHER$
4680 WEATHER$ = MID$(WEATHER$,1,1)
4690 IF WEATHER$ < "0" OR WEATHER$ > "4" THEN GOTO 4660
4700 LSET WEATHERF$ = WEATHER$
4710 PUT #1,I : PRINT "Record has been updated"
4720 NEXT I
4730 CLOSE : RETURN
4740 ' ********************************************************************
4750 ' THIS SECTION WILL PROMPT FOR THE KEY RECORD VALUES AND FIND THE   *
4760 ' REQUESTED RECORD IN THE FILE                                      *
4770 ' ********************************************************************
4780 FOUND$ = "N"
4790 LINE INPUT "Enter team type PRO(1) or COLLEGE(2) :";TTYPE$
4800 IF TTYPE$ = "" THEN FOUND$ = "Q" : RETURN
4810 IF TTYPE$ <> "1" AND TTYPE$ <> "2" THEN GOTO 4790
4820 LINE INPUT "Enter season year :";SEASON$
4830 IF SEASON$ = "" THEN GOTO 4790
4840 SEASON$ = MID$(SEASON$,1,2)
4850 SEASON = VAL(SEASON$)
4860 IF SEASON < 0 OR SEASON > 99 THEN GOTO 4820
4870 LINE INPUT "Enter week number :";TWEEK$
4880 IF TWEEK$ = "" THEN GOTO 4820
4890 WEEK$ = SPACES$(2) : LSET WEEK$ = TWEEK$
4900 WEEK$ = MID$(WEEK$,1,2)
4910 IF WEEK$ = "P1" OR WEEK$ = "P2" OR WEEK$ = "P3" OR
WEEK$ = "P4" OR WEEK$ = "P5" THEN GOTO 4940
4920 WEEK = VAL(WEEK$)
4930 IF WEEK < 1 OR WEEK > 52 THEN GOTO 4870
4940 LINE INPUT "Enter team name :"; TTEAMA$
4950 IF TTEAMA$ = "" THEN GOTO 4870
4960 TEAMA$ = SPACES$(30) : LSET TEAMA$ = TTEAMA$
4970 RECNO = 0
4980 RECNO = RECNO + 1
4990 IF RECNO > GAMECNT THEN PRINT "Record not found" : GOTO 4780
5000 GET #1,RECNO
5010 IF TTYPEF$ <> TTYPE$ THEN GOTO 4980    ' NO MATCH ON TEAM TYPE
5020 IF SEASONF$ <> SEASON$ THEN GOTO 4980  ' NO MATCH ON SEASON YEAR
5030 IF WEEKF$ <> WEEK$ THEN GOTO 4980      ' NO MATCH ON WEEK NUMBER
5040 IF TEAMAF$ <> TEAMA$ THEN GOTO 4980    ' NO MATCH ON TEAM NAME
5050 FOUND$ = "Y"
5060 RETURN
```

```
5070 ' ********************************************************************
5080 ' THIS SECTION WILL PROMPT FOR THE DISK DRIVE DESIGNATOR        *
5090 ' ********************************************************************
5100 LINE INPUT "Drive the datafile will be on :";TDISK$
5110 IF TDISK$ = "" THEN PRINT "The default drive will be used": RETURN
5120 IF MID$(TDISK$,1,1) < "A" OR MID$(TDISK$,1,1) > "P" THEN GOTO 5100
5130 DISK$ = SPACE$(2)  : LSET DISK$ = MID$(TDISK$,1,1)+":"
5140 RETURN
5150 ' ********************************************************************
5160 ' THIS SECTION WILL READ THE SCREEN HEIGHT AND WIDTH SIZES FROM THE *
5170 ' PARAMETER FILE .. IF NO PARAMETER FILE EXISTS PROMPT FOR THE      *
5180 ' VALUES AND CREATE ONE FOR NEXT TIME .. IN ANY CASE SET THE VARS.  *
5190 ' SCREENHEIGHT AND SCREENWIDTH AND RETURN                          *
5200 ' ********************************************************************
5210 OPEN "R",#1,DISK$+"PARAMTER.FIL",8
5220 FIELD #1,4 AS SCREENHEIGHT$,4 AS SCREENWIDTH$
5230 I = 1 : GET #1,I
5240 SCREENHEIGHT = CVI(SCREENHEIGHT$)
5250 SCREENWIDTH  = CVI(SCREENWIDTH$)
5260 IF SCREENHEIGHT > 1 THEN CLOSE : RETURN
5270 LINE INPUT "Enter screen height value (1-24) :"; SCREENPARM$
5280 SCREENHEIGHT = VAL(SCREENPARM$)
5290 IF SCREENHEIGHT < 1 OR SCREENHEIGHT > 24 THEN GOTO 5270
5300 LINE INPUT "Enter screen width value (1-80) :"; SCREENPARM$
5310 SCREENWIDTH = VAL(SCREENPARM$)
5320 IF SCREENWIDTH < 1 OR SCREENWIDTH > 80 THEN GOTO 5300
5330 LSET SCREENHEIGHT$ = MKI$(SCREENHEIGHT)
5340 LSET SCREENWIDTH$  = MKI$(SCREENWIDTH)
5350 I = 1
5360 PUT #1,I
5370 CLOSE : RETURN
5380 ' ********************************************************************
5390 ' THIS SECTION WILL HANDLE THE HELP REQUEST FROM THE MAIN MENU       *
5400 ' ********************************************************************
5410 CHGFIELD$ = MID$(CHGFIELD$,2,2)
5420 CHGFIELD = VAL(CHGFIELD$)
5430 IF CHGFIELD < 1 OR
CHGFIELD > 7 THEN
PRINT "Help is available for all commands by typing ?x where x = 1 to 7" :
RETURN
5440 ON CHGFIELD GOSUB 5460,5470,5480,5490,5500,5510,5520
5450 RETURN
5460 PRINT "This command is used to enter information about a game." :RETURN
5470 PRINT "This command is used to enter results of played games." :RETURN
5480 PRINT "This command is used to update information about a game.":RETURN
5490 PRINT "This command is used to delete information about a game.":RETURN
5500 PRINT "This command is used to report on team performance." :RETURN
5510 PRINT "This command is used to report all data stored in the file":RETURN
5520 PRINT "This command is used to leave the program."           :RETURN
5530 ' ********************************************************************
5540 ' THIS SUBROUTINE WILL REORG THE GAMES FILE AND ELIMINATE ALL RECORDS*
5550 ' WITH A TEAM TYPE OF "0" .. WHICH IS AN INVALID VALUE              *
5560 ' ********************************************************************
5570 OPEN "R",#1,DISK$+"GAMES.DAT",79
5580 FIELD #1,1 AS OTYPEF$,78 AS ORESTF$
5590 OPEN "R",#2,DISK$+"NEWGAMES.DAT",79
5600 FIELD #2,1 AS NTYPEF$,78 AS NRESTF$
5610 IF GAMECNT > 0 THEN GOTO 5630
5620 PRINT "No game records " :
LINE INPUT "Enter return to continue :";CHGFIELD$ :CLOSE : RETURN
5630 J = 0
5640 FOR I = 1 TO GAMECNT
5650 GET #1,I
5660 IF OTYPEF$ = "0" THEN GOTO 5710
```

```
5670 J = J + 1
5680 LSET NTYPEF$ = OTYPEF$
5690 LSET NRESTF$ = ORESTF$
5700 PUT #2,J
5710 NEXT I
5720 PRINT "Old file had " (I-1) " game records.
New file has " J " game records."
5730 CLOSE
5740 GAMECNT = J : GOSUB 5890        ' GO SAVE NEW GAME CNT
5750 KILL DISK$+"GAMES.DAT" : NAME DISK$+"NEWGAMES.DAT" AS DISK$+"GAMES.DAT"
5760 LINE INPUT "Enter return to continue :";CHGFIELD$
5770 RETURN
5780 ' ****************************************************************
5790 ' This subroutine will open the game count file and the game file*
5800 ' ****************************************************************
5810 OPEN "R",#1,DISK$+"GAMES.CNT",4
5820 FIELD #1,4 AS GAMECNT$
5830 I = 1 : GET #1,I
5840 GAMECNT = CVS(GAMECNT$)
5850 CLOSE #1
5860 OPEN "R",#1,DISK$+"GAMES.DAT",79
5870 FIELD #1,1 AS TTYPEF$,2 AS SEASONF$,2 AS WEEKF$,
30 AS TEAMAF$,30 AS TEAMBF$,1 AS WEATHERF$,4 AS PTSAF$,
4 AS PTSBF$,1 AS FAVOREDF$,4 AS SPREADF$
5880 RETURN
5890 ' ****************************************************************
5900 ' This subroutine will save the current value of the GAMECNT field
5910 ' ****************************************************************
5920 OPEN "R",#1,DISK$+"GAMES.CNT",4
5930 FIELD #1,4 AS GAMECNT$
5940 LSET GAMECNT$ = MKS$(GAMECNT)
5950 I = 1 : PUT #1,I
5960 CLOSE #1
5970 RETURN
5980 ' ****************************************************************
5990 ' This subroutine will print the contents of the REPORT.FIL file·*
6000 ' on the console or printer depending on the value of OUTTYPE$      *
6010 ' ****************************************************************
6020 OPEN "I",#2,DISK$+"REPORT.FIL"
6030 J = 0
6040 IF EOF(2) THEN GOTO 6100
6050 J = J + 1
6060 LINE INPUT #2,A$
6070 IF OUTTYPE$ = "2" THEN LPRINT A$ : GOTO 6040
6080 IF J MOD (SCREENHEIGHT - 1) = 0 THEN
LINE INPUT "Enter return to continue :";CHGFIELD$
6090 PRINT A$ : GOTO 6040
6100 CLOSE #2 : FOR J = 1 TO 4 : PRINT : NEXT J
6110 RETURN
```

CHAPTER
ELEVEN
PROFITS IN
SUPPORT

A few years ago, a software company sold a lot of programs and, as a result, nearly went bankrupt. The company offered a great program, had it priced to be exceptionally profitable, offered free support, but hardly made any money. The company brought in consultants. It didn't take the consultants long to discover that customer support, which was being given away free, was costing the company *several hundred thousand dollars* a year. Since it had agreed to free support, the company saw bankruptcy fast approaching.

The consultants examined the user documentation and discovered it simply wasn't readable. New documentation that clearly explained how the program was used was written. The training staff used the new documentation to develop new classes, and suddenly people who attended the new classes didn't call for help in every procedure. All the "old" users were retrained and given new manuals. The company's telephones stopped ringing with problems. The support costs dropped to below $10,000 a year for "hand-holding." The program became as profitable as everyone always knew it to be.

Today, support is important to making a personal computer or software sale. Clients want to know if support will be available if they need help. They want to be sure they'll be able to use their purchases. They want proper training. It means profitable opportunities for those with the right skills.

PROFITS IN DOCUMENTATION

Good documentation is vital to a profitable program. Many PC manufacturers evaluate a description of a program before asking for code, so the description has to be well written. Mail order houses, too, want to see a user manual to evaluate the program. Software companies need good documentation to avoid backbreaking support costs. If you sell your own programs, you'll need it, too.

A free-lance writer, experienced in documenting software, earns between $20.00 and $50.00 per hour.

Preparing documentation, really, is at the end of a good writer's job. A writer becomes involved in a project when a program is first designed. The writer becomes an end-user's advocate. He or she looks at the program from the user's viewpoint and offers suggestions for missing areas, points out illogical and inconsistent prompting, and helps make the operation as user-friendly as possible.

At an early stage, the writer begins to develop the conceptual framework for presenting the program. The developer and programmers have ideas about the program, but these may be of a very detailed nature. It's up to the writer to stand back and develop a concise, readily understandable overview. The writer also helps to identify sales features and capabilities.

As the program is developed, the writer refines this overview and becomes the programmer's chief critic. He or she ensures that all details are consistent, and works to make the software friendlier. The writer starts taking notes for the manual.

Writers also may work with marketing people to help them understand the program and its audience. Often, the writers themselves will prepare brochures, data sheets, descriptions, and sales aids.

Finally, the writer prepares the user manual. An early draft is given to training personnel, who use it to develop classes, when necessary. Ideally, the program, documentation, and training, then are all consistent.

Documenting software *well* is an art. You need writing skills and an understanding of an application. You do not need to know how to program. This is one opportunity, in fact, in which knowing programming can hurt you. If you know programming, you may automatically include that which is meaningful to you, but which would make no sense to an end user who *doesn't* know how to program.

Learning this art is difficult. Schools continue to focus on developing programmers. Very few schools, colleges, graduate schools, or adult education programs offer any classes in how to document software. It is widely accepted that many thousands of programs will be written in the years ahead, but the question of who will document all that software is left unanswered.

Today, most people learn the art on the job. Essentially, successful software documentation specialists keep reinventing the wheel.

Repeat work is built into this business because programs generally are updated, and the changes must be documented, too. You can handle distributing the changes to program users with your *Programs for Profit* Mail List Program. To start a documentation business, you will use the advertising and direct mail techniques already presented to contact software companies, hardware manufacturers, and programmers.

A new market is also emerging. The major publishing houses are publishing user manuals in conjunction with PC manufacturers and software companies. Houses have found they don't have enough qualified writers to do this work. The manufacturers and companies need the books to gain exposure for their products. The houses need the books to enter the PC field. The result is a new and profitable opportunity for anyone with the skill to document software.

PROFITS IN TRAINING

Karen is a popular, highly paid technical representative in charge of training customers to use a program. She teaches her classes how to use the program and they invariably leave with smiles on their faces. People call her with problems when they sit down to use the program, and she merrily tells them how it's done. She tells her students again and again, because though Karen is a warm, wonderful person, she's an awful teacher.

Teaching isn't easy, but it, too, is a valuable skill that can be used in many profitable ways. In industry, people involved with computer training earn between $20,000 and $50,000 a year.

TRAINING IN THE CLASSROOM

Personal Computer classes no longer are limited to schools and colleges. Computer stores hold classes in many subjects from computer literacy to specialized applications. One store devotes its main efforts to one-on-one tutorials to develop students' fluency in programming and PC operation. As more application programs become available, more teachers will be needed for training. High school teachers presently teaching PC courses easily can earn a sizable extra income by contacting a store and offering to teach the same classes to adults.

Classes can be held for a variety of new subjects, too, including how to document software, teach PC skills, repair hardware, and, using this text, make money with PCs.

Today classes also are held to help buyers choose the right PC. Many of these classes are conducted with manufacturers' materials, or even by a representative of a manufacturer. (Guess which PC they suggest is right for everybody?) *Independent* classes can be held to help a novice objectively select the best machine for his or her needs. Similarly, classes can be held to help buyers select the right software for their particular needs.

Can you show how PCs can be applied to specific jobs? Can you teach word processing? Do you know how to explore the ramifications of this new technology? These and similar subjects are being taught in adult or continuing education classes. What you earn teaching an adult education class depends on the number of people who register for it.

You don't even need a formal classroom to teach your subject. You also can hold seminars by renting a room and charging a fee for your instruction. On a smaller scale, you can offer tutorial services.

Classes also are held in companies. Software companies hold classes in client companies to train people to use their programs. Your business can be to teach the use of these programs. A software company's application programs also can be taught at computer and software stores. To start this business, you should prepare direct mail letters for software companies. You do not need to be geographically near the company. In fact, a location far from the company can help you to represent it in your "remote" territory. Teaching classes for a software company offers you the best money of these opportunities.

TEACHING THE TEACHERS

Training a company's personnel and consultants to teach classes in software use is a very profitable business. Once the training program is defined, supporting materials and aids also must be prepared. These can include texts, homework assignments, practice PC sessions, and graphic slides for presentations. Teachers must be trained to use these materials and conduct the classes. Periodically, ongoing classes are held to train new teachers. Refresher courses, at which program changes are explained, also are held for graduate teachers.

It's an art to develop these classes. The time necessary for instruction should be as short as possible because end users won't be earning anything for their companies while attending the classes. But the classes must be comprehensive. Likewise, the training programs should be just as short and comprehensive. The material should also be economically presented in, if possible, a way that holds interest. This training also is crucial to limiting support costs for hand-holding. Companies, consequently, will pay dearly for people with these skills.

At one extreme are highly paid consultants who go to large companies with in-house training departments and teach them how best to set up courses for their teachers. These consultants do not set up specific classes themselves, but present general guidelines for others to set the classes up.

Consultants may also offer to develop specific courses for a company. In this situation, you also will prepare the teaching aids and train teachers to conduct the classes and use your materials correctly.

PUBLISHING TEXTBOOKS

Personal computer-related courses taught in schools, colleges, graduate schools, technical schools, and adult education classes rely on textbooks, many of which remain to be written.

Writing a good textbook can be very profitable. Widely used texts have made millionaires of their authors. Even lesser used texts may earn their authors substantial amounts ($10,000 to $50,000) each year. Each incoming group of students must buy new textbooks, and so profits build long after the work is done. Once written, the textbook may need revision, which means updated texts must be bought to replace the old ones.

A writer is paid on a royalty basis for a textbook. He or she first submits to a publishing house a proposal that presents the book's market, outlines its contents, presents the writer's credentials for authoring the book, and includes at least two sample chapters.

DEVELOPING SELF-INSTRUCTIONAL PROGRAMS

In college, I learned economics with a "programmed" text. Key words were missing from the text and I had to write them in. When I was finished with a lesson, I looked up the right answers. Today, PCs enable this "self-instruction" to be far more interesting. Instead of writing in a text, a student can respond to a program prompt and *immediately* know if the answer is correct before continuing. Graphics, sound, and voice output are available to hold the student's attention. These programs can be used at any time, for as long as the student wishes, in the classroom, at work, or in the home.

Most "old" programmed texts still need to be converted into self-instructional programs. As with textbooks, many new self-instructional programs remain to be written, too.

TEACHING ONLINE

Modems enable PCs to communicate with one another over great distances. This technology has enabled a new form of teaching to evolve—teaching online.

A major drawback of the self-instructional programs is the requirement that a student's answer *exactly* match the program's answer. Though major software development efforts are attempting to provide some latitude so that answers that come close also are acceptable, no one has been able yet to overcome this problem.

Online teaching goes around it. In this case, the teacher prepares a lesson and transmits it to PCs in the students' homes or dorm rooms. Whenever the student wishes, he or she does the lesson, answers the teacher's questions, and transmits work back to the teacher, who corrects it the following day. The corrected lesson is transmitted to the student with the new lesson. This approach allows all participants—teachers and students—to schedule their own time and still receive a teacher's individual attention.

Cable television and video recording machines present possibilities for adding online visuals. The lesson programs must be written. Textbooks that support the lessons also need to be published.

These programs still are in the experimental stage, but it does present a promising opportunity for working out of your home.

TROUBLE-SHOOTING SOFTWARE

One of the most irritating experiences in life is to buy a program, use it for 2 months so a lot of data is accumulated, and then discover you can't do something you need to do. If training or documentation is shoddy, a user needs somebody to turn to in order to do the simplest task. You can make money by handling these problems.

Today, people primarily support software that has been installed for business applications. As consumer programs become more sophisticated and better integrated into the home, the need for software support people will increase.

Software support can be a full-time business or you can use it to underwrite other activities. Consultants who support software are paid a fixed fee by a company for being available to trouble-shoot problems, and often another fee for actually resolving a specific problem. A lot of free time results. The first fee, consequently, can help support you in other activities, such as program development. On the other hand, you can support many programs for different companies and accrue fees for a full-time business.

Software support sometimes is offered via an 800 telephone number "hot line." Technically, any software problem should be resolvable over the telephone. However, users inexperienced with technical vocabularies often become inarticulate when it comes to describing and correcting a problem. Local, on-site support is required, which presents profitable opportunities.

Many companies require that a store offer support before allowing it to sell software. You can contact stores that sell software and offer to support it. You also can contact mail order houses, software companies, and people running classified ads in PC magazines.

If you become accredited to support different companies' software, you can run your own ad listing those companies in the telephone directory Yellow Pages for your general area.

REPAIRING HARDWARE

Personal computers and peripherals break down, and someone has to fix them. As with software, many companies require that a store offer hardware repair facilities before allowing their equipment to be sold. You can contact stores that sell PCs and equipment with an offer for repairing hardware.

You also can make your services available to anyone with a PC. For various reasons, people may acquire equipment that should have hardware support, but doesn't. When an equipment problem occurs, a major dilemma is faced. If you have the skills to repair such equipment, you can help. The best way to make people aware of your service is to run an ad once a week in your local paper, and another in your telephone directory Yellow Pages.

In addition to repairing equipment, you can offer your own fixed-fee warranties to do all work necessary for a specific time period (usually 1 year). Few of the warranties will require you to do actual repair work, so you can pocket quite a profit.

CHAPTER
TWELVE
TIMING
PROFITS:
A TICKLER
PROGRAM

Timing the long-term activities of our lives is just about impossible. Lives, today, are very complicated. We focus our attention in one area, wake up one day, and ask, "Where did the time go?" Your Tickler Program gives you the ability to stay on top of these activities, which can be very profitable.

USING YOUR TICKLER PROGRAM

Your Tickler Program is the most versatile program in *Programs For Profit*. It can be used to start a business, in a business you've already started, in your career, and even in your personal life.

Your Tickler Program lets you time telephone calls and mail to people. The timing of the contact is defined to each person's schedule and individual needs. That may not sound like much, but it gives you the ability to make money in a lot of ways.

STARTING A BUSINESS

Professionals and business people will pay to have their customers' memories "tickled" with reminders. Dentists recommend 6-month checkups and teeth cleaning. Yearly checkups also are recommended by doctors for people over a certain age. You can mail these reminders for people to come in.

Veterinarians administer drugs to some animals on a periodic basis. A dog, for example, may need a shot 8 months after his first one. The pet owner needs to know when to bring the animal in, and you can send out the reminder.

A car's oil should be changed every 3 months and its engine tuned every 6. Gas stations that do repair work don't send out reminders, but if you offered to do it for them—and pointed out that they would benefit from a steady flow of dependable, repeat business—many would be interested.

Resorts, inns, and travel agents, too, can use this service to tickle ex-customers' memories with a reminder of the goods that were enjoyed. A note received just before plans are made is beguiling and easily could turn into a tradition: "Oh, yes, every winter we go there!" All it takes to ensure this repeat business is a note mailed around somebody's vacation time, which usually occurs about the same time every year.

Businesses that rely on subscribers, such as newsletters and the many services that offer repair and maintenance contracts, can use this service. Subscribers sign up at different times, and pay annually. Your program lets you offer these businesses the ability to send out renewal notices at the right time without much trouble.

All the Tickler Program applications mentioned so far have reminder periods of a year or less, but the period can be *anything* appropriate to a business you want to serve. Most painters, for example, strive to do a good job painting a house (interior or exterior) and hope to get referrals. A paint job is good for only 3 to 5 years, but when the house needs to be repainted, the painter fails to contact the family or new owner—he simply doesn't have the time to go back through his records to see what happened 3 years ago. Most of the families for whom the painter did work don't keep records, so they don't call the painter back—they don't remember who he was. As a result, the painter loses repeat business that his hard work really earned. Your service will help him get those customers back, which will make the painter's life much easier.

To start a service with your Tickler Program, use your Mail List Program to send out letters to prospective customers in the area on which you want to focus your first efforts. An example of a letter that can be sent to gas station owners and managers is shown in Fig. 12-1. Use it as a model for letters to send to other businesses.

When you contact these businesses, you should bring along reminders you already have written for the business. Such a reminder is shown in Fig. 12-2. You should offer to have the reminders typeset and printed. Once a contract is signed, print enough reminders to last a year.

USING THE PROGRAM IN YOUR BUSINESS

If you already have a business of your own, you may find people interested in your offer, but unable to use it now. They may ask to be called back in a few months, but in a few months, you may have a distraction—new business or pressing work—and the follow-up call is forgotten and the easy sale missed, so all the preparatory work is needlessly thrown away.

Your Tickler Program makes following up on a sales call easy. When you're asked to come back, use the program to record a reminder. Every morning, look at the notes you've left yourself for the day. The program will show you the reminder, the customer's name, address, and telephone number, and the date you originally entered the reminder. It even will print a mailing label so you can get off a letter in a hurry.

You can leave yourself reminders about anything. The Tickler Program, for example, can help keep your customers happy by reminding you of commitments you have made, and would have otherwise forgotten. Your reputation for reliability and service will grow and so will your business.

If you have employees, you can use the program to store dates for employee reviews. Timely reviews boost morale and improve productivity.

Your business can be given a distinctive personal touch with reminders about important customers' birthdays and anniversaries, which were mentioned in passing, as well as the birthdays of those you work with.

All these reminders are adjustable to your life. If you fall behind schedule a week because you're sick, or too busy to act on a reminder, you don't need to do a lot of paperwork juggling, which just will compound your problems. One Tickler Program command moves all your reminders from one day to another. It's that easy.

Month 00, 19XX

Address
Telephone number

Address lines _____
_____
_____

Dear Mr. Jamison,

Periodic oil changes and tune-ups benefit your customers and are profitable to you, but how do you find the time to remind your customers that their cars are due for service?

Sending out these reminders is my specialty. All you have to do is tell me when a customer comes in for service. I'll send him (or her) a reminder for an oil change and lube job every 3 months and a tune-up every 6—or as often as you like. You'll gain a steady flow of work and your customers will appreciate your help in keeping their cars running better.

By using my own computer, I'm able to offer this service very inexpensively.

In a few days, I'll be giving you a call to discuss this offer. Please think it over. I'm looking forward to talking to you.

Sincerely,

Your Name

(Note: In states that require yearly auto emissions tests, include the line: "I'll also remind your customers to come in for a pre-examination auto emissions checkup each year.")

Fig. 12-1 A letter introducing a Tickler Program service.

JACK'S SERVICE STATION

Our records show your vehicle is due for an engine tune-up.
To ensure proper maintenance, prolong your vehicle's life, and
reduce costs for major work, please call us at 555-5555 to
arrange an appointment.

289 Mulberry St., Hancock, Vt.

Fig. 12-2 A reminder note.

Individual notes also can be easily moved up. If somebody isn't in when you call, you simply change the date on the reminder and you'll see it again. This capability makes it easy to record a reminder, send out a letter when you see it, change the date to the following week, and make a follow-up call to your letter. A reminder about a birthday or anniversary, too, can be transferred to a new year by changing the date, saving you the trouble of reentering all the information.

USING THE PROGRAM FOR YOUR CAREER

Efficiently organizing reminders can help your career, too. Many jobs require extensive dealing with other people each day. It's hard enough to return calls made the same day. Getting back weeks later to *all* the people you promised to call may be impossible without having to ask a few people, in an embarrassed voice, "What did I promise you?" Your Tickler Program takes away the worry that you'll forget to get back to somebody. People you do get back to will praise your diligence and dependability, and that will help advance your career.

Your Tickler Program lets you reliably extend commitments over months or years, so you can confidently seize opportunities for the future that would be intimidating before.

You can set goals for yourself and use your Tickler Program to set an agenda to reach those goals. Each morning, you'll look at what you have to accomplish during the day to meet your overall goal. You'll fully use the time that's available to you to move ahead.

In this same way, the Tickler Program can be used to help manage complex projects. You can set reminders for checking on how work is progressing in various small tasks that all must come together at the end. You'll even be able to manage two or more complex projects at the same time, which would be difficult without the program.

USING THE PROGRAM AT HOME

Commitments are made at home as well as at work. A promise can be made to return something to a neighbor, attend a recital with your spouse, or play tennis. Forgetting is easy. Forgetting to pick up your children who are waiting for you is not good parenting. Your Tickler Program will ensure you don't forget.

It's fairly easy to remember your immediate family's birthdays, but it gets more difficult when brothers and sisters have children. Neighbors' birthdays and anniversaries are impossible to remember. This information, too, can be recorded and brought to your attention on the right day.

Best of all, home and business reminders can be stored on the same disk. Scheduling conflicts will be brought to your attention so you can adjust your plans.

HOW YOUR PROGRAM HELPS YOU

Capabilities have been built into the Tickler Program to help in each of its many applications. For a service, your Tickler Program prints labels and reports for dates of your choice. Each piece you mail will be timed to reach an individual on the proper date. The reports let you offer prospects the ability to make follow-up calls to the mailings. A person may receive a letter, for example, stating that somebody will call in a few days to discuss the offer. The report lists telephone numbers or addresses of the people to whom pieces were mailed, so the calls are perfectly timed to coincide with the letters in a very effective sales technique.

The CHANGE command lets you move all reminders from one day to another. The CHANGE command's flexibility also allows you to preview your upcoming reminders and move them around to the demands of your schedule. So, if you can't call all the people you wanted to on Monday, you can choose which ones to move to a day later in the week. The entire reminder won't have to be reentered—only the date will need to be changed. The Tickler Program adjusts to your life—you don't have to conform to its dictates.

If you'll be using the Tickler Program to keep track of your own records, you'll be happy to find an automatic delete capability which removes the need for disk maintenance. Specifically, after 7 days, old reminders *automatically* are flagged for deletion. On any day you can override the deletion for records you want to save. This capability assures that you always will have space on your disk for all your reminders.

These capabilities make your Tickler Program very simple to use.

OPERATING YOUR TICKLER PROGRAM

Your Tickler Program records reminders that automatically are brought to your attention. The appearance of the reminder is defined by a "trigger" which you set. Specifically, a "trigger" date is entered for each reminder to set the day the program will show you the information.

The program automatically flags for deletion all reminders 7 days after the trigger date. That is, after you are shown the reminder, it stays on your disk for 7 days before it is flagged. During that time, you decide whether or not you want to save it. The records are flagged when you end program operation, so even on the seventh day after a trigger date you still can change the trigger date and save the reminder *before* you end program operation. The records are cleaned from your disk whenever the DELETE command is used.

If your Tickler Program is used for a service, you should store each customer's reminders on a separate disk. Label the disk cover with the customer's name, address, and telephone number. Each week, ask your customers for a list of people to be added. This list usually can be developed from the customer's invoice copies.

If you're using the program to keep track of reminders for yourself, both business and home reminders can be stored on the same disk.

You're ready to use the Tickler Program. Once you've accessed the program, you may:

- Add reminders
- Change information on a reminder, including the trigger date
- Delete a reminder
- Print reports for the present day, or any day you want
- Print mailing labels

The procedures for these activities are presented below.

ACCESSING THE TICKLER PROGRAM

To access the Tickler Program, type **RUN TICKLER** in response to your system prompt:

A: **RUN TICKLER**

The Tickler Program will be loaded. You will specify the drive with your data disk and the current date. The menu of Tickler Program commands, then, will be displayed:

```
* * * * * * * * * * * * * * * * * * * * * * * * * * * * * * * * * * * * * * * * * *
                          TICKLER

                      CHOICES ARE:

               1  -  ADD
               2  -  CHANGE
               3  -  DELETE
               4  -  TELEPHONE REPORT
               5  -  ADDRESS REPORT
               6  -  ALL RECORDS
               7  -  MAILING LABELS
               8  -  EXIT TO SYSTEM
* * * * * * * * * * * * * * * * * * * * * * * * * * * * * * * * * * * * * * * * * *
```

The following procedures provide all you will need to know to use these commands effectively.

ADDING A REMINDER

The ADD command (1) is used to add a new reminder. A trigger date first is specified for the reminders to be added. You then record as many reminders as you wish for this date.

Only a name for each reminder needs to be entered. Your application determines any additional information you'll need to record. If your program is used for a service, you'll record all information requested. If your program is used for your business or career, you'll record only the person's telephone number and a note. If your program is used at home, you may record only a note for a person.

At a later time, additional information can be stored on the reminder with the CHANGE command.

The procedure for adding a reminder is:

1. COMMAND CHOICE: Type 1 for the ADD command.
2. ENTER TRIGGER DATE: Type the date that you want the reminders for. This may not be the actual date on which you want to schedule an activity. If a dentist uses your service, for example, you may want to set this date at 5½ months after the last checkup so the reminder can be mailed with an adequate lead time to schedule an appointment at 6 months.
3. ENTER NAME: Type the person's name that you want to recall on the trigger date, using 17 or less characters.
4. ENTER COMPANY: Type the name of a company using 15 or less characters.
5. ENTER PHONE: Type the person's telephone number.
6. ENTER STREET ADDRESS: Type the person's street address using 23 or less characters.
7. ENTER TOWN OR CITY: Type the city in which the person will be when contacted, using 15 or less characters.
8. ENTER TWO-DIGIT STATE CODE: Type the postal code for the state. These codes are listed in Appendix B.
9. ENTER ZIP: Type the zip code.
10. ENTER SUBJECT: Type the subject for the reminder or a note using 28 or less characters.
11. ENTER NAME: Type the name of the person if you want to store another reminder for this date and repeat steps 4 through 11; or, if you have no more reminders for this date, press the carriage return.
12. ENTER TRIGGER DATE: Type another trigger date if you wish

to store more reminders. If you have no more to store press the carriage return and you'll be returned to the Menu Level.

If you do not wish to respond to a prompt, press the carriage return and nothing will be stored for that line. The date you entered a reminder will be stored automatically for you.

The procedure for adding a reminder is illustrated in Fig. 12-3.

CHANGING INFORMATION

The CHANGE command (2) changes information on a reminder. All reminders triggered by one date can be changed to another trigger date. This capability allows you to adjust your "triggers" quickly if your schedule is unexpectedly disrupted. Trigger dates also can be changed one at a time. Lines on any reminder can be changed, too.

The CHANGE command also can be used to review all reminders you have for a person.

The procedure for changing information is:

1. COMMAND CHOICE: Type 2 for the CHANGE command.
2. ENTER   TYPE   OF   CHANGE: [T]RIGGER   DATE   OR [N]AME: Type **T** if you want to move *all* reminders from one trigger date to another. In this case, you will be prompted for the old trigger date (under which the reminders now are stored) and the new date on which you want to see the reminders. When you type the new date, all pertinent reminders will be changed and you will start this step again. When you are done adjusting the trigger dates, respond to ENTER TYPE OF CHANGE by pressing the carriage return and you will be returned to the Menu Level.

    Type **N** if you want to change a trigger date for *only* a specific reminder or any of the information you entered for a reminder. You will be prompted for the name of a person. Type the name under which the reminder is filed. The program will display the first reminder you stored for this person:

        =
        1. Trigger Date: 051883
        2.   Name: KATHY MARKLE
        3.   Company: KRM INC.

* *

TICKLER

CHOICES ARE:

```
1 – ADD
2 – CHANGE
3 – DELETE
4 – TELEPHONE REPORT
5 – ADDRESS REPORT
6 – ALL RECORDS
7 – MAILING LABELS
8 – EXIT TO SYSTEM
```
* *

COMMAND CHOICE FROM ABOVE [1–8 or
?1–?8]: **1**

The ADD command is chosen.

ENTER TRIGGER DATE [MMDDYY] **041885**

A trigger date is set for April 18, 1985. The reminder that is to be added will be printed in that day's report.

ENTER NAME **KATHY MARKLE**
ENTER COMPANY: **KRM INC.**
ENTER PHONE: **2035556999**
ENTER STREET ADDRESS: **355 ORANGE
  STREET**
ENTER TOWN OR CITY: **NEW HAVEN**
ENTER 2 DIGIT STATE CODE: **CT**
ENTER ZIP: **06511**
ENTER SUBJECT: **MEETING WITH
  ACCOUNTANT**

All information for the reminder is typed.

ENTER NAME ⟨**CR**⟩
ENTER TRIGGER DATE [MMDDYY] ⟨**CR**⟩

No more reminders for this date or any other are to be added now.

At this time, you will be returned to the Menu Level.

Fig. 12-3 Adding a reminder.

4.   Phone: 2035556999
5.   Street: 245 ORANGE STREET
6.   City: NEW HAVEN
7.   State: CT
8.   Zip: 06511
9.   Subject: MEETING WITH ACCOUNTANT
= =
Date Entered: 04 / 14 / 83

10. *Look for different record*

You then will be prompted CHANGE WHICH ITEM? :. If this is not the reminder you wish to change, type 10 and you will be shown the next one stored. If you continue typing 10, you will see every reminder you have added for this person. After the last one is displayed, you will be prompted for a new name.

If the reminder is the one you want, type the number of the line you want to change and you will be prompted for the new line. Change as many lines as you wish. When you're finished, respond to CHANGE WHICH ITEM? : by pressing the carriage return and you will be returned to the Menu Level.

The procedure for moving all reminders from one trigger date to another is illustrated in Fig. 12-4. The procedure for changing a specific line on a specific record is illustrated in Fig. 12-5.

DELETING A REMINDER

The DELETE command (3) deletes reminders from your disk. All or only selected reminders for a person or a company can be deleted at a time. The command makes it easy to remove all reminders for a company or person who stops doing business with you.

Reminders with trigger dates 7 or more days old automatically are flagged for deletion so you do not need to spend time removing them. Though reminders are flagged, they will be cleaned from your disk only when you use the DELETE command. If you never use the DELETE command, these old reminders will collect until you will be unable to store new ones. Consequently, about once a month, at least enter the DELETE command, look at

COMMAND CHOICE FROM ABOVE [1–8 or   The CHANGE command is
   ?1–?8]: **2**   chosen.

ENTER TYPE OF CHANGE:
     [T] RIGGER DATE or [N] AME   **T**   All reminders for April 18, 1985
                                                      are to be moved to another
                                                      date.

ENTER TRIGGER DATE: **041885**   The old date is defined.
ENTER NEW DATE: [MMDDYY] **051885**   The new date is defined.
ALL OCCURENCES OF   04 / 18 / 85 CHANGED
  TO   05 / 18 / 85

ENTER TYPE OF CHANGE:
     [T] RIGGER DATE or [N] AME ⟨**CR**⟩   No more changes are to be made.
                                                         At this time, you will be
                                                         returned to the Menu Level.

Fig. 12-4 Moving reminders to a new trigger date.

any reminder, but don't delete it. The command will engage the cleaning process and your old reminders will be removed.

The procedure for deleting a reminder is:

1. COMMAND SELECTION: Type **3** for the DELETE command.
2. DELETE BY [N]AME OR [C]OMPANY? : Type **C** to delete reminders for a person. Type **C** to delete reminders for all people who work at a company.
3. DELETE [A]LL RECORDS OF THAT NAME OR JUST [S]ELECTED RECORDS? : Type **A** and all reminders for the name (whether person or company) will be flagged. Type **S** and you will be shown the reminders, one at a time, for that name and asked which ones you want deleted.
4. ENTER NAME: Type the name of the person or company that you're deleting records for. If all records are to be deleted, the program immediately flags all reminders with the specified name, cleans them from your disk, and returns you to the Menu Level. If only selected ones are to be deleted, the program will display the first reminder that you stored for that name and ask DELETE THIS RECORD? If you want to flag it, type **Y**. If not, type **N**. In either case, the next reminder then will be displayed. After the last one has been displayed, cleaning will be started, the flagged reminders will be removed, and you will be returned to the Menu Level.

The procedure for deleting a selected record is illustrated in Fig. 12-6.

COMMAND CHOICE FROM ABOVE [1–8 or
   ?1–?8] : **2**

The CHANGE command is
chosen.

ENTER TYPE OF CHANGE:
    [T] RIGGER DATE or [N] AME **N**

A reminder for only one person is
to be changed.

ENTER NAME: **KATHY MARKLE**

That person is identified.

```
= = = = = = = = = = = = = = = = = =
 1. Trigger Date: 041885
 2.       Name: KATHY MARKLE
 3.    Company: KRM INC.
 4.       Phone: 2035556999
 5.       Street: 355 ORANGE  STREET
 6.        City: NEW HAVEN
 7.        State: CT
 8.         Zip: 06511
 9.     Subject: MEETING WITH ACCOUNTANT
= = = = = = = = = = = = = = = = = =

 Date Entered: 04 / 14 / 85


10. *Look for different record*
```

—The first reminder that was added
for Kathy Markle is displayed.

Change which item? [1–9] **4**

The street address will be
changed.

ENTER NEW STREET: **245 ORANGE STREET**

The new address is typed.

```
= = = = = = = = = = = = = = = = = =
 1. Trigger Date: 041885
 2.       Name: KATHY MARKLE
 3.    Company: KRM INC.
 4.       Phone: 2035556999
 5.       Street: 245 ORANGE  STREET
 6.        City: NEW HAVEN
 7.        State: CT
 8.         Zip: 06511
 9.     Subject: MEETING WITH ACCOUNTANT
= = = = = = = = = = = = = = = = = =
Date Entered: 04 / 14 / 85

10. *Look for different record*
```

—The revised reminder is displayed.

Fig. 12-5 Changing a reminder for a person. (*Cont. on following page.*)

Change which item? [1–9] ⟨**CR**⟩

> No more changes are to be made to this reminder. At this time, you will be returned to the Menu Level.

Fig. 12-5 *Cont.*

COMMAND CHOICE FROM ABOVE [1–8 or
?1–?8] : **3**

> The DELETE command is chosen.

DELETE BY [N]AME OR [C]OMPANY? **N**

> Reminders for a person will be deleted.

DELETE [A]LL RECORDS OF THAT NAME
OR JUST [S]ELECTED RECORDS? **S**

> Reminders will be reviewed before a decision is made about deletion.

ENTER NAME: **CINDY PARSONS**

> The person is identified.

= = = = = = = = = = = = = = = = =
1. Trigger Date: 050585
2.   Name: CINDY PARSONS
3.   Company: CP INC.
4.   Phone: 2035559999
5.   Street: 133 SHERMAN AVENUE
6.   City: HARTFORD
7.   State: CT
8.   Zip: 06777
9.   Subject: CALL KATHY
= = = = = = = = = = = = = = = = =
  Date Entered: 04 / 14 / 85

> The first reminder added for Cindy Parsons is displayed.

DELETE THIS RECORD? **Y**

> Permission is given to delete this reminder.

CLEANING IN PROGRESS . . . .

> This reminder is the only one stored for Cindy Parsons, so cleaning is started as soon as the screen is cleared.

CLEANING COMPLETE

> At this time, you will be returned to the Menu Level.

Fig. 12-6 Deleting a reminder.

PRINTING REPORTS

Three Tickler Program reports can be printed:

1. A Telephone Report, which, for a specific day, lists all the people you wanted to remember. The report gives each person's telephone number, the reason for return call, and the date the reminder was added. The TELEPHONE REPORT command (4) prints this report. An example of one is shown in Fig. 12-7.
2. An Address Report, which lists people, addresses, and reminders. The report is intended for use when traveling to the person's home or company for an appointment. The ADDRESS REPORT command (5) prints this report. An example of one is shown in Fig. 12-8.

TELEPHONE REPORT
FOR
05/18/85

NAME	TELEPHONE	DATE	SUBJECT
KATHY MARKLE	(203) –555–6999	04/14/85	MEETING WITH ACCOUNTANT
MARY E. COSTIN	(203) –555–8744	04/14/85	MEETING WITH KATHY

END OF REPORT

Fig. 12-7 A Telephone Report.

ADDRESS REPORT
FOR
05/18/85

NAME	STREET CITY	STATE	ZIP	SUBJECT
KATHY MARKLE	245 ORANGE STREET NEW HAVEN	CT	06511	MEETING WITH ACCOUNTANT
MARY E. COSTIN	1212 CHAPEL STREET NEW HAVEN	CT	06512	MEETING WITH KATHY

END OF REPORT

Fig. 12-8 An Address Report.

3. The All Records Report lists all the reminders stored from a specified date to the present date. With this report, you're able to look ahead at reminders for upcoming days (see Fig. 12-9). Note that the trigger dates for these records usually will be in the future.

These three reports are printed using the same procedure:

1. COMMAND CHOICE: Type the number of the command that prints the report you want.
2. REPORT FOR WHAT DATE? : Press the carriage return and all reminders for the present day will be printed, or type a date and the report for *that* day will be printed. In the case of the ALL RECORDS command, this date defines for the report the first day on which reminders were stored. The last date in the period is the present date. That is, reminders will be printed from the specified date through the present date.

At this time, you will be prompted to set up your printer. When it's ready, press the carriage return and the report will be printed. You then will be returned to the Menu Level.

PRINTING MAILING LABELS

The MAILING LABELS command (7) prints labels.

NOTE:

If you're using your Tickler Program for a service, failure to change the trigger date after labels are printed can result in the customer's reminders being deleted automatically. *Be sure to move up the trigger date for the next mailing **before** ending program operation.*

If you're using the program for a service, you should provide your customer with either a Telephone or Address Report of the people you've contacted. The report will serve as documentation of your service.

Labels are printed in the same way as reports. You enter the command, then the date for which you want the labels. The program gives you an opportunity to load labels in your printer. When you're ready, press the carriage return, the labels will be printed, and you'll be returned to the Menu Level.

ALL RECORDS ONLINE
AS OF
05/18/85

TRIGGER DATE: 05/18/85
= = = = = = = = = = = = = = = = = = = =

     Name: KATHY MARKLE
  Company: KRM INC.
      City: NEW HAVEN
    State: CT
      Zip: 06511
  Subject: MEETING WITH ACCOUNTANT
= = = = = = = = = = = = = = = = = = = =
Date Entered: 04/14/85

TRIGGER DATE: 05/18/85
= = = = = = = = = = = = = = = = = = = =

     Name: MARY E. COSTIN
  Company: MEC INC.
      City: NEW HAVEN
    State: CT
      Zip: 06512
  Subject: MEETING WITH KATHY
= = = = = = = = = = = = = = = = = = = =
Date Entered: 04/14/85

TRIGGER DATE: 04/20/85
= = = = = = = = = = = = = = = = = = = =

     Name: TIMMY MARTIN
  Company: TM INC.
      City: WEST HAVEN
    State: CT
      Zip: 06502
  Subject: EMMISSIONS TEST
= = = = = = = = = = = = = = = = = = = =
Date Entered: 04/14/85

TRIGGER DATE: 05/05/85
= = = = = = = = = = = = = = = = = = = =

     Name: TAVIAN MAYER
  Company: TAVIAN MAYER, E

Fig. 12-9 An All Records Report. (*Cont. on following page.*)

City:	ROYALTON
State:	VT
Zip:	05777
Subject:	COURT APPEARANCE

= = = = = = = = = = = = = = = = = = = =

Date Entered:	04 / 14 / 85

END OF REPORT

Fig. 12-9 *Cont.*

END PROGRAM OPERATION

When you're done with the Tickler Program, respond to COMMAND CHOICE by typing 8 to EXIT TO SYSTEM. At this time, reminders that are 7 days old or older will be flagged for deletion. You then will be returned to the operating system level.

TICKLER PROGRAM COMMAND SUMMARY

Command Number and Name	Function
1–ADD	Adds new reminders to the disk.
2–CHANGE	Moves reminders from one trigger date to another and changes lines on a specific reminder. The command also can be used to review all reminders entered for a specific person.
3–DELETE	Removes all or only selected reminders for a person or a company.
4–TELEPHONE REPORT	Prints a list of the people mentioned in reminders that are triggered by a specified date. Each person's telephone number, the reason for the call, and the date the reminder was added also are shown.
5–ADDRESS REPORT	Prints a list of the people mentioned in reminders that are triggered by a

Command Number and Name	Function
	specified date. The report also shows each person's address and the reason for the reminder.
6–ALL RECORDS	Prints a list of all reminders stored between a specified date and the present date. All information is printed for each reminder.
7–MAILING LABELS	Prints mailing labels.
8–EXIT TO SYSTEM	Ends program operation and sets deletion flag for 7-day-old reminders.

TICKLER PROGRAM SOURCE CODE

```
10 CLEAR
20 REM ROUTINE: SET PARAMETERS FOR THE END USER'S PARTICULAR
30 REM COMPUTER SCREEN.  SINCE THE PROGRAMS PRESENTED IN THIS
40 REM BOOK HAVE BEEN DESIGNED TO RUN ON A NUMBER OF  DIFFERENT
50 REM MACHINES WHICH MAY DIFFER IN HEIGHT AND WIDTH  FROM  THE
60 REM "STANDARD" 24 x 80,  THIS ROUTINE ALLOWS THE END USER  TO
70 REM CREATE A FILE ("PARAMTER.FIL") THAT STORES THE HEIGHT AND
80 REM WIDTH INFORMATION,  ("SCRSIZE" & "SCRHITE") AS WELL AS  A
90 REM FLAG ("PARMSETFLAG") THAT KEEPS THE COMPUTER FROM RUNNING
100 REM THE ROUTINE EVERY TIME THE PROGRAM IS RUN.
110 REM ******************************************************
120 DIM SELECT$(10)
130 ON ERROR GOTO 390
140 OPEN "I",#1,"PARAMTER.FIL"
150 INPUT #1,PARMSETFLAG
160 CLOSE #1
170 IF PARMSETFLAG>0 THEN 440
180 PRINT "HOW MANY CHARACTERS WIDE IS YOUR SCREEN?  ";
190 LINE INPUT SCRSIZE$
200 IF SCRSIZE$="?" THEN GOSUB 310
210 IF SCRSIZE$="?" THEN 180
220 PRINT "HOW MANY LINES LONG IS YOUR SCREEN?  ";
230 LINE INPUT SCRHITE$
240 IF SCRHITE$="?" THEN GOSUB 310
250 IF SCRHITE$="?" THEN 220
260 SCRSIZE=VAL(SCRSIZE$):SCRHITE=VAL(SCRHITE$):PARMSETFLAG=1
270 OPEN "O",#1,"PARAMTER.FIL"
280 PRINT #1,PARMSETFLAG,SCRSIZE,SCRHITE
290 CLOSE #1
300 GOTO 440
310 PRINT: PRINT  "ANSWER THIS QUESTION WITH A NUMBER.  IF  WIDTH  IS
320  PRINT "ASKED FOR,  GENERALLY THE ANSWER WILL BE BETWEEN  40
330  PRINT  "AND 132.  IF HEIGHT IS CALLED FOR,  GENERALLY  THE
340  PRINT  "ANSWER  WILL BE BETWEEN 16  AND 66.  AFTER  YOU'VE
350  PRINT "ANSWERED,  REMEMBER TO PRESS THE 'RETURN' OR 'ENTER'
360  PRINT "KEY"
370  PRINT
380 RETURN
390 CLOSE:PRINT ERR,ERL
400 OPEN "O",#1,"PARAMTER.FIL"
410 PRINT #1,PARMSETFLAG,SCRSIZE,SCRHITE
420 CLOSE #1
430 RESUME 140
440 REM ******************************************************
450 REM ROUTINE: MONITORS USER'S  REQUESTS FOR PROGRAM ACTION
460 REM BY PRESENTING A MENU OF AVAILABLE CHOICES OR ACTIONS.
470 REM  THE PROGRAM WILL ALWAYS RETURN TO THIS ROUTINE AFTER
480 REM COMPLETING ANY OTHER ROUTINE IN THE PROGRAM.
490 REM ******************************************************
500 OPEN "I",#1,"PARAMTER.FIL"
510 INPUT #1,PARMSETFLAG,SCRSIZE,SCRHITE
520 CLOSE #1
530 FOR LOOP=1 TO SCRHITE:PRINT:NEXT LOOP: REM clears the screen
540 IF DATE$<>"" THEN 580
550 LINE INPUT "PLEASE ENTER TODAY'S DATE [MMDDYY]: ";DATE$
560 LINE INPUT "Please enter DRIVE that datafile is on: ";DRIVE$
570 FILE$=DRIVE$+":TKLRDATA":GOTO 530
580 FOR LOOP=1 TO SCRSIZE:PRINT "*";:NEXT LOOP: REM creates a border
590 CENTER=(SCRSIZE/2):REM allows all screen display to be centered
    within givenscreen width. Used in conjunction with string lengths.
600 PRINT:PRINT
```

```
610 PRINT TAB(CENTER-6);" TICKLER "
620 PRINT:PRINT:PRINT
630 PRINT TAB(CENTER-6);"CHOICES ARE:"
640 PRINT:PRINT:PRINT
650 PRINT TAB(18);"1 - ADD"
660 PRINT TAB(18);"2 - CHANGE"
670 PRINT TAB(18);"3 - DELETE"
680 PRINT TAB(18);"4 - TELEPHONE REPORT"
690 PRINT TAB(18);"5 - ADDRESS REPORT"
700 PRINT TAB(18);"6 - ALL RECORDS"
710 PRINT TAB(18);"7 - MAILING LABELS"
720 PRINT TAB(18);"8 - EXIT TO SYSTEM"
730 PRINT:PRINT:FOR LOOP=1 TO SCRSIZE:PRINT "*";:NEXT LOOP
740 PRINT:LINE INPUT "COMMAND CHOICE FROM ABOVE [1-8 or ?1-?8]: ";
    COMMAND$
750 IF LEFT$(COMMAND$,1)="?" THEN COMMAND=VAL(MID$(COMMAND$,2,2))
    ELSE 780
760 WIDTH SCRSIZE
770 ON COMMAND GOSUB 820,840,850,890,900,910,920,930
780 COMMAND=VAL(COMMAND$)
790 ON COMMAND GOSUB 970,2000,2670,3390,3730,4100,4470,4740
800 GOTO 580
810 FOR LOOP=1 TO SCRSIZE:PRINT "*";:NEXT LOOP
820 PRINT "1- ADD:  ALLOWS YOU TO ADD NEW INFORMATION TO THE
    TICKLER LIST AND
830 PRINT "PROMPTS AS IT GOES.":GOTO 950
840 PRINT "2- CHANGE: ALLOWS YOU TO EDIT ANY INFORMATION THAT
    HAS ALREADY BEEN ENTERED.":GOTO 950
850 PRINT "3- DELETE: ALLOWS YOU TO ERASE ANY INFORMATION THAT
    IS NO LONGER ACCURATE OR
860 PRINT "NEEDED.":GOTO 950
870 PRINT '
880 PRINT '
890 PRINT "4- TELEPHONE REPORT: LISTS NAMES AND NUMBERS FOR ANY
    GIVEN TRIGGER DATE":GOTO 950
900 PRINT "5- ADDRESS REPORT: LISTS NAMES AND ADDRESSES FOR ANY
    GIVEN TRIGGER DATE":GOTO 950
910 PRINT "6- ALL RECORDS: FINDS ALL RECORDS THROUGH A GIVEN DATE":
    GOTO 950
920 PRINT "7- LABELS: PRINTS NAMES AND ADDRESSES ON ENVELOPE LABELS":
    GOTO 950
930 PRINT "8- EXIT: EXITS THE PROGRAM RUN, AND RETURNS TO THE
    OPERATING SYSTEM."
940 FOR LOOP=1 TO SCRSIZE:PRINT"*";:NEXT LOOP
950 LINE INPUT "PRESS 'RETURN' TO CONTINUE.....";DUMMY$
960 GOTO 580
970 '    ************** A D D   R O U T I N E **********************
980 '    This routine prompts the user for each item of mailing data.
990 '    It allows the user to add info to the list
1000 '   ***********************************************************
1010 '
1020 '    VARIABLES USED:
1030 '    T$=TRIGGER DATE (6)
1040 '    N$=MAILING NAME (17)
1050 '    CO$=COMPANY (15)
1060 '    P$=PHONE NUMBER (10)
1070 '    S$=STREET ADDRESS (23)
1080 '    C$=TOWN OR CITY (15)
1090 '    ST$=STATE (2)
1100 '    Z$=ZIPCODE (5)
1110 '    SUBJ$=REFERENCE ITEM (28)
1120 '    DA$=DATE ENTERED (6)
1130 '    D$=DELETE FLAG (1)
1140 '    R=CURRENT RECORD COUNTER
```

```
1150 '
1160 '    FILES USED
1170 '    TKLRDATA: AN R/A FILE
1180 '
1190 '  FILE INTITIALIZATION
1200 FILE$=DRIVE$+":TKLRDATA"
1210 OPEN "R",1,FILE$
1220 OPEN "R",2,"TCOUNTER.FIL",5
1230 FIELD 1, 6 AS TF$,17 AS NF$,15 AS COF$,10 AS PF$,23 AS SF$,
     15 AS CF$,2 AS STF$,5 AS ZF$,28 AS SUBJF$,6 AS DAF$,1 AS DF$
1240 FIELD 2,5 AS RF$
1250 R=VAL(RF$)
1260 FOR LOOP=1 TO SCRHITE:PRINT:NEXT LOOP
1270 ' ********************************
1280 ' LOCATE LAST USED RECORD
1290 ' ********************************
1300 R=R+1
1310 ' *****************
1320 ' DATA ENTRY MODULE
1330 ' *****************
1340 IF T$<>"" THEN 1390
1350 '
1360 LINE INPUT "ENTER TRIGGER DATE [MMDDYY] ";T$
1370 IF T$="" THEN 1720
1380 FOR LOOP=1 TO SCRHITE:PRINT:NEXT LOOP
1390 LINE INPUT "ENTER NAME ";N$
1400 IF N$="" THEN T$="":GOTO 1260
1410 LINE INPUT "ENTER COMPANY: ";CO$
1420 LINE INPUT "ENTER PHONE: ";P$
1430 LINE INPUT "ENTER STREET ADDRESS: ";S$
1440 LINE INPUT "ENTER TOWN OR CITY: ";C$
1450 LINE INPUT "ENTER 2 DIGIT STATE CODE: ";ST$
1460 LINE INPUT "ENTER 5 DIGIT ZIP: ";Z$
1470 LINE INPUT "ENTER SUBJECT: ";SUBJ$
1480 D$="L"
1490 ' ********************
1500 ' MOVE DATA TO BUFFER
1510 ' ********************
1520 LSET TF$=T$
1530 LSET NF$=N$
1540 LSET COF$=CO$
1550 LSET PF$=P$
1560 LSET SF$=S$
1570 LSET CF$=C$
1580 LSET STF$=ST$
1590 LSET ZF$=Z$
1600 LSET SUBJF$=SUBJ$
1610 LSET DAF$=DATE$
1620 LSET DF$=D$
1630 ' *********************
1640 ' COPY BUFFER INTO FILE
1650 ' *********************
1660 PUT 1,R
1670 ' *********************
1680 ' MORE DATA TO ENTER?
1690 ' *********************
1700 GOTO 1260
1710 ' *********************
1720 ' CLOSE FILE
1730 ' *********************
1740 LSET RF$=STR$(R):CLOSE 2
1750 CLOSE 1
1760 GOTO 530
1770 ' *************************
```

```
1780 '   READ/PRINT THE ENTIRE FILE
1790 '   **************************
1800 FOR LOOP=1 TO SCRHITE:PRINT:NEXT LOOP
1810 OPEN "R",1,FILE$
1820 FIELD 1, 6 AS TF$,17 AS NF$,15 AS COF$,10 AS PF$,23 AS SF$,
     15 AS CF$,2 AS STF$,5 AS ZF$,28 AS SUBJF$,6 AS DAF$,1 AS DF$
1830 R=0
1840 R=R+1:GET 1,R
1850 PRINT:PRINT TF$:PRINT"------------------------------":PRINT
1860 PRINT NF$
1870 PRINT COF$
1880 PRINT PF$
1890 PRINT SF$
1900 PRINT CF$;" ";STF$;"  ";ZF$
1910 MO$=MID$(DAF$,1,2):DY$=MID$(DAF$,3,2):YR$=MID$(DAF$,5,2)
1920 PRINT "ADDED TO FILE: ";MO$;"/";DY$;"/";YR$
1930 PRINT:LINE INPUT "Press RETURN to continue";X$
1940 FOR LOOP=1 TO SCRHITE:PRINT:NEXT LOOP
1950 IF EOF(1) THEN 1970 ELSE 1840
1960 '
1970 CLOSE 1
1980 GOTO 530
1990 '
2000 '********** C H A N G E   R O U T I N E *************
2010 'This module allows changes to be made to the
2020 'data in the EVENTLST file.
2030 '*************************************************
2040 '
2050 FOR LOOP=1 TO SCRHITE:PRINT:NEXT LOOP
2060 T$="":    PRINT "ENTER TYPE OF CHANGE:"
2070 LINE INPUT "      [T]RIGGER DATE or [N]AME   ";TYPE$
2080 IF TYPE$="T" OR TYPE$="t" THEN
     LINE INPUT "ENTER TRIGGER DATE: ";T$:GOTO 2110
2090 LINE INPUT "ENTER NAME: ";N$:PRINT:PRINT:PRINT
2100 N$=N$+STRING$(17-LEN(N$),32)
2110 OPEN "R",1,FILE$
2120 FIELD 1, 6 AS TF$,17 AS NF$,15 AS COF$,10 AS PF$,23 AS SF$,
     15 AS CF$,2 AS STF$,5 AS ZF$,28 AS SUBJF$,6 AS DAF$,1 AS DF$
2130 IF LEN(T$)=6 THEN 2600
2140 R=0
2150 R=R+1:GET 1,R
2160 IF LEN (T$)<> 6 THEN IF NF$<>N$ OR DF$="D" THEN 2340
2170 '
2180 '
2190 '
2200 PRINT "1.  T R I G G E R   D A T E: ";
     MID$(TF$,1,2)+"/"+MID$(TF$,3,2)+"/"+MID$(TF$,5,2)
2210 PRINT "=============================
2220 PRINT "2.      Name: ";NF$
2230 PRINT "3.   Company: ";COF$
2240 PRINT "4.     Phone: ";PF$
2250 PRINT "5.    Street: ";SF$
2260 PRINT "6.      City: ";CF$
2270 PRINT "7.     State: ";STF$
2280 PRINT "8.       Zip: ";ZF$
2290 PRINT "9.   Subject: ";SUBJF$
2300 PRINT "=============================
2310 PRINT " Date Entered: ";
     MID$(DAF$,1,2)+"/"+MID$(DAF$,3,2)+"/"+MID$(DAF$,5,2)
2320 PRINT:PRINT "10. *Look for different record*"
2330 GOTO 2360
2340 IF EOF(1) THEN 2350 ELSE 2150
2350 GOTO 2400
2360 PRINT:PRINT:PRINT:INPUT "Change which item? [1-9] ";C
```

```
2370 IF C=10 THEN FOR LOOP=1 TO SCRHITE:PRINT:NEXT LOOP:GOTO 2340
2380 ON C GOSUB 2580,2420,2440,2460,2480,2500,2520,2540,2560,2580
2390 PUT 1,R
2400 CLOSE 1
2410 GOTO 530
2420 LINE INPUT "ENTER NEW NAME: ";N$
2430 LSET NF$=N$:FOR LOOP=1 TO SCRHITE:PRINT:NEXT LOOP:GOTO 2200
2440 LINE INPUT "ENTER NEW COMPANY: ";CO$
2450 LSET COF$=CO$:FOR LOOP=1 TO SCRHITE:PRINT:NEXT LOOP:GOTO 2200
2460 LINE INPUT "ENTER NEW PHONE NUMBER: ";P$
2470 LSET PF$=P$:FOR LOOP=1 TO SCRHITE:PRINT:NEXT LOOP:GOTO 2200
2480 LINE INPUT "ENTER NEW STREET: ";S$
2490 LSET SF$=S$:FOR LOOP=1 TO SCRHITE:PRINT:NEXT LOOP:GOTO 2200
2500 LINE INPUT "ENTER NEW CITY: ";C$
2510 LSET CF$=C$:FOR LOOP=1 TO SCRHITE:PRINT:NEXT LOOP:GOTO 2200
2520 LINE INPUT "ENTER NEW STATE: ";ST$
2530 LSET STF$=ST$:FOR LOOP=1 TO SCRHITE:PRINT:NEXT LOOP:GOTO 2200
2540 LINE INPUT "ENTER NEW ZIP: ";Z$
2550 LSET ZF$=Z$:FOR LOOP=1 TO SCRHITE:PRINT:NEXT LOOP:GOTO 2200
2560 LINE INPUT "ENTER NEW SUBJECT: ";SUBJ$
2570 LSET SUBJF$=SUBJ$:FOR LOOP=1 TO SCRHITE:PRINT:
     NEXT LOOP:GOTO 2200
2580 LINE INPUT "ENTER NEW TRIGGER DATE: ";T$
2590 LSET TF$=T$:FOR LOOP=1 TO SCRHITE:PRINT:NEXT LOOP:GOTO 2200
2600 LINE INPUT "ENTER NEW DATE: [MMDDYY] ";T2$
2610 R=0
2620 R=R+1:GET 1,R:IF TF$=T$ THEN LSET TF$=T2$:PUT 1,R
2630 IF EOF(1) THEN 2640 ELSE 2620
2640 PRINT "ALL OCCURENCES OF  ";
     MID$(T$,1,2)+"/"+MID$(T$,3,2)+"/"+MID$(T$,5,2);
     " CHANGED TO  ";
     MID$(T2$,1,2)+"/"+MID$(T2$,3,2)+"/"+MID$(T2$,5,2)
2650 PRINT
2660 CLOSE:GOTO 2000
2670 '***** D E L E T E    R O U T I N E **************
2680 '  This routine flags an item as deleted.
2690 '  NOTE: The item is not actually deleted. It
2700 '  is simply flagged as such.
2710 '************************************************
2720 '
2730 FOR LOOP=1 TO SCRHITE:PRINT:NEXT LOOP
2740 LINE INPUT "DELETE BY [N]AME OR [C]OMPANY? ";DEL$
2750 PRINT "DELETE [A]LL RECORDS OF THAT ";:
     IF DEL$="N" OR DEL$="n" THEN PRINT "NAME "
     ELSE PRINT "COMPANY "
2760 LINE INPUT "OR JUST [S]ELECTED RECORDS?  ";DC$
2770 IF DEL$="N" OR DEL$="n" THEN LINE INPUT "ENTER NAME: ";
     RT$ ELSE LINE INPUT "ENTER COMPANY: ";RT$
2780 FOR LOOP=1 TO SCRHITE:PRINT:NEXT LOOP
2790 OPEN "R",1,FILE$
2800 FIELD 1, 6 AS TF$,17 AS NF$,15 AS COF$,10 AS PF$,23 AS SF$,
     15 AS CF$,2 AS STF$,5 AS ZF$,28 AS SUBJF$,6 AS DAF$,1 AS DF$
2810 R=0
2820 R=R+1:GET 1,R
2830 IF DEL$="C" OR DEL$="c"
     THEN RT$=RT$+STRING$(15-LEN(RT$),32):GOTO 2850
2840 RT$=RT$+STRING$(17-LEN(RT$),32)
2850 IF DEL$="N" OR DEL$="n" THEN IF NF$<>RT$ THEN 3040
2860 IF DEL$="C" OR DEL$="c" THEN IF COF$<>RT$ THEN 3040
2870 IF DF$="D" THEN 3040
2880 PRINT "T R I G G E R   D A T E: ";
     MID$(TF$,1,2)+"/"+MID$(TF$,3,2)+"/"+MID$(TF$,5,2)
2890 PRINT "==============================="
```

```
2900 PRINT "1.      Name: ";NF$
2910 PRINT "2.   Company: ";COF$
2920 PRINT "3.     Phone: ";PF$
2930 PRINT "4.    Street: ";SF$
2940 PRINT "5.      City: ";CF$
2950 PRINT "6.     State: ";STF$
2960 PRINT "7.       Zip: ";ZF$
2970 PRINT "8.   Subject: ";SUBJF$
2980 PRINT "===============================
2990 PRINT " Date Entered: ";
     MID$(DAF$,1,2)+"/"+MID$(DAF$,3,2)+"/"+MID$(DAF$,5,2):
     PRINT:PRINT
3000 IF DC$="A" THEN PRINT "RECORD DELETED":
     FOR I=1 TO 1300:NEXT I:GOTO 3030
3010 PRINT:PRINT:PRINT:LINE INPUT "DELETE THIS RECORD? ";A$
3020 IF A$<> "Y" THEN FOR LOOP=1 TO SCRHITE:
     PRINT:NEXT LOOP:GOTO 3040
3030 D$="D":LSET DF$=D$:PUT 1,R
3040 IF EOF(1) THEN 3050 ELSE 2820
3050 CLOSE 1
3060 '
3070 '****** C L E A N   R O U T I N E ***************
3080 '  This routine clears out all records flagged
3090 '  as DELETED (DF$="D").  The routine does its
3100 '  job with no prompting and with few messages.
3110 '  It is designed simply to conserve disk space.
3120 '***********************************************
3130 '
3140 PRINT "CLEANING IN PROGRESS . . . . . . ."
3150 OPEN "R",1,FILE$
3160 OPEN "R",2,DRIVE$+":CLEANLST"
3170 FIELD 1, 6 AS TF$,17 AS NF$,15 AS COF$,10 AS PF$,23 AS SF$,
     15 AS CF$,2 AS STF$,5 AS ZF$,28 AS SUBJF$,6 AS DAF$,1 AS DF$
3180 FIELD 2, 6 AS TFN$,17 AS NFN$,15 AS COFN$,10 AS PFN$,
     23 AS SFN$,15 AS CFN$,2 AS STFN$,5 AS ZFN$,28 AS SUBJFN$,
     6 AS DAFN$,1 AS DFN$
3190 R=0
3200 R=R+1:GET 1,R
3210 IF DF$="D" THEN 3340
3220 LSET TFN$=TF$
3230 LSET NFN$=NF$
3240 LSET COFN$=COF$
3250 LSET PFN$=PF$
3260 LSET SFN$=SF$
3270 LSET CFN$=CF$
3280 LSET STFN$=STF$
3290 LSET ZFN$=ZF$
3300 LSET SUBJFN$=SUBJF$
3310 LSET DAFN$=DAF$
3320 LSET DFN$=DF$
3330 PUT 2
3340 IF EOF(1) THEN 3350 ELSE 3200
3350 CLOSE 1,2
3360 KILL FILE$: NAME DRIVE$+":CLEANLST" AS FILE$
3370 PRINT "CLEANING COMPLETE":FOR I=1 TO 750:NEXT I
3380 GOTO 530
3390 '****** TELEPHONE REPORT ROUTINE *************
3400 'This routine prints names, numbers, and subjects
3410 '*********************************************
3420 '
3430 Y=1
3440 FOR LOOP=1 TO SCRHITE:PRINT:NEXT LOOP
3450 LINE INPUT "REPORT FOR WHAT DATE? ";REP$
```

```
3460 IF REP$="" THEN REP$=DATE$
3470 OPEN "R",1,FILE$
3480 FIELD 1, 6 AS TF$,17 AS NF$,15 AS COF$,10 AS PF$,23 AS SF$,
     15 AS CF$,2 AS STF$,5 AS ZF$,28 AS SUBJF$,6 AS DAF$,1 AS DF$
3490 PRINT "SET PAPER AT TOP OF PAGE,"
3500 PRINT "PRESS RETURN TO START . . .":A$=INPUT$(1)
3510 LPRINT:LPRINT
3520 LPRINT TAB(25);"TELEPHONE REPORT"
3530 LPRINT TAB(31);"FOR"
3540 LPRINT TAB(30);
     MID$(REP$,1,2)+"/"+MID$(REP$,3,2)+"/"+MID$(REP$,5,2)
3550 LPRINT:LPRINT
3560 LPRINT
     "NAME                 TELEPHONE      DATE      SUBJECT"
3570 LPRINT
     "                                                                "
3580 R=0
3590 R=R+1:GET 1,R
3600 IF DF$="D" THEN 3690
3610 IF TF$<>REP$ THEN 3690
3620 PHONE$="("+MID$(PF$,1,3)+")-"+MID$(PF$,4,3)+"-"+MID$(PF$,7,4)
3630 DAY$=MID$(DAF$,1,2)+"/"+MID$(DAF$,3,2)+"/"+MID$(DAF$,5,2)
3640 LPRINT NF$;"  ";PHONE$;"      ";DAY$;"      ";SUBJF$
3650 LPRINT
3660 Y=Y+1:IF Y<30 THEN 3690 ELSE LPRINT CHR$(12):Y=1
3670 LPRINT
     "NAME                 TELEPHONE      DATE      SUBJECT"
3680 LPRINT
     "                                                                "
3690 IF EOF(1) THEN 3700 ELSE 3590
3700 LPRINT:LPRINT "END OF REPORT"
3710 CLOSE 1
3720 GOTO 530
3730 '******** ADDRESS REPORT ROUTINE *************
3740 '
3750 'This routine prints names, addresses,
3760 'and subjects entered.
3770 '*********************************************
3780 '
3790 '
3800 Y=1
3810 FOR LOOP=1 TO SCRHITE:PRINT:NEXT LOOP
3820 LINE INPUT "REPORT FOR WHAT DATE? ";REP$
3830 IF REP$="" THEN REP$=DATE$
3840 OPEN "R",1,FILE$
3850 FIELD 1, 6 AS TF$,17 AS NF$,15 AS COF$,10 AS PF$,23 AS SF$,
     15 AS CF$,2 AS STF$,5 AS ZF$,28 AS SUBJF$,6 AS DAF$,1 AS DF$
3860 PRINT "SET PAPER AT TOP OF PAGE,"
3870 PRINT "PRESS RETURN TO START . . .":A$=INPUT$(1)
3880 LPRINT:LPRINT
3890 LPRINT TAB(25);"ADDRESS REPORT
3900 LPRINT TAB(31);"FOR
3910 LPRINT TAB(30);
     MID$(REP$,1,2)+"/"+MID$(REP$,3,2)+"/"+MID$(REP$,5,2)
3920 LPRINT:LPRINT
3930 LPRINT
     "NAME                 STREET                       SUBJECT"
3940 LPRINT
     "                     CITY           STATE   ZIP"
3950 LPRINT
     "                                                          "
3960 R=0
3970 R=R+1:GET 1,R
3980 IF DF$="D" THEN 4060
```

```
3990 IF TF$<>REP$ THEN 4060
4000 LPRINT NF$;"      ";SF$;"        ";SUBJF$
4010 LPRINT "                        ";CF$;STF$;"      ";ZF$
4020 LPRINT
4030 Y=Y+1:IF Y<30 THEN 4060 ELSE LPRINT CHR$(12):Y=1
4040 LPRINT
     "NAME                ADDRESS                      SUBJECT"
4050 LPRINT
     "_____                      _____"
4060 IF EOF(1) THEN 4070 ELSE 3970
4070 LPRINT:LPRINT "END OF REPORT"
4080 CLOSE 1
4090 GOTO 530
4100 '************A L L   R E C O R D S***************
4110 'This routine prints all records, all info through
4120 'a given date.
4130 '*************************************************
4140 Y=1
4150 FOR LOOP=1 TO SCRHITE:PRINT:NEXT LOOP
4160 LINE INPUT "REPORT FOR WHAT DATE? ";REP$
4170 IF REP$="" THEN REP$=DATE$
4180 OPEN "R",1,FILE$
4190 FIELD 1, 6 AS TF$,17 AS NF$,15 AS COF$,10 AS PF$,23 AS SF$,
     15 AS CF$,2 AS STF$,5 AS ZF$,28 AS SUBJF$,6 AS DAF$,1 AS DF$
4200 PRINT "SET PAPER AT TOP OF PAGE,"
4210 PRINT "PRESS RETURN TO START . . .":A$=INPUT$(1)
4220 LPRINT:LPRINT
4230 LPRINT TAB(25);"ALL RECORDS ONLINE
4240 LPRINT TAB(31);"AS OF
4250 LPRINT TAB(30);
     MID$(REP$,1,2)+"/"+MID$(REP$,3,2)+"/"+MID$(REP$,5,2)
4260 LPRINT:LPRINT
4270 R=0
4280 R=R+1:GET 1,R
4290 IF DF$="D" THEN 4430
4300 IF DAF$>REP$ THEN 4430
4310 LPRINT "T R I G G E R   D A T E: ";
     MID$(TF$,1,2)+"/"+MID$(TF$,3,2)+"/"+MID$(TF$,5,2)
4320 LPRINT "=========================
4330 LPRINT "       Name: ";NF$
4340 LPRINT "    Company: ";COF$
4350 LPRINT "       City: ";CF$
4360 LPRINT "      State: ";STF$
4370 LPRINT "        Zip: ";ZF$
4380 LPRINT "    Subject: ";SUBJF$
4390 LPRINT "=========================
4400 LPRINT " Date Entered: ";
     MID$(DAF$,1,2)+"/"+MID$(DAF$,3,2)+"/"+MID$(DAF$,5,2)
4410 LPRINT
4420 Y=Y+1:IF Y<6 THEN 4430 ELSE LPRINT CHR$(12):Y=1
4430 IF EOF(1) THEN 4440 ELSE 4280
4440 LPRINT:LPRINT "END OF REPORT"
4450 CLOSE 1
4460 GOTO 530
4470 '*************** L A B E L S ***********************
4480 '
4490 'This routine prints names & addresses on one-up,
4500 'mailing labels.
4510 '*******************************************
4520 '
4530 '
4540 Y=1
4550 FOR LOOP=1 TO SCRHITE:PRINT:NEXT LOOP
4560 LINE INPUT "LABELS FOR WHAT DATE? ";LAB$
```

```
4570 IF LAB$="" THEN LAB$=DATE$
4580 OPEN "R",1,FILE$
4590 FIELD 1, 6 AS TF$,17 AS NF$,15 AS COF$,10 AS PF$,23 AS SF$,
     15 AS CF$,2 AS STF$,5 AS ZF$,28 AS SUBJF$,6 AS DAF$,1 AS DF$
4600 PRINT "SET LABELS AT TOP OF FIRST LABEL,"
4610 PRINT "PRESS RETURN TO START . . .":A$=INPUT$(1)
4620 R=0
4630 R=R+1:GET 1,R
4640 IF DF$="D" THEN 4710
4650 IF TF$<>REP$ THEN 4710
4660 LPRINT NF$
4670 IF ASC(LEFT$(COF$,1))>0 THEN LPRINT COF$ ELSE 4680
4680 LPRINT SF$
4690 LPRINT CF$;STF$;"   ";ZF$
4700 LPRINT:LPRINT:LPRINT:IF NOT COF$>"" THEN LPRINT
4710 IF EOF(1) THEN 4720 ELSE 4630
4720 CLOSE 1
4730 GOTO 530
4740 FOR LOOP=1 TO SCRHITE:PRINT:NEXT LOOP
4750 OPEN "R",1,FILE$
4760 FIELD 1, 6 AS TF$,17 AS NF$,15 AS COF$,10 AS PF$,23 AS SF$,
     15 AS CF$,2 AS STF$,5 AS ZF$,28 AS SUBJF$,6 AS DAF$,1 AS DF$
4770 R=0
4780 R=R+1:GET 1,R
4790 IF DF$="D" THEN 4830
4800 POSDEL$=MID$(TF$,5,2)+MID$(TF$,1,2)+MID$(TF$,3,2)
4810 REVDATE$=MID$(DATE$,5,2)+MID$(DATE$,1,2)+MID$(DATE$,3,2)
4820 IF VAL(POSDEL$)+7<=VAL(REVDATE$) THEN D$="D":LSET DF$=D$:PUT 1,R
4830 IF EOF(1) THEN 4840 ELSE 4780
4840 CLOSE 1
4850 RESET:SYSTEM
```

CHAPTER THIRTEEN

SELLING HARDWARE

The most obvious way to make money with personal computers is by selling them. Unfortunately, opportunities related to hardware sales generally require the investment of a lot of money. If you have the money, however, you can make more with PC hardware.

OPENING A COMPUTER STORE

A computer store primarily sells personal computers and peripherals. Software and services (e.g., training, repair) also may be offered. The stores usually sell PCs from various manufacturers. Most manufacturers have stringent requirements that must be met before you will be authorized to sell their products. Checks will be made on your credit and character. If you measure up, you then must stock an inventory of PCs from the manufacturers you represent. Often, a manufacturer requires a *sizable* initial purchase of inventory and scheduled, monthly purchases.

Though inventory will be your largest single investment, you also will need to pay for rent of a store, equipment (cash registers, counters, displays), help, utilities (heat, electricity, telephone, water), and advertising. You also face competition from large retail chains that offer general merchandise, such as Sears.

Stores with established reputations offer franchises for an additional cost. With business training often provided with the franchise, this additional cost may be very worthwhile as an investment.

Many people, however, have made money by opening stores on their own. They direct their main sales efforts to businesses, which like having local support.

To open a store, contact the manufacturers of the PCs you're interested in selling for specific requirements.

DISTRIBUTING HARDWARE

Between the computer store and the manufacturer may stand a hardware distributor. The distributor warehouses huge inventories of hardware for stores. The warehouse also may stock replacement parts. The investment required for this business is much greater than for a computer store, but the profits are larger, too.

For more information about becoming a distributor, contact the manufacturers you wish to represent for specific details.

DEVELOPING NEW HARDWARE

Personal computers with new capabilities and cheaper prices will be developed. Some already are being developed by companies no one has ever heard of—yet. Be assured, you will hear of them. Some of these new companies will become as commonly known as IBM, Apple, and Texas Instruments are now. It seems foolhardy to go up against such competition, but people who think they can offer better products do, and some achieve epic success.

It never will be too late to develop new hardware or take on one of the giants. You don't need a fancy research lab to create new hardware. You can design your machine on an old desk in the bedroom and take the plans to the bank for financial backing. Prototypes have been and will continue to be made in cellars and garages.

Personal computers are just one hardware area for development. Disk drives, modems, conversion cards for operating systems, graphic peripherals (e.g., light pens, pucks, tablets), and PC multiplexers are other areas.

Money is not required to get started. Substantial capital, however, generally is necessary to start manufacturing and selling hardware. It is best to get expert financial advice on obtaining this funding and creating a detailed business plan. You should talk to an officer in your bank or reply to an ad offering venture capital, as advertised in major newspapers and financial papers.

ADAPTING HARDWARE FOR PERSONAL COMPUTERS

The evolution of the PC industry has presented many companies with a major problem: What is to be done with all the terminals they have bought?

Manufacturers such as IBM offer parts to transform terminals, traditionally used to communicate with mainframe computers, into stand-alone PCs. An estimated 1.5 *million* IBM terminals in use today can be adapted. Many other manufacturers also have these terminals in the field.

Other mainframe hardware can be adapted, too. Someone has to make the transformations. The manufacturers can do it, but if you have the skills, you could do it, too. You first need to obtain the proper hardware supplies. You then contact companies and offer to adapt their hardware.

SUPPLYING HARDWARE PARTS

When a piece of equipment breaks down, a PC user can return the equipment to the manufacturer and wait—and wait—for it to be repaired. Or, the user can get the replacement part.

Supplying hardware parts is a natural adjunct to offering a hardware repair service. As more equipment is sold, supplying the hardware alone will become a very profitable business. To enter the business, you need to stock an inventory of parts. This inventory can be obtained from a distributor or equipment manufacturer.

SELLING PERSONAL COMPUTER TIME

Time may sound like an odd thing to sell, but it's not. Actually, time to operate a PC is what is sold. The price for this privilege is a small fraction of the price of the equipment. In this way, someone who can't afford a PC, or who simply doesn't want to buy one, can use one.

Buyers of PC time include people investigating various machines, students, people who have only occasional and limited use for a PC, and program developers who need many different ones for a variety of projects.

Some libraries are beginning to install PCs for this purpose. Soon you may be able to walk into a library, and for some change use the PC, just as you now may pay to use a copying machine.

The trickiest problem to overcome in this business is pricing. Many people try to recoup their "investment" in equipment too quickly and charge a price that is so high, a person is better off buying a machine. The price should be set *low* to attract users. This low price means you need nearly constant use of the PC to make money, which is why a library with a constant flow of people is an ideal place to offer PC time.

Anyone can go into this business, but few individuals will make a profit. And, do you want a constant flow of people tracking through your living room? Do you want to be on the telephone constantly making appointments to use your PC? Do you want to be around all the time to monitor people in your home? Charging only a few dollars an hour, is it worth it to you? Since you also need to pay for advertising, can you expect to make *any* money?

You may be the exception who can make money if you live near a college or university. Computer equipment still is in short supply at these institutions. Many students would be happy to pay for an opportunity to use a PC when they want and not wait for a small, scheduled interval in the overcrowded computer lab. In this case, you can inexpensively make posters and tack them up in college dorms. You also can run an ad very inexpensively in the college paper. Without altering your lifestyle too much, you should be able to show a small profit.

This business is best suited to supplement other activities. If you program, for example, you may offer your machine when you're not using it. The

PC time business won't pay for your equipment, but it can help you pay your other bills.

As with the other opportunities in this chapter, this one also requires an initial investment—for the equipment.

RENTING AND LEASING EQUIPMENT

As well as selling it, you can rent and lease PC equipment. From a customer's point of view, renting and leasing make a lot of sense. The industry is undergoing rapid technological changes. Buying a machine means committing oneself to equipment that very likely soon will be outdated. It also means committing one's business to a particular computer before it's known whether the machine is right for the business, something that only can be learned by actual in-business use.

Today, computer stores offer leasing agreements that lead to purchases. The few computer stores that offer rentals charge a price so high as to all but make the rental uneconomical (charges generally range from one-fourth to one-third of the total machine price per month, so after only a few months the machine is paid for, but you don't own it). These practices are understandable because these stores are in the business to sell PCs and make large profits.

A few stores recently have opened that specialize in rentals. They have attractively priced the rentals. These stores should do very well because a market for renting and leasing does exist. As the industry changes, it will become more economical to lease and rent used equipment. Many more of these stores can open.

To offer an attractive deal, you should have PCs from many manufacturers, and price the rental low. All your equipment should be insured for damage.

The business also can be conducted very profitably with selling hardware. The hardware first can be offered at a very low price to allow monthly use on a test basis. If a user likes the equipment after using it in business, the user then purchases it. If not, he or she has no obligation to buy.

Software can be rented or sold with the equipment for an increased price. If you offer a low price for software during a trial period, you virtually lock a customer into a sale because after a few months the customer's business already will be converted to the system.

Some books and articles have suggested that an individual can make money by renting his or her PC. This is not really a valid opportunity. To attract people, the rental price should be low, which means a nearly constant flow of renters is necessary to show a profit. It is difficult to assure that all these people will care for your machine, so accidents are likely. Any profits you may earn easily can be eaten up by advertising costs and costs of repairing damage. If the damage is bad enough, you may have to buy a new computer. Since it isn't economical to insure one PC, you'll have to pay the full cost for a replacement. The small profit, if any, that you can hope for simply doesn't justify taking this risk with a single PC.

Programs For Profit has shown you many safer and more profitable ways to make money with your PC. In fact, selling your PC at a tag sale is more sensible than renting it to strangers.

CHAPTER FOURTEEN
PUTTING IT ALL TOGETHER

About now, a feeling of uneasiness may be overtaking you. You may be inclined to read this last chapter very slowly because you may not feel ready to start your own profitable business yet—and you shouldn't.

All the preceding chapters merely have introduced you to opportunities, techniques, and facts. Before you can make money with them, you have to shape them into a personal plan.

PUTTING TOGETHER A COMPREHENSIVE PACKAGE

Jeremy sells personal computer application programs to dentists. He wrote to many, asking if he could show them how his PC application programs could help their businesses. One day, he had sold a dentist on his programs' many benefits.

"When can we get started?" the dentist asked.

"I can install my programs right now," Jeremy said. "Where's your PC?"

"I don't have one yet," the dentist said.

"Well, there's no sense talking to me until you get one," Jeremy said.

He left, asking to be called when the dentist finally made up his mind to get a computer.

Jeremy actually missed a very profitable opportunity. He has focused his business so sharply that he has stopped listening to his prospective customers, which is a major mistake. A person may have ideas about what to offer, but *the customer is the one who defines the offer.*

What should Jeremy have done? If he was open to money-making opportunities, he would have heard the dentist asking to be sold software *and a PC.*

You can succeed where Jeremy failed by offering *comprehensive* packages.

Today, most small businesses still lack PCs. If you aim your efforts at only businesses having them, you will encounter stiff and established competition, and you will miss a sizable market.

Likewise, most people, especially those unfamiliar with PCs, prefer to deal with a single source that they can turn to for hardware, software, and service. They are so involved in their businesses that they don't have time to stay on top of the evolving hardware and software markets to make sound decisions.

Most small business people, finally, suspect PCs can benefit them, but they don't know how. They avoid contacting PC representatives and going into computer stores out of fear of the unknown. They want to avoid asking simple-minded questions. They're reluctant to change the way they do business. They're afraid they'll be laughed at for trying to introduce PCs to a business as small as theirs. If you actively seek out these people and present an attractive, introductory offer for hardware, software, *and* service to them, you can develop a sizable and profitable business.

One approach to such a business is to sell hardware and software by first renting them at a very modest, introductory price. You will train people in the use of the equipment and software. If they like it, they can buy it. You will also offer a contract for hardware and software support. In short, you will offer a total package.

You can contact, for example, gas station owners with the offer to introduce them to computer benefits for their businesses. Out of plain curiosity, many will talk to you and that's all you need to get in the door. Invite your prospective customers to use a personal computer and customized software for a month or two at a nominal fee. If, at the end of that time, they aren't interested, you'll remove the system. If, after working with it, clients like it, they can buy it. It's an offer hard to resist. What does the client have to lose? You will be also offering a service contract for hardware and software support, and will keep the client informed of enhancements and pertinent, new application programs—which you'll also sell for a profit.

How, for example, do you computerize a gas station? Bookkeeping can be put on the PC—you have software for it from *Programs For Profit*. A car maintenance program can be set up with the *Programs For Profit* Tickler File Program so that customers are sent reminder letters for tune-ups every 6 months, increasing repeat business.

Clients should be given only a few programs to start, otherwise they may become bewildered by taking on too much too soon. You will have to introduce someone unfamiliar with PCs to them very slowly. You'll point out, though, that these start-up programs can be supplemented by others, such as programs for inventory, and word processing, and payroll. If your customer is interested in continuing a business relationship, you'll be his or her guide through the perplexing world of PC.

When clients agree to your offer, you initially enter all the data to make them operational. You will write up specific procedures and train users.

You are investing a lot of time, but the risk really isn't as great as it first appears. Personal computers do benefit small businesses and your customers will see that when they begin using them themselves. After a month or two, the PC will become an integral part of the business, and so *removing* it will be disruptive.

In this same way, you can introduce PC technology to doctors, dentists, veterinarians, auto repair shops, diners, clothing stores, home furnishing stores, lawn care services, and most other small businesses.

The profits in one sale are appreciable. You charge for:

1. The hardware, which you mark up. Assume the PC, printer, and disk drive cost $3,000. With a 15 percent markup, you earn $450. Your profit can be greater if you buy directly from a manufacturer or distributor, or if you arrange a deal with the manager of a computer store for large-volume discount purchases.
2. The software, which you also mark up. You can sell the programs in *Programs For Profit* and keep the complete price. You also can provide a copy of the book as an instruction manual, but you'll mark up that price.
3. Initial data entry.
4. Training.
5. The ongoing service contract, which will be paid on a scheduled basis, giving you a predictable cash flow.
6. Supplemental software and training.

To start, you have to identify the market you will direct your efforts at. You will place ads and begin a direct mail campaign to these people. For your first prospect, you do not have to invest in a new PC and peripherals. You can install your equipment as a demonstration model. When the customer buys, you will replace the demonstration model with new equipment, thus reducing your financial exposure.

You then will have to investigate supplemental programs. You can go through ads in computer magazines and send for catalogs from manufacturers and mail order houses. When you find the programs you want, you can order them for specific customers as needed. If your experiences with the programs are good, you can write to the owner of the software and ask for permission to represent and service it, allowing you to make more money on each sale. This permission should enable you to buy the software at a discount and you may be able to obtain a fee for servicing the software from the program's owners.

Once in the door, you also can look for ways to apply PCs that haven't been done before. You then can create your own program for national distribution.

You should offer your comprehensive package with flexibility. You may encounter somebody, for example, who already owns a PC, but who really doesn't know how to use it. You certainly don't need to sell this person a new computer. You will offer your software, training, and service so the client can effectively use the computer he or she already owns.

Many comprehensive packages can be created. Instead of basing one on a hardware sale, for example, you might base it on service. In this case, you'll provide the client with the benefits of computerization, but he or she will never have to actually use a computer. You'll go to the client, collect data, enter it on your machine, and deliver reports for bookkeeping, inventory, general ledger, and mailing labels, and so on.

By offering a comprehensive package, you can dramatically expand your market and increase your profits. You'll get the most from every sales call you make.

PUTTING *YOUR* PLAN TOGETHER

In a sense, *Programs For Profit* is a generalized program for making money in the personal computer field that now must be customized to you. Only you can shape the money-making program best suited to your needs and abilities.

The first step in putting your plan together may surprise you because it has nothing to do with you.

First, you should think about a single, idealized *customer*. If you haven't been in business before, you probably haven't had the opportunity to think of other people as customers. In business, you may think of people as bosses, co-workers, or vendors, but thinking of them as customers may be something new.

Customers *always* define profitable offers. The smartest marketing manager at a giant company may have an idea of what will sell, but he or she can't make a single customer buy. In the marketplace, the customer decides what sells and what doesn't.

However, right now don't worry about what a customer will buy. Just keep thinking about this customer as you create your plan. The specific offer will come along in time.

The reason for this beginning is simple. The only way to make money in your own business is to help a customer in a way that's profitable for you. Thus, the focus of your efforts should not be on the offer, but on your customer, whom your eventual offer must help. Aim your plan at one person. This person, not your offer, will lead you to another customer and another. In this way you should be able to avoid putting together an offer perfectly tailored to your needs and abilities—that no one will buy.

The second step is to review the opportunities open to you. You should decide on the ones that are affordable and easiest for you and that you believe will interest a customer.

You must feel comfortable with your business. Don't try to "force fit" yourself into a great new money-making career. An elementary software design principle is to create a program that operates according to a user's habits. If the user has to change too much, he or she will resist and the program will be a failure. The same is true for your life, also. If you have to change too much, you'll resist and your business will fail.

If you're really into programming, for example, but shy away from directly dealing with others and aren't interested in the *business* of a business, you will not be very successful in a business that requires you to attend a lot of meetings and present many proposals that may need to be negotiated. You will be much better off either working with a partner who can handle the "talking" and the business, or selling your programs through mail order house catalogs, PC magazines, and manufacturers.

There is an exception. There may be something you have always wanted to do that you know you can do given the chance. You may be teaching, but deep down you know you really want to make money by selling software. Or, you may work in a support department, and find that no one listens to your ideas about new programs. You just know your ideas are sound and you can design your own very profitable program.

This is your chance! If no one else gives you the opportunity to become who you want, give yourself the chance.

You then should be ready to sketch in your offer and the market for it. You now should be familiar with how to do this very well. For each program in *Programs For Profit*, offers and markets have been defined. These case studies have explored potential markets and focused on the most profitable opportunities in them. You can do the same thing.

It's time, now, to stand back and ask yourself if this business is feasible for you. Do you have the time and money to proceed? What are your social, financial, and time obligations to your mate, children, parents, friends, and pets? To your job? To other organizations? Can you make the time to go into your own business? If you can't start a full-time business—and only a few people can—you may be able to go into a part-time one that you can turn into a career later on.

The business may look good to you, but ask other people, especially successful ones, to listen to your plans. They may be able to see problems you have overlooked. These conversations also will help you objectively think through what you've planned. You'll gain excellent feedback and as you begin to talk about your business, you'll begin to feel more confident about actually starting it.

At this point, you should review the first half of *Programs For Profit* and pin down exactly what you intend to offer and to who. Change your original offer if you think you can make it more salable. Review it to make sure you still can handle it. Give yourself enough time to figure out what you're doing. Play through a couple of the famous "what-if" cases by varying your offer. Work through the consequences on paper. You may be interested, for example, in selling software through a catalog, but you should also consider selling it through PC magazine classified ads or locally yourself.

It's not advisable, on the other hand, to spend the rest of your life defining your offer. To start, you don't need to have a perfect, all-encompassing offer. Do the best you can to create an offer a customer will buy.

Using the techniques presented earlier, you then will have to decide:

1. How to charge for your offer
2. How much to charge
3. How best to introduce your offer, i.e., ads, direct mail, letters, etc.

When these questions are answered, you will be ready to introduce your offer and make your first sale. From the time you first began thinking about customers, it may take only a few evenings to reach this point for service-oriented businesses, such as hardware repair. Months or even years may be required for other businesses. A new PC, for example, may take 2 or 3 years to bring to market.

After your first sale, are you finished planning? Hardly. You should go back and improve your offer. Review what was successful and note the areas that need work.

Once you've gained the wonderful experience of making money in your own business, you can begin looking ahead. You'll be in a position to meaningfully ask yourself what you hope to achieve in a few years. You already will have succeeded in a noteworthy effort. You already will have overcome obstacles. New and distant challenges now must be set to give you direction. Can you achieve the best support service in your state? Why not in the country? Where will these achievements lead you to in 10 years? Freedom to do what you want? Security? A magnificent home on an exclusive beach?

It's not unusual for successful people to find themselves surpassing their goals in only a few years. They look back in wonder and ask why they ever set their goals so low.

A detailed, step-by-step plan to achieve your long-range goals isn't recommended. It will take a lot of time to create such a plan; time that can better be spent making money. You should make short-range plans for 6 months to a year. Detailing plans beyond a year isn't wise. You'll change as you experience new success. Computer technology will change. Setting a rigid plan is a way to assure yourself of disappointment. As things change in ways you haven't foreseen in your grand plan, you'll question your abilities to ever reach your goals and possibly give up when all you really had to do was adapt to new circumstances. Paradoxically, without a rigid, long-range plan, you'll reach your long-range goal.

WHEN TO QUIT YOUR JOB

In a moment of frustration, everyone I know has told themselves, "I'm going to quit this job." Quitting and moving on to something better always has been a dream. Opportunities that PCs are making possible today actually let you do it. But when should you head out?

There are no rigid rules. People's situations are different. A single young woman living at home with her well-off parents very well may be able to begin a full-time business immediately. An older man with children and a mortgage may have to be more cautious and work his business in the evenings and weekends until he's sure it's a money maker.

Before quitting your job, you should ask yourself if you can survive if everything you have lined up goes wrong. How much tolerance do your plans have for disasters?

Most people, unfortunately, have a tendency to stay too long at a job before moving on to their own business. Partings *always* are going to be difficult, even when you leave people you dislike. Only months after people leave do they wonder why they stayed so long. By then, they're building their own business and looking for employees.

MAKING YOUR BUSINESS GROW

Randy started his own software consulting business. He sent out 300 letters that introduced his service, and within a month he had more business than he could handle. He honestly was surprised by how much money he was making. Clients told others who called Randy with more business. After a year, though, his income had leveled off. He still had a few referrals now and then, but his business had stopped growing. He didn't know how to get it moving again.

Many people, especially part-timers, have this same problem. They have early success, but it fades and they just can't seem to make any headway.

There are a number of things you can do about this. The most common cause of this problem is that people forget what made them successful in the beginning. Randy, for example, started his business by sending out direct mail, but he never did it again, even though his experience and credentials would have won him a larger response than his first one. Direct mail can be sent to prospects at any time. You could be in business 40 years and still send out introductory letters to new prospects. And, you can mail pieces to people who haven't replied to earlier ones.

You should always stick to your basics. The practices that brought you success before will work again, no matter how big you are.

The first test of your management ability will be how well you manage your own time. You will have to make time in your busy schedule for "growth" activities. Just meeting your commitments with ongoing business may be profitable, but it won't keep your business growing.

At some point, you may need to hire help to make your business grow. You simply may not be able to do all the work yourself. You may want somebody else to start taking over some of the business side so you can do your work. This process will be very difficult—the first time you do it. You'll wonder if you can afford the help. Will you have enough work for two people? The answer is "Yes," and you'll find it becomes easier and more profitable once you've hired your first person.

As you attain success, you also may be able to create new offers. You may be able to enter new PC markets or offer more comprehensive packages. You may find it advantageous to work with another company. Or, another company may buy you out.

You, finally, should seek out successful people and ask them for guidance. Many retired business people have faced these same problems in other businesses. They'll be happy to talk to you and what they have to say about "the old battles" they fought will prove very helpful.

LOOKING AHEAD

As a person who owns his or her own business, you will find that you have to respond to the world as it is today and as it will be tomorrow. Personal computers have created opportunities, some of which allow a lot of money to be made very quickly. As the technology evolves—and it's doing so very quickly—new opportunities will be created as others are left behind.

You will have to build your business as the field is today, but you should keep an eye open to the future where there are already some discernible trends changing the field:

1. The general public's awareness of software is increasing. As recently as 2 years ago, I had to explain to a very well educated, aware group what software was. They really didn't have any idea! Most people today at least have heard the term. In the coming years, the general public will be able to distinguish between programs. Software will be advertised more. You may even hear a talk show host asking, "Will you show us a few routines from your latest program?" But he won't be talking to a television star. He'll be talking to a programmer.
2. As the public's awareness of software increases, there will be software stores and more software outlets.
3. In the business environment, PCs will be linked to mainframes in increasingly powerful networks. Computers will be simpler to use so that even unskilled people will be able to create sophisticated applications. A

conflict will occur in most large businesses between adapting existing mainframe software, in which large amounts of money as well as careers are invested, and buying new software designed to take advantage of PC characteristics.

4. Software companies will go into more specialized application areas.

5. There will be significantly fewer PC operating systems and variations in programming languages as more companies aim at the mainstream market.

6. The PC support industries (training, documentation, service) will grow rapidly. As these computers find their way into more homes and businesses, the need for support will becoming more important. It is estimated that of the $14 billion likely to be spent on PCs by 1986, $3 billion will be for training alone.

7. The use of intercomputer communication will increase. New software should allow PCs to enter more homes. A great many PCs are necessary to make many telecommunications services and opportunities possible. Major problems must be overcome. What is the communications media to be—telephone lines, cable, or something else? Pricing is another problem area. If these serious problems can be overcome, it is feasible that most people will be able to work at home (in fact, it is now estimated that over 55 percent of the population will be able to do so by the end of the decade). The glamorous corporate office buildings that surround us today will become relics. A few of these communications opportunities have been looked at in previous chapters, but the consequences of linking PCs on a broad basis are so staggering as to be hard to envision. Should interpersonal computer communications become commonplace, one thing, at least, is certain. *Programs For Profit* will be revised with many new opportunities.

We are in the midst of a personal computer revolution that will transform the world as much as, if not more than, automobiles changed it nearly a century ago. It's still a field where a person working in a cellar or a garage can start a multimillion dollar company that could change the direction of this infant industry.

This frontier, like all the others before it, won't be open forever. Some people, in years to come, will look back at this time when there were so many possibilities. Others will achieve great success by crossing over into this field while it's still new and fresh, and starting their own profitable businesses.

You can be one of the successes.

APPENDIXES

A. A WORD PROCESSING INTERFACE PROGRAM

B. POSTAL CODES

C. PROGRAMS AND FILES

APPENDIX A
A WORD PROCESSING INTERFACE PROGRAM

The Word Processing Interface Program enables you to access with your Word Processing Program the data you've stored with your *Program For Profit* software. Your data, then, can be used in letters or reports without the need for reentry.

This program may be used with the Mail List, A/R, and Tickler Programs. *Your original data will not be affected in any way.* The program copies the name, company (when available), street, city, state, and zip code and sets up a standard data file with comma delimiters and one record per line. This file then can be used with WordStar or any of the other many word processing programs that use such files.

The name of the file that's created is WSCONDAT.DTA.

NOTE:

Only one WSCONDAT.DTA file can be set up on a disk at a time. Whenever a file is copied, any old data is replaced. You, of course, can set up as many WSCONDAT.DTA files as you like on *different* disks, one per disk.

The Word Processing Interface Program is accessed by typing **RUN WSCON** in response to the system prompt:

A: **RUN WSCON**

The program will be loaded and the following procedure started:

1. NAME OF DATA FILE TO CONVERT: Each of the three programs has a file which contains the data you want. If you want:

Data for:	Type:
MAIL LIST PROGRAM	**MAILLIST**
A/R PROGRAM	**CUSTOMER**
TICKLER PROGRAM	**TKLRDATA**

2. DATA THAT [your specified file] IS ON: If you haven't already done so, load the data disk in a drive. Type the letter of the disk drive with the data.

At this time, the data will be copied and the WSCONDAT.DTA file created. You will be informed that the operation is complete by the message:

THERE IS NOW A FILE ON DRIVE [the one you specified] CALLED WSCONDAT.DTA CONTAINING ALL OF THE INFORMATION IN [the name of the program file you specified] IN A WORDSTAR COMPATIBLE FORMAT

At this time, you will be returned to the BASIC Level. You now can use the file with your Word Processing Program.

NOTE:

Though the message mentions only WordStar, the WSCONDAT.DTA file can be used with *any* Word Processing Program that uses a data file with comma delimiters and one record per line.

WORD PROCESSING INTERFACE
PROGRAM SOURCE CODE

```
10 LINE INPUT "NAME OF DATA FILE TO CONVERT: ";FILE$
20 PRINT "DRIVE THAT ";FILE$;" IS ON: ";:LINE INPUT DRIVE$
30 OPEN "O",1,DRIVE$+":WSCONDAT.DTA"
40 OPEN "R",2,DRIVE$+":"+FILE$
50 IF FILE$="TKLRDATA" THEN
    FIELD 2,6 AS TF$,17 AS NF$,15 AS COF$,
    10 AS PF$,23 AS SF$,15 AS CF$,2 AS STF$,
    9 AS ZF$,28 AS RF$,6 AS DAF$,1 AS DF$
60 IF FILE$="MAILLIST" THEN
    FIELD 2,20 AS NF$,20 AS CF$,20 AS SF$,
    15 AS TF$,2 AS STF$,9 AS ZF$,20 AS I1F$,20 AS I2F$,1 AS DF$
70 IF FILE$="CUSTOMER.DAT" THEN GOSUB 300:GOTO 100
80 IF FILE$="TKLRDATA" THEN GOSUB 160
90 IF FILE$="MAILLIST" THEN GOSUB 230
100 PRINT "THERE IS NOW A FILE ON DRIVE ";DRIVE$;" CALLED"
110 PRINT:PRINT "WSCONDAT.DTA"
120 PRINT:PRINT "CONTAINING ALL OF THE INFORMATION IN"
130 PRINT:PRINT FILE$
140 PRINT:PRINT "IN A WORDSTAR COMPATIBLE FORMAT"
150 PRINT:END
160 X=0
170 X=X+1:IF EOF(2) THEN 220
180 GET 2,X
190 N$=NF$:C$=COF$:S$=SF$:CT$=CF$:ST$=STF$:Z$=ZF$
200 PRINT #1,N$;",";C$;",";S$;",";CT$;",";ST$;",";Z$;",";CHR$(13)
210 GOTO 170
220 CLOSE:RETURN
230 X=0
240 X=X+1:IF EOF(2) THEN 290
250 GET 2,X
260 N$=NF$:C$=CF$:S$=SF$:T$=TF$:ST$=STF$:Z$=ZF$
270 PRINT #1,N$;",";C$;",";S$;",";T$;",";ST$;",";Z$;",";CHR$(13)
280 GOTO 240
290 CLOSE:RETURN
300 REM ******************************************
310 REM OPEN CUSTOMER FILE RANDOM               *
320 REM ******************************************
330 OPEN "R",#2,DISK$+"CUSTOMER.DAT",120
340 FIELD #2, 4 AS IDF$,20 AS COF$,20 AS NAF$,15 AS DEPF$,
    15 AS STREETF$,15 AS CITYF$,2 AS STATEF$,9 AS ZIPF$,
    10 AS PHONEF$,4 AS BALF$,10 AS PONUMF$
350 X=0
360 X=X+1:IF EOF(2) THEN 410
370 GET 2,X
380 N$=NAF$:C$=COF$:S$=STREETF$:CT$+CITYF$:ST$=STATEF$:Z$=ZIPF$
390 PRINT #1,N$;",";C$;",";S$;",";CT$;",";ST$;",";Z$;",";CHR$(13)
400 GOTO 360
410 CLOSE:RETURN
```

APPENDIX B
POSTAL CODES

State	Code	State	Code
ALABAMA	AL	NEBRASKA	NE
ALASKA	AK	NEVADA	NV
ARIZONA	AZ	NEW HAMPSHIRE	NH
ARKANSAS	AR	NEW JERSEY	NJ
CALIFORNIA	CA	NEW MEXICO	NM
COLORADO	CO	NEW YORK	NY
CONNECTICUT	CT	NORTH CAROLINA	NC
DELAWARE	DE	NORTH DAKOTA	ND
DISTRICT OF COLUMBIA	DC	OHIO	OH
FLORIDA	FL	OKLAHOMA	OK
GEORGIA	GA	OREGON	OR
HAWAII	HI	PENNSYLVANIA	PA
IDAHO	ID	PUERTO RICO	PR
ILLINOIS	IL	RHODE ISLAND	RI
INDIANA	IN	SOUTH CAROLINA	SC
IOWA	IA	SOUTH DAKOTA	SD
KANSAS	KS	TENNESSEE	TN
KENTUCKY	KY	TEXAS	TX
LOUISIANA	LA	UTAH	UT
MAINE	ME	VERMONT	VT
MARYLAND	MD	VIRGINIA	VA
MASSACHUSETTS	MA	VIRGIN ISLANDS	VI
MICHIGAN	MI	WASHINGTON	WA
MINNESOTA	MN	WEST VIRGINIA	WV
MISSISSIPPI	MS	WISCONSIN	WI
MISSOURI	MO	WYOMING	WY
MONTANA	MT		

APPENDIX C
PROGRAMS AND FILES

You will be storing files that should not be erased on your disks. These files are listed by program below.

File Name	Contents
All Programs	
PARAMTER.FIL	The Parameter File, which defines a screen size. Only one is necessary for programs on the same disk.
Mail List Program	
MAILLIST.BAS	This file contains the program.
MCOUNTER	A counter file.
MAILLIST.DTA	The Mail List data file.
A/P Program	
PAYMENT.BAS	This file contains the A/P "monitor" program, including code for command no. 13.
PAYMENT1.BAS	This file contains code for command no. 1.
PAYMENT2.BAS	This file contains code for command nos. 2 and 3.
PAYMENT3.BAS	This file contains code for command nos. 4 and 5.
PAYMENT4.BAS	This file contains code for command nos. 6, 7, and 8.
PAYMENT5.BAS	This file contains code for command nos. 9, 10, 11, and 12.
BILLS.DAT	This file contains transaction data.
TOTALS.DAT	This file contains year-to-date totals.
CHECK.FIL	This file contains the last check number.
RATE.FIL	This file contains the mileage rate.
A/R Program	
INCOME.BAS	This file contains the A/R "monitor" program, including code for command no. 14.
INCOME1.BAS	This file contains code for command no. 1.
INCOME2.BAS	This file contains code for command nos. 2 and 3.

File Name	Contents
INCOME3.BAS	This file contains code for command no. 4.
INCOME4.BAS	This file contains code for command nos. 5 and 6.
INCOME5.BAS	This file contains code for command no. 7.
INCOME6.BAS	This file contains code for command nos. 8 and 9.
INCOME7.BAS	This file contains code for command nos. 10, 11, 12, and 13.
CUSTOMER.DAT	This file contains customer cards.
CUSTOMER.KEY	This file is used for locating customer records.
TRANSACT.DAT	This file contains invoice transactions.
PAYMENT.DAT	This file contains details about invoice payments.
CASH.DAT	This file contains the cash transactions.

Football Program

FOOTBALL.BAS	This file contains the football program.
GAMES.DAT	This file contains data about games.

Tickler Program

TICKLER.BAS	This file contains the program.
TCOUNTER	A counter file.
TKLRDATA.DTA	This file contains reminders.

Word Processing Interface Program

WSCON.BAS	This file contains the program.
WSCONDAT.DTA	This file contains information in a format suitable for a word processing system.

INDEX

INDEX

Catalog

If you are interested in a list of fine Paperback
books, covering a wide range of subjects
and interests, send your name and address,
requesting your free catalog, to:

McGraw-Hill Paperbacks
1221 Avenue of Americas
New York, N.Y. 10020